THE BEGINNINGS OF
NYASALAND
AND NORTH-EASTERN
RHODESIA
1859–95

THE BEGINNINGS OF
NYASALAND
AND
NORTH-EASTERN RHODESIA
1859–95

BY

A. J. HANNA

Lecturer in History in the
University of Southampton

OXFORD
AT THE CLARENDON PRESS
1956

Oxford University Press, Amen House, London E.C.4

GLASGOW NEW YORK TORONTO MELBOURNE WELLINGTON
BOMBAY CALCUTTA MADRAS KARACHI CAPE TOWN IBADAN

Geoffrey Cumberlege, Publisher to the University

PRINTED IN GREAT BRITAIN
AT THE UNIVERSITY PRESS, OXFORD
BY CHARLES BATEY, PRINTER TO THE UNIVERSITY

PREFACE

THIS is a story of British activity overseas, small in scale, but culminating in the creation of new political unities, embryonic states, in the interior of tropical Africa. The so-called 'partition' of Africa was not the tearing apart of a previously united continent, for, with the exception of a few native states like Buganda and Barotseland, effectively controlled by a powerful monarch, there was only a medley of little tribes, themselves lacking in effective organization. The work of state-building in Africa has for the most part been done by Europeans. The lines of partition, and indeed the fact of partition itself, may have been unfortunate, but this is of minor importance compared with the work of consolidation and unification which it has been possible to carry forward in the large tracts of territory which were brought under a single rule when the Europeans, British and others, took control. By their administrative achievement the colonial Governments have done in Africa what the medieval monarchies did in western Europe: they have made it possible for men's loyalties to become increasingly national rather than parochial in scope. In so far as African national consciousness has yet developed, even when it is characterized by anti-colonial emotion, it owes its existence to the creation of public order within defined frontiers by an alien authority.

The British interest in Nyasaland began with Livingstone's explorations and culminated in the assumption of political control in 1889–91. At first it was limited to private individuals and to Christian missions, and the involvement of the British Government came later and proceeded slowly. By 1891 the boundaries of the Nyasaland Protectorate had been defined on paper, but it was not until another four or five years had passed that the authority of the Administration became effective throughout the country, and it was not until 1894 that the British Government fully accepted the responsibilities of its position as the ruling power. In this book I have traced these developments in considerable detail, giving particular attention to the building up of the Administration and to the lines of policy which it pursued.

North Eastern Rhodesia, which afterwards became part of a united Northern Rhodesia, was closely connected with Nyasaland in its early history as a region of British activity, and it is therefore included in the present study.

I have presented the available evidence with the minimum of comment, because I think the duty of an historian is to try to re-create the past as it was and to refrain from pontificating about it with the spurious wisdom of hindsight.

◦   ◦   ◦

In spelling African names I have, on the whole, been guided by common usage. Other things being equal, I have preferred aesthetic considerations to strict logical consistency. For instance, it would seem proper that the prefix 'Wa' or 'Ba' or 'A', meaning 'people', should either be attached to the name of every African tribe or be omitted from them all.[1] But 'Yao' sounds less disagreeable than 'Wayao', besides being much more frequently used; and 'Tonga' is shorter and simpler than 'Atonga'. On the other hand, 'Ngoni' and 'Nkonde' seem altogether out of place on a page of English prose, so I have called them 'Angoni' and Wankonde'.

It appears to be a principle of 'scientific spelling' that no letter should ever be unnecessarily doubled. Thus 'Senna', 'Tette', and 'Quillimaine', which were often used in the pioneering days, gave way in due course to 'Sena', 'Tete', and 'Quilimane'. Likewise, 'Nyassa' was superseded by 'Nyasa', and this triumph of the scientific spirit has had the unforeseen result that most English-men now pronounce the word as 'Nye-a-za', whereas it ought to have only two syllables, and a soft 's', thus: 'Nya-sa'.

Sir Harry Johnston was an enthusiast in the cause of scientific spelling. Indeed, he made it plain in more than one letter that if he could have had his choice (or 'tshoice') he would have played merry havoc with the appearance of the English language in the sacred cause of science. Since, however, he lacked opportunity to trans-literate the entire vocabulary, he had to confine his reforming acti-vities to the more restricted sphere of African proper names. It was he who cajoled a conservative Foreign Office into dropping the second 's' from 'Nyassa', a step which had by this time (the early 1890's) been taken by the local missions. He also used his most dulcet arts of persuasion to induce them to replace 'ch' with 'tsh', on the grounds that the latter could only be pronounced in one way, whereas 'ch' could also signify 'sh' or 'k'. He adopted the 'tsh' in

[1] The latter course is followed by the anthropologists, who also write 'Cewa' when they mean 'Chewa'.

his dispatches, and the practice was tolerated for a time: as Lord Rosebery remarked, 'I understand the proposal to be that Johnston shall spell the word Tshindi and we shall reply with Chindi—well and good'. In 1894, however, he was officially instructed to adopt an orthodox 'ch'.

In quotations, I have not adhered to the punctuation of the original if I have thought an alteration would make for clarity or readability. I have also sometimes ventured to expand abbreviated words without encumbering them by putting square brackets round the letters I have supplied. But I have not interfered with the spelling of proper names, and I have retained capital letters wherever I found them.

This book is based on a thesis which I presented to the University of London for the Degree of Doctor of Philosophy in 1948. My available leisure during the intervening years has been occupied with revision and rewriting.

I owe much to the guidance of Professor V. T. Harlow and Professor W. P. Morrell, who supervised my research when I was preparing my thesis, and I have received helpful advice from Miss Margery Perham, Dame Lillian Penson, and the late Sir Reginald Coupland. Dr. J. A. Barnes, the authority on the Angoni, has very kindly and patiently tried to educate me in some of the elements of anthropology.

I am especially grateful to Sir Dougal Malcolm, President of the British South Africa Company, who has assisted me to the utmost of his power. When I told him that I was interested in his Company's relations with the African Lakes Company, he at once made arrangements to provide me with typed copies of the various agreements and of the land transfers which those agreements involved. I am also greatly indebted to Dr. Roland Oliver, who is writing a biography of Sir Harry Johnston, for placing at my disposal his typed copies of the relevant material in the Cape Town office of the South Africa Company: a glance at the footnote references in the concluding subsection of my book will show how valuable this information has been.

I wish to express my cordial thanks to Miss Fletcher, the librarian of the London Missionary Society, for taking unlimited pains to help me when I was consulting the records of the Tanganyika Mission; and to Dr. Stewart, the Africa Secretary of the Church of Scotland, for doing everything he could to assist me when I presented myself at the offices of the Church. The Rhodes Trustees kindly permitted me to consult the Rhodes Papers, and in working on them and on the Cawston Papers in Rhodes House, Oxford, I was much helped by the friendly co-operation of the library staff. I should also like to record my sincere appreciation of the kindness and consideration shown by the staff of the Institute of Historical Research, and particularly by Professor V. H. Galbraith, who was its Director while I was working there. And perhaps my greatest debt of all is to the late J. E. Todd, Professor of History in Queen's University, Belfast, in my years as an undergraduate: whose magnanimity, eloquence, and passion for truth were an imperishable inspiration to me, as to most others who had the privilege of studying under him.

A. J. H.

14 January 1955

CONTENTS

LIST OF ILLUSTRATIONS

FACSIMILE (REDUCED) OF TREATY WITH TONGA CHIEFS AND HEADMEN

The original is 12″ × 8″

TREATY made at *Bandawe* in *British Central Africa,*
this *23rd* day of *February* in the year 189*4*, between
the undersigned paramount chiefs & headmen of Bandawe
and of Tshitotshi being the Representative chiefs of the whole
along line and Alfred Sharpe Her Majesty Vice Consul.

for and on behalf of Her Majesty the Queen of Great Britain and Ireland,

Empress of India, &c., &c., her heirs and successors, on the one part, and

the Undersigned, *paramount chiefs and headmen of*
Bandawe and of Tshitotshi. B.C.A. for *their*

heirs and successors, on the other part.

We , the Undersigned, *chiefs and headmen* do in the presence of *our*

Headmen and people assembled at this place hereby cede to Her Majesty the

Queen of great Britain and Ireland, Empress of India, &c., &c., all *our*

Sovereign and Territorial rights absolutely and in perpetuity and without

reservation, save that on all lands hitherto belonging to us which may

be leased or sold by Her Britannic Majesty's Representative a percentage of ten

per centum on the selling price or the annual rent shall be paid to *us* or

to whomever shall be recognised by Her Britannic Majesty as chief in *our*

place; and further on the condition that none of our existing villages or

plantations shall be disturbed or alienated without our full consent and proper

indemnification.

We also agree to obey all laws and regulations instituted by Her Britannic

Majesty for the proper governance of the British Central Africa Protectorate.

Done at _Bandawe_ this _twenty third_ day of
February, 1894

Alfred Sharpe
Br Vice Consul

Signed in the presence of

C. Hope Robertson
Lieut Comr RN
S.N.O Lake Nyasa.

I __ the Undersigned, do swear that ✓ have truly and honestly
interpreted the terms of the foregoing Agreement to the Contracting Parties,
in the _Tchinyanja_ language.

Kolumbo Njalezu

Witness to signature:

Alfred Sharpe

Tshikuru ✕ ~~his mark~~

Fuka ⁓⁓⁓ all ~~his mark~~

Marenga ⁓⁓ his mark

Ngombo ⁓⁓⁓ his mark

Kasuna ⁓⁓ his mark

his mark

Mpembi ⁓⁓⁓ his mark

Mubarenga ⁓⁓ his mark

Tshujere ✕ his mark

Kamkumba (Malete) ✕ his mark

Kangoma (Tshulutshi) his mark

Longwe (") his mark

Sawora (") his mark

Nganda (") his mark

Tshmyeule (") his mark

Ngurungaru (") his mark

Kasunga (") his mark

Yagama (") his mark

Tshomani (") his mark

Witnessed — all the above Eighteen signatures
pa Tshiposiola
Kolimbo Nyaleza.

I

CHRISTIANITY, COMMERCE, AND CIVILIZATION, versus THE SLAVE-TRADE

1. *Genesis*

THE great lakes of Central Africa did not become known to the civilized world until after the middle of the nineteenth century. Yet much of the African coast had been under European sovereignty for more than three hundred years, and, although she did not realize it, Portugal held the chief gateway to the vast interior. The Zambesi, it is true, was too shallow to be an ideal waterway; yet, with its tributary the Shiré, it offered access to Lake Nyasa, and from the north end of Nyasa to the south end of Tanganyika the land journey was relatively short and free from natural obstacles.

Such facts, however, were unknown to the handful of fever-ridden Portuguese[1] who occupied the forlorn little settlements of Tete, Sena, and Quilimane. These men were not voluntary emigrants, resourceful and enterprising, adventurously seeking a bright and tolerably honest fortune in the undeveloped regions of the world. For the maintenance of her imperial position Portugal relied on men transported for their misfortunes or their crimes: 'beggars embittered by hardship, thieves, assassins, incorrigible soldiers and sailors, together with a sprinkling of respectable men suffering for their political offences';[2] as for the administration, it was conducted by officials whose salaries were miserably inadequate and usually far in arrears.[3]

It is not surprising, therefore, that when, in 1856, Dr. Livingstone visited the Portuguese settlements on the Zambesi, he found their condition melancholy indeed. He was making his way towards the east coast, in the course of the historic journey across

---

[1] Livingstone commented that they would have been a good deal more healthy if they had lived a less indolent life.

[2] M. V. Jackson, *European Powers and South-East Africa*, p. 23.

[3] Ibid., pp. 32–33; Livingstone, *Missionary Travels* (John Murray edition, 1857), p. 659.

Africa which was to capture the imagination of the British people and establish his position as a national hero. Reaching the confluence of the Luangwa and the Zambesi, he found the natives so sullen and suspicious that he thought his life was in serious danger. This attitude was probably not unconnected with the fact that they had, as they told him, had the 'Bazungu'—white men—living in their midst in days gone by. 'They have reason', he admitted, 'to be distrustful of the whites.' This had in fact been the site of the Portuguese settlement of Zumbo; but now all that remained of it was some ruins built of stone, including a church, beside which lay a broken bell. The place was admirably chosen, yet the failure had been complete. The priest's success had been no greater than the trader's, for the natives 'used the same term for the church bell as they did for the diviner's drum'.[1]

Proceeding to Tete, he found that it consisted of some thirty European houses and 1,200 wattle-and-daub huts. It was the chief bulwark of Portuguese power in the interior of East Africa, and had a garrison of about eighty men; the Portuguese civilians living there were less than twenty in number. The place had formerly enjoyed a certain modest prosperity, exporting about 130 pounds of gold each year, as well as 'considerable quantities' of grain, coffee, and other products. Then, preferring quick profits to a steady annual return, the merchants had sold their slaves for export and thus robbed themselves of their own labour force, so that the total amount of gold they could now obtain had dwindled to a mere eight or ten pounds a year.[2]

'I thought the state of Tete quite lamentable,' wrote Livingstone, 'but that of Senna was ten times worse. At Tete there is some life; here everything is in a state of stagnation and ruin. The fort, built of sun-dried bricks, has the grass growing over the walls.'[3] A Zulu tribe, known locally as Landeens, levied tribute upon the Portuguese in Sena, and the commandant could offer no resistance to them, because the only forces at his disposal were the native militia, and these were utterly unreliable. The place was very unhealthy, being built on swampy ground.

Sena was the lowest point on the Zambesi occupied by the Portuguese, apart from a station, with a garrison of four, at

[1] *Missionary Travels*, pp. 585–7.   [2] Ibid., p. 631.
[3] Ibid., p. 658. There is a contemporary photograph in Sir R. Coupland, *Kirk on the Zambesi*, facing p. 127.

Mazaro near the delta,[1] and an old stone house below the Shiré confluence at a place called Shupanga, which afterwards became the burial-ground of Livingstone's wife, and a sort of shrine where homage was paid by British wayfarers in years to come. Travellers did not usually enter or leave the river by any of its mouths, for the approaches to most of them were blocked to a greater or less extent by a shallow bar, and the only really navigable one, the Chinde, was not discovered till long afterwards.[2] North of the delta the Portuguese had built the village of Quilimane, and made it their port of entry to the Zambesi valley. It was situated on a mud-bank at the mouth of the River Kwakwa, whose slimy banks, with their mangrove trees and their torrid heat, were the breeding-ground of myriads of mosquitoes, the nightmare of every traveller[3] who had to spend several days in their haunts before his canoe reached the point nearest to Mazaro, where the Zambesi and the Kwakwa were only about three miles apart, and were, indeed, connected in time of flood.

In 1858 Livingstone returned to the Zambesi.[4] On this expedition he did not travel alone, as previously; he was now at the head of a little group of pioneers chosen by himself and financed from public funds, and he bore the Queen's commission as consul accredited to the independent rulers beyond the limits of Portuguese jurisdiction, and also to the Governor of Quilimane. He enjoyed the enthusiastic support of both Government and people, and in particular of the Foreign Secretary, Lord Clarendon. His expedition's instructions from the Foreign Office were drafted by himself, and his second-in-command, Dr. John Kirk, commented that 'the sum of them is—live at peace with the natives, obtain all the information we can, and try to bring civilisation among them by introducing arts and commerce as far as may seem proper'. Livingstone's purpose was not merely to satisfy his own curiosity, and that of Europe, about matters of geography. It was to open a highway along which he could be followed by European civilization, and especially by Christianity, whose influence upon the European mind he seems to have exaggerated. He had high hopes

---

[1] E. D. Young, *Nyassa*, pp. 231–3.   [2] See below, p. 142.

[3] For one comment out of many see Young, *Nyassa*, pp. 234–8.

[4] This account of the Zambesi expedition is based mainly on Coupland, *Kirk on the Zambesi*, and on Livingstone's own *Narrative of an Expedition to the Zambesi and its Tributaries*.

that the Zambesi would provide access to the regions beyond
Zumbo, the last point at which Portugal had any vestige of jurisdiction. He had even called it 'God's highway' to the land of the
Barotse in the far interior, with whose Makololo rulers he had
established friendly relations on his previous journey. Kirk
facetiously referred to it as 'his pet river'. It was therefore with
bitter disappointment that he found its navigation interrupted by
the Kebrabasa Rapids, which were fully 120 miles downstream
from Zumbo. If a regular means of communication was to be
opened with the interior, it could not be by the Zambesi itself; it
must be by one of its tributaries. That was why the expedition
turned its attention to the Shiré, and why the culmination of its
work was the discovery of Lake Nyasa in September 1859. The
word 'Nyasa' is itself simply the native name for any broad expanse
of water.

A few weeks before reaching this inland sea, Livingstone had
recorded in a private letter his impressions of the region he was
now exploring.[1]

The country is exactly the same as I found the middle of the continent: exceedingly fertile, and abounding in running streams: but while
the middle country was flat, this is mountainous, and the mountains the
finest I ever saw. They are all green and well wooded, and one, Zomba,
6,000 feet high at least, is inhabited, and has a top about 15 miles
broad. . . .

The Portuguese never went up the Shiré more than a few miles, and
know nothing of the people there except what slaves tell them. We are
on the best terms with them, but they are jealous of our discoveries and
wish to make all appear as their country on the ground of some unknown
documents in their archives.

The exploration of Lake Nyasa could not be undertaken at once,
and about two years elapsed before Livingstone was able to ascend
the Shiré a second time and to launch a sailing-boat upon the lake.
Even then he was compelled to turn back, owing to shortage of
food, while still a considerable distance from the northern end.[2]
From this point until its recall in 1863, the main interest of the
expedition does not lie in any positive achievement, but in the light
it threw upon the working of the slave-trade.

On his return to the Shiré in 1861, he found that the Portuguese

---

[1] F.O. 84/1082: Livingstone to Shelborne, 9 Aug. 1859.
[2] Coupland, *Kirk on the Zambesi*, p. 208.

had turned his discoveries to their own account during his absence of two years. To them, his contribution to geographical knowledge implied merely an extension of their slave-preserve into a district in which they could conveniently operate from their base at Tete. Tete itself had improved considerably[1] since Livingstone had first seen it in 1856, and it appeared to owe its improvement to the energy of its Governor, Antonio Tavares d'Almeida, a brother of the Governor-General. But this unusually active official did not attempt to curb the slave-trade; instead, he took the lead in organizing it. On 16 July 1861 Livingstone and his party found themselves face to face with a slave-caravan at a village on the Lower Shiré. They released the captives and arrested the leader, whom they recognized as a slave of Livingstone's old friend and benefactor, Major Tito Sicard, lately commandant at Tete. A day or two later they released another party of slaves. 'The head of this gang, whom we knew as the agent of one of the principal merchants of Tette, said that they had the licence of the Governor for all they did. This we were fully aware of without his stating it. It is quite impossible for any enterprise to be undertaken there without the Governor's knowledge and connivance.'[2] But the most astonishing feature of this Portuguese effrontery was the frankness shown by Governor Almeida in an interview with Dr. Kirk in the following May, when he bluntly declared that he had communicated with his brother, the Governor-General, and had received from him a confirmation of his own view that Portuguese legislation against the slave-trade applied only to the export of slaves by sea, and that slave-hunting in the interior of the continent was still perfectly legal. He accordingly warned Kirk that any further interference with slave-caravans would be resisted by armed force.[3] This was the merest casuistry. The Cortes had enacted that the state of

[1] 'Two good roads or streets have been made, which is something new for this country. The Governor himself is nearly walked off his feet looking after them. There are some hundreds of black soldiers in the town, who are very much better clothed than a tithe of the number used to be in former years. We were told, on what seemed good authority, that Tette now costs the Home Government £3,000 a year, and yields an annual revenue of £300. The ivory-trade has declined very materially, from the elephants being nearly all killed, or driven off from the part of the country formerly hunted.' (Livingstone, *Narrative of an Expedition to the Zambesi and its Tributaries*, p. 421.)
[2] Livingstone, op. cit., p. 359.
[3] Extract from Kirk's Journal in Coupland, *Kirk on the Zambesi*, p. 233. The facts were published by Livingstone, op. cit., p. 420.

slavery—not merely the slave-trade, but the state of slavery itself
—should end in 1878, and that slaves owned by the Government
should receive their freedom in 1864.[1] As Livingstone put it, in an
official dispatch,[2] 'the employment of the Tette slaves in reducing
their fellow-countrymen to bondage, which these two precious
Governors so complacently contemplate, is but a sorry education
for freedom'. In a dispatch written some months later,[3] he expressed his melancholy conclusion: 'Having seen how men
apparently of good and humane principles, as the present Governor-General was, sink helplessly into the general corruption, . . . I
feel sad in the conviction that, as the Portuguese were the first to
begin the slave trade, they will be the last to abandon it.'

North of the Portuguese possessions, from Cape Delgado as far
as the desert of Somaliland, the East African coast was officially
regarded by Britain and France as being subject to the jurisdiction
of the Sultan of Zanzibar.[4] The wealth of Zanzibar rested primarily
on the trade in slaves, for whom there was a ready market in the
region of the Persian Gulf. The traffic was financed by Indian
traders (who were British subjects), and was conducted by Arabs
and Arab half-castes whose caravans penetrated farther and farther
into the interior, reaching Lake Tanganyika and even ranging
widely in the country known as Manyema to the west of it. At
Ujiji, on the coast of Tanganyika, they established a depot which
grew into an important settlement, and their main trade-route was
from Ujiji overland to the coast opposite Zanzibar. But they were
also at work as far north as Uganda, and in the south they were
active on either side of Lake Nyasa. On the western shore of that
lake, one of them, called Jumbe (that is, 'Prince'), established
himself as a chief, styled himself 'Sultan of Marimba', and made
his settlement at Kota-Kota an important port of call for caravans
about to cross the lake on their way to the seaboard.

The first Europeans to reach the 'Sea of Ujiji'—Lake Tanganyika—were Captain Richard Burton and J. H. Speke, in 1858.
But it was Livingstone, in the last years of his life, who made
known to the people and Government of Britain how cruelly the

[1] Coupland, op. cit., p. 85; Livingstone, op. cit., p. 421.
[2] F.O. 84/1177: Livingstone to Malmesbury, No. 2, S.T., 27 June 1862.
[3] F.O. 84/1200 (for the year 1863): undated dispatch marked 'Separate'.
[4] The history of Zanzibar is related in Sir R. Coupland, *East Africa and its
Invaders*, and its sequel, *The Exploitation of East Africa, 1856–90*.

people of Central Africa were being afflicted by the Arabs, just as he had previously exposed the misdeeds of the Portuguese. He found that the Arabs, like the Portuguese, relied much less upon their own raiding than upon the willingness of Africans to sell prisoners of war, or even members of their own family, in return for the cloth and other trade goods which the Arabs supplied. In a dispatch to the Foreign Secretary, Lord Clarendon,[1] written from the eastern shore of Lake Nyasa, he explained what he had found out on his journey inland:

The process of depopulation goes on annually. The coast Arabs from Kilwa come up with plenty of ammunition and calico to the tribe called Waiyau or Ajawa, and say that they want slaves. Marauding parties immediately start off to the Manganja or Wa-nyassa villages, and, having plenty of powder and guns, overpower and bring back the chief portion of the inhabitants; those who escape usually die of starvation. . . .

The perpetrators of the great annual mischief would themselves be shocked were the guilt not sub-divided. The Kilwa and Zanzibar slave traders do not themselves make forays. These are the work of the Waiyau or Waiau known in the Shire valley as Ajawa. Those who perish by starvation after a foray are probably never seen by the marauders after their flight from the villages. Then those who die on their way to the coast, do so piecemeal. The only victims who might disturb the Arab conscience are those who are tied to trees and allowed to perish. We saw three adult bodies fastened by the neck to trees and their hands secured. It was declared by all the country people that the Arabs, when vexed at losing their money by a slave being able no longer to march, vent their spleen in this inhuman way; but it is probably only the work of those vile half-castes that swarm about every caravan.

Many years afterwards, Captain Lugard quoted with approval what had become a current saying, that 'if you freed three slaves today, two of them, given the opportunity, would sell the third to-morrow'; and he also quoted Dr. Laws, the great missionary, as having commented that 'experience amply confirms this'.[2]

[1] F.O. 84/1265: 20 Aug. 1866.

[2] F. D. Lugard, *The Rise of Our East African Empire*, vol. i, p. 28. Cf. Consul Sharpe's bitter comment on some foolish remarks in a pamphlet by Horace Waller: 'What are the FACTS!! The native *won't* even help himself, and won't take our help. Why? Because it would be himself we should have to help him against. Who is the great upholder of slaving? *The African*. . . . What's HIS [Waller's] little idea of how to stop the native from selling his mother to his cousin?'—Encl. in Johnston to Anderson, 13 Nov. 1894 (in F.O. 2/68).

Passing round the south end of Lake Nyasa, on his westward journey, Livingstone met some of the chiefs of the aggressive Yao tribe—the tribe which he called Ajawa or Waiyau[1]—among them Mponda and Kawinga. When he remonstrated with them for their slave-raiding, they replied, 'What could we do without Arab cloth?' and it was in vain that he retorted 'Do what you did before the Arabs came into the country'.[2] There was no reason to hope that any amount of preaching or persuasion would prevail upon such people to renounce their economic interest in the slave-trade. If, however, they could obtain calico in return for some form of export other than human beings, it was not impossible that they might reconsider where their economic interest lay. The only 'legitimate' export of any importance was ivory: but the ivory-trade, far from competing with the slave-trade, made it more lucrative, since the slave-gangs provided free transport for the elephants' tusks which the dealers bought in the interior and sold at the coast. If some efficient, civilized agency would undertake to supply manufactured goods and to provide means of transport for ivory and any other exports which might be produced, the slave-trade would be undermined.

The idea that 'legitimate' trade would be of great value in counteracting the slave-trade had grown up in the early days of the British anti-slavery movement, and had been powerfully advocated by Buxton.[3] It was championed by Livingstone, and came to be generally accepted by philanthropists and officials. As late as 1894, Acting-Commissioner Sharpe wrote semi-privately to the Foreign Office that 'under the present conditions of transport in Central Africa, ivory and slaves must always to a certain extent be inseparable. Whenever the day comes when there are plenty of Banyan (Indian) merchants settled on Lake Nyasa, . . . then there will be no inducement for the ivory caravans to carry their freight beyond Nyasa, and therefore they would no longer require slaves for the journey to the coast.'[4] It may well have been, however, that slaves—often called 'black ivory'—would have continued to be in demand for their own value. The issue was never put effectively to the test, for legitimate trade was not introduced on the required

---

[1] The prefix 'A' or 'Ba' or 'Wa' means 'people'.
[2] *Last Journals*, vol. i, p. 104.
[3] Coupland, *Kirk on the Zambesi*, pp. 28–39.
[4] F.O. 2/66: Sharpe to Hill, 24 May 1894.

scale until after the *Pax Britannica* had been imposed at the point of the bayonet.

Firmly as Livingstone believed in the need for an economic transformation if Africa was to be freed from the curse of the slave-trade, he was far from imagining that economic progress was all that Africa required. Spiritual and cultural advancement were needed too, and must be promoted with the same vigour as legitimate trade. Christianity, commerce, and civilization must all be introduced, for all were desperately needed. Livingstone's hope for the people whom he served was contained in this famous formula of the 'three C's'.

Before he became an explorer he had been a missionary in the service of the London Missionary Society, and to the end of his life he remained a missionary at heart, driven forward in all his endeavours by his belief that the Bible is 'the Magna Carta of all the rights and privileges of modern civilisation'.[1] During his visit to Britain after his journey across Africa, he had issued his call to the University of Cambridge to see that the door which he was opening was not allowed to close; and Cambridge had responded by founding, in association with the Universities of Oxford, Durham, and Dublin, the 'Universities' Mission to Central Africa'. A High Church Anglican mission had been formed through the initiative of a Scottish Presbyterian. Its first bishop, Charles Frederick Mackenzie, proceeded in 1861 with a party of eight missionaries to the Shiré Highlands—Livingstone himself acting as guide—and settled at a place called Magomero. As it happened, however, the venture was begun at the worst possible time, for the country was being harried and conquered by the Yao,[2] who found the Manganja inhabitants an easy prey. Influenced by Arab traders, who had been visiting them for a long period of time, the Yao descended upon the Shiré Highlands from their homeland north of the Rovuma, slaughtering, burning, and enslaving, and driving the surviving Manganja to inaccessible places, where they were soon in the grip of famine. The Tete merchants then sent up supplies of food, which some of the people were able to purchase

[1] *Missionary Travels*, p. 678.
[2] For the customs and previous history of the Yao see J. C. Mitchell, 'The Yao of Southern Nyasaland', in *Seven Tribes of British Central Africa* (ed. E. Colson and M. Gluckman, O.U.P., 1951).

by surrendering their kinsfolk in exchange. Mackenzie was so grieved and angered by the sufferings inflicted upon the Manganja that he not only used his rifle to defend them, but twice put himself at the head of a war party and took the offensive, with successful results. Not long afterwards, on 31 January 1862, he died of fever, and three weeks later another of the missionaries followed him to the grave. Before his successor, Bishop Tozer, arrived in the middle of the following year, two more had died, and the Yao had recovered their courage and resumed their raids. When Tozer arrived, it did not take him long to reach the conclusion that the mission must withdraw entirely from the Zambesi valley. He decided to establish a station on the island of Zanzibar, and to make it a base from which to build up a chain of stations extending farther and farther into the interior, until the Nyasa country could again be reached, and the work resumed with better prospects of success.[1]

It was not only the English universities who were roused to action by Livingstone's appeal. In 1860 an Edinburgh medical student named James Stewart resolved to plant a mission in the country in which the Zambesi expedition was then at work. Being a member of the Free Church of Scotland,[2] he approached its Foreign Missions Committee and urged them to send him and two of his friends to Central Africa. They felt unable to do so. But Stewart, with astonishing perseverance, brought together by his own exertions and persuasions an influential committee of twenty men, and with their help he raised the funds he needed for a journey to the Zambesi. He spent three months exploring the country east of the Shiré, and long afterwards described it as

a lonely land of barbarism, of game and wild beasts, of timid and harried but not unkindly men, harassed by never-ending slave raids and inter-tribal wars. . . . We had passed through many villages burnt and deserted, just as their unhappy occupants had left them when they fled for life—that is, those of them who were not speared or shot or captured.

[1] For a fuller account see Coupland, *Kirk on the Zambesi*, pp. 185–259.
[2] Formed in 1843, as a result of the famous 'Disruption' of the Established Church, when several hundred of its ministers and about a third of its members seceded from it in the conviction that the secular control was being tightened to such an extent as to strangle its spiritual freedom. The Free Church was notable for the vigour of its work in overseas missions. It was reunited with the Established Church in 1929; the records of both bodies are now to be found in the Church of Scotland's Offices, Edinburgh.

We saw in these villages heaps of the ashes of charred poles in circles like the shape of the huts, broken pottery, a good many bones, but no bodies—the hyenas had attended to that.[1]

So he turned to the Upper Zambesi in the hope that it might provide a better opportunity for the planting of a mission, and proceeded beyond Tete as far as the Kebrabasa Rapids, only to return in the conviction that it was, after all, to the Shiré that any future mission must go out.[2] But when he reported to his committee at home the conditions which he had found there, it decided that no action could usefully be taken; and indeed his own recommendation to them was that action should at least be postponed. Since his scanty financial resources were now exhausted, he had to put aside all thoughts of returning to Central Africa. A few years later, in 1867, he went to the Eastern Province of Cape Colony to take charge of the mission-college of Lovedale.

Yet it was on his initiative that the first successful mission to Nyasa was eventually undertaken. In 1874, having returned to Britain to raise money for his college, he was able to be present in Westminster Abbey when, on 18 April, the embalmed remains of Livingstone were buried there.

On my return to Scotland from that funeral [he wrote], I consulted with some friends as to whether the time had not now arrived to again take up the idea of the projected mission. The subject was carefully considered through an entire summer night, and only when daylight was beginning to appear was the matter finally concluded. But the resolve was made to reopen the question of the South African Mission, and give it the name of LIVINGSTONIA. . . . The mission would thus be a memorial of Livingstone, and the one of all others which I knew very well he would have himself preferred.[3]

When the General Assembly of the Free Church met in May 1874, Dr. Stewart proposed to it the establishment, 'in a carefully selected and commanding spot in Central Africa', 'of an institution at once industrial and educational, to teach the truths of the gospel

---

[1] J. Stewart, *Dawn in the Dark Continent*, p. 209.

[2] His own record of these experiences has been published, together with various letters, as a volume in the Oppenheimer Series, under the title *The Zambesi Journal of James Stewart, 1862–3*, ed. J. P. R. Wallis. See also his biography by J. Wells, *Stewart of Lovedale* (Hodder & Stoughton, London, 1908).

[3] Quoted by Wells (op. cit., p. 125) from Stewart's *Livingstonia, Its Origins*, printed privately in 1894 (copy in library of Church of Scotland Offices).

and the arts of civilised life to the natives of the country'.[1] As it happened, some such project was already under consideration by that Church's Foreign Mission Committee. In the previous March the Committee had been urged by Sir Bartle Frere, a distinguished imperial statesman who could speak with considerable authority on matters concerning East Africa, to send a mission to Somaliland. Further inquiries, however, showed that Somaliland was not promising as a mission-field; and the coast between Somaliland and the River Rovuma was 'already more or less occupied, or in course of being so, by several Societies'. The East African field was thus being narrowed, and it was natural that Stewart's advocacy of Nyasaland should receive increasing attention, especially as it was supported by Sir John Kirk,[2] Livingstone's former companion on the Zambesi, who was now British Consul-General in Zanzibar and a most influential personality. Stewart was accordingly asked to confer with certain laymen whose interest in the scheme had been aroused, and who were willing to contribute generously towards its finances.

This meeting, held in November, unanimously recommended that the Foreign Mission Committee should press forward with the project.[3] It also suggested that the leadership of the mission-party should be entrusted to E. D. Young, of the Royal Navy, who had already visited Lake Nyasa on two occasions. These recommendations were gladly accepted. The Livingstonia Mission was launched.

Meanwhile, the Foreign Mission Committee of the Established Church of Scotland was likewise considering the idea of sending a mission to Africa. The subject was first mooted on 2 June 1874, but the precise reasons which caused it to be brought before the Committee have apparently been lost to history. A sub-committee was appointed, and the Convener, Dr. Macrae, went to London to consult Sir Bartle Frere, Dr. Kirk, and others who could provide helpful information. On 22 December the Committee resolved that it was the duty of the Church 'to take all proper steps for carrying out the proposed Mission without undue delay', and that the co-operation of the Free Church should be invited. Accordingly, in the following February (1875), a joint meeting was held

[1] Wells, op. cit., p. 125.
[2] Mins. Free C. of S. For. Miss. Comm., 17 Mar. and 21 July 1874.
[3] Ibid., 17 Nov. 1874.

by the representatives of the two denominations, who resolved as follows:[1]

As the slave-hunting region around Lake Nyassa is so large and populous as to afford abundant scope for many Missions, it is expedient, under present circumstances, that each Church should appoint its own staff of Agents, and have its own stores and supplies as well as its distinct settlement and field of labour.

The settlements, however, should not be so far from each other as to render easy intercourse at all difficult, it being most desirable that they should render each other all possible assistance. . . .

The Established Church, however, had difficulty in recruiting staff for its new mission, and was only able to send one lay representative to accompany the Livingstonia party when it sailed for Africa. This was Henry Henderson,[2] a man who had acquired a pioneer's experience in Australia, and whose task was to find a suitable site to which the missionaries of his Church could proceed in the following year.

The Livingstonia party was led by Young, to whom the Admiralty had granted two years' leave of absence. The second-in-command was Dr. Robert Laws, a medical missionary; there were also four Scottish artisans and an English seaman.[3] These seven men, accompanied by Henderson, left London in May 1875, travelling by the Cape, and sailed over the bar of the Kongone mouth into the waters of the Zambesi on the evening of 23 July.[4] From that date until 12 October, when they reached the lake, they spent their time to good effect. They had brought with them the sections of a small steamer, which had to be put together on the banks of the Kongone, navigated up the Zambesi-Shiré as far as the Murchison cataracts, taken to pieces, distributed among some 800 native porters, carried a distance of sixty miles over rugged and roadless country, and reassembled in a locality haunted by fever and mosquitoes, whence it could steam without further difficulty into the deep waters of the lake. This little vessel was called the *Ilala*, after the place at which Livingstone had died. It drew only three feet of water, so as to be capable of negotiating the

[1] Ibid., 16 Feb. 1875.
[2] For an interesting biographical sketch see W. Robertson, *The Martyrs of Blantyre*, ch. 1.
[3] W. P. Livingstone, *Laws of Livingstonia*, pp. 41–42.
[4] E. D. Young, *Nyassa*, p. 19.

mud-banks of the Zambesi, and therefore, although it was admirably built, it was rather too light for service on Nyasa, which is sometimes lashed by tremendous gales.[1]

The safety of the *Ilala* had to be the missionaries' first concern, and determined their choice of a site for Livingstonia station. The south end of Lake Nyasa is divided into a fork by the promontory known as Cape Maclear, and here they found a satisfactory harbour. This appealed so strongly to Young that he gave the place credit for a healthiness to which it had little claim, for it was as hot as a furnace. Another disadvantage of Cape Maclear was that it had few native inhabitants, so that the missionaries had little scope for their work of preaching and teaching.[2] But the site was probably as wise a provisional choice as was possible at that time, when as yet the lake had never been properly explored. In spite of its shortcomings, it provided Dr. Laws and his colleagues with a base from which to become thoroughly familiar with the nearby country and with the entire Nyasa shore, to win the confidence of the people, to learn the language, and in every way to establish the foundations of their future usefulness.

Young had not forgotten the disasters which had befallen the Universities' Mission, and he realized that it was essential to the very survival of the mission that its members should be properly housed, since, if they neglected this precaution, they would be very likely to die of fever. By the time the rainy season began on 10 November, a large and durable building had already been erected, and they were ready to explore the lake.

Leaving Livingstonia on the 18th,[3] with Young, Laws, Henderson, and three others on board, the *Ilala* steamed up the east coast, past the towering, majestic cliffs of the Livingstone Mountains, past the flat, marshy plain at the north end, and down the west coast towards Cape Maclear, where they arrived, safe, though exhausted by the gales they had encountered, on 12 December.

Young remained at Livingstonia for some months longer. He supervised the erection of a log fort in which the missionaries could, if necessary, protect themselves against an attack by slave-raiders, and he had the ground cleared of trees and brushwood for

---

[1] E. D. Young, *Nyassa*, p. 66.

[2] R. Laws, *Reminiscences of Livingstonia*, p. 16. Cf. Young, op. cit., pp. 68 and 76.

[3] The date given by Young (op. cit., p. 92). W. P. Livingstone gives it as the 19th (op. cit., p. 75).

a considerable distance, so as to deprive any marauders of cover, and in any case to rid the settlement of some of its snakes and vermin. He saw to the cutting of a deep, wide drain, securely lined with logs, to carry away the water which collected during the rainy season on a flat piece of ground near the station, making it marshy and unhealthy. He constructed a timber slipway on which the *Ilala* could be hauled for repainting and for security against storms. By October 1876 his work was done, and he began his journey home.

○   ○   ○

At the end of 1875 or the beginning of 1876, a citizen of Leeds named Robert Arthington offered an exceptionally generous donation to the London Missionary Society, provided that it would agree to found a mission on the shores of Lake Tanganyika. The L.M.S. was already strongly established in South Africa, and its Directors were considering the practicability of opening up a new field in the centre of the continent, perhaps on Victoria Nyanza. They were therefore favourably disposed towards Arthington's proposal, although they were not altogether ignorant of the 'peculiar difficulties' with which the project would be beset. The offer was accepted.[1] Roger Price, an experienced missionary from the South African field, and the sole survivor of a disastrous attempt to plant a mission on the Upper Zambesi, was sent out to report on the route. On 2 December 1876 his report was considered by the appropriate committee, and early in the following year the expedition sailed.

In June 1877 it left Saadani, on the coast opposite Zanzibar, and began its slow progress overland towards Ujiji. The distance was enormous—on a subsequent journey Captain Hore, the most notable member of the mission, measured it with a measuring wheel, and found it to be 836½ miles.[2] For the transport of its stores the expedition relied upon carts and wagons drawn by large numbers of oxen; but the oxen were bitten by tsetse fly, which Price had inexplicably failed to recognize when he made his reconnaissance in the previous year, and one by one they sickened and died. It became necessary to organize a caravan of porters, and to abandon the idea of using any more efficient mode of transport

---

[1] Mins., L.M.S. Southern Comm., 18 Nov. 1875, 20 Jan. 1876, 1 Feb. 1876.
[2] E. C. Hore, *Tanganyika*, p. 175. This book contains a detailed account of the first eleven years of the mission's history.

until a railway was eventually built, or until an alternative route could be opened by the Zambesi and Lake Nyasa. This latter possibility would to a large extent substitute water transport for portage overland, the distance between the north end of Lake Nyasa and the south end of Lake Tanganyika being only about 200 miles. The country between the two lakes was as yet unexplored, but the suggestion that this might prove to be the most convenient way of reaching Tanganyika had been put forward at a meeting of the Royal Geographical Society in February 1877 by Captain Wilson, a naval officer who had co-operated with Livingstone at the time of the Zambesi expedition, and who was an active supporter of missions to Africa. Wilson's suggestion came to the notice of Captain Hore, who turned it over hopefully in his mind as he plodded forward on the long Ujiji road.[1]

2. The Nyasa and Tanganyika Missions

In October 1876 Dr. Stewart took charge of Livingstonia. After the visit to Britain during which he had successfully launched the mission, he had returned to his duties at Lovedale, and it was from that place that he now proceeded to Nyasa, via Quilimane. He was accompanied by four volunteers from among the students he had trained, and one of these four Kaffirs, named William Koyi, was to do work of the highest importance in the service of the Livingstonia Mission.

They took with them a considerable quantity of tools and miscellaneous equipment, for, as Stewart said, they were 'going as civilisers as well as preachers'. He saw little good, and a possibility of harm, in the kind of emotional evangelism which was not brought to bear upon the plain realities of secular life. 'The reason and object of our industrial training', he explained, 'are not the [economic] value of the labour, but the principle that Christianity and idleness are incompatible.' Livingstonia, then, was to be an 'industrial' mission: that is, the natives should be trained to be competent craftsmen and agriculturists.[2]

With Dr. Stewart and his Kaffirs came a doctor and three artisans as reinforcements for Livingstonia, and also the first contingent of the Church of Scotland mission, consisting of a doctor and five artisans. The first grim year of struggle against savage

---

[1] L.M.S., C.A., Box 1, passim.
[2] Wells, Stewart of Lovedale, pp. 134, 174, 209.

nature was now at an end, and life on the station became more comfortable and happy. It was now possible to undertake regular mission work with more energy than hitherto. A beginning had already been made: on 2 March 1876 Dr. Laws had carried out the first surgical operation in the history of Central Africa, and its success enormously increased his prestige and caused people to come from a considerable distance to be treated by the white man's medicine.[1] The primitive African, understanding little of the laws of cause and effect, regarded medicine as synonymous with magic, believing that if he possessed the appropriate charm or drug he would be immune from the danger of lions or crocodiles;[2] and when Dr. Laws visited the Tonga on the west coast of Nyasa, they asked for 'war medicine' which would make them strong and valiant in battle. The Doctor's medical achievements thus secured for him an extraordinarily high place in the respect of the natives, and went far to open the way for his evangelical and educational work. Rapid, satisfying progress was out of the question in face of what he called 'the blank open-mouthed stare of wondering ignorance which knows nothing about spiritual things and cares less';[3] but he was able to hold informal conversations with those who came to the station, to show them pictures, and especially to try to undermine their implicit faith in the *mwavi* ordeal: the drinking of poison by suspects—especially persons suspected of trying to bewitch their chief—who, if they vomited it, were deemed innocent, and if not, were 'proved' guilty. But Laws placed his greatest hope in the regular instruction of the children, and he had already managed to bring a little class together before Dr. Stewart arrived to take charge of the mission. Long afterwards, he contrasted those humble beginnings with the situation which existed in 1931, 'when there were, in the Livingstonia Mission alone, 644 schools, with 1,347 native teachers and 28,330 pupils'.[4]

Early in 1877 the school was enlarged by the arrival of a number of children from the Shiré: sons of the Makololo chiefs who ruled over the country north of the Ruo and in the vicinity of the

[1] W. P. Livingstone, *Laws of Livingstonia*, pp. 93–102.
[2] For a dramatic illustration of this belief see A. J. Swann, *Fighting the Slave-Hunters*, p. 91. Swann also tells how a native, who had refused to believe that an iron vessel could float, explained the buoyancy of the *Good News* with the disdainful remark: 'You put medicine into it!' (Ibid., p. 102.)
[3] Quoted by Livingstone, op. cit., p. 94.
[4] R. Laws, *Reminiscences of Livingstonia*, p. 64.

Murchison Cataracts. These chiefs were men who had been brought
by Livingstone from Barotseland on the Upper Zambesi, then
under Makololo rule. Taking advantage of the state of turmoil in
the much-raided Shiré valley, they had put themselves at the head
of the Manganja and established a group of strong, well-stockaded
villages capable of bidding defiance to the Yao, and, indeed, to the
Portuguese, against whom they bore a bitter animosity because
one of their number had been killed by a half-caste slave-raider
named Bonga.[1] Their hatred of the Portuguese was equalled by
their respect for the fellow-countrymen of Livingstone, and this
fact, together with the strategic position of their territory, which
occupied the approaches to the lake, was to make them a factor of
exceptional importance in determining the future of Nyasaland.
They ruled their subjects with a rod of iron, and even their
panegyrist, E. D. Young, admitted that their punishments were
harsh.[2] But they were distinguished from all the neighbouring
tribes by their firm refusal to have anything to do with the export
slave-trade, and this fact caused their villages to become cities of
refuge to those who feared that they were about to be sold to some
passing caravan.

The Makololo children who were sent to Livingstonia were
extremely wild, and the difficulty of dealing with them was enhanced by the fact that they were accompanied by a score of their
slaves, who were entirely under their authority and whom they
were at liberty to murder if they should desire a little practice in
the royal art of shedding blood. The slaves were put into the school
along with their young masters, and one of them afterwards became the first convert of the Livingstonia Mission.

Of all the problems which confronted the mission, the greatest
was the attitude it should adopt to the slave-trade. Fortunately for
Livingstonia, the site which had been provisionally adopted on
Cape Maclear was fairly remote from the routes of the slave-
caravans, and the missionaries were able to use it as 'a safe observation post and a quiet training ground, away from the main lines of
native activity and traffic'.[3] The smallness of the population was,
from a long-term point of view, an insuperable obstacle to effective

---

[1] Young, *Nyassa*, pp. 39–40.
[2] Ibid., pp. 46–47. For an ugly example of their cruelty see Livingstone, op.
cit., p. 62.   [3] Ibid., p. 184.

work at that place; but in the short term it was a decided advantage, because it simplified difficulties which would otherwise have been overwhelming. Dr. Laws was able to observe the working of the slave-trade with an objectivity which would have been unattainable without a certain measure of detachment. He collected, from native informants, the following facts about the prices which were current on the lake at that time (1877):[1]

A young unmarried girl	.	.	.	56 yards of calico.
A young woman with baby	.	.	.	36 „ „
(32 for the mother, 4 for the baby)				
A strong young man	.	.	.	. 40 „ „
A toothless old man	.	.	.	. 2 „ „

The natives were willing enough to work hard for the mission in return for calico, and Laws was confirmed in the conviction that the slave-trade could be undermined if they were encouraged to develop such products as cotton and were given the cloth and other commodities which they required in exchange. He even came to the conclusion that the mission itself would be justified in acting as a trading agency, and was impatient with the idea that he and his colleagues would thus be 'soiling our fingers and staining the holy garments of Christian prejudice in the country from which we have come'.[2] He already had much buying and selling to do, merely in connexion with providing food for the missionaries and the hundred or more natives who had settled round the station; on one journey he brought back 2,570 lb. of maize from Makanjira's town on the east coast; in a single year he expended a total of fifteen miles of calico.[3]

However necessary these activities might be, they seriously interfered with the mission's real work, and their deliberate extension in the interests of the African population would have added still more to the weight of the burden, even if Laws was not mistaken in thinking that, in other respects, this course would be judicious. Dr. Stewart was profoundly dissatisfied. 'All this work', he complained, 'pleasant to see, and beneficial as it will be in its

---

[1] Ibid., p. 119.
[2] Quoted by Livingstone, op. cit., p. 121. 'No one', continued Laws, 'has complained of the manual work I have done: I have hauled ropes, driven an engine, sawed wood, while a medical missionary at home or in India would have been making pills or writing sermons. The nature of the case not only justifies but renders such conduct necessary.'   [3] Ibid., p. 120.

results, is material only. It begins and ends with time.'[1] He wrote
to James Stevenson, the Convener of the Livingstonia Sub-Committee of the Free Church's Foreign Mission Committee, urging
how desirable it was in every way that a regular store should be
opened at Livingstonia. Stevenson was a Glasgow merchant, and
himself took up the matter, with the cordial approval of the
Foreign Mission Committee. The problem of supplies involved
a need for adequate means of transport: for a small steamer to
ply on the Zambesi and the Lower Shiré, and also for a road
to link Katunga, at the foot of the Murchison Cataracts, with
Matope, the limit of navigation on the upper part of the river.

In the following April (1878) John and Frederick Moir, sons of
an Edinburgh doctor who was a member of the Committee, expressed a strong desire to trade on Lake Nyasa and asked for the
Church's support. Stevenson accordingly drew up a draft prospec-
tus for a limited Company, and on 21 June the Livingstonia
Central Africa Company was launched. It bought the *Lady
Nyassa*, the paddle-steamer which had by this time been provided
for the river, and hired the *Ilala* from the mission.[2] By September
the Moirs had reached Quilimane. They spent the next few weeks
assembling the sections of the *Lady Nyassa* on an evil-smelling
mud-bank near the town, and then waited until the annual rise in
the Zambesi would fill the Balambwana Channel, which separated
the great river from the Kwakwa at Mazaro. In March 1879 the
flood-water was sufficiently deep to enable them to take the little
vessel across to the Zambesi under her own steam.[3]

During the intervening period, when the steamer was immobi-
lized near Quilimane, Frederick Moir proceeded up-river by boat
and canoe to visit Livingstonia and the lake. By this time Dr. Laws
was in charge of the station at Cape Maclear. Dr. Stewart had gone
back to Lovedale in December 1877, and though he remained
nominal head of the mission,[4] he never found it possible to return.

[1] Wells, op. cit., p. 141.
[2] Ibid., p. 139; Livingstone, op. cit., pp. 143–5; F. L. M. Moir, *After Livingstone*, p. 8; Mins., F.C. of S. For. Miss. Comm., 17 July 1877, 20 Nov. 1877,
18 Dec. 1877, 16 Apr. 1878, 18 June 1878, 16 July 1878. For a photograph of the
Lady Nyassa see Moir, op. cit., facing p. 33.
[3] Moir, op. cit., pp. 9–13, 30.
[4] There was a certain difficulty about Dr. Laws's position, because he was not
himself a member of the Free Church. He had been lent to that body, and his
salary had been provided, by the United Presbyterians, a denomination whose
component sects, united in 1847, had broken away from the Church of Scotland

But his cousin—also named James Stewart—had come to Livingstonia in the previous January. This visitor was a civil engineer in the Indian Public Works Department, and wished to spend his furlough in the service of the mission.[1] At the time of Moir's arrival, Laws and Stewart were preparing to explore the highland plateau which lies behind the west coast of the lake, and to visit its dominant inhabitants, the Angoni. Accordingly, Moir accompanied them on their journey.[2]

The Angoni were comparatively recent immigrants, having lived in Natal until about half a century earlier. They had fought their way northward in two separate migrations, routing all who resisted them by Zulu methods of attack, slaughtering and plundering without mercy, and augmenting their own numbers by impressing their prisoners into their ranks. In the country north of the Zambesi they became divided into half a dozen or more separate communities: one of these became the scourge of the country east of Lake Nyasa, while several others settled west of that lake, on or near the watershed which afterwards became the boundary between Nyasaland and Northern Rhodesia. These Angoni tribes terrorized where they did not rule, and it was only the Bemba, a people as cruel and virile as themselves, occupying the plateau farther west, who were able to withstand their attacks. 'I have seen', wrote Dr. Elmslie, 'an army, ten thousand strong, issue forth in June and not return till September, laden with spoil in slaves, cattle, and ivory, and nearly every man painted with white clay, denoting that he had killed someone.'[3]

Could these bloodthirsty warriors be brought into willing

during the eighteenth century. Relations between the two Churches were excellent—in 1900 they combined with one another to form the United Free Church—but Laws's connexion with Livingstonia was necessarily of a somewhat provisional character, since the Free Church could not be quite sure that the United Presbyterians would not withdraw him for service in another field. In Nov. 1877, however, it was undertaken that no one other than Dr. Stewart should 'be sent out to supersede him in seniority', and in May 1886 he was definitely appointed 'missionary in principal charge'.

[1] Livingstone, op. cit., pp. 109–10.
[2] For an account of this journey see below, pp. 37–38.
[3] W. A. Elmslie, *Among the Wild Ngoni*, p. 79. In his first chapter Dr. Elmslie gives a useful account of the Angoni migrations. A list of authorities on this subject is given by Dr. J. A. Barnes in a footnote on p. 194 of *Seven Tribes of British Central Africa*, edited by E. Colson and M. Gluckman (O.U.P., 1951). I am indebted to Dr. Barnes for communicating to me a great deal of valuable information about Angoni history.

subjection to the rule of law? Upon that question depended the future of Livingstonia and western Nyasaland. But, momentous though it was, Moir and the company he represented were in no position to give any effective help to the missionaries in meeting its challenge. There was no means of opening up a regular trade with the Angoni, even if they had been prepared to beat their spears into pruning-hooks in order to produce commodities with which to pay for the goods they wanted from the Europeans—and this they were certainly not prepared to do. Their country was far from Quilimane, and the company's resources were quite insufficient to enable it to operate on any substantial scale over so long a route in addition to taking up supplies to the mission at Cape Maclear and the Established Church's mission which had by this time been begun in the Shiré Highlands. Its capital amounted merely to £20,000, which Moir admits was far from adequate.[1] Its weakness was shown by the terms of an agreement which was signed on 16 June 1879 by Rev. Duff Macdonald and both the Moir brothers, and which gave the company the use of the storehouse erected by the Established Church's mission at its station, Blantyre. 'We had no agent residing here [Blantyre] regularly to represent us', declared John Moir to the Church's Commission of Inquiry in 1880. 'When we happened to be here during intervals between our journeys, we resided with one or other of the members of the mission. We paid the mission a certain sum per annum for the use of the store and the watching of our property in it.'[2] This was, it

[1] Moir, op. cit., pp. 8–9.

[2] F.O. 84/1565: enclosed in O'Neill to Granville, No. 13, Consular, 18 Nov. 1880. A copy of the agreement forms part of the enclosure. Other points dealt with were the following: A passage upstream, from Mazaro to Blantyre, was to cost £10; for the same journey downstream the charge was £6. 13s. 4d.; a return fare was £15. This did not include baggage, for which the ordinary rate was charged: £12 a ton, either from Quilimane to Blantyre or from Blantyre to Quilimane. The mission was to pay the company £10 per annum for carrying its mails. From these figures it will be seen that Central Africa was a decidedly expensive place in which to live in 1879, especially if the depreciation of the pound since that date is borne in mind.

By a further provision, the Company undertook to pay a third of the expense of repairing the road which had been made from Matope (north of the cataracts) to Katunga via Blantyre, a total distance of about sixty miles. This road had been built by the two missions' (Livingstonia and Blantyre) sharing the expense (Livingstone, op. cit., p. 132). Its construction enabled Livingstonia to dispense with the porterage over the exceedingly difficult country along the bank of the Shiré. But it was not an ideal highway, as Mr. R. C. F. Maugham discovered when he travelled over it as late as 1894. 'The road was an awful one,' he wrote. 'It

is true, a provisional and temporary arrangement, and the Company afterwards erected a store and headquarters of its own on a site, to which they gave the name of Mandala,[1] about a mile distant from the mission. But if the Moirs had been able to draw upon a larger capital, and consequently to engage a larger staff,[2] such a makeshift would never have been necessary. One of its effects was to make the Blantyre mission responsible for the checking of supplies brought up by native porters from Katunga, the limit of navigation on the Lower Shiré, and the missionaries little foresaw the consequences which the acceptance of this and other secular responsibilities would bring upon their heads.

On 23 October 1876 the first party of missionaries sent out by the Church of Scotland established their encampment in a pleasant, well-watered place in the Shiré Highlands, situated some 3,000 feet above sea-level, and surrounded by seven hills.[3] They had been guided by Henry Henderson, the pioneer who had accompanied the Livingstonia expedition in 1875, and who, after sailing round Lake Nyasa with Young in the *Ilala*, and discovering no site which satisfied him, turned south to the country which had been occupied for a time by the unfortunate Bishop Mackenzie. The

had been clearly constructed with little regard either for gradient or camber. Now ascending almost precipitously to some tree-clad shoulder, now descending a forbidding ravine, farther on following round the contour of some majestic mountain, it presented for the most part the appearance of the dry bed of some rock-strewn torrent.' (R. C. F. Maugham, *Africa as I have known it* (John Murray, London, 1929), pp. 73–74.)

[1] 'Mandala' is the Yao word for a flash of light, and the natives applied it to John Moir because they were intrigued by the glinting of the sun on his spectacles. So, in effect, the Company's headquarters were named after John Moir who was the senior of the two brothers.

[2] In 1879 there were only five Europeans serving the Company in Africa, and of these two were required to work the *Lady Nyassa*. This meant that when one of them went on a journey to the north end, there were only two left to look after stores, correspondence, and everything else, and it was only by working far into the night that they were able to carry on their business at all. They had, in addition, their share of tropical fevers and other illness. Their numbers were, indeed, somewhat increased in 1882 (Moir, op. cit., pp. 62–64). But at the end of 1884 Acting-Consul Goodrich informed the Foreign Office that there were still only seven Europeans employed by the Company, including two at Mandala but not including those on the steamer (F.O. 84/1662: Goodrich to Granville, No. 16, Africa, 20 Dec. 1884). In these circumstances the Company could hardly be expected to introduce any very revolutionary changes into the economic life of Central Africa.

[3] A. Hetherwick, *The Romance of Blantyre*, pp. 21–22; J. Buchanan, *The Shiré Highlands*, pp. 201–4.

site he chose was, according to Dr. Laws's biographer, none other than Magomero itself; but the missionaries, weary and feverish, did not proceed so far up-country, but remained where they had happened to spend the night.[1] They called the place Blantyre, after the town where Livingstone was born.

No clergyman accompanied the expedition. The future of Blantyre rested in the hands of a little group of artisans, a young and inexperienced doctor, and Henderson, who, though an invaluable assistant, was quite unfitted for leadership. The country had to some extent settled down since Livingstone's time, because the Yao had established their predominance over the whole of it except those parts near the river where the Makololo ruled. But the slave-trade still flourished, conditions remained unsettled and demoralizing, and there was no paramount chief to establish a single strong rule.

Henderson was fully aware of his own inadequacy, and thinking that his work for Blantyre was done, he wrote home asking to be relieved.[2] Accordingly the Committee resolved, on 13 February 1877, 'to advertise for a Superintendent—clerical or lay—for the Mission'. Strange as it seems, this is the first mention in the Committee's minutes of the idea that a clergyman should be associated with an enterprise whose predominant purpose was the expansion of Christianity. There was, however, a shortage of ordained ministers for the Church's missionary work elsewhere, and on 31 May the General Assembly formally expressed regret that 'so many stations in India still remain very insufficiently manned, and that no ordained missionary has yet been procured for Africa'. They authorized the Committee, therefore, 'to make a direct official call upon ministers and licentiates who may be judged suitable for either country'.[3] A Church which cannot produce a sufficient number of worthy missionaries is a Church which is dying on its feet, and the state of affairs which these words reveal is not creditable to the condition of the Scottish Establishment at that time. By the middle of the following January (1878) the Committee had succeeded in inducing the Rev. Duff Macdonald to give up his charge at Pulteneytown to become their chief agent in Central Africa. In the light of subsequent developments, it is ironical and pathetic to observe the feeling of intense relief to which they now gave ex-

[1] Livingstone, op. cit., p. 106.
[2] Mins., C. of S. For. Miss. Comm., 13 Feb. 1877. [3] Ibid., 5 June 1877.

pression.[1] They were in no position to ask themselves whether or not Macdonald was a man of the right calibre for such an appointment; all they knew or cared was that he was an ordained minister, and they were heartily glad to get him.

Meanwhile, at Blantyre, Henderson had grown desperate. On 1 December 1876, hearing that Dr. Laws was on his way to Quilimane on business, he sent a messenger to the Shiré with a letter in which he begged the Doctor to come and take charge of the station.[2] The appeal was entirely unwelcome, for the responsibilities of the Livingstonia staff were already quite heavy enough; but the path of duty was clear. Livingstonia must not allow Blantyre to collapse if she could by any means prevent it. Dr. Stewart, who was with Laws in the *Ilala*, concurred, and together they ascended the rugged slopes, over which no road had yet been made, and found their fellow missionaries living in a cluster of native huts and quite at a loss as to what to do next. An agreement was therefore drawn up by Dr. Stewart, accepted by all present, and afterwards approved by the Committees of both Churches. By its terms, Livingstonia was to lend one of its missionaries to Blantyre for a provisional period of a year. Dr. Stewart himself took charge at first, and in May 1877 he left the station in the hands of his cousin, who remained responsible for it, except for one short interval when he was relieved by Dr. Laws, until Macdonald arrived in July 1878.[3]

While James Stewart was at Blantyre, he used his professional skill to good effect in the planning of the settlement, the construction of terraces to facilitate gardening, and the making of the road between Katunga and Matope. John Buchanan, the mission's agriculturist, was impressed by the terraces, and more than half a century afterwards Hetherwick paid tribute to the manner in which Stewart laid out the station.[4] Unfortunately, he had other work to do of a less agreeable character.

---

[1] Having made the appointment and the arrangements connected with it: 'The Committee then engaged in prayer, returning thanks to Almighty God for having heard their supplications and supplied the long desired want of an Ordained Missionary to be head of their Blantyre Mission.' (Mins., C. of S. For. Miss. Comm., 15 Jan. 1878.)

[2] The letter is printed by Livingstone, op. cit., p. 105.

[3] Livingstone, op. cit., pp. 106, 113, 116; Mins., F.C. of S. For. Miss. Comm., 17 Apr. 1877. The date of Macdonald's arrival is given in his deposition, in F.O. 84/1565: enclosed by O'Neill to Granville, No. 13, Consular, 18 Nov. 1880.

[4] Livingstone, op. cit., pp. 131-2; Hetherwick, op. cit., p. 29; Buchanan, op. cit., p. 64.

There was so much pilfering of goods, both from the missionaries and on the road from Katunga, that when Dr. Stewart was on
his way to the coast in December 1877, bound for Lovedale, he
had written to Laws: 'This thieving must be brought to an end or
it will end us.'[1] Central Africa, with its fevers and its vermin, was
what Laws called a 'notably cantankerous country',[2] and it was not
unnatural that when, after suffering on several other occasions,
James Stewart lost his best suit of clothes, he resolved to make an
example of the first thief whom he could catch. In February 1878
a man was caught in the act. He was a subject of Ramakukan, one
of the Makololo, and the station natives demanded that he should
be sent to his chief, who could be relied upon to attend to his
speedy execution. Stewart, however, demurred; but he himself
sentenced the man to eight dozen lashes and six weeks in the
stocks.[3] Such is the account of the matter given by Mr. W. P.
Livingstone, who does not state his sources; but two of the artisans
who were eyewitnesses formally declared that a day or two after
being flogged, the man received a second flogging of at least equal
severity, and that salt and water were rubbed into his back after
the first flogging in order to harden it for the second. One of them,
Fenwick, added: 'At first the instrument used was a hammock clue,
but Mr. Stewart said it was not half heavy enough, and substituted
for it a whip made of several ropes mounted on a stick, with knots
at the end of each rope.'[4]

Such was the precedent established for Macdonald's guidance
when he reached Blantyre in July 1878. The only other guidance
he received was contained in the address given him by the Rev.
Dr. Macrae, the Convener of the Blantyre Sub-Committee of the
Church of Scotland's Foreign Mission Committee, before he left
Scotland. Macrae had told him that Blantyre was to be a Christian
colony with people under its protection; and this view had been
embodied in the instructions sent to Henry Henderson in a letter
dated 17 October 1876, 'to act as the General Director, and Christian Magistrate, of the settlement'. The mission, by the time of
Macdonald's arrival, possessed a tract of land some thirty or
thirty-five miles long, and of unspecified breadth, which had been

[1] Livingstone, op. cit., p. 134.
[2] Quoted by Livingstone, op. cit., p. 165.   [3] Ibid., p. 135.
[4] F.O. 84/1565: Depositions enclosed by O'Neill to Granville, No. 13, Consular, 18 Nov. 1880. Supplementary depositions were enclosed by O'Neill to
Granville, No. 15, Consular, 5 Dec. 1880 (in same vol.).

procured from Chief Kapeni in return for 'calico and other articles', and on which some seven villages had sprung up, occupied for the most part by fugitive slaves, whom the mission had willingly received. Its action in so doing was in accordance with the policy at headquarters, for the *Missionary Record* of July 1878 described Blantyre as an asylum for the slave. These fugitives, however, were not themselves innocent of selling slaves: for instance, Kumalomba, the headman of the first village to be founded near Blantyre, had sold one of his wives. The land had been bought by Macklin, the mission doctor, who expressed to Macdonald the opinion that ownership carried with it the right of jurisdiction; a similar opinion was held by Henry Henderson. Thus, by the will of Dr. Macrae and by the principles of native law, Macdonald found himself enjoying the dignity and prerogatives of a Yao chief. He did not relish the position, realizing that it was inconsistent with his duty as an ordained Christian minister, and he did his best to devolve its responsibilities on Macklin and the artisans.

The idea with which I came here [he declared] was that I was to act as Head in much the same way as a minister does in his Kirk-session in Scotland. I expected that each artisan would be practically independent in his own department. I did not know that they had been requested to obey my instructions until I saw the written agreement which had been made with Mr. Duncan. I saw it first at Quilimane in May, 1878. I relied on Dr. Macklin, in consideration of his experience, taking the leading charge of secular matters. I was advised in a letter from Dr. McRae to Dr. Macklin, soon after my arrival, that this charge should be left much to him.

He added that no written agreement had ever been presented to him on behalf of the Church for signature. Thus, with a carelessness and improvidence which can scarcely be believed, Macrae and his Committee launched a weak man into a welter of undefined responsibilities.[1]

Macdonald had considerable ability and some excellent qualities of character, and might have done useful missionary work as second-in-command to a strong and judicious head. He had a real affection for the natives, especially the children whom he had gathered round him in his school, and was never happier than on the two occasions when he took them for an annual picnic to the

[1] Depositions, loc. cit. For Macdonald's own not unreasonable comments on his treatment see Duff Macdonald, *Africana*, vol. ii, pp. 203–10, 259–61.

top of a nearby mountain. He made a diligent study of the languages, and of the customs and folk-lore of the Yao tribe.[1] It is with the utmost good humour that he relates how he found that his house-boy had been in the habit of playing football with the cloth which was used to strain the milk; how the white ants surmounted every obstacle in order to devour his food; and how, throughout the night, a horde of rats kept up a continuous dance on his biscuit-tins, at the same time emitting vocal noises which resembled human laughter.[2] What he lacked was the determination to strike out a line of policy in accordance with his own principles, and to pursue it in the face of opposition with inflexible tenacity of purpose.

About the beginning of 1879 Fenwick, one of the artisans, found the body of a murdered woman lying in the middle of the stream which flowed through the station. Chief Kapeni was called upon to help in finding the murderer, but he was offended by the mission's policy of harbouring runaway slaves, and temporized. Some weeks later one of the natives at the station reported that he had heard two men who had been trained as carpenters openly boasting in another village that they were the murderers; so, when they returned to Blantyre, they were set to work to make a pair of stocks, and, having completed their task, were arrested and secured in them. They received some sort of trial from the white men, acting together with Kumalomba and the other headmen of the villages which had been built on the mission's land, and it was unanimously agreed that they were guilty and must die. The missionaries, however, were reluctant to execute the sentence, and were disposed to hand the men over to Kumalomba. While they were trying to make up their minds as to what precisely was required of them by the powers of civil jurisdiction which they had assumed, the prisoners remained in the stocks, and the rats bit holes in their feet. Then, on 19 February (1879), one of them escaped. 'As the villagers seem to fear that we are interposing between these men and their punishment,' wrote Macdonald in his diary, 'the other one, Manga, must be executed immediately.'

So, on 20 February, a grave was dug and the condemned man

---

[1] Duff Macdonald, *Africana*, vol. i and Appendix to vol. ii, *passim*.
[2] Ibid., vol. ii, pp. 75–77, 122–33. Macdonald's diary records (under date 6 Aug. 1879) that 168 rats were killed in a single afternoon when the school was given a holiday for that purpose.

was led to the head of it. He was then informed by the minister that he was not being killed because of any feeling of vindictiveness, but because the Word of God required it. When Macdonald had completed his explanations, a squad of natives were ordered to fire, and they obeyed the command with a clumsiness of which the details are sickening to read.

Some time before this, when a carrier in charge of a load of the company's beads had arrived at the station, it had been found that his load had been opened and some of the beads removed. The man received no trial: his guilt was assumed: he was at once stripped, tied to a tree, and flogged simultaneously by two natives under the supervision of Macdonald and the artisan Buchanan. When he had received what appeared to one witness to be over a hundred strokes, he was asked to confess, which he did. He was then bidden to lead his captors to the place where he had hidden the beads. He led them for some distance, but no beads could be found, so he was flogged again and put in the stocks with the men who were condemned to death. When the alleged murderer was executed, he was forced to witness the scene, and naturally thought he was to suffer a similar fate. Instead, however, he was given another flogging at the head of the grave, and when most of the skin had come off his back he was set free. One of the whips used on him eventually reached the Foreign Office, and was thus described by T. V. Lister: 'It has a bamboo handle and 3 thick rhinoceros hide thongs which would cut out strips at every blow. It is not suitable for riding or driving and looks as if it were specially made for flogging men.'

Afterwards, it was found that the missing beads had been extracted by John Moir himself, who, in the blundering way in which he seems to have managed everything he did, forgot to send an explanatory note to Blantyre. The carrier was entirely innocent.

A fortnight later, on 7 March, another alleged thief was given seventy-five lashes by one of the artisans, who then decided that he had had enough and was about to let him go. Before he could do so Buchanan rushed up, bellowing that he had 'not had half enough', and that the man who was flogged on the previous occasion had had far more. In other words, the standards of justice which had then been established constituted a precedent which had now to be maintained. Buchanan accordingly took charge, and bade two native workmen to lay on lustily, otherwise they would lose their week's wages. At the end of the punishment the prisoner was left in the store to recover. By five o'clock he was dead. Dr. Macklin, to hush the matter up, said he must have been diseased in some way, and Macdonald records this view in his private diary, thereby showing that he apparently believed it to be true; but Macklin admitted privately that it was the flogging alone which had caused the man to die.[1]

These were not the only instances of maltreatment, but they were by far the worst.[2] Macdonald seems to have felt thoroughly uncomfortable about the whole matter. 'I may mention,' he pleaded, 'that when I first saw a flogging I expressed sympathy with the man so much that Dr. Macklin had to tell me not to do so or else the flogging would lose its proper effect.' And Robert Henderson, the engineer of the *Lady Nyassa* (and not to be confused with Henry Henderson), declared:

In reply to the question what part Mr. McDonald took as head of the Mission, in these cases he was nowhere. I believe he was always consulted, but that Dr. Macklin and Buchanan guided him. . . . I always thought him soft, and that he hid his softness by sticking through thick and thin to whatever he had once agreed to.

The soundness of Henderson's view was shown when Macdonald and Fenwick visited a chief named Mitioche, who had robbed a party of carriers bearing calico to a sub-station which had been started by Buchanan on Mount Zomba. Before setting out, Macdonald had sought advice from Dr. Laws, who had warned him to avoid bloodshed and to be cautious, adding shrewdly that 'to overpower the natives with the arms you have would be a comparatively easy matter compared with fighting the public at home for the rest of your life'.[3] But Macdonald's idea of caution was to walk into Mitioche's village at 4 a.m., the hour when, as Fenwick warned him, any visit would be interpreted as a raid. The cry of 'War, War,' was raised, and soon the mission party was surrounded by a yelling, menacing mob. 'I felt sorry for Mr. MacD.', said Fenwick. 'He certainly did look out of his element,

---

[1] Depositions; Diary; F.O. 84/1564: O'Neill to Granville, No. 34, Confidential, 28 Apr. 1880: minute by Lister.

[2] Shocking as the Blantyre floggings were, the guilt of their perpetrators was not unique. Floggings equally savage were inflicted at Frere Town by the representatives of the Church Missionary Society. A report on the subject by Consul Holmwood is enclosed in Kirk to Granville, No. 91, 21 July 1881, in F.O. 84/1600.   [3] Livingstone, op. cit., p. 170.

and I believe he felt like a fish on dry land. For one thing, he caught hold of my arm and said, "Oh, if you fall I shall never get back to Blantyre."' They were, however, able to withdraw after the villagers had worn themselves out with leaping and jeering; but they were pursued, and there was a running fight for the first two miles of their retreat. On reaching Blantyre, Macdonald went to bed for a week in a state of complete physical and nervous exhaustion.

On the day after his return, while he was in this condition, and burning with humiliation, he ordered Fenwick and another artisan to lead a party of natives to set fire to Mitioche's village; but the only result of this mad act was that one of the enemy was killed and several were wounded, for the artisans called off the attack as soon as one of their own followers was hit by a bullet.

Macdonald reported both the execution and the fighting to his Committee, and he seems also to have sent them some information about the floggings. They at once disavowed all responsibility for the infliction of capital punishment, but refrained from passing judgement until they had considered the matter further and sought advice from the Free Church.[1] Meanwhile Macrae wrote to Macdonald, expressing the hope that 'the example will strike a salutary terror'; and as late as 4 February 1880 he thus expressed himself:

We have come no nearer to the resolution of the civil and criminal questions. Until we do, you must just act as you have hitherto done, justly and according to circumstances. . . . At all our meetings I have declared, and strenuously, the justice and scripturalness of your acts; have declared that I share all your responsibility, and have declared that had the murderer been allowed to escape it would in my mind have been to the lasting infamy of the Mission at Blantyre.[2]

But, having obtained legal advice, the Committee made the belated discovery that if British subjects took the law into their own hands in regions where there was no settled government, they could be made to answer for their actions in a British court of justice. So, on 23 March 1880, they directed that Macdonald should be told to abandon all civil jurisdiction, which must be left to the native headmen.[3]

There the matter might have rested, had not a Fellow of the

[1] Mins., C. of S. For. Miss. Comm., 28 May 1879.
[2] Quoted by Macdonald in Supplementary Depositions, loc. cit.
[3] Mins., C. of S. For. Miss. Comm., 23 Mar. 1880.

Royal Geographical Society named Andrew Chirnside, who had been visiting Nyasaland, published a pamphlet,[1] disclosing all that had happened. When this came before the Committee, the Rev. Dr. Rankin was appointed to go to Blantyre and investigate the charges, and was given full powers to alter the character of the mission or even, if necessary, to suppress it altogether. In particular he was to inquire how best the missionaries could be dissevered from magisterial functions. 'Government', he was told, 'is indispensable; evildoers must be restrained and punished, but the power should not be in the hands of those who have gone forth as the Ambassadors of Christ's Gospel.' A letter was also sent to Lord Granville, the Foreign Secretary, asking that O'Neill, the British consul at Mozambique, should be instructed to accompany Dr. Rankin and assist him in his work.[2] The Foreign Office promised to send the necessary instructions, but, in the event, O'Neill was prevented by illness from carrying them out.[3] But a lawyer named Pringle volunteered to accompany Rankin at his own expense, and was appointed to act as Deputy Commissioner.

The result of the Commissioners' work was the recall of the entire staff except one or two of the artisans. Blantyre had virtually to be refounded.

When Chirnside reached Mozambique on his way home from Blantyre, he called on Consul O'Neill and told him about the atrocities which he had seen. The consul was astounded and dismayed. He at once sent a friendly private letter to Macdonald asking for an explanation, and at the same time wrote to the Foreign Secretary, pleading for instructions:

I confess, my Lord, I am at a loss to know how to proceed in such a matter, and respectfully request that instructions be given me as to whether further enquiries should be made, and whether those enquiries should be of an official character. If there be truth in what we hear of the harsh and inhumane treatment of natives, it should be stopped before the Portuguese authorities hear of them and institute enquiries

---

[1] *The Blantyre Missionaries: Discreditable Disclosures by Andrew Chirnside, F.R.G.S.*

[2] Mins., C. of S. For. Miss. Comm., 1 June, 15 June, and 20 July 1880.

[3] He was, however, provided with a copy of the depositions and of Pringle's (though not of Rankin's) report. These were forwarded to London and are now with O'Neill's dispatches in the Public Record Office. See reference above, p. 26, n. 4.

which will bring a storm of abuse upon the whole mission, throw discredit upon all our mission work, and give occasion for abundant sneering in the Portuguese press, which they will not be slow to indulge in, with respect to our humanitarian policy in East Africa and on the coast.[1]

The Foreign Office decided to take no action until it received Macdonald's reply to O'Neill's letter. The reply, when it came, was such a feeble attempt to make light of the whole matter that they read it with anger and contempt. T. V. Lister thought it would be undesirable to send O'Neill to Blantyre, which was not in his consular district.

As he would have no power [added Lister], it seems very important that neither he, nor the F.O. thro' him, should have any responsibility for the doings of the Mission.

Mr. Macdonald, to judge from his letter, would have made an admirable inquisitor, and would have delivered over his prisoners to the civil power with tender and well understood instructions for their treatment.

But Lord Tenterden was not content to dismiss the matter with a jibe. 'Can anyone go to Central Africa and do as he likes?' he asked. 'What does Pauncefote think of the case?'

Lister replied that he was very unwilling to communicate with the Church of Scotland 'until we have an overwhelmingly strong case', especially as they had already appointed a Commissioner.

They are very rancorous and have a widespread influence, and would resent most bitterly any attempt to expose the misdeeds of their missionaries.

... I am not aware of our having any means to prevent British subjects from torturing and murdering people in Central Africa, if the Central Africans will let them do it.

Sir Julian Pauncefote, however, corrected him on this point, but thought it improbable that sufficient evidence could be obtained to secure a conviction. It was by his advice that O'Neill was told to go to Blantyre, lest 'our *inactivity* may damage us in the estimation of the Portuguese at Mozambique, who know all about it; and may be difficult to defend here by and by'.[2]

Afterwards, when the depositions reached London, Lister com-

---

[1] F.O. 84/1564: O'Neill to Salisbury, No. 11, S.T., 3 Feb. 1880.
[2] F.O. 84/1564: O'Neill to Granville, No. 34, S.T., Confidential, 28 Apr. 1880: minutes.

mented that no action need, or could, be taken until they had been considered by the Church.[1] In all probability the Foreign Office was well satisfied by the decisions finally reached, and was only too pleased to find that the Augean stables had been cleansed without its help.

    ⌒   ⌒   ⌒

At Livingstonia the problem of civil jurisdiction was not acute, because the settlement was small. The Blantyre depositions, indeed, contain a statement by Robert Henderson to the effect that two of the Livingstonia artisans, who had gone down to Katunga, discovered a case of fornication and reported it to the local chief, after whom the place was named. Katunga was one of the Makololo, and in their country, as Young testified with great satisfaction, strict chastity was the universal rule.[2] Accordingly, the chief ordered the woman to be tortured, and under torture she named another woman who had similarly offended, whereupon the two women had their heads crushed between poles and slowly bled to death. The artisans, of course, had no direct responsibility for the barbarities inflicted by Katunga; but they were indirectly responsible, for they made no attempt to secure the women's release, and one of them boasted to Henderson that 'he would do the same again if similar circumstances occurred'.[3] But such a mentality was in no way representative of the mission's leaders. Dr. Laws once ordered a native to receive twenty lashes as a punishment for raping one of the girls from the school, but he stopped the flogging after the thirteenth stroke, and on no other occasion did he ever order a native to be flogged.[4] As for Dr. Stewart, he disapproved entirely of flogging, and strongly resented the allegation, which had been made at Blantyre when the depositions were being taken, that it was he who was responsible for introducing the system in the first place.[5] This allegation had,

[1] F.O. 84/1565: O'Neill to Granville, No. 13, Consular, 18 Nov. 1880: minute.   [2] E. D. Young, *Nyassa*, pp. 47–50.

[3] Supplementary Depositions, loc. cit.   [4] Livingstone, op. cit., pp. 136–8.

[5] Stewart to Macrae, 5 Jan. 1880. This was read by Macrae at a joint meeting of the Blantyre and Livingstonia Sub-Committees, and is reproduced in Mins., F.C. of S. For. Miss. Comm., 17 Feb. 1880. 'My view, without any doubt,' added Dr. Stewart, 'and my recommendation or advice, would be that no mission should take the power of life and death into its hands, but rather hand over the culprits to their own chiefs, if they have them, or deport them out of the country, if they have none. If a regular civil administration were set up in the country, the case would be different.' In effect, it must be noted, expulsion

presumably, been made by someone who confused him with his cousin and namesake.

Livingstonia would have suffered to a far greater extent than it did from the ills of Blantyre had it adopted the Blantyre policy of becoming a sanctuary for runaway slaves. Fortunately the missionaries, unlike those of the Established Church, had been provided with detailed and prudent instructions, drawn up for the most part by Dr. Stewart; and these, while allowing them a certain amount of discretion, strictly forbade forcible interference with the slave trade.[1] This necessarily meant that they must withhold their protection from fugitive slaves. Dr. Laws appreciated the wisdom of this provision, but it was naturally at variance with his intense desire to set the captive free.

However much non-interference is correct theoretically [he wrote to his Committee],—and I uphold it as the best order that could have been given on the subject—there is still in the breast of every free-born Briton such a hatred of the horrid traffic in human flesh and blood that when one comes across a gang of poor, half-starved, wayworn fellow-creatures on their way to the coast, and is morally certain that a word from his lips or a flash from his eye is enough to set them all at liberty, need it be wondered at that the temptation to do what is at the moment good for these creatures should overcome the patient waiting which the judgment of calmer moments pronounces to be the better and surer plan to obtain ultimate success?[2]

Accordingly, he provisionally adopted, and the Committee sanctioned, the following rule: If a fugitive came to the station, he should be given sanctuary, unless his owner claimed him within one month and proved that he had committed some crime. The slave must, however, be willing to work to earn the cost of his ransom.

This should be, in a given case, the price paid for the slave by his master, or, if this cannot be ascertained, then the current price of slaves

from the mission was really a severer sentence than one of flogging, for, as Mr. Livingstone points out (op. cit., p. 124), if the offender was sent back to a Makololo chief, he would be executed, while Dr. Laws himself remarked that a man who was banished and who had no village and no kin to protect him would be fairly sure to fall into the hands of a slave-dealer (quoted by Livingstone, op. cit., p. 171). Yet the only alternative to this course was the intolerable one of assuming powers of civil jurisdiction. In these circumstances it is small wonder that the Livingstonia mission repeatedly pressed the Government to set up some sort of protectorate.

[1] Livingstone, op. cit., p. 44; J. W. Jack, *Daybreak in Livingstonia*, p. 40.
[2] Quoted in Mins., F.C. of S. For. Miss. Comm., 17 Feb. 1880.

in the district. When the price is paid for, it should be paid over to the master on application by him for it.

My reasons for proposing and now insisting on a ransom being wrought for are that it gives compensation to the slave-holder, as Britain herself has done, and, next, that it is a test of the sincerity of the slave. If a man does not think his liberty worth a little self-denial to procure, he is unworthy of it, and would most probably give us a good deal of trouble after he had got it.[1]

It was well that this painful question had been settled, for the time was approaching when Livingstonia must leave the relative seclusion of Cape Maclear and establish itself in a populous district, where its opportunities of doing good—and also its dangers of committing a disastrous blunder—would be greatly increased. The work had, indeed, been growing at Cape Maclear: for example, in 1880 Dr. Laws had 776 patients, some of whom had come a long distance to be healed. Still, by 1881 the time had come to move. The question of a new site had been under consideration since 1877, when Dr. Stewart and Dr. Laws had made a careful search on the west coast without reaching any definite conclusion. The place eventually chosen was called Bandawe, on a low ridge near the shore of the lake. By October 1881 the mission and all its movable property had been transferred to it, and Old Livingstonia was left under the control of a native headman, with a court of seven to administer native law and a native teacher to teach the children in the school.[2]

Before its removal, the mission had lost no fewer than five of its staff through death, and several others had retired or been invalided home. So, in spite of having been reinforced, it consisted only of Dr. and Mrs. Laws and two artisans. But its worst difficulties did not arise from its lack of staff but from the political conditions of the country.

When the Angoni warrior-horde had arrived in the vicinity of Lake Nyasa, the original inhabitants had been broken and dispersed. The survivors had sought refuge in the most inaccessible places they could find, and lived like sea-birds on narrow ledges of rock on the sheer face of the mountains, or eked out an unspeakably wretched existence on tiny rocky islands in the lake, north of Bandawe; while others built their villages in pestilent swamps

[1] Quoted in Mins., F.C. of S. For. Miss. Comm., 17 Feb. 1880.
[2] W. P. Livingstone, *Laws of Livingstonia*, pp. 182–9.

where Dr. Elmslie had afterwards to be carried from door to door through a morass of 'semi-liquid, black, stinking mud'.[1] No one, however, in that region dared to defy the Angoni, until, a year or two before the arrival of the mission, there was a desperate revolt among the Tonga, their subjects, who successfully established several independent villages on the shore of the lake. Such was Livingstonia's new mission-field. The Tonga were demoralized by the frequent raids made upon them by their former masters, who bitterly resented their rebellion and were determined that they should either be annihilated or subdued. In their mortal peril the Tonga were constantly bickering among themselves, and, although they had suffered so greatly from the inhumanity of others, they were actively engaged in the export of slaves across the lake. Their villages were 'kept without exception in a most filthy condition';[2] and Dr. Laws declared that they were given to 'a wickedness and degradation of which the people at home have no conception'.[3] In such circumstances he realized the need for the greatest caution, and resolutely withstood all temptation to assume authority for the purpose of putting some sort of order and decency in place of the anarchy and depravity which he saw around him. He entirely abandoned the practice of receiving slaves, and would not even give them sanctuary for a night. Still less would he yield to the plea of the Tonga that he should lead them against the Angoni, though it was hard to answer their argument that 'you cannot hold a discussion with a wild beast; you can only go to it with a gun'. He advised them to unite in their own defence, but he refused to be himself their rallying-point.[4]

There was only one way in which the mission could properly help the Tonga to survive their perils, and that was by securing a moral influence over the Angoni raiders themselves. Dr. Laws had been in touch with them for several years. Some of them had visited the station on Cape Maclear, apparently in 1877, and had received as hospitable a reception as it was possible to offer. William Koyi, one of the Kaffirs whom Dr. Stewart had brought up from Lovedale, was able to converse freely with them in their own language, and Laws at once appreciated how valuable this

---

[1] W. A. Elmslie, *Among the Wild Ngoni*, pp. 83–89.
[2] F.O. 84/1702: Goodrich to Granville, No. 1, 19 Feb. 1885.
[3] Quoted by Livingstone, op. cit., p. 186.
[4] Ibid., pp. 186–91.

might prove. Towards the end of 1878 he set out for Angoniland with James Stewart, Fred Moir, William Koyi, and the native headman of the village at Livingstonia station, taking also eight armed natives and the necessary carriers. Their first visit was to Chikusi, chief of the southern Angoni, whose people were amazed at the temerity of these strangers who calmly walked into their village and sat down beside the cattle kraal. The white men, they protested, must have come in order to bewitch the chief. He himself was so much dominated by this idea that for several days he refused to grant an interview.[1] When at length he came forward, he seemed to Dr. Laws to bear the appearance of 'a determined, cruel man, deeply under the power of superstitious fear'.[2] Before venturing to show himself, he had caused a man, a dog, and a fowl to drink *mwavi* to determine whether or not the white men had evil intentions; and it was well for the visitors that in every case the poison was vomited, so that their innocence was 'proved'. As a result of the interview, Chikusi asked for a copy of the Bible, which, as far as he could judge from what the Doctor had said of it, seemed to be 'medicine' of no ordinary value; and Laws very properly refused to comply. Nothing more could be achieved on a first visit, and the party returned to the lake.[3] It was not, however,

[1] In his book, Fred Moir does not mention this first visit to Chikusi; perhaps his recollection as to the order in which events occurred was growing rather confused. But he tells us that he was at Chikusi's some years afterwards, and saw with his own eyes the evidence of this man's obsession with the idea of witchcraft and his consequent inordinate recourse to the poison ordeal. Six of his wives were made to drink *mwavi* during Moir's visit. 'Two of the six women died, and their bodies were left exposed, and parties of young men armed with spears and clubs immediately dashed off to kill their relatives and seize their property. That night the plain resounded with the yells of hyenas as they fought over the corpses.' When Moir was about to leave, he saw a long column of the ordinary tribesmen being marshalled for the ordeal. 'We estimated that there were two hundred in sight, and more were to come later on.' (Moir, *After Livingstone*, chap. viii.)

[2] R. Laws, *Reminiscences of Livingstonia*, p. 67. Moir obtained his waist measurement by promising to send him a shirt: it was four feet seven inches (Moir, op. cit., p. 56). 'Like most chiefs', wrote Dr. Laws (op. cit.), 'he was gross and unwieldy in body, being an inveterate drinker.' The drink in which the chiefs indulged so freely was *pombé*, the native beer. Young mentions that Mponda, the Yao chief at the south end of Nyasa, required the assistance of one of his wives, who stood behind him and stroked his stomach, with what Young described as 'a sort of shampooing action', during his potations (Young, *Nyassa*, p. 63). Dr. Elmslie gives an amusing description of Mombera, more than half hidden behind his *pombé*-pot, in *Among the Wild Ngoni*, pp. 109–11.

[3] Except where otherwise stated, this account of the visit to Chikusi is based on Livingstone, op. cit., pp. 146–50.

until 1886 that Livingstonia was in a position to establish a sub-station in Chikusi's country, and when the tyrant died, seven of his wives were buried with him, and thirty of his subjects succumbed to the *mwavi* ordeal. His country lay far to the south of Bandawe, and, after the removal of the mission, it was with the northern Angoni, under Mombera, that an understanding had to exist if Livingstonia was to remain.

In January 1879 Dr. Laws succeeded in obtaining access to that potentate, taking with him the same companions as on the visit to Chikusi. Mombera, who, apparently without realizing it, was the very personification of insolence, showed a not unfriendly interest in his Scottish visitors, asking them if they wore clothes because they were ashamed of their white skins; and, when Dr. Laws told him that by obeying 'the Book' and giving up war and plunder, his people would become richer and greater than they were, he expressed the wish that the mission should establish its headquarters at his village. He protested, however, against the founding of an observation post at Bandawe. This had been done some weeks earlier, as a tentative step towards the removal of the mission from Cape Maclear to that place. To Mombera and his arrogant Angoni it was incomprehensible, and something of an insult, that the white men should reside among their rebellious slaves rather than among themselves. Dr. Laws explained that the Gospel was for the Tonga as well as for them, but what doubtless was more intelligible and acceptable to them was the argument that the missionaries required to have a port to which the steamer could bring their supplies. He also made it plain that they would be strictly neutral in the quarrel between the Angoni and the Tonga. He expressed his regret that it was not yet possible to send them a European missionary, but promised that as soon as possible they should have a native teacher such as Koyi.

This visit was of incalculable importance for the future, even though more than three years elapsed before it could be followed up by the establishment of a permanent sub-station. The deep respect with which Mombera ever afterwards regarded Dr. Laws gave the mission an opportunity to take up its work among the northern Angoni with some prospect of success. Its first member to undertake the task was Koyi, who was afterwards joined by James Sutherland (an artisan), and later by Dr. Elmslie. These three men had much to endure, for a considerable part of the tribe was eager to murder them, and they owed their lives to the protection afforded by the chief himself. The Angoni could not understand why the missionaries remained with them when nothing was being achieved, and taunted them with the futility of their work. They frequently forced their way into the missionaries' hut and insolently demanded presents; in this respect Mombera was no less offensive than any of his subjects. With the passing of time, however, some of the people became more friendly, largely because of Elmslie's medical work, and in 1885 Mombera and his councillors at last gave permission for the opening of a school. But two years later a crisis developed, and the whole Livingstonia Mission was in mortal danger. Mtwaro, the chief's powerful brother, and other notables insistently demanded the abandonment of Bandawe, while at Bandawe the terrified Tonga kept Dr. Laws a virtual prisoner. In October the situation seemed desperate. Neither the Angoni nor the Tonga would be satisfied unless the missionaries would take sides in their feud, and the Tonga would not allow them to withdraw to another part of the lake until passions cooled. Then, at a great meeting of the assembled Angoni headmen, after hours of tedious debate, the whole matter was settled when the missionaries offered to open a sub-station at Mtwaro's—a step which they had for years been desiring to take, but had been prevented from taking by Mombera's determination to keep them under his own supervision so that he could monopolize whatever benefactions it might be possible to wring from them.

Peace had been secured, and it was permanent. There were no more raids on the Tonga. The work of the mission went forward steadily among the Angoni, and in 1897, after the death of Mtwaro, who had succeeded Mombera on the latter's death in 1891, the people elected Mtwaro's son as their chief, although he was not only a Christian but an ordained elder in the native church. In 1896, when one of the old war-leaders made a last attempt to rouse the people for war, the young men quietly refused to listen to him and to those veterans who wished to follow him, and the agitation served only to show that the old order had passed away.

It was now possible for the harassed people whom the Angoni had driven to the mountain-ledges to return from their barren places of refuge, for their former persecutors were ready to welcome them as friends. On the shore of the lake, the Tonga abandoned the large squalid settlements in which they had huddled for defence, and dispersed in small communities where they could settle down with confidence to a normal village life.[1]

⚬   ⚬   ⚬

The clergyman appointed by the Church of Scotland to take charge of its mission at Blantyre after the dismissal of Macdonald was David Clement Scott, a mystic and an idealist who, according to his colleague, Rev. Alexander Hetherwick, was in the habit of using language so lofty that it was unintelligible to most white men, and still more so to the Yao whom he was sent out to teach— but who could nevertheless inspire respect and win loyalty even from those who were very imperfectly able to grasp what he had in mind.[2] Scott was responsible for an amazing achievement—the construction of Blantyre Church, a building of rare dignity and beauty, rising majestically amidst hundreds of miles of wild countryside where, except for the houses of the missionaries and the fortified store which had been erected (in 1882) at Mandala, nothing had ever been built except the wattle-and-daub huts of the primitive inhabitants. Scott himself acted as the architect, though he had never been trained as such, and he kept the project hidden from the knowledge of his Committee until it had been completed, in the belief, which he probably had every reason to entertain, that they would forbid him to proceed with it on the ground that it was utterly impracticable. The church was opened in 1891.[3]

The instructions with which the Committee furnished its new missionaries showed how thoroughly it had learnt its lesson from the bitter experiences of the preceding months. 'You must always keep in view', the missionaries were told, 'the fact that you are labouring to found and build up a Christian Church, and not laying the foundations of a British Colony or of a small State. . . . Carefully avoid every temptation to act as judges or rulers in the land. Let it be perfectly and extensively understood that you will take no

[1] Elmslie's book, *Among the Wild Ngoni*, contains a fascinating account of this part of the mission's history. See also Livingstone, *Laws of Livingstonia*, and Laws's own *Reminiscences of Livingstonia*.

[2] Hetherwick, *The Romance of Blantyre*, pp. 33–37. Hetherwick relates (p. 34) that a devout elder of Aberdeen, after hearing Scott preach, gravely remarked to his minister: 'God forbid that I should presume to understand him.'

[3] W. P. Livingstone, *A Prince of Missionaries*, pp. 67–70. For photographs see also Hetherwick, *The Romance of Blantyre*, frontispiece, and facing pp. 144 and 242; also Lugard, *The Rise of Our East African Empire*, vol. i, pp. 44 and 474.

part in native quarrels.' Fugitive slaves must be told that if they
were claimed by their owners they would be given up. If the
missionaries caught a criminal, they must hand him over to his
chief—'in no such case must the law be taken into your hands'—
and, although they might be justified in recommending that the
punishments prescribed by native law should be made less severe,
they should do nothing to undermine respect for that law, and
should teach their converts 'to obey and respect the laws of their
country as far as Christians ought to do'.[1]

There is, however, reason to doubt whether these admirable
precepts were faithfully carried out by the new missionaries to
whom they were addressed. Certainly there were no more scandals
or reports of cruelty. But in 1892, when a British protectorate had
been declared over Nyasaland, H. H. Johnston, the Queen's representative, replied to a spate of malicious accusations which were
being made by Scott and Hetherwick (especially the latter) against
himself and his officials, by asserting that the reason why a vendetta
existed between the Blantyre Mission and the Administration was
simply 'that this mission cannot divest itself of a wish to acquire
and exercise magisterial functions in the Shiré province'. Being
narrowly theocratic in outlook, it could not reconcile itself to being
divested of all temporal power by a purely secular authority. He
supported this charge by referring to an incident which had occurred
a short time previously, when seventeen Africans living at the
mission were armed with sticks and led out by the organist to
'arrest' a man charged with setting fire to a house and to bring him
before Scott for 'examination'. The incident 'ended in broken
heads and a riot which brought all parties concerned into the
consular court'.[2]

In their instructions the missionaries were also warned to 'Be
careful not to invoke the secular arm of Europe even when you can
do so, to punish an affront or deed of persecution'. This can only
mean that they were to refuse any offers of Portuguese assistance—
offers which, if accepted, would involve the permanent establishment of Portuguese jurisdiction in their mission-field.

They were directed to make themselves thoroughly acquainted

---

[1] The instructions and supplementary instructions are reproduced in full in
Mins., C. of S. For. Miss. Comm., 13 July 1881.
[2] F.O. 84/2197: Johnston to Salisbury, No. 11, C.A., 10 Mar. 1892; ibid.,
J. to S., No. 24, C.A., 7 July 1892.

not only with the native language but also with native laws, customs, and beliefs; for 'as a rule, our missionary failures are due in great measure to lack of proper appreciation of those whom we desire to evangelise. It is not enough to know a heathen's want: you must understand himself, his modes of thinking, and his most cherished beliefs, before you can hope to supply his spiritual wants.' These words might well be pondered by those who hold that nineteenth-century missionaries were hopelessly blind to all that was good in the unconverted tribesman's way of life.

A further set of regulations governed the internal management of the mission. One of Duff Macdonald's gravest perplexities had been his undefined relationship to the lay members of the staff, and his diary clearly shows how much trouble it caused him. In future, the ordained minister was to have unquestioned authority over the other missionaries, though he was to consult them at regular meetings about all the mission's affairs, and to send a record of these meetings to the Committee. 'Subordination of office', it was explained, 'is necessary to good order in every section of the Church militant; but it need not infringe self-respect, as it does not imply personal inferiority.'

The medical and educational as well as the religious aspects of the mission's work were covered by detailed and carefully considered provisions, but there was no mention of an 'industrial' department such as was one of the most characteristic features of the work of Livingstonia. In this respect the Committee had taken altogether too much to heart the belatedly discovered truth that the mission, to be successful, must as far as possible be dissociated from secular responsibilities. It remembered only too well how the agreement with the Moir brothers had placed the missionaries under the necessity of protecting the Company's stores from theft, and had provided the occasion for the barbarous floggings of suspected native offenders. It therefore placed the following clause among its supplementary instructions:

5. No contracts implying permanent arrangements should be entered upon without sanction of the Home Committee. Caution and circumspection should be observed in your relation to Traders or Trading Companies, whether British, Portuguese, Arab, or other. The members of the Mission must keep themselves clear of all transactions that would involve themselves or the Mission in responsibility.

In so far as this refers at all to 'industrial' work, it is by implication. Ten years later, however, in July 1891, Dr. Rankin, who had been the Church's Commissioner during the troubles at Blantyre, placed before the Committee a number of suggestions for the reorganization and reform of the mission, and in one of these he expressed the belief:

That when, in 1881, by order of the General Assembly, the original industrial side of the Mission was suppressed, this was overdone.

He suggested that a number of boys should be trained as gardeners, carpenters, brick-makers, and printers, and that afterwards it might be possible to provide training as blacksmiths, tailors, and shoe-makers. The Committee agreed that this was a wise proposal,[1] and the only serious error in the arrangements made in 1881 was thus, it seems, put right. The vital importance of inculcating the habit of diligent and patient work into the mind of the volatile and improvident African had been powerfully urged by both Consul O'Neill and Captain Lugard, who knew from experience as well as from common sense that emotional religion, doctrinal instruction, and general moral precepts would produce no lasting effect whatever on the native mind, except possibly to unsettle it and so do actual harm instead of good—unless such theoretical instruction was complemented by a practical training in the living of a purposeful and useful life.[2] Even from the standpoint of the mission's own interests it was far more satisfactory that its requirements should, as far as possible, be met with goods produced locally, than that such goods should, at enormous cost, be transported all the way from Britain.[3]

There can be no doubt that, under D. C. Scott's leadership, Blantyre became a model village, an oasis of civilization in the midst of the African wilderness. On this there is unanimity among all who passed through it and recorded their impressions. Captain Lugard, for instance, praised its houses, 'most admirably built of sun-dried bricks, with sawn-wood joists, and very neat thatches,' and declared that 'the spotless clothes of the children, the neatness, and order, and discipline enforced, were like nothing I have ever

---

[1] Mins., C. of S. For. Miss. Comm., 17 Nov. 1891.
[2] H. E. O'Neill, *The Mozambique and Nyassa Slave Trade*, p. 19; F. D. Lugard, *The Rise of Our East African Empire*, vol. i, pp. 70–71.
[3] Mins., C. of S. For. Miss. Comm., 28 Feb. 1893.

seen elsewhere in Africa'.[1] A sub-station was established at Domasi, near Zomba, in 1884, and another was begun on Mount Mlanje in 1890.

◇   ◇   ◇

During the first years of its existence, the L.M.S. mission had no link of any kind with the Scots in Nyasaland. Ujiji, where its original members arrived at last on 23 August 1878, lay far to the north; the next two stations to be opened were in the Uguha country, to the west, and at Urambo, hundreds of miles away on the road to Zanzibar. The general policy of the mission was to use boats to visit and teach the peoples dwelling all around the thousand-mile shore of the lake. At first sailing-boats were used, but early in 1881 the Directors agreed to provide a small steamer, which would be called the *Good News*. In the event, however, the dispatch of this vessel marked the beginning of the end of the very policy it was meant to serve, and set in motion a gradual change of emphasis from itinerating round the lake to residence at permanent stations at or near its southern end.

The Livingstonia Central African Company, which had renamed itself the African Lakes Company, undertook to convey it in sections by the Zambesi–Shiré–Nyasa water-route to the north end of Lake Nyasa, and thence across the plateau to the south end of Lake Tanganyika, thus reducing the overland journey to about a quarter the distance from Saadani to Ujiji. The first European to traverse the Nyasa–Tanganyika plateau, at any rate in the nineteenth century, had been Joseph Thomson, who had made his way across it in 1879.[2] It had then become apparent to the Directors of the L.M.S. that the water-route to their mission-field would be, or rather ought to be,[3] much less expensive and fatiguing than the long overland march to Ujiji, and they had accepted a proposal, made by James Stevenson, that they should co-operate with the company in establishing a trade-route between the lakes. Stevenson himself contributed £4,000 for the construction of a road, and the L.M.S. undertook to build a station on the line which the road was to follow, though they refused to give a binding assurance, which

---

[1] Lugard, *The Rise of Our East African Empire*, vol. i, pp. 43, 72.

[2] Thomson's own account of his journey is given in his book, *To the Central African Lakes and Back*, vol. i, chap. vii.

[3] For the service which they in fact received from the African Lakes Company see below, pp. 87–88.

he desired, that they would entirely abandon the overland route and import everything they required by way of Nyasa.[1]

The Stevenson Road, as it came to be called, was carried forward some seventy miles from its starting-point at Karonga, near the north end of Lake Nyasa. There it stopped. But the remainder of the route lay along the fairly level plateau, over which travellers were able to pass without much inconvenience, so that a few years later there was a well-defined track made by the passage of innumerable native carriers. Commissioner Johnston, writing in 1895, declared that the road 'has had very little existence except on paper';[2] but although he added that he was 'not in any way intending to disparage Mr. Stevenson's philanthropic efforts', it may be that his hearty dislike of the company led him to exaggerate a little. Whatever its deficiencies as a feat of engineering, it served its primary purpose of linking the Tanganyika and the Nyasa missionfields.

For some years, indeed, the L.M.S. continued to use the long portage to Zanzibar as well as the water-route, and although it abandoned Ujiji in 1883 and Uguha in 1885, its decision to concentrate its efforts at the south end of the lake was not taken until 1889. But fever and death prevented it from building up its numbers sufficiently to enable it to disperse its efforts without thereby rendering them fruitless,[3] and it was driven reluctantly to the conclusion that the policy of itinerating must be abandoned. In choosing to settle at the south end rather than elsewhere, it was influenced partly by an intense desire to be as far removed as possible from the influence of the Arabs and 'coast-men', and partly by the fact that it had come to rely mainly upon the Nyasa rather than the Zanzibar line of communications. Niamkolo, its station on the shore of the lake, was occupied temporarily in 1885, and permanently in 1889. Its other station was at Fwambo, some fifty miles inland from Niamkolo on the road to Nyasa.

Up to this time the main achievement of the mission had been to survive. Its history had been one of missionaries dying of fever or invalided home, often before they had time to do any useful work, and of stations founded only to be abandoned a few years

[1] Mins., L.M.S. Southern Comm., 17 Mar. 1881 and 25 Apr. 1881.

[2] F.O. 2/88: Johnston to Kimberley, No. 73, C.A., 8 June 1885. Cf. L. M. Fotheringham, *Adventures in Nyassaland* (Sampson Low, London, 1891), p. 9.

[3] Of the 36 missionaries sent out between 1877 and 1894, 11 died, 16 retired owing to illness or (as in Hore's case) after long service, and 9 remained.

later. But from then on, having struck root in a single locality, it began to achieve distinct success in all branches of its work—evangelical, educational, medical, and industrial. In the first decade of the present century it was able to begin extensive and valuable work among the large and once formidable Bemba tribe, on the plateau to the south; about the same time the terrible mortality which had crippled its work in the pioneering days began to be sharply reduced. Such achievements have, indeed, been modest in comparison with the efforts, the hopes, and the sacrifices of its heroic age, and in this more recent period it has been merely one of a score of separate missions working with varying degrees of co-operation in Northern Rhodesia. But they have been more than sufficient to justify the founding of the mission, and to vindicate the faith of those who suffered and died to keep its work alive.

⃝ ⃝ ⃝

The problem of civil jurisdiction did not arise for the L.M.S. Tanganyika mission until about 1890. Captain Hore showed himself fully aware of the dangers inherent in it when, at the time of the withdrawal from Niamkolo in 1885, the people who had settled there begged him to take them with him to Kavala Island, which was then his headquarters. 'This I cannot do', he reported, 'tho' I fain would, for troubles would in time be sure to arise, and in spite of all efforts I should be regarded as chief of the new settlers.'[1]

The Fwambo station, founded in 1887, was situated about a mile from the nearest village, that of the chief after whom it was named. Why D. P. Jones, the missionary in charge of it, should have chosen to settle in open country rather than among the people whom he had come out to serve is an unexplained mystery.[2] He hoped that instead the people would come to him, and felt disappointed and frustrated when those who sold him produce or labour went home as soon as they received their pay. In March 1889 he opened a school, and several youths arrived as pupils; Jones began by explaining that this was a form of work for which

[1] L.M.S., C.A., 6.4.C: Hore to Thompson, 18 Oct. 1885.
[2] There was no missionary in charge of the whole mission: each individual did what he thought proper, subject to the general control of the infrequently convened committee of all the missionaries in the field. The result was a good deal of wasted effort and working at cross-purposes, not to speak of personal animosities.

they would not receive any calico, whereupon they arose in disgust and went away.[1]

It was after the reoccupation of Niamkolo, early in 1889, that members of the mission began to be increasingly involved in the cares of village administration. The natives were overjoyed at their return, and, fearing renewed slave-raids by the Bemba, they hastened in growing numbers to build their huts round the station. Swann, Hore's successor as head of the 'marine department', built a stockade round the settlement, and announced to his Directors that, whether or not he was overstepping their instructions, he would protect his people against the Arab slave-hunters and their native associates.[2] In September 1890 Jones reported that the village which had grown up behind Swann's fortifications was now probably the strongest in Ulungu. Early in the following year he erected a stockade around his own station at Fwambo, in the hope that people would seek shelter behind it.[3] His hope was realized. Thus, at both stations, the beginnings of regular mission work were accompanied, if not indeed made possible, by the acceptance of secular commitments which could not be satisfactorily reconciled with it.

When repeated attacks were made on the Niamkolo villagers by the followers of an Arab named Kakungu, who lived on the eastern shore of Lake Tanganyika, Swann lost patience. Enlisting the help of two agents of the African Lakes Company, who, early in 1890, had formed a station at Kituta, a few miles from Niamkolo, he organized a native assault on what he called 'this den of brutes'.[4] The attack was successful, and it brought much more peaceful conditions to the country. Though the natives still feared an attack from the Bemba—as well they might, for they themselves did not scruple to make furtive raids upon that hated tribe—by 1895 they had gained enough confidence to begin to venture to settle in small groups in the open country, outside the stockades. Yet the missionaries knew that the action taken, however good the reasons for it might have been, was inconsistent with the pacific and non-

[1] L.M.S., C.A., 7.3.C: Jones to Thompson, 1 May 1888; 7.4.B: Jones to Thompson, 1 Apr. 1889.

[2] Ibid., 7.4.C: Carson to Thompson, 27 June 1889; 8.1.A: Swann to Thompson, 26 Feb. 1890; 8.1.C: Swann to Thompson, 19 June 1890.

[3] Ibid., 8.2.B: Jones to Thompson, 19 Sept. 1890; 8.3.C: Jones to Thompson, 15 Apr. 1891.

[4] A. J. Swann, *Fighting the Slave Hunters*, pp. 255–69.

political character of their Society, and they refrained from reporting it to the Directors—who in fact condemned it when news of it eventually reached them.[1]

On the organization of life in these stockaded settlements we have little information. Swann was content to define the missionaries' relations with the people in a single phrase: 'We are their fathers and friends, but not their chiefs.'[2] This may have been so at the beginning—Swann wrote those words in June 1890 —but it could scarcely be expected that the military protection of a collection of undisciplined fugitives would not develop into the exercise of some measure of political authority. In April 1891 the situation at Niamkolo was described by Jones in the following terms:

The responsibility of the people's temporal welfare lies entirely in the missionaries residing there—it being in fact a *missionary* village; but alas! their spiritual and moral welfare, the very object for which we are in the country, has to a certain extent to be neglected, from necessity, the harvest being great and the workers few.[3]

And in October 1894 an artisan named Purves declared that he did not 'believe in missionaries becoming native chiefs', and that he had become unpopular with his colleagues because he had disputed the right of one of them 'to act as law-maker and judge without appeal'.[4] Clearly this is a partisan statement, but it cannot be entirely discounted. The exercise of judicial as well as administrative functions was almost certain to follow from the decision to protect the natives; for, as Swann put it, they were 'not a penitent lot'.[5]

In 1898 one of the missionaries, Dr. G. J. Mackay, strongly criticized this exercise of chiefly powers by his colleagues. He reported that they used long thick strips of hippopotamus hide to inflict punishment by flogging, and declared that in so doing they established a false relationship—one based chiefly on fear—between themselves and their people, thereby becoming demoralized themselves. Wardlaw Thompson, who corresponded with the missionaries on behalf of the Directors, replied that the administration

---

[1] Mins., L.M.S., Southern Comm., 19 Mar. and 23 Apr. 1894.
[2] L.M.S., C.A., 8.1.C: Swann to Thompson, 20 June 1890.
[3] Ibid., 8.3.C: Jones to Thompson, 15 Apr. 1891. Cf. Mins., L.M.S. Southern Comm., 27 Feb. 1893.
[4] L.M.S., C.A., 9.2.E: Purves to Thompson, 2 Oct. 1894.
[5] Ibid., 8.1.A: Swann to Thompson, 26 Feb. 1890.

of justice should be left entirely to the civil authorities—which at that time meant the officials of the British South Africa Company. But the system remained in existence until 1905, when it was resolved that 'in the judgment of the Directors no missionary should be involved either directly or indirectly in the flogging of adult natives for offences of any kind'.[1] In this connexion it should be mentioned that the country had been nominally under British administration since 1891. That such powers should have been wielded by the missionaries as late as 1905 is a remarkable illustration of the time-lag which separated the development of Northern Rhodesia from that of Nyasaland.

3. British Consuls and the Slave-trade

Apart from sponsoring Livingstone's expedition to the Zambesi, the British Government did nothing to interest itself in the hinterland of Portuguese East Africa until the last quarter of the nineteenth century. But its zeal for the suppression of the slave-trade led it to extort Portugal's consent, in 1842, to a treaty by which British warships were permitted to search dhows flying her flag if they were suspected of carrying slaves; and in 1847 the effectiveness of this treaty was greatly increased by a protocol whereby British vessels operating against the slave-trade were given access to Portuguese territorial waters, though on the explicit understanding that Portuguese sovereignty should be scrupulously respected. This provision was for a period of three years, and in 1850 it was renewed for a similar period. The Portuguese Government, however, refused to renew it a second time, alleging that the British naval forces had abused the rights previously given them. The British Government denied this charge, and its ambassador in Lisbon hinted that it might be prudent not to risk arousing the wrath of Parliament in such a way, lest Parliament should call in question Portugal's right to sovereignty over those parts of the coast which she neither occupied nor ruled.[2] But the outcome was that after 1853 British cruisers were again excluded from the coastal waters, which became once more, as they had been of old, a slave-dealers' Paradise.

---

[1] Quoted by W. P. Livingstone in *Laws of Livingstonia*, p. 174, footnote.
[2] *British and Foreign State Papers*, vol. 36, pp. 588–90; vol. 44, pp. 1355–62. For the history of the slave-trade in Portuguese East Africa see Jackson, *European Powers and South-East Africa*, *passim*.

As the shipment of slaves across the Atlantic diminished and eventually ceased entirely, new markets came into being which were fully able to absorb the available supply. These were in the French islands of Réunion, Mayotte, and Nossi Bé. The French did not, indeed, buy 'slaves': they engaged 'free emigrants', and stoutly maintained that the difference was more than terminological. Having sanctioned this system in 1854, the Portuguese Government condemned it a year later;[1] but no notice of the condemnation was taken at Mozambique. The British consul, John Lyons McLeod, officially informed the Governor-General 'that at Ibo, slaves are supplied to the so-called Free Labour ships at forty dollars a head, and that these slaves are afterwards sold at Réunion for from eighty to 120 dollars each'.[2]

McLeod was the first British consul at Mozambique, and his experiences during his brief tenure of the post showed clearly how important a place the slave-trade continued to hold in the local economy. Colonel Almeida, who became Governor-General a few months after McLeod's own arrival early in 1857, so infuriated the colonists by his action in seizing a French ship engaged in the 'free labour' trade—an action which, incidentally, involved his Government in a public humiliation at the hands of Imperial France[3]—that they sent their slaves to throw stones at his band as it played before the palace in the evening; and the Governor-General was sufficiently impressed by the hostility he had aroused to make no further effort to interfere with the export of slaves. McLeod, whose zeal in the cause of freedom was expressed in the most haughty and peremptory manner, now found his position becoming increasingly difficult and disagreeable. As his consulate was not on the island of Mozambique but on the mainland opposite, he had to use a boat to communicate with the Governor-General, and his neighbours were therefore able to render him practically helpless by taking steps to make it impossible for him to obtain a crew. They likewise spirited away his servants, leaving him and his wife to be their own hewers of wood and drawers of water, exposed to the ridicule not only of the Portuguese but even of their slaves. On more than one occasion stones were hurled

---

[1] Coupland, *Exploitation of East Africa*, pp. 135–6; *Kirk on the Zambesi*, p. 85.
[2] Copy encl. in McLeod to Clarendon, No. 1, S.T., 3 Oct. 1857 (in F.O. 84/1019).
[3] Coupland, *Kirk on the Zambesi*, pp. 266–8; F.O. 84/1050: McLeod to Clarendon, No. 4, S.T., 1 Nov. 1858, with enclosures.

through his windows. When his wife was dangerously ill the surgeon refused to visit her and forbade his assistants to do so until the Governor-General, acting on a formal representation made by the consul, ordered the surgeon to attend. But Almeida, irritated by McLeod's imperious attitude as well as being anxious to appease the colonists, was careful to reduce his assistance to the barest minimum required by diplomatic decorum. In the end the consul was starved out of Mozambique, having found it impossible for many weeks to buy flour for his household. On 18 May 1858 he left his post, hurled his defiance at the Governor-General in a bitter farewell note, and sailed for home on a British warship.[1]

In view of these events, it is not surprising that the Foreign Office allowed seventeen years to pass before it repeated the experiment of sending a consul to Portuguese East Africa. And Frederic Elton, whom it appointed in 1875, was incomparably better suited to his task than McLeod had been.

Within a few weeks of his arrival he reported that the police force did not exist except on paper, and that street brawls were of frequent occurrence on the island of Mozambique itself, where numerous public houses, most of them kept by convicts, supplied cheap liquor in unlimited quantities to the slaves. And, although the Governor-General had three old gunboats at his disposal, there were 'no sailors, no soldiers, no money, no authority, and consequently no power' which he could employ against the slave-traders whose dhows sheltered in the creeks and rivers of the long and desolate coast. On one occasion, when one of the gunboats was required for active operations, the other two had to be left with only three sailors to guard them both. Elton realized that in these circumstances it was necessary to proceed with the greatest tact and caution, relying on the good faith of the Governor-General and endeavouring to secure his confidence and respect.[2] During the two years which he spent at Mozambique, he worked for the suppression of the slave-trade with energy, understanding, and good judgement.

To achieve his object he had to obtain accurate and timely information of the whereabouts of the slave-dhows, and then, having

---

[1] F.O. 84/1050: McLeod to Clarendon, No. 1, S.T., 1 Jan. 1858, with enclosures, and to Malmesbury, No. 5, S.T., 9 Nov. 1858, with enclosures. The date of his departure is given in his dispatch of 20 Jan. 1859 in F.O. 84/1082.

[2] F.O. 84/1411: Elton to Derby, No. 14, S.T., 21 July 1875, with confidential enclosure; No. 16, S.T., 24 July 1875.

communicated it to the Governor-General, he had to arrange as best he could for action to be taken to capture the vessels before they could escape. José Guedes de Carvalho e Menezes, the Governor-General with whom he had to deal, was a sincere opponent of the slave-trade, and was disposed to welcome the co-operation of the British Navy in suppressing it. Though the British ships had no longer any right, recognized by treaty, to enter Portuguese territorial waters, they could operate there on specific occasions at the invitation of the Governor-General. And Menezes frankly admitted to Elton on one occasion that he fully appreciated the value of a British cruiser as a bulwark of Portuguese authority, when that authority was challenged by slave-dealing natives on the coast over which he nominally ruled.[1] In August 1875, at his suggestion, H.M.S. *Thetis* accompanied the Portuguese gunboat *Sena* on a thorough search of the mouths of the rivers Moma and Kisungo, in the course of which a dhow was captured and two others forced to flee without having had time to take aboard any slaves.[2] Elton was exceedingly gratified by this co-operation, which gave the slave-traders cause to wonder whether they had not underestimated the dangers of their work.

Yet, when on subsequent occasions he offered British naval support for a similar purpose, the offer was politely declined on the ground that the Portuguese Navy, unaided, was equal to the task. In fact, through inefficiency and half-heartedness, it repeatedly allowed slavers to escape when they might very well have been captured. Eventually, in June 1877, Menezes confessed that he had received from Lisbon 'special instructions upon the matter of co-operation with the British naval forces'. He called Elton's attention to a debate held in the Cortes on the previous 28 February, when the Colonial Minister, replying to criticisms of the decision to invite British co-operation in 1875, had taken refuge in the assertion that the naval action on that occasion had been so effective that the slave-trade had been completely extinguished, and that the force now available at Mozambique was strong enough to police the coast unassisted by the British fleet.[3]

Clearly there was small inducement for a Governor-General of

---

[1] Elton's No. 16 of 1875.
[2] A. & P., 1876, lxx, p. 624: Elton to Derby, 16 Aug. 1875; ibid., pp. 628–32: E. to D., 13 Sept. 1875.
[3] A. & P., 1878, lxvii, pp. 708–9: Elton to Derby, 23 June 1877.

Mozambique to act with vigour and honesty of purpose against the slave-trade, when by so doing he would not only injure the vested interests of the local colonists[1] but would also be likely to fall foul of the nationalist demagogues in the Cortes.

On 3 July 1877 Elton set out from Mozambique on a journey to the interior, from which he did not live to return. A suitable successor was hard to find, and almost two years elapsed before the consulate was reopened by Henry E. O'Neill, who at the time of his appointment had been serving as a lieutenant in one of the cruisers operating in East African waters. The Governor-General whom he found in office, Francisco Maria da Cunha, showed himself completely unwilling to court unpopularity by taking any effective action against the slave-trade. O'Neill was therefore helpless until Cunha was compelled by illness to return to Portugal in February 1880. While his office was vacant, the Secretary-General of the province, named Sarmento, acted as his deputy. The result of this change of leadership was immediate. A series of small but swift and unexpected expeditions were launched against the slave-dealers, several of whom were captured and brought to trial. And Sarmento gladly accepted as much help from British cruisers as they were able to provide. He also published a pamphlet about the Mozambique slave-trade, estimating that the average number of slaves then being exported annually was between two and four thousand. 'For the bold and honest manner in which the actual state of things has been proclaimed by Senhor Sarmento', declared O'Neill, 'I feel we owe him a great debt.'[2] His Government rewarded him for his endeavours by abruptly recalling him early in 1881, in response to the intrigues of those in Lisbon—notably the Geographical Society—who, as the British ambassador put it, wished 'to make out that the Mozambique Slave Trade is a mere hallucination of Her Majesty's Consuls'.[3] It is scarcely remarkable, therefore, that the next Governor-General, Agostinho Coelho, quietly resumed the ways of Cunha, while assuring O'Neill of his zealous concern for the suppression of the slave-trade, an object

---

[1] Menezes's successor, Cunha, candidly told the senior British naval officer that Menezes had rendered himself extremely unpopular among the colonists by his co-operation with the British Navy in 1875: Cunha himself took care not to incur similar odium. F.O. 84/1539: O'Neill to Salisbury, No. 26, S.T., Confidential, 17 Aug. 1879.

[2] A. & P., 1882, lxv, pp. 476–83: O'Neill to Granville, 27 Feb. 1881, with enclosures.   [3] Ibid., p. 458: Morier to Granville, 25 Apr. 1881.

which, he averred, 'has always received the most serious attention of the Portuguese Government'.

〇 〇 〇

When Consul Elton left Mozambique to visit Livingstonia, he was an angry and frustrated man. Three days before his departure he had had to report the ludicrous failure of the Portuguese gun-boats to deal with a slave-dhow, after he had been assured that British help would not be needed. 'By such abortive attempts', he declared, 'with ineffective means to assert jurisdiction over the coast, and the rejection of British co-operation for the suppression of the export Slave Trade in Portuguese territorial waters, . . . the Lisbon Government absolutely encourage the promoters of the Traffic to maintain their hold upon their slaving stations on the Mozambique coast.' By so doing they prolonged indefinitely the heavy British expenditure on naval action, while 'Her Majesty's servants, both naval and Consular, are compelled to remain in-active spectators, powerless . . . to grapple with a Slave Trade which . . . imperatively demands the employment of prompt and decisive measures for its repression.'[1]

If the most assiduous and tactful attempts to collaborate with the Portuguese were doomed to failure, or at best to an occasional ephemeral success, could better results be obtained by direct British action in the interior, where the slave-trade had its roots, and where the Portuguese had no jurisdiction? Elton's thoughts must have turned in this direction in the course of his travels, for although he did not live to make an official recommendation, he wrote in his journal that it was his 'deliberate belief' that it was necessary for the British Government, as part of its struggle against the slave-trade, to adopt 'some definite policy . . . with regard to the Nyassa and its neighbourhood'. 'I believe', he de-clared, 'an immensity of good might be effected by a commissioner, whose aim should be to detach the chiefs from the Arab Slave Trade influences, and attach them to a policy of legitimate trade and progress.'[2]

Apart from Livingstone, who was given consular status, Elton was himself the first British official to visit the Nyasa country. On his way to Livingstonia and during his sojourn there he visited the more important chiefs of the Shiré valley and the Nyasa coast, for

[1] A. & P., 1878, lxvii, p. 714: Elton to Derby, 30 June 1877.
[2] J. F. Elton, *Lakes and Mountains of Eastern and Central Africa*, pp. 238-9.

the purpose of establishing friendly relations with them, and so facilitating the work of the mission while also, perhaps, exercising some influence in restraint of the slave-trade. From Livingstonia he was conveyed by Dr. Stewart in the *Ilala* to the north end of the lake, which he reached on 12 October; thence he proceeded northwards and eastwards in order to open up unexplored country while returning to the coast. His choice of this route was made in response to the prompting of Dr. (later Sir) John Kirk, who had been the companion of Livingstone when he discovered Lake Nyasa, and was now Consul-General at Zanzibar. Kirk was watching with keen interest the attempts which were beginning to be made to open up regular European communications between Zanzibar and Central Africa; for, at the same time as the L.M.S. was making its attempt to introduce ox-drawn wagons and, as he put it, apply 'the South African mode of travel . . . to the tropical regions', a second enterprise, commercial-cum-philanthropic in character, and sponsored by Sir William Mackinnon, was starting to construct a road from Dar-es-Salaam in the direction of the north end of Lake Nyasa—'in the hope', as Kirk said, 'that trade will spring up'. If we had not in our own time experienced the ground-nut fiasco, perpetrated in the same region, we would marvel at the folly of setting out to build a road hundreds of miles long across country which had never been explored, still less surveyed. Kirk last referred to it in 1881, when it had been constructed for a distance of 73 miles, and had encountered a belt of tsetse fly but 'no highway of commerce'. 'And', Kirk admitted, 'the local trade, although fast increasing, is still small.' The country beyond was too mountainous and steep to serve as a convenient route to Lake Nyasa, and 'in all probability the trade of the Nyassa district will pass in time along the Shiré and Zambesi and not by land'.[1] But in the meantime Elton had sacrificed his life in attempting to explore the country which the road was intended to traverse. Passing through a region devastated by native wars, he suffered great privations, and on 19 December 1877 he died.

Elton's interest in the Nyasa country was shared by Kirk, who, in a dispatch dated 15 September 1877, declared: 'It is from the districts surrounding this Lake that the greater part of the supply of slaves to Zanzibar and the Mozambique [coast] is still derived,

[1] F.O. 84/1484: Kirk to Derby, No. 114, 26 July 1877; F.O. 84/1599: Kirk to Granville, No. 30, 28 Feb. 1881.

and the district thus rendered of interest to us as a nation.'[1] By this time Kirk had succeeded to a large extent in bringing the Sultan of Zanzibar into line with the British policy of suppressing the slave-trade. A treaty which he had imposed upon the Sultan in 1873, under threat of naval blockade, together with a decree issued at his instance in 1876, had made the traffic in slaves, though not their ownership, completely illegal. These measures were vigorously enforced, for the Sultan welcomed the opportunity to use British naval support and a British-officered and British-equipped military force to acquire for himself an autocratic position which he and his predecessors had not formerly enjoyed. Whereas in the past Zanzibar had exported 20,000 slaves a year, after satisfying its own very considerable requirements as well as those of the neighbouring island of Pemba and the plantations on the coast, the number annually exported now dwindled to a few hundred, or at most a few thousand.[2] This sudden constriction of the outlet disorganized the work of the slave-dealers in the interior. Kirk was told—by some Europeans who had accompanied Elton on his journey to-wards the coast, and who had survived to reach their destination—that the Nyasa chiefs spoke of the traffic as 'ruined'.[3] Six months previously he had received information, presumably from the Livingstonia mission, that the Nyasa chiefs, 'those most inveterate of all slave dealers', were looking for an outlet on the Portuguese part of the coast rather than hoping for more favourable conditions on the more northern part; and afterwards he heard that Nyasa slaves who had for some time been kept near the lake as unsaleable were now on their way to the coast: some of them, indeed, to the Zanzibar port of Kilwa, but others to the Portuguese possessions.[4]

The temporary slump in the demand for slaves near Lake Nyasa, coming as it did immediately after the Sultan's decree of 1876, strongly suggests that at the time when Livingstonia was founded the people captured or bought in the surrounding country were being taken to destinations north rather than south of Cape Delgado.

[1] F.O. 84/1486: Kirk to Derby, No. 133, 15 Sept. 1877.

[2] F.O. 84/1548: Kirk to Salisbury, No. 149, 12 Nov. 1879. The number of slaves liberated by the British Navy off the Zanzibar coast steadily declined from 491 in 1876 to 73 in 1879 (F.O. 84/1574: K. to S., No. 20, 23 Feb. 1880). But Kirk reckoned that not more than 5 per cent. of the slaves who were shipped could be intercepted and liberated at sea.

[3] F.O. 84/1514: Kirk to Derby, No. 28, 7 Feb. 1878.

[4] F.O. 84/1486: Kirk to Derby, No. 123, 22 Aug. 1877; F.O. 84/1514: K. to D., No. 63, 3 May 1878.

If, therefore, the slaves exported from the Portuguese part of the coast were not being obtained in the Nyasa country, they were presumably being found in the regions east and south of it: for example, in the Makua country, where Consul O'Neill conjectured in 1881 that the slave-dealers, though plying their business on a small scale, accumulated an annual total of many hundred people.[1] How large a proportion of the Nyasa slaves were diverted to the Portuguese coast from 1877 onwards it is impossible to estimate. Certainly the demand on the Zanzibar coast, though sharply reduced, was by no means ended. Kirk himself admitted in 1879 that 2,000 slaves a year would scarcely satisfy local requirements, without leaving any for export;[2] and, until the slave-caravans reached the coast, there was no means of interfering with them.

Dr. Laws was able to give O'Neill much information about the Nyasa slave-trade, and in a letter which the consul received in December 1879 he stated that at least three routes were being used: one was through Mponda's, at the south end of the lake; another had its headquarters at Jumbe's town of Kota-Kota; the third crossed the lake farther north. But he was unable to ascertain the destination to which the slaves were being taken.[3]

In September 1881 he estimated that the number of slaves being taken across Lake Nyasa, from its western shore, was between two and three thousand a year; a few months later he wrote that it 'seems to be increasing very much'.[4]

The reason, or at least one of the reasons, for this revival of demand was pointed out by O'Neill in a dispatch dated 3 November 1880.[5] In the district of Ibo, the most northerly part of the Portuguese possessions, there had been such a notable growth in the production of oil-seeds that the revenue of the district provided a surplus for the central Treasury at Mozambique: a state of affairs which, in Portuguese East Africa, was quite unique. But the labour employed was slave-labour. The status of slavery had, indeed, been formally brought to an end a few years earlier, and consequently Portuguese property-owners who lived in or very near the coastal settlements were unable to obtain slaves except

[1] A. & P., 1883, lxvi, p. 332: O'Neill to Granville, 19 Nov. 1881.
[2] F.O. 84/1548: Kirk to Salisbury, No. 149, 12 Nov. 1879.
[3] Quoted in O'Neill to Granville, 13 Dec. 1879, in A. & P., 1881, lxxxv, p. 524.
[4] Quoted in O'Neill to Granville, 12 Jan. and 30 May 1882, in A. & P., 1883, lxvi, pp. 333, 344.   [5] A. & P., 1881, lxxxv, p. 580.

with difficulty and at considerable risk; but the half-caste Portuguese, or 'Mouros', as they were called, maintained a profitable slave-system by adopting the simple precaution of establishing themselves at least two hours' journey in the interior, where the Governor of Ibo, however hostile to the slave-trade he might be, had no power to reach them. As O'Neill put it: 'At this day, the Portuguese Settlements on the coast rather stand in the position of "cities of refuge" outside a slave-holding State, than as centres of Government within a province where all have been proclaimed free.'

Kirk, after reading this report when it passed through his hands on its way to London, commented that the situation it revealed in the northern part of the Portuguese coast was closely similar to that existing in the southern part of the Sultan's dominions. It appeared, he remarked, that the actual state of things in the Portuguese settlements, where slavery was nominally abolished, and in the Zanzibar territories, where it was still legally recognized, remained much the same, 'the great impetus lately given to legitimate commerce having in each case led to the employment of slave labour'.[1]

O'Neill even went so far as to express the opinion that at least half the slaves who were now being brought to the coast were not meant to be taken any farther.[2] And, in addition, there was what he called the 'interior Slave Trade', whose victims passed up the Zambesi by way of Tete and were sold for ivory to other tribes—slave-holding being an important custom among Africans themselves. E. D. Young attached great and probably exaggerated importance to this traffic,[3] and Elton had information about it too.[4] From all this it followed that only a minority of slaves were ever intended to be put aboard dhows; only a minority, therefore, had any chance of being liberated at sea. And of that minority only a fraction could in fact be intercepted by the British Navy, encumbered as it was in its difficult operations by the obstructionism of the Portuguese. By the beginning of the eighties it had become evident that naval action was a clumsy and ineffective weapon to employ against the slave-trade of South-East Africa. The trade could go on for ever in spite of it.

[1] F.O. 84/1575: Kirk to Granville, No. 131, 12 Nov. 1880.
[2] A. & P., 1882, lxv, pp. 468–9: O'Neill to Granville, 31 Dec. 1880.
[3] F.O. 84/1504: Young to Morier, 1 Mar. 1877, enclosed in Morier to Salisbury, No. 13, S.T., Confidential, 15 May 1878.
[4] A. & P., 1878, lxvii, p. 694: Elton to Derby, 23 Apr. 1877.

And the full extent of the havoc which was wrought could not be measured by the number of slaves who reached their destination, wherever it might be. It was necessary also to take account of those who were speared or shot in the slave-raids, or perished of hunger after their crops had been destroyed, or died of exhaustion and maltreatment on the march. The numbers of these unfortunate people are even more difficult to estimate than those of the slaves who were sold, but there is no doubt that they were very large. Even those who were not themselves raided were forced to live under the shadow of a constant dread, so that, in the words of Dr. Laws, writing in 1882, 'These slavers are the bane alike of mission work and lawful commerce in this country.'[1]

The futility of the navy's costly and arduous endeavours was rendered peculiarly ironical by the attitude of the fortunate few among the victims of the traffic who were released from captured dhows and placed under the care of the missions after being taken to Natal or Zanzibar.[2] In the eyes of the white men they were now free, but in their own eyes this freedom was meaningless: they had not even a word in their vocabulary with which to express it. In primitive barbarism, quite as much as in modern totalitarian barbarism, the individual counts for nothing, and collective society alone has status. The bond of primitive society is that of blood relationship: hence the only 'freedom' which the African tribesman could understand consisted in being with his kin, and he did not regard himself as having been liberated until he was restored to them. If they had all been slaughtered or enslaved when he was taken prisoner, it was impossible for any power on earth to set him free. In such circumstances he was unlikely to 'make good'.[3] When Archdeacon Johnson, as the missionary in charge of a little colony of released slaves on the mainland near Zanzibar, complained about them in conversation with Sir John Kirk, the Consul-General replied: 'Remember, Moses tried for forty years with released slaves, and was beaten by them.'[4]

◇   ◇   ◇

In the course of his report on the demand for slaves near Ibo, O'Neill reminded the Foreign Office of Elton's proposal that a

---

[1] Quoted in O'Neill to Granville, 30 May 1882, in A. & P., 1883, lxvi, p. 344.
[2] The Foreign Office did not think it safe to entrust them to the authorities at Mozambique: A. & P., 1876, lxx, p. 619: Bourke to Elton, 1 July 1875.
[3] Lugard, op. cit., vol. i, pp. 188–92; W. P. Johnson, *My African Reminiscences, 1875–95*, pp. 34–36, 75–76.   [4] Johnson, op. cit., p. 35.

'slave trade commissioner' should be appointed to work in Central Africa, though he admitted that the difficulties which would confront such an official would be 'enormous'. And in January 1882 he asked permission to undertake the task of exploring the route by which the slaves were taken from the Nyasa country to the district of Ibo. The Foreign Office refused, partly because an official visit to the interior by the consul accredited to Portuguese East Africa might seem to imply an admission that the regions visited were under Portuguese jurisdiction, and partly, perhaps mainly, through fear of what the Treasury would say if it were asked for the £200 necessary to cover his travelling expenses. But O'Neill was so eager to undertake the journey that in November he offered to make it at his own expense, with the help of a grant from the Royal Geographical Society, during the five months' accumulated leave to which he was now entitled. This self-sacrificing offer was gladly accepted.

Setting out in June 1883 he proceeded overland and explored the country round Lake Shirwa, discovering two smaller lakes named Amaramba and Chiuta. In February 1884 he was back at his post,[1] from which he forwarded a long report[2] containing an enormous amount of information, mainly geographical. But his most important discoveries were connected with the slave-trade, and were decidedly discouraging. He found that the 'Africanos', or Portuguese half-castes, were extending Portuguese influence as far inland as the shores of Lake Shirwa, whereas he had hitherto been under the impression that it did not extend far beyond the coastal settlements. Of course, influence is a very different matter from jurisdiction; nevertheless, it was sufficiently serious that these traders should be disposing of large quantities of guns and powder in return for slaves, and that the natives should be 'learning to look upon the English as their enemies, who have come to subvert their customs and prevent them from getting those supplies which they are most eager to obtain'. And, if the Portuguese did not bring caravans to the slave-trading chiefs, the chiefs sent caravans to the

---

[1] F.O. 84/1671: O'Neill to Granville, No. 1, Africa, 3 Feb. 1884. (It is pleasing to note that on receiving this dispatch, which reported that he was ill after his travels, the Foreign Office showed its appreciation of his services by restoring him the six months' leave on full pay which he had sacrificed in order to visit the interior.)

[2] Written at various times during his journey, and bound in F.O. 84/1671 without a covering dispatch.

Portuguese. This was done, for instance, by Matapwiri, a Yao chief who lived on the slopes of Mount Mlanje, which was afterwards included within the Nyasaland Protectorate. Matapwiri could have bought beads and calico at the nearby British settlement of Blantyre, but he preferred to buy powder at the much more distant coast,[1] and for that purpose he sent no less than five hundred tusks of ivory to the Portuguese port of Angoche in the year 1882.[2]

O'Neill summed up the position with regard to such chiefs as this by declaring that 'slaves are their chief stock in trade: these they cannot sell to the English; powder and guns they require in large quantities: these the English do not sell'.[3] He had thus made the painful discovery that, in the struggle between the slave-trade and legitimate trade, the scales were heavily weighted in favour of the former.

○　　○　　○

While O'Neill was exploring the country around Lake Shirwa, his Government was taking a decision which, in effect, amounted to the adoption of his suggestion that a 'slave trade commissioner' should be sent to the Nyasa country. On 1 October 1883 Captain Foot, who had for several years been in command of a British cruiser in East African waters, was appointed 'to be Her Majesty's Consul in the territories of the African Kings and Chiefs in the districts adjacent to Lake Nyassa'. 'The primary object of your appointment', he was told, 'is the suppression of the Slave Trade.' He was not, however, to use force to achieve this end, or to take action which might endanger his own life or the lives of the Europeans who resided on the lake. Instead, he was to do his utmost to secure the confidence of the chiefs and to persuade them that the slave-trade was ruinous to their own interests, which could best be served by the development of legitimate trade. It was stated in his instructions that the Government attached much importance to the efforts he would make 'to develop the general civilization and commerce of the country', and that he was to report on 'all matters of commercial or scientific interest'. Such work, however, was not to include trading on his

---

[1] Perhaps, also, he did not like the prices charged by the African Lakes Company, for whose business methods see below, pp. 86–88.

[2] F.O. 84/1671: O'Neill to Granville, No. 6, Africa, Confidential, 20 Feb. 1884.　　　　　　　　　　　　　　　　　　　　[3] Ibid.

own account, and was moreover subsidiary to his 'special duties' of using his influence to undermine the slave-trade. To the missionaries who were established in his consular district—whose territorial limits were in no way defined—he was to afford all the support in his power.[1]

The Portuguese Government were informed of this appointment, and the conviction was expressed that they would cordially recognize in it a proof of Britain's desire to co-operate with them, by land as well as by sea, in checking the slave-trade and encouraging the growth of legitimate commerce, and, consequently, of civilization.[2] We may be quite certain that the hard-headed Sir Percy Anderson, who drafted these remarks, intended them merely as a sugar-coating for what would, to the Portuguese, be a very bitter pill. Indeed, the only reason why they were told of the matter lay in the fact that Captain Foot had to go through Quilimane on his way to his post, and it was desired that the Lisbon authorities should instruct their officials in that port to pass his luggage and goods 'freely and without delay' through the customs house. It is significant that Anderson deleted a sentence in the draft by Sir Clement Hill suggesting that a copy of Foot's instructions should be communicated to the Portuguese Government, for they might have interpreted such a civility as a tacit admission that his consular district lay within their dominions.[3] As it was, their Foreign Minister, Bocage, while granting the British request for a free pass, took the opportunity to declare that this act of grace implied no inclination on their part to relinquish what he called 'the rights held by the Portuguese Crown to the possession of territories which have always been looked upon as subject to its dominion and sovereignty'.[4] He may well have suspected, and probably with good cause, that one reason for the creation of the Nyasa consulate was that it should enable the Foreign Office to keep a watchful eye and exercise a restraining influence not only upon the slave-dealers but also upon the Portuguese authorities themselves, who had already extended their jurisdiction as far up the Shiré as its tributary the Ruo, and were not unlikely to press

[1] A. & P., 1884, lxxv, p. 370: Lister to Foot, 1 Oct. 1883.
[2] Ibid., p. 373: Granville to Baring, 23 Oct. 1883. Draft in F.O. 84/1639, No. 41, Africa.
[3] See draft, loc. cit.
[4] F.O. 84/1639: enclosed in Baring to Granville, No. 78, Africa, 10 Nov. 1883.

on northwards, if the British Government and their own finances permitted, to the shores of the lake itself.[1]

To the Free Church of Scotland, the news of Foot's appointment was entirely welcome, and at the request of the Foreign Office a letter was sent to Livingstonia directing the missionaries to give him all the assistance in their power. The new consul and his wife visited the Church's offices before sailing for Nyasaland.[2] Ever since the foundation of Livingstonia, both the missionaries on the lake and their Committee in Edinburgh had been doing everything possible to draw the British Government into Central Africa in their wake. First they had requested a consular position for E. D. Young, chiefly because this would enable him to report officially to Dr. Kirk at Zanzibar on the movements of Arab slave-dealers;[3] but the Foreign Office refused on the ground that 'there is a manifest inconvenience in conferring the title of Consul where there are, as yet, in fact, no Consular duties to perform, and so investing with an official character what is, in reality, a tentative expedition, started by private subscription, and not subject to Government control'.[4] Two years later, at Dr. Stewart's suggestion, the Government were asked to appoint 'a Consul of their own at Lake Nyassa, in order that the residents there may be under *a kind of British Protectorate*'.[5] Stewart, writing to Captain Elton, made clear his attitude:

On the point of any recommendations home about protection on the Lake—there is only one reason for that, and it is not the natives. If we are wise we shall not require it, so far as they go. It is, if our Portuguese friends are to claim all we may have done, 10 or 12 years hence.[6]

In November 1876 a traveller named Cotterill, who was very closely associated with the missionaries, had expressed the opinion that, to forestall the Portuguese, it would be wise 'to declare the whole region at once under British jurisdiction'. Referring to a proposal strongly urged by Young, that a gunboat should be placed on the lake to intercept the dhows which ferried slaves

[1] See below, pp. 123–5.
[2] Mins., F.C. of S. For. Miss. Comm., 16 Oct. 1883.
[3] Ibid., 22 Feb. 1876.
[4] Derby to Cowan, 14 May 1875. This is bound, with other papers, in a volume entitled *The Livingstonia Mission, 1875–1900*, compiled by Dr. Stewart.
[5] Mins., F.C. of S., For. Miss. Comm., 17 Apr. 1877. (Italics are the author's.)
[6] F.O. 84/1479: enclosure, dated 15 Apr. 1877, in Elton to Derby, No. 20, S.T., 28 May 1877.

across it, he commented: 'It would be a grand move, and tanta-
mount to proclaiming British authority here.'[1] And Elton's own
view had been stated vigorously and unequivocally:

Should the Portuguese declare Lake Nyassa their territory, 'Livingstonia' would inevitably have to retire in the face of the restrictions,
duties, petty annoyances, and difficulties that would undoubtedly be
thrown in the way of the Scotch Mission's progress by interested and
jealous officials.[2]

The Free Church did not allow the question of jurisdiction to
slumber. It had, as time went on, an additional reason for desiring
to have a British official stationed in the vicinity of the mission,
for, as the number of the natives settled around the station increased, it was beset by the problem of what to do with thieves and
other offenders, and wished to avoid the necessity of inflicting
punishment by having at hand someone who could, without im-
propriety, exercise the powers of civil jurisdiction. With this end
in view it made renewed representations in June 1880.[3] Though it
would be entirely untrue to suggest that the action taken in 1883
was dictated primarily by a desire to meet the wishes of the Free
Church, there can be no doubt that the presence on the lake of
British subjects who were supported by an influential section of
British public opinion was a factor which contributed powerfully
towards the making of that decision, and that the Government
would not have ventured to embark on such a course had not the
way been shown and the ground prepared by the Scottish pioneers.

⌒   ⌒   ⌒

In February 1884 the Makololo country was disturbed by an
event of exceptional local importance. The artisan Fenwick, who
had been dismissed by the Church of Scotland's Commission of
Inquiry in 1880, had not returned to Britain, but had been taken
into the service of the African Lakes Company. In view of his
persistent misconduct, and of the fact that on one occasion he had
threatened to shoot John Moir, he again found himself without
employment in 1883; so he established himself as a private trader.
He took down-river to Quilimane some ivory belonging to Chipa-

[1] F.O. 84/1479: enclosed in Elton to Derby, No. 4, S.T., Confidential,
3 Feb. 1877. Some information about Cotterill and his reasons for visiting
Nyasaland is given below, p. 107.
[2] F.O. 84/1479: Elton to Derby, No. 5, 1 Mar. 1877.
[3] Mins., F.C. of S. For. Miss. Comm., 17 June 1879 and 22 June 1880.

tula, the Makololo chief whose village, at Chiromo, commanded the confluence of the rivers Ruo and Shiré, and returned with the goods which he had obtained as payment. According to the statement afterwards made by Fenwick's native servant, Chipatula and Fenwick indulged in a prolonged drinking bout, and quarrelled violently the next morning when business was discussed. Finding the chief unreasonable in his demands, Fenwick shot him dead and then tried to escape; but after a time he was hunted down and killed.

Chipatula was succeeded by his son Chikusi (not to be confused with the ruler of the southern Angoni), an arrogant, drunken youth of about twenty. Chikusi sought to improve upon the occasion by demanding that Fenwick's wife, who was then at Blantyre, should be handed over to him. Thus the entire British community in the Shiré Highlands became involved in the dispute; and, to make matters worse, Chikusi was given a measure of support by Ramakukan, who exercised a shadowy paramountcy over the other Makololo chiefs. It was unfortunate that Moir, some time previously, had withheld part of the payment for a tusk which he had bought from that chief, on the ground that Ramakukan had received goods to the same value, which had been stolen from the company. To this grievance—legitimate or otherwise—was added the resentment which the Makololo felt because it was Moir who had brought back Fenwick when he was about to leave the country. The little group of settlers at Blantyre and Mandala thus found themselves in some danger of armed attack; but what was of more immediate importance was the closing of river communications with the outer world. In April 1884 a foolish attempt to bring up the *Lady Nyassa* from the Zambesi had resulted in Chikusi's seizing and plundering the vessel and sending her captain to Mandala, dressed only in a palm leaf,[1] to present the young despot's outrageous demands.

Fortunately for all concerned, Captain Foot had arrived at Blantyre early in January to take up his consular duties. He at once set to work to secure the friendship of Ramakukan, and was entirely successful. The old chief declared that he had no quarrel with either the consul or the missionaries, but that he hated Moir. His feelings in this respect were, however, appeased when, on Foot's advice, Moir paid him the trade goods which had been held

[1] D. J. Rankin, *The Zambesi Basin and Nyassaland*, p. 83.

back. Ramakukan had already dissociated himself from the seizure of the steamer, and he now determined to assist the white men to recover her, and to compel Chikusi to adopt a reasonable attitude. He had, he declared, been a chief in his own country on the Upper Zambesi, from which he had accompanied Dr. Livingstone, and he meant to assert his authority over Chikusi, who was a mere boy, and whose father, Chipatula, had originally been his slave. With his help the *Lady Nyassa* was refloated from the mud-bank on which she had been driven, and the river was again opened to navigation. Chikusi was compelled to acknowledge his claim to be the paramount chief of the Makololo; and the other Makololo chiefs assured Foot of their friendship for the English and their willingness to co-operate with Ramakukan and with the consul.[1]

Captain Foot's last dispatch was dated 7 August 1884 and showed that the negotiations were almost complete. He was then, as he reported, suffering severely from fever, and on 16 August he died.[2] From then until the arrival of his successor the work of the consulate was carried on with the utmost energy by his assistant, Lawrence C. Goodrich, whom the Foreign Office, through Sir John Kirk, authorized to assume this responsibility.[3]

❧   ❧   ❧

Blantyre lay dangerously near to southern Angoniland, and the Yao who occupied the surrounding country had neither the military discipline nor the social cohesion to withstand a raid by the warriors of Chikusi. Kapeni, the chief from whom the mission had obtained its land, was old and incapable of commanding respect among his subjects, and Buchanan wrote that 'whenever there is a report of war, Kapeni's first move is to get to the top of [Mount] Soché with the bulk of his wives, and there wait in fear and trembling'.[4] In 1884 a war-party of Angoni swept across the Shiré Highlands, which they devastated as far eastward as Lake Shirwa; but they spared Blantyre and the natives connected with it, because D. C. Scott, hearing that an attack was impending, had just paid a visit to Chikusi to try to avert the blow. The mission

<hr>

[1] F.O. 84/1662: Foot to Granville, No. 1, Africa, 18 Jan. 1884; No. 6, Africa, 8 Mar., 19 Mar., and 5 Apr.; No. 7, Africa, 28 Apr.; No. 8, Africa, 30 Apr.; No. 9, Africa, 9 May; No. 11, Africa, 9 June; No. 12, Africa, 26 June; and No. 14, Africa, 7 Aug. 1884.

[2] A. & P., 1884–5, lxxiii, pp. 406–7: O'Neill to Granville, 3 Oct. 1884.

[3] A. & P., 1884–5, lxxiii, p. 462: Kirk to Granville, 23 Oct. 1884.

[4] J. Buchanan, *The Shiré Highlands*, p. 99.

became a sanctuary for hundreds of fugitives, whom the Angoni commander did not dare to attack because his chief was on friendly terms with the white man. After some days, during which the raiders scoured the surrounding country, Scott went out to meet them and induced them to return home—though they took with them a large number of Yao captives.[1]

They returned in July 1885, but before they could cross the Shiré they were met by Goodrich, who told them that though the English wished to be the friends of Chikusi and his people, 'they could not look on Chikusi as their friend if he allowed his people to come and capture and kill the Yao in whose country they lived'. They had come, Goodrich explained, 'to trade with and to teach the people', and it was impossible for them to carry on such work if the country was disturbed by incessant wars. The Angoni agreed to withdraw on condition that Goodrich promised to visit their monarch and explain the position to him.[2] Accordingly, a visit was paid to Chikusi in June 1886 by Consul Hawes, Captain Foot's successor, who had now relieved Goodrich. Gratified, no doubt, by an exceptionally large present from the British representative, Chikusi not only expressed his willingness to give every facility to a missionary from Livingstonia who desired to settle with him, but solemnly undertook, in the presence of his assembled councillors, that there should be no more raids upon the Shiré Highlands. 'If I break my word, white man', he declared, 'you may come and spit in my eyes.'[3] This promise was faithfully kept as long as he lived, and the Angoni did not again menace Blantyre until 1896. When that time came, there was in existence a British administration with the resources and the will to inflict swift and exemplary chastisement upon the aggressor.[4]

◦   ◦   ◦

On 28 August 1886 there was another murder at Chiromo, occasioned by another quarrel about the price of ivory. A trader named Hinkleman, Austrian by birth but apparently British by nationality, had come up the Shiré selling firearms and cheap gin, the latter commodity being, as Sir Percy Anderson remarked, 'rank poison'.

  [1] Hetherwick, *The Romance of Blantyre*, pp. 50–52; F.O. 84/1679: Goodrich to Kirk, 28 Aug. 1884, and 6 Sept. 1884, enclosed in Kirk to Granville, No. 140, 25 Oct. 1884.
  [2] F.O. 84/1702: Goodrich to Salisbury, No. 7, Africa, 9 Aug. 1885.
  [3] F.O. 84/1751: Hawes to Rosebery, No. 20, C.A., 1 July 1886.
  [4] R. C. F. Maugham, *Africa as I have known it*, pp. 165–79.

Consul Hawes and the missionaries strongly disapproved of these proceedings, but had no authority to interfere. This man insulted Chikusi after the arrogant young chief had disagreed with him about the terms of trade, and Chikusi retaliated by letting loose his followers upon Hinkleman, who was clubbed, slashed with a knife, and speared in the stomach. Then—according to an Englishman who was with him, and whom Chikusi allowed to go free—his heart was torn out, and eaten, before his body was thrown to the Shiré crocodiles.[1]

'Faults on both sides', commented Sir Percy Anderson, when he read the consul's report. 'We must hope Hawes will be able to do something. This is the second white man killed in the Makololo country. They were neither much loss, but the precedent is dangerous.'[2]

In fact it soon became apparent that Chikusi had overreached himself. His tyranny made his rule hated by his own people, and his crime on this occasion aroused a feeling of shame and resentment amongst the other Makololo chiefs. Ramakukan sent a message to Hawes, expressing the intention to capture Chikusi and send him to Quilimane for punishment, but Hawes replied that the Portuguese would interpret this as an acknowledgement of their sovereignty. Several weeks passed, and Ramakukan took no action. Chikusi meanwhile wrote to the consul, stating that he wished to be friendly with the English. But Hawes could not forget that the murdered man had been in possession of 200 guns, 900 pounds of ivory, and several bales of goods and casks of powder, all of which had been seized as loot; and he realized that if so profitable a crime could be committed with impunity, it would in all probability be repeated.[3] At the Foreign Office, Anderson thought the situation was one which called for vigorous action.

Impress on Mr. Hawes [he wrote] that unless the English settlers have sufficient influence to cause murder of whites and theft of their property to be punished, it will be impossible for H.M. Govt. to resist offers of Portuguese Govt. to chastise the offenders even if their so doing should lead to their occupation of the country.

[1] F.O. 84/1751: Hawes to Iddesleigh, No. 26, C.A., 28 Aug. 1886; No. 27, C.A., 4 Sept.; No. 28, C.A., 7 Sept.; No. 30, C.A., 18 Sept. 1886.
[2] Minute on Hawes's No. 30, C.A., of 1886, loc. cit.
[3] F.O. 84/1751: Hawes to Iddesleigh, No. 32, C.A., 24 Sept. 1886; No. 37, C.A., 19 Oct. 1886.

At the same time approve his not acting himself where he cannot be sure of doing so with effect.[1]

At the end of November, however, Ramakukan moved against Chikusi, whose country was overrun without difficulty and with little bloodshed. Chikusi fled, but was captured and put to death.[2] 'A good riddance of a drunken vagabond, so long as it has not been brought about by the Portuguese': such was the not inappropriate comment of E. W. Wylde when a telegram from Delagoa Bay brought the news to the Foreign Office.[3]

Ramakukan did not appoint a successor to Chikusi, but brought the country round Chiromo under his own direct control.[4]

◇　◇　◇

The routine work of the consul for Nyasa was to collect information about the slave-trade and to try to persuade the chiefs in his district to resist the temptations placed in their way by the slave-dealers. Such work involved frequent and prolonged journeys. Acting-Consul Goodrich, carrying out, as he said, the plans formed by the late consul, made a journey of over 2,000 miles, of which more than a thousand were traversed on foot.[5] Before setting out, he had written to Kirk that there were 'years and years of work here and great possibilities; work indeed for half a dozen consuls between the Ruo and Tanganyika. The slave-trade is more active in these parts than it has been for years, and now that Matapwiri has got a lot of Arabs permanently settled in his village, it is not likely to lessen.'[6] He realized that he could not accomplish much by a single visit, but he hoped that it would be possible 'by gradually getting them to regard you as a friend, [to] gain influence with them'.[7] Setting out early in 1885, he sailed up the west coast of the lake to Kota-Kota, where he had an interview with Jumbe, the Arab who had established himself as ruler over that place, with

[1] Minute on Hawes's No. 37, C.A. of 1886, embodied in F.O. to Hawes, No. 32, 31 Dec. 1886 (in F.O. 84/1751).
[2] F.O. 84/1751: Hawes to Iddesleigh, No. 43, C.A., 19 Nov.; No. 44, C.A., 20 Nov.; No. 45, C.A., 29 Nov.; No. 46, C.A., 2 Dec.; No. 47, C.A., 8 Dec. 1886.
[3] F.O. 84/1829: minute on Hawes's telegram of 22 Jan. 1887.
[4] Hawes's No. 45, C.A., of 1886, loc. cit.
[5] F.O. 84/1702: Goodrich to Granville, No. 5, 15 June 1885.
[6] F.O. 84/1662: Goodrich to Kirk, 18 Dec. 1884. Matapwiri has already been referred to above, p. 62.
[7] Goodrich's letter of 18 Dec. 1884, loc. cit. (The word 'you' refers, of course, to the person paying the visits.)

its surrounding territory of Marimba. In the presence of about 3,000 people, of whom at least a hundred were Arabs, he presented letters from the Sultan of Zanzibar and from Sir John Kirk. Jumbe, as was to be expected, was very polite. He excused his active slave-trading practices—for which he kept no fewer than six dhows—on the ground that if he grew produce instead of selling slaves, no one would come to buy it: this was the usual answer of Central African chiefs, except those who were so much afraid of the unknown powers of the white man that they strenuously denied having ever sold a slave. At the same time he promised to plant any seeds that were given him, and repeated many times the suave protestation: 'All my country belongs to the Seyed [i.e. the Sultan of Zanzibar] and his friends the English.'

Continuing his journey from Kota-Kota, Goodrich proceeded northwards to Bandawe in order to visit the Tonga villages in that region; he then crossed the lake and called at the village of the exceptionally powerful Yao chief, Makanjira, who dominated the entire south-east coast. He found that the chief's residence was 'a handsome building with substantial carved doors such as one sees in Zanzibar', and that there were a considerable number of half-caste Arabs in the village. Here also he presented letters from the Sultan and from Kirk: and here also he received an assurance of 'great friendship for the English, and much gratitude to Her Majesty's Government for sending a Consul to live on the Lake'.[1] The future was to show only too clearly how much these civilities were worth.

After making the acquaintance of various other chiefs on the east coast of Nyasa, the acting-consul returned to Bandawe and went on to Mombera's. Mombera assured him that the Angoni never sold slaves: they incorporated conquered peoples in their own tribe. 'Send me any slaves you may release', said the chief, 'and I will make them free men in my country.' When urged to abandon his destructive raids, Mombera replied: 'How will my people get cattle except by fighting?' He was told that the answer lay in the cultivation of oil-seeds for sale to the white man, but he displayed little interest in so unorthodox a project; instead, he 'asked a great many questions about England and begged for a great many things'.[2] Returning to the Tonga country, Goodrich

---

[1] F.O. 84/1702: Goodrich to Granville, No. 2, Africa, 19 Mar. 1885.
[2] F.O. 84/1702: Goodrich to Granville, No. 3, Africa, 24 Apr. 1885.

was received in a most unfriendly manner by Chigau, the foremost slave-dealer of the district, whom he was now visiting for the third time, and who, he concluded, was irritated and alarmed by his interest in the chief's misdeeds.[1]

By the middle of June 1885 Goodrich was back at Livingstonia on his way to Blantyre. In September he again made a tour of the lake, and on 19 October, a few days after his return, Hawes arrived and assumed the duties of the consulate.[2]

Before leaving London, Hawes had obtained permission to erect a house at the public expense, because without it he would have had to live in a tent or a grass hut unless he obtained hospitality from the missionaries or the African Lakes Company.[3] A month after his arrival at Blantyre he had chosen a site which he recommended because it lay close to the great slave-route from the south end of Lake Nyasa to the Portuguese coast south of Ibo.[4] Here, on the slopes of Mount Zomba, about forty miles north of Blantyre, the Church of Scotland Mission had formerly established a sub-station, with John Buchanan, the artisan, in charge. After his well-deserved dismissal in 1880 Buchanan had remained at this place, where he had created an extensive coffee and sugar plantation. In 1885, when Hawes arrived, he had just returned from a visit to Britain, bringing with him a sugar-mill and coffee-pulping machinery.[5] It is to be regretted that we do not know more of this remarkable man, whose harshness towards suspected thieves in 1879 stands out in striking and apparently inexplicable contrast with the position of honour and esteem which he occupied in later life. It would, of course, be possible to offer the slick explanation that the world always respects those who prosper, or the equally shallow theory that his humiliation led to a complete change of heart. There is probably an element of truth in both these explanations, but it seems more reasonable to suggest that a rugged probity and a puritanical rectitude of character are not inconsistent with a complete absence of gentleness and charm, and with an inexcusable heavy-handedness towards evildoers. However that may be, it

---

[1] F.O. 84/1702: Goodrich to Granville, No. 4, Africa, 1 June 1885.
[2] F.O. 84/1702: Goodrich to Salisbury, No. 10, Africa, 7 Oct. 1885; Hawes to Salisbury, No. 2, Africa, 30 Oct. 1885.
[3] F.O. 84/1702: Hawes to Granville, 15 May 1885; F.O. to Hawes, 15 July 1885.
[4] F.O. 84/1702: Hawes to Salisbury, No. 4, Africa, 19 Nov. 1885.
[5] Ibid.

was Buchanan who introduced the cultivation of coffee to Nyasaland, thereby providing the country with its chief source of wealth during the early years of the Protectorate. It was from him that Hawes bought 100 acres of land—an area for which the consul paid very little, 'as the value of ten acres or one hundred acres is at present out here practically the same'.[1] It was he also who erected, at very reasonable cost, a large and attractive building as the British Consulate. This building was afterwards taken over by Commissioner Johnston as his Residency; and thus the lonely site on the slopes of Zomba became the capital of a British dependency. The Residency, in the words of Mr. R. C. F. Maugham, was 'situated in a wonderfully beautiful gorge some distance up the mountain'. 'I have always stated it as my opinion', adds Maugham, 'that of the many attractive spots which I have seen in Africa, Zomba is the loveliest of all.'[2]

During his first few months in Nyasaland, Hawes confined his activities to the country between Zomba and Chiromo. In June 1886, however, as already related, he visited southern Angoniland. On his way, he passed through the villages of two of the most important Yao slave-trading chiefs, Liwonde and Mponda. Liwonde's settlement was situated on the Shiré, between Zomba and Lake Nyasa; Mponda's was at the point where the Shiré emerges from the lake. At the former place he found the people living in dread of the attack which, it was believed, the Angoni were about to launch, and their fear caused them to give the consul a friendly welcome. Mponda, however, proved to be entirely under the influence of the numerous coastmen who had settled at his village, which, because of its geographical position, was a thriving entrepôt of the slave-trade. Between it and the Angoni country lay an uninhabited forest; nevertheless, Mponda found it expedient to pay tribute to Chikusi to secure immunity from Angoni raids. But these raids, directed against others, were probably a source of considerable profit to Mponda, providing most of the slaves who passed through the village on their way to the coast. The chief, in spite of these interests and connexions, 'expressed great friendship for the English, and promised to maintain the same friendly feeling towards the African Lakes Co. that his predecessor [who had died

[1] F.O. 84/1751: Hawes to Salisbury, No. 1, C.A., 4 Jan. 1886, with enclosures.
[2] R. C. F. Maugham, *Africa as I have known it*, p. 93. There is a photograph of the landscape, ibid., facing p. 104.

earlier in the year] had shown'.[1] As an illustration of how this
'friendly feeling' towards the Company had operated in the past,
we may cite the experience of A. J. Swann, who had passed down
the Nyasa–Shiré route on his way home to England in 1884. The
captain of the *Ilala* told Swann that he always had trouble with the
Arabs when passing this place: and on this occasion a tree had
been felled so as to form a boom across the river. All on board
congregated aft, so as to raise the steamer's bows, and when she
struck the boom they rushed forward, and, in Swann's words, 'the
little craft struggled over, with a heavy list into deep water on the
other side. This was marine steeplechasing; the wonder was it did
not break the vessel's back. In those days no one stood at trifles.
Things *had* to be done. . . . The rage of the people at the success
of the captain's strategy may be well imagined. They fired guns at
us, but no one knew where the bullets went to; certainly they never
struck anything near us.'[2]

In his report on the first part of his journey to southern Angoniland, Hawes mentioned that the country between Blantyre and
Zomba, in the heart of the Shiré Highlands, was completely de-
populated.

Though well watered by numerous streams [he wrote], and possessing
good soil well suited for the cultivation of coffee, there is neither sign of
habitation nor cultivation. The dread of raids from Angoni Land is so
great that the people, instead of occupying the rich plains, prefer to
cluster together in small villages on mountain slopes where they cultivate only sufficient for their wants. A bad harvest would be to them undoubtedly a source of serious distress.

In the same dispatch he made an interesting suggestion. He said
that a chief, who admitted having sold slaves from time to time,
and to whom he had pointed out the advantages of growing coffee
as an alternative means of obtaining supplies, had shown considerable interest in the idea, but had objected that he could not afford
the initial outlay. Hawes admitted that this was true, and asked the
Foreign Office if it had at its disposal any funds which could be
employed to subsidize the enterprise of native chiefs. He had to be
told, however, that there were no funds available for this purpose.[3]

[1] F.O. 84/1751: Hawes to Rosebery, No. 19, C.A., 3 June 1886; No. 21, C.A.,
7 July 1886.   [2] Swann, *Fighting the Slave-Hunters*, pp. 136–7.
[3] F.O. 84/1751: Hawes to Rosebery, No. 19, C.A., 3 June 1886; ibid., F.O. to
Hawes, No. 16, 22 Sept. 1886.

After his return from Chikusi's, the consul did not embark upon another long journey for more than a year; and when, in October 1887, he at length did so, the attempt was a failure. He wished to visit the Gwangwara, or eastern Angoni, but his porters were so much afraid of these formidable marauders that they deserted on the way, and he was compelled to abandon his purpose.[1]

It seems, indeed, that Hawes had never intended to visit the north end of Nyasa, for, at the beginning of 1886, he had asked that a vice-consul should be appointed to deal with the affairs of that part of his huge district: a request which had been turned down for the usual reason—lack of funds.[2] In effect, therefore, his district was, for practical purposes, reduced to an area which comprised little more than the Shiré Highlands, and when he visited the southern Angoni and attempted to visit the Gwangwara it was primarily because these tribes were terrorizing the region in which he was trying to establish peace and promote the growth of commerce and civilization.

In the relatively restricted sphere to which he thus confined himself he had, as it proved, not only plenty of work but a steadily increasing burden of troubles. Scarcely had he arrived in Nyasaland at the end of 1885 when he found that 'some British subjects' had been disregarding the claim of the native chiefs to one of the tusks of every elephant shot within their territory.[3] A tax of 50 per cent. on all ivory shot—which is what this rule amounted to—was undoubtedly severe: still, it was the custom of the country, and foreigners had no right to break it. Hawes gives only one instance of such high-handedness: that of an Englishman named Pettitt, the partner of Hinkleman. Pettitt had given offence in this way to Katunga, the Makololo chief who lived at the foot of the Murchison Cataracts; but Hawes persuaded him to give Katunga his lawful due.[4] He had to rely on persuasion, for he had no administrative or judicial authority whatever.[5] It is improbable that there were any other offenders of this kind in the country. If relations between the white men and the natives were steadily deteriorating, the fault,

---

[1] F.O. 84/1829: Hawes to Salisbury, No. 44, C.A., 5 Oct. 1887; No. 45, C.A., 16 Nov. 1887.
[2] F.O. 84/1751: Hawes to Salisbury, No. 2, C.A., 9 Jan. 1886; F.O. to Hawes, No. 3, 22 Apr. 1886.
[3] F.O. 84/1702: Hawes to Salisbury, 7 Nov. 1885, Confidential.
[4] F.O. 84/1702: Hawes to Salisbury, No. 5, Africa, 1 Dec. 1885.
[5] Minute on dispatch of 7 Nov.

it is safe to say, rested chiefly with the natives, and with the slave-dealing Swahilis and coastmen who exploited their *naïveté*. Such an assertion, made by a white man relying entirely on the evidence of another white man, may appear to have little weight: but the fact is that Hawes had no conceivable interest in misrepresenting the facts, since he was the servant of a Government which had no intention of annexing Central Africa, or of applying any force whatever to make the natives conform to its will; so that all its hopes for the advancement of civilization and of trade in those regions were conditional upon the friendship of the inhabitants. And, obviously, friendship can only be possible where there is just dealing.

The Government's intention not to use force had been made clear from the beginning. At the time of the troubles occasioned by Fenwick's murder of Chipatula, Consul Foot had suggested that it would have a salutary effect on the light-headed and cowardly rabble of Manganja whom the Makololo chiefs had gathered round them if a few British bluejackets were sent up-river to the scene of the disturbances. In reply, he was firmly told that no such suggestion could be considered, and that he must rely entirely on his own tact.[1]

It was precisely this total absence of even a shadow of armed power which made it inevitable that the white man's prestige would decline. Even among civilized nations, diplomacy is always backed by force. A strong Power is valued as a friend and feared as an enemy, and so long as it does not abuse its strength and thus consolidate opposition to itself its influence in the counsels of the nations will be proportional to its might. It could not be otherwise in tropical Africa. When the British first arrived, they were received with the respect which primitive man accords to the unknown: but familiarity bred contempt. That uncritical negrophilist, E. D. Young, in his account of his expedition's journey up the Shiré,[2] recorded enthusiastically that nothing whatever had been stolen, although theft would have been easy. Now, however, Goodrich and Hawes reported that thefts were of constant occurrence. The Lakes Company did not take the precaution of putting a white man in charge of their caravans—presumably because they

[1] F.O. 84/1662: Foot to Granville, No. 9, Africa, 9 May 1884; ibid., F.O. to Foot, 5 Sept. 1884.
[2] See above, p. 13.

could not afford this expense—and the natives too often yielded to the temptation to run away with their loads.[1]

At first, the British consuls had been honoured, because they came as representatives of the Queen. But by 1887 this feeling had worn off, and in June of that year Hawes was bluntly asked, by a petty chief near Zomba, what he could do if the chief chose to buy slaves from a passing caravan.[2] In the previous April he reported that people were being enslaved in the vicinity of Zomba by a powerful Yao named Kawinga, who lived at the north end of Lake Shirwa and who had never even consented to receive a visit from him. He asked the Foreign Office what he should do if Kawinga captured one of his own servants: Wylde's minute on this dispatch is worth quoting:

This is rather a prickly question. If Kawinga seizes a mission [sic] servant as a slave, there is no way of getting the man back—as Kawinga will not see Europeans—short of telling Hawes to pitch into him, and that we cannot do.

Answer that it is difficult to give advice in such matters inasmuch as during the time communications are taking place, new and different phases of a question may be entered upon; and that Lord Salisbury has confidence in Consul Hawes' tact and general management of the natives in his district, and looks to him to keep clear of any unnecessary embarrassments.[3]

With the other powerful Yao chiefs the position was little better. It will be remembered that Acting-Consul Goodrich had been given a very friendly reception at Makanjira's village early in 1885: now, in April 1887, Hawes was received without actual discourtesy but with a distinct lack of hospitality. It was obvious that the chief was entirely in the hands of his Arab counsellors. When Hawes pressed for a reply to the British offer of friendship which he had conveyed, it was given in the following terms:

The chief does not see his way to giving up slavery and confining himself to what you call lawful trade, and on this account he is unable to accept unreservedly the friendship of England.[4]

[1] F.O. 84/1662: Goodrich to Granville, No. 16, Africa, 20 Dec. 1884; F.O. 84/1751: Hawes to Iddesleigh, No. 29, C.A., 17 Sept. 1886.
[2] F.O. 84/1829: Hawes to Salisbury, No. 27, C.A., 27 June 1887.
[3] F.O. 84/1829: Hawes to Salisbury, No. 20, C.A., 25 Apr. 1887, with minute. A dispatch on the lines suggested was sent to him on 9 Aug. (this also is in F.O. 84/1829).
[4] F.O. 84/1829: Hawes to Salisbury, No. 15, C.A., 8 Apr. 1887. Obviously

As for Matapwiri, the most important of the Yao who dwelt among the fastnesses of Mount Mlanje, he would not even receive the messengers who came to tell him that Hawes wished to visit him; but his influential brother, Mange, sent word that if the English consul came, he would be shot, for 'the English are my enemies'. The immediate reason for this hostile attitude is of some interest. Hawes, like most Europeans on their first arrival in Central Africa, had thought it necessary to provide himself with a few men from Zanzibar. In March 1886 he had declared that 'their services could not be dispensed with'. Now these men had run away, had robbed the company's store at Mandala, and had taken up residence with Mange, under whose protection both they and their loot were safe. Some weeks later Moir attempted to communicate with Matapwiri to try to recover his property, only to be told that 'if the English wanted the stolen goods, they could come and fight for them'. The consul, realizing that it would be disastrous to ignore such an open challenge, asked the Foreign Office to request the Portuguese to come to his help, although, as Sir Percy Anderson observed, 'at other times he has deprecated [Portuguese influence] as the worst evil that could be introduced'.[1]

'This despatch', commented Sir Villiers Lister,[2] 'raises doubts in my mind (not for the first time) as to the utility of the Lakes Consulate.'

While Matapwiri was challenging the British to make war upon him if they could, Kawinga was continuing his raids in the vicinity of Zomba. Reporting this, Hawes made what Anderson called the 'despairing' suggestion that Britain should resort to force, without which, the consul admitted, 'I do not see much hope for an improvement in the present deplorable state of affairs.' He went on to make proposals which, in effect, amounted to nothing less than the establishment of British rule:

To interfere with what may be termed domestic slavery would, I

the phraseology here employed is Hawes's own, but presumably the substance of the communication is authentic. Hawes lacked all insight into the native idiom. W. P. Johnson relates that the consul, when visiting Mponda, said to Buchanan, who was acting as interpreter: 'Will you please tell the Chief that if he continues to act in this way there will be strained relations with the Foreign Office.' (Johnson, *My African Reminiscences*, p. 149.)

[1] F.O. 84/1829: Hawes to Salisbury, No. 5, C.A., 25 Feb. 1887, and No. 9, C.A., Confidential, 4 July 1887, with minutes; also F.O. 84/1751: H. to S., No. 10 C.A., 9 Mar. 1886.   [2] As T. V. Lister had become.

believe, be unwise, but I feel confident that a check could very effectually be placed on the export of slaves by the presence of a few armed steamers on Lake Nyasa, and of a small military force at Zomba to keep in control the slave markets held at the villages of Kawinga and Matapwiri. This would, I believe, strike at the source of the present evil, and completely drive the Arab dealers from these territories.

'We can only print this', was Anderson's gloomy comment.[1]

A dispatch was, however, sent to Hawes comforting him with the assurance that he was 'rendering valuable service by ascertaining the truth as to the direction and origin of these raids and as to the dispositions of the chiefs'. But, even if moral influence produced no effect, he must continue to rely on it alone. To call in the Portuguese would merely antagonize the missionaries and traders, while Britain herself could not send forces to a country to which she had no access except through the possessions of a foreign Power.[2]

In August of the same year (1887) the exhausted and frustrated consul applied for leave of absence, which was granted.[3] It was while awaiting the result of this application that he set out on his unsuccessful attempt to visit the Gwangwara. Arriving back at Zomba in November, he received news of disturbances which were to prove more serious than any with which he had yet been called upon to deal.

4. *The Arab War*

It was not until June 1884 that the African Lakes Company established a permanent station at Karonga, on the west coast of Lake Nyasa, near the north end.[4] The agent who was put in charge of it was L. Monteith Fotheringham, by far the best man who served the Company during the early years of its existence.[5]

---

[1] F.O. 84/1829: Hawes to Salisbury, No. 31, C.A., 9 July 1887, with minute.
[2] F.O. 84/1829: F.O. to Hawes, No. 22, 22 Oct. 1887. The attitude to Nyasaland prevailing in the Foreign Office is well illustrated by Lister's comments on a request for a dozen rifles and 5,000 rounds of ammunition: 'How is all this to be paid for? . . . Hawes will be conquering Africa if we don't take care.' (F.O. 84/1829: Hawes to Salisbury, No. 22, C.A., 7 May 1887: minutes.)
[3] F.O. 84/1829: Hawes to Salisbury, No. 36, C.A., 15 Aug. 1887, with minute.
[4] L. M. Fotheringham, *Adventures in Nyassaland*, p. 12.
[5] Lugard describes him as 'a man of strong character, actuated by high principles', and declares that 'he had a very great influence with the tribes around' (F. D. Lugard: *The Rise of Our East African Empire*, vol. i, p. 53). When he took

Karonga was the terminus of the Stevenson Road, along which it was Fotheringham's task to forward supplies to the Free Church of Scotland's station at Mwiniwanda, some sixty miles distant, and to the agents of the London Missionary Society on Lake Tanganyika; at the same time he collected ivory from the surrounding country and sent it by the *Ilala* on its way to the markets of the world. Apart from two journeys to Tanganyika, his first three years were uneventful.[1]

The Wankonde people, who inhabited the fertile country around Karonga, were probably the most attractive tribe in Central Africa. Though they were so unsophisticated that they wore nothing whatever except a belt of copper wire and ankle-bells, they were scrupulously clean in their habits, and their huts, in the construction of which they used sun-dried bricks, were skilfully and neatly built, in pleasant contrast to the miserable hovels which were usually to be found elsewhere. To their visitors they were friendly, frank, and hospitable.[2]

Attracted by the market for their ivory which the Karonga station afforded, Arabs and Swahilis came long distances to transact business with Fotheringham. Since he often did not have enough goods in stock to pay for the ivory which they brought, they found it convenient to establish themselves in the neighbourhood on a permanent footing. The numerous followers of these half-caste Arabs were mere brigands, adorned with necklaces of human teeth, and they had a most agreeable time in the Wankonde country, terrorizing and plundering the peace-loving people.[3]

The first of the so-called 'Arabs'—in reality Swahili half-castes —to settle near Karonga was named Mlozi, whom Fotheringham described as a 'sly diplomat, with professions of the warmest friendship to the natives'.[4] Mlozi gradually consolidated his posi-

supplies to Tanganyika, Swann at once recognized a kindred spirit. 'Mr. Monteith', he wrote (for Fotheringham was often called 'Monteith') 'appears to be thoroughly interested in our work, and his especial duty is to superintend the transport of our goods north of Nyassa, which duty he appears to be well qualified for, and we may expect better things in future if he is not interfered with by Mr. J. Moir, the Manager (so called).' L.M.S., C.A., 5.5.C: Swann to Thompson, 28 Oct. 1884.

[1] Fotheringham, op. cit., pp. 13–20.
[2] Ibid., chap. ii; Lugard, op. cit., p. 52; Swann, *Fighting the Slave-Hunters*, pp. 122–3; also—most memorable of all—J. Thomson, *To the Central African Lakes and Back*, vol. i, pp. 266–76. For a modern anthropological study see G. Wilson, *The Constitution of Ngonde* (Rhodes-Livingstone Papers, No. 3, 1939).
[3] Fotheringham, op. cit., pp. 12, 19–20, 37.   [4] Ibid., p. 32.

tion, erecting a stockade round his village and increasing the numbers of his armed robbers. Two other black Arabs, named Kopa-
Kopa and Msalema, established fortified villages, somewhat
smaller than Mlozi's, a few miles away from his. As the Arabs
became stronger they became more violent, and in July 1887 their
followers murdered a Wankonde sub-chief. Fotheringham's media-
tion prevented the outbreak of hostilities which would otherwise
have followed; but on 4 October another chief was murdered, and
this time the result was war. Fotheringham afterwards expressed
the conviction that the murder was a deliberate act of provocation:
that the Arabs had decided that the time was ripe to sweep the
country of its population with the help of their allies, the Henga,
a native tribe who lived on the shore of the lake about twenty miles
north of Karonga.[1] His view is supported by the fact that the
Arabs now adopted an overbearing and menacing attitude towards
himself, while at the same time Mlozi assumed the title of 'Sultan
of Nkonde'.

In the three weeks following the second murder, the Arabs and
their followers stormed village after village, plundering, slaughtering, and taking captive. The culmination of these atrocities occurred
on 27 October. A large number of the Wankonde had fled to the
Kambwe lagoon, a stagnant swamp overgrown with reeds, and
only a short distance from the Company's station. The Arabs surrounded the lagoon, and poured volley after volley into the reeds.
There was no escape. The attackers gradually advanced, and fired
the reeds. Then Mlozi, Kopa-Kopa, and Msalema climbed into
trees to obtain the best possible view of the scene, where hundreds
of people who had never done them wrong had to choose between
being burned alive, being shot in the open, or being seized by the
waiting crocodiles in the lagoon.[2]

A special fate was reserved for an old witch-doctor, whom the
Arabs hated because he had 'made medicine against them'. The
story was afterwards told by Fotheringham to Swann, and can best
be related in Swann's own words:

They surrounded his rocky retreat, and forced him to capitulate
through hunger. The poor wretch was tied to some very light pith-wood
trees, used by fishermen as buoys for their traps; the raft was then
placed on the lagoon, with fresh-cut goat's meat to attract the crocs.
His tormentors sat on the bank, watching the crocs fight for his body.

[1] Ibid., chap. iii.   [2] Ibid., chaps. iv and v.

This being firmly lashed, the creatures could only snap at him; the buoyant wood prevented them from carrying him under water. It is said they tore him to pieces, and one can imagine what torture he must have suffered as he lay helplessly looking at the green-eyed monsters swimming around the raft and trying to get a favourable opportunity of biting off a limb. When he was nearly torn to pieces, the Arabs amused themselves, as they sat, by firing at the crocodiles.[1]

$$\diamond \qquad \diamond \qquad \diamond$$

When the fighting, or rather the massacres, began, Fotheringham was the only white man at Karonga. He had little ammunition, and was in no position to defend himself if attacked. He at once sent a messenger to Mwiniwanda, the Livingstonia mission's station on the Stevenson Road, asking the Rev. Bain, the missionary there, to come down and join him. Bain arrived on 8 October, and work was hastily pressed forward on the building of a fortification round Karonga. Mlozi was at this time too preoccupied to raise objections, but two days after the attack on the Kambwe lagoon he sent a message demanding that this work should cease. It was nearly complete, and to avoid giving any provocation Fotheringham complied.

There were still some villages left to raid, however, and it was not until 23 November that the Arabs began the long-expected siege of the station. J. L. Nicoll, an agent of the Company, had in the meantime arrived from Tanganyika, and as soon as the attack began he was sent off to the Mwamba country, at the north end of the lake, to try to enlist the support of its numerous and warlike inhabitants. On 4 November Fotheringham and Bain had been reinforced. The *Ilala* had gone south with news of the Arab rising, and had now brought back four volunteers to assist in the defence. One of these was a solicitor named Alfred Sharpe, who had come to Africa to hunt big game; and another was Consul O'Neill.[2]

O'Neill's presence on Lake Nyasa was occasioned by other business, but when he arrived at Old Livingstonia (Cape Maclear), on 30 October 1887, he received word of the upheaval at the north end, and was profoundly alarmed by it.

Your Lordship has doubtless been made aware [he wrote to Lord Salisbury, the Prime Minister and Foreign Secretary] of the remarkable growth of Arab power during the past three years in East Central

---

[1] A. J. Swann, *Fighting the Slave-Hunters*, p. 278.
[2] Fotheringham, op. cit., chaps. iv–vi.

Africa, and learnt from other sources the bloodshed and ruin and desolation that has been the direct accompaniment of that growth. . . . This destructive wave, which has hitherto taken a westerly direction, being apparently directed towards the countries of the Congo Free State, is now, I deeply regret to say, taking a Southerly course and threatening to devastate well-populated districts around the North end of Lake Nyassa.

He accordingly determined to proceed at once to the scene of the disturbances, and not to wait for Consul Hawes to return from the Gwangwara country. 'I trust', he added, 'that all may be settled without force or bloodshed, which I shall do my utmost to check.'[1]

Immediately after the arrival of the reinforcements, work on the defences of the station was resumed. Two days later, on 6 November, some sixty starving and emaciated natives were given shelter, and others were brought in on the 17th. This was purely an act of mercy, but when Consul Hawes heard of it he disapproved, on the ground that it was a provocation to Mlozi.[2] One is inclined to retort that it was a strange kind of provocation: indeed, it could not even, strictly speaking, be described as an interference in native politics, since Mlozi was as much a foreigner in Central Africa as Fotheringham or O'Neill. And yet, in a sense, Hawes was right. By refusing to recognize the usurper, and by giving sanctuary to his victims, these British subjects were inevitably setting themselves up in his country as a rival power, and sooner or later there must be a fight to the finish. In other words, there was, in the last analysis, only one choice for the white men: either they must assume responsibility for the establishment and maintenance of order and justice in those regions, putting forth a sufficient effort to break the power of Mlozi and his kind, or they must acquiesce in the intensification of the reign of terror, and its prolongation as far into the future as it was possible to foresee.

Already, long before Mlozi had become a power in the land, the Lakes Company had taken the measure of the situation, and, with more boldness than prudence, had decided on its course. In August 1885 John Moir had informed Acting-Consul Goodrich that he had induced many of the chiefs of the Nyasa district to put their mark on two memorials, 'one praying Her Majesty's Government

---

[1] F.O. 84/1846: O'Neill to Salisbury, No. 57, Africa, 31 Oct. 1887. O'Neill's views on the Arab menace are discussed below, pp. 97–100.

[2] F.O. 84/1883: Hawes to Salisbury, No. 3, C.A., 16 Jan. 1888.

to declare a Protectorate over their territory, and the other asking the African Lakes Company to grant them protection should Her Majesty's Government refuse their petition'.[1] As soon as Hawes arrived at Quilimane, a few weeks after this conversation, he received a letter from Moir enclosing copies of eight documents, of which the originals had already been sent to England. These documents were dated May 1885 and purported to show that the Makololo chiefs had ceded their territory and their rights of jurisdiction to the company. Moir also stated that he was about to proceed to England to lay before the Foreign Office petitions and treaties to the same effect, made by seventeen Yao chiefs, by fourteen of the chiefs on the shores of the lake, and by two chiefs on the Stevenson Road.[2]

Ramakukan and another of the Makololo chiefs sent messages to Goodrich, asking the meaning of what they had signed. Goodrich, in reply, denied that either he or the British Government was in any way responsible for Moir's action.[3] Writing to the Foreign Office, he declared that Moir had told the Makololo that the Portuguese were about to take their country and that British protection was the only sure way to avert this calamity; he added that in his opinion this action was 'exceedingly indiscreet, as everything that passes between the English and the Makololo is reported to the Portuguese authorities at Quilimane through the medium of a Frenchman who has for the last eighteen months lived with Ramakukan'.[4] Not long afterwards, when making his second tour of the lake, the acting-consul found that Jumbe's suspicions had been aroused by the news that Moir had concluded treaties with the Tonga, to whose country Jumbe pretended to have some sort of claim. 'Tell me all that is in your mind', he repeatedly urged Goodrich, in the conviction that Moir had been acting on official instructions. As for the Tonga themselves, they were quite convinced that the act of signing the treaties would be sufficient to safeguard them from any further Angoni raids.[5]

The action of the Makololo and the Tonga is intelligible enough: protection was desired, in one case against the Portuguese, in the

[1] F.O. 84/1702: Goodrich to Salisbury, No. 8, Africa, 9 Aug. 1885.
[2] F.O. 84/1702: Hawes to Salisbury, No. 1, Africa, 17 Sept. 1885, with enclosure.
[3] Goodrich's No. 8, Africa, of 1885, loc. cit.
[4] F.O. 84/1702: Goodrich to Salisbury, No. 9, Africa, 29 Aug. 1885.
[5] F.O. 84/1702: Goodrich to Salisbury, No. 10, Africa, 7 Oct. 1885.

other, against the Angoni. But it is not easy to suggest why any of the Yao signed the treaties, if, as is doubtful, they knew what they were doing.

Consul Hawes visited the Makololo in November 1885, and asked the chiefs for their opinions. They all denied that they had signed away their sovereignty. Hawes therefore brought Ramakukan and John Moir to a meeting at Mandala, and asked Moir to read the documents. When this was done, Ramakukan refused to admit that he had accepted any such provisions.

He understood, he said, that the paper he had put a mark to simply contained a statement that he was the paramount chief of the Makololo tribes, that there were so many chiefs under him, and that he would be friendly to any Englishman who might come to his country. Mr. Moir read over the documents a second time and pointed out the various signatures attached to them; the chief however repeated what I have above stated and persisted most emphatically that he had never signed documents of that nature. He added that he thought it would be very good to be under the English Queen, and on his return to the river he would consult with the other chiefs about it. Mr. Moir stated that he felt sure the chiefs clearly understood the nature of the documents at the time they signed them; that no trouble had been spared to fully explain to each of them the exact meaning of both the petition and treaty, and he could not account for their having now repudiated them. I am not aware myself of any reason, but it appears to me very evident that the feeling of the Makololo Chiefs towards the African Lakes Company is far from cordial, and from the numerous minor complaints that were made to me whilst I was at the river, I am of opinion that the influence of the company has been greatly lessened by the conduct of some of its employés, who I may add are in some cases men of a very inferior stamp.[1]

The Foreign Office had no objection in principle to the treaties, but it wished to satisfy itself that the company was capable of discharging honourably and efficiently the great responsibilities which that body was seeking to assume. On this point the evidence was not encouraging. Hawes, although convinced that 'the introduction of a protectorate and efficient administration would tend largely towards the civilization and progress of the country', reported that after thoroughly discussing the project with John Moir, he had 'unhesitatingly told him that, under its present constitution, the

[1] F.O. 84/1702: Hawes to Salisbury, No 5, Africa, 1 Dec. 1885.

Company is, in my opinion, totally unable to carry out successfully the undertaking'.[1]

This was indeed true. When all possible excuses have been made for it—the difficulty of pioneer conditions, its lack of capital, and its consequent shortage of staff—there is still no doubt that it was grossly mismanaged. Its refusal to sell liquor to the natives was, indeed, greatly to its credit; and Dr. Laws, in his memoirs, said of the Moir brothers: 'They established a standard of commercial relationship and trust which has been of the utmost importance for Nyasaland. . . . Commercial adventurers, arriving later, found that they could not do as they liked, but had to conform to the standard of justice already existing.'[2] But Laws was an uncommonly sympathetic observer, since the company was an offshoot of the mission which he served, and the relations between the two bodies remained close, as Kirk noticed when he had a conversation with James Stewart—Dr. Stewart's cousin—in 1880. He was, he remarked, 'much struck . . . with the undisguised jealousy with which independent English traders who visit that region are viewed by the Missionaries as being rivals, in trade, with the affiliated Livingstonia trading company. Speaking of an English trader who left Zanzibar and who has now reached the Lake, Mr. Stewart said that had he known his object was trade he certainly would not have given him the assistance he did.'[3]

Competition was the spur that the company needed, but, thirteen years after Kirk's encounter with Stewart, George Cawston, a Director of the British South Africa Company, related that its Directors in Glasgow had told a new company which was trying to start a steamer service on the Zambesi–Shiré route that they intended to run it out of business. 'The Company', declared Cawston, 'is composed of a number of the most bigoted Scotch, most difficult to move and most difficult to interfere with. . . . They don't care much about money, but they have been in Nyasaland for the last fifteen years and they will not allow anyone else to come up there.'[4]

While its monopoly lasted, the company abused it shamefully. When Consul Foot travelled up the Zambesi in its steamer in 1883,

[1] F.O. 84/1751: Hawes to Rosebery, No. 13, C.A., 30 Mar. 1886.
[2] *Reminiscences of Livingstonia*, pp. 100–1.
[3] F.O. 84/1575: Kirk to Granville, No. 97, 24 Aug. 1890.
[4] Cawston Papers, vol. iv: copy of letter, recipient unspecified, dated 1893 (? May).

he found that the vessel had no cook, no cabin, and no awnings; it had no firebars in the furnace and therefore could not keep up steam, and its bottom leaked so badly that constant bailing was needed day and night, which prevented sleep.[1] Instances could be multiplied of the company's complete indifference to the health and comfort of its passengers on the river and of its inexcusable carelessness in its treatment of other people's goods. For the wretched service which it rendered it charged extortionate prices, and carried its niggardliness to the verge of dishonesty—if not a little farther. 'A more rotten commercial concern which contrives to make a big noise and cackle in the world I have never seen'—so Joseph Thomson informed Cecil Rhodes in 1890.

From no person [he added] have I heard a good thing said in its favour—beyond that it is recognised that its *intentions* have been good —but that is just it. It is entirely made up of good intentions, good aims, great schemes for the benefit of the natives, and lives in a perfect atmosphere of philanthropy and religion, while they utterly fail to carry out their commercial engagements, and do things which would ruin the reputation of any third-rate house, while giving their employees starvation wages and housing them in the most miserable fashion, having at places boxes to do for chairs and tables, their jack-knives for their cutlery, etc. . . . The type of men they have got out is utterly unsuited for the work to be done. They think £60 a year and the privilege of engaging in mission work amply sufficient to pay men who are to face fevers, isolation from society, the work of slaves, who are to be ready to be all things, face all things, know what to do in all sorts of ticklish situations. That so much has been accomplished under the circumstances is a marvel.[2]

H. H. Johnston, writing privately to Sir Percy Anderson in 1893, said that he was encouraging every possible rival to the Lakes Company, because, left in its hands, 'British trade on Lake Nyasa will always be kept in a crippled condition'.

If you ask me how this can be [he continued], I am at a loss for a general theory, except that it seems as though the riff-raff of Glasgow is not the best material with which to develop the commerce of British Central Africa. There have been in the past and possibly there are now one or two decent men in the Lakes Company's service,[3] but the bulk of

[1] F.O. 84/1677: Kirk to Granville, No. 19, 21 Jan. 1884 (summarizing a private letter from Foot).

[2] Rhodes Papers, Charters, 3A, 29: Thomson to Rhodes, 8 Aug. 1890.

[3] Johnston himself had by that time drawn the best of the company's men into his own Administration, with the exception of Fotheringham.

their employés seem to devote the whole of their talents to the cheating of all men, white, black, and yellow; to supplying you with bad articles instead of good, to intriguing against you, deceiving you, and disappointing you. Yet it is hard to see what they expect to gain by this policy. They do not even seem to know themselves.[1]

For the British Government to have conferred powers of jurisdiction on such a body would have been irresponsible and inexcusable. It did not, however, make its refusal final and irrevocable: it merely took note of the fact that the company itself, in deference to the opposition of the missions (or at least of Blantyre), had 'agreed that the Treaties concluded by Mr. Moir with the Makololo chiefs are [not] to be for the present in operation'.[2] So, when the Arabs opened fire on Karonga on the morning of 23 November 1887, and attempted to storm it on the following day, they were, probably unwittingly, measuring their strength against that of a body which still reserved its claims to set up a protectorate over a large part of the Shiré Highlands and of the west coast of the lake.

◦   ◦   ◦

The defence of Karonga was resolutely and skilfully maintained for several days in conditions of great difficulty and extreme discomfort. Then, early in the morning of 28 November, the attackers quietly withdrew. Soon afterwards, Nicoll came up with a force of no less than 5,000 Mwamba spearmen, and it was resolved to follow up the Arab retreat. It was found that the nearest of their villages had been deserted, so this was set on fire and its stockade was pulled down. But no more could be done. The Mwamba were disheartened by their failure to make contact with the enemy, and were afraid that their own country would be raided in their absence. Persuasion was of no avail: they were determined to go home. Realizing that it would be impossible to withstand another siege, Fotheringham and O'Neill resolved to abandon Karonga and accompany their unstable but indispensable allies to the north

---

[1] F.O. 2/54: Johnston to Anderson, 21 Jan. 1893. Cf. L.M.S., C.A., 5.5.A: Hore to Thompson, 25 Aug. 1884, and many other letters in the L.M.S. papers; F.O. 84/1662: Goodrich to Granville, No. 16, Africa, 20 Dec. 1884; Mins., C. of S. For. Miss. Comm., 14 June 1885, 12 July 1887, and 3 Mar. 1891; W. P. Johnson, *My African Reminiscences*, pp. 92, 160; D. J. Rankin, *The Zambesi Basin and Nyassaland*, p. 87.

[2] F.O. 84/1751: F.O. to Hawes, No. 11, Confidential, 24 July 1886; cf. Hawes to Rosebery, No. 13, C.A., 30 Mar. 1886, with enclosed letter from Hetherwick.

end. Here, at the beginning of the rainy season, they encamped beside a pestilent and mosquito-infested swamp.[1]

On 9 December the *Ilala* arrived, bringing Consul Hawes and John Moir. Meanwhile, information had been received that the Arabs had sent to Senga, about eight days' journey west of Karonga, for reinforcements and supplies with which to take the British camp. Accordingly, the British decided to strike first. A strong force of Mwamba was again enlisted, and on 23 December Mlozi's stockade was stormed, his people driven out, and his village burned. The Mwamba, however, having come merely for the sake of loot, at once fell upon the stores and rushed homewards with what they could carry. The victory, therefore, could not be followed up. Mlozi had lost much of his wealth but little of his power, and the menace which he represented had not been materially diminished.[2] A meeting of the white men was therefore held, and Hawes proposed that they should withdraw from the Konde country; but Fotheringham dissented strongly from this suggestion, declaring that it would involve abandoning their Mwamba allies, and also the missionaries at Fwambo, to the blood-lust of the Arabs. Accordingly, it was decided that he and four others should fortify themselves at Mwiniwanda, and hold it until reinforcements could be brought up to renew the war. John Moir gave Fotheringham a written promise that fifteen white men and a sufficient supply of munitions would come up before the end of April (1888). He also gave a verbal promise that the *Ilala* would come back in a fortnight, bringing ammunition for those who had undertaken to hold out till reinforcements came. Consul Hawes wrote to Moir 'to caution him to be most careful to confine his action to those who have been hostile towards his agents at Karonga's and to avoid in any way extending the area of disaffection beyond its present limits', and, having received an assurance that this would be done,[3] he took no further steps either to encourage or to restrain the company in the preparations which it had set afoot.

In addition to the two Scottish missions, the Lakes Company, Buchanan, and the consul for Nyasa, there was now another British

[1] Fotheringham, op. cit., chap. vii.
[2] F.O. 84/1883: Hawes to Salisbury, No. 1, C.A., 11 Jan. 1888; No. 3, C.A., 16 Jan. 1888, with enclosures.
[3] Ibid.; Fotheringham, op. cit., pp. 123–6.

agency at work on the lake. The Universities' Mission to Central Africa had returned to the country for which it had originally been intended. The credit for initiating this achievement must be given to Edward Steere, a man whose qualities of character, practical-mindedness, and versatility were comparable with those possessed by Dr. Laws of Livingstonia. Steere had formerly been called to the Bar, but he had become absorbed in social service work and afterwards took Orders as an Anglican priest. He was a friend of W. G. Tozer, and when Tozer went to Africa as Bishop of the Universities' Mission, Steere accompanied him. In 1873 Tozer resigned, and in the following year Steere was consecrated as his successor.[1]

While energetically carrying on the work which had been begun at Zanzibar, the new bishop, assisted by an increased staff, set himself to extend the mission's sphere to the Yao country east and south of Lake Nyasa. In 1875, accompanied by Chuma, one of the natives who had brought Livingstone's body to the coast, he himself reconnoitred the overland route as far as the village of Mataka, not far from the lake.[2] In the following year he established a station at Masasi, north of the Rovuma and about a hundred miles from the coast, and in 1880 he was in a position to follow up his own pioneer journey by sending W. P. Johnson to the Yao hills. Illness and the hostility of slave-dealing natives caused Johnson's first attempt to fail, but in 1881 Steere sent him back, accompanied by another missionary named Charles Janson. Janson died of fever on the shore of the lake in February 1882, but Johnson continued to explore the Yao country with a philosophic indifference to hardship and ill health until it became urgently necessary to sail across to Bandawe to receive medical treatment from Dr. Laws. When he recovered, he went down to Blantyre, where he found a message summoning him to England for consultations.[3]

He arrived in England in the summer of 1884, and was entirely successful in the appeal which he launched for a steamer to carry an itinerating missionary around Nyasa. The vessel was afloat in January 1886, and was named the *Charles Janson* to honour the memory of Johnson's fellow pioneer. Its headquarters were the

---

[1] G. H. Wilson, *History of the Universities' Mission to Central Africa* (U.M.C.A., London, 1936), pp. 35–36.

[2] Ibid., pp. 42–43.

[3] Ibid., pp. 43, 51–54, 60–64; W. P. Johnson, *My African Reminiscences*, chaps. v–x.

island of Likoma, which is situated near the east coast of the lake. From then on, the mission was continuously at work both on the island itself and on the mainland for a distance of about eighty miles south of Likoma, where the steamer visited seven or eight large coastal villages almost every week. The itinerating work was done by Johnson, while his friend, Chauncy Maples, was placed in charge of Likoma.[1] The urbane and eloquent Maples was in some ways very different from the unpolished and almost inarticulate Johnson, but the two men were united not only by a heroic spirit and by a strong personal affection but also by a common policy. This policy differed from that of the other missions by its almost exclusive emphasis upon direct evangelical work[2] and by the importance which was attached to itinerating rather than to the routine building up of stations and sub-stations. On the latter point, indeed, Johnson's views were much more extreme than those of Maples, for he saw a positive danger in the growth of stations which, by the very success achieved in making them large, well-ordered, and prosperous, might lose their capacity for exercising spiritual influence on the impoverished natives in the surrounding countryside.[3] As late as 1928 he wrote in the following characteristic terms:

Root objection to station life is expense of system; there must be three whites plus white food plus white houses. These are the things that take money hand over hand: so it must be, but to what degree?[4]

Probably, however, the course of the mission's development was not greatly affected by the too restricted view of their work which these missionaries adopted, under the influence of their own single-minded devotion to their primary object. Thus, although they probably did not realize that medical services were an invaluable method of winning the respect and confidence of the native, they recognized the need to heal the sick, and set up a dispensary on Likoma, where a medical missionary took up residence in 1889.[5] Again, they discovered, when they set up a printing press

---

[1] Wilson, op. cit., chap. xv; B. H. Barnes, *Johnson of Nyasaland* (U.M.C.A., London, 1933), chap. iv; Chauncy Maples, *Journals and Papers*, pp. 173–4.

[2] It is noticeable that Maples's paper 'On the Method of Evangelising Uncultured Races' (*Journals and Papers*, pp. 175–88)—an admirable paper in its way—makes no mention of any kind of mission work other than the directly evangelical.   [3] Barnes, op. cit., pp. 143–8.

[4] Quoted by Barnes, op. cit., p. 151.   [5] Ibid., p. 82.

in 1888, that if it was to have any value they would have to teach the natives to read.[1] They needed carpenters on the station, and so, from necessity and not from choice, they gave some of the natives an industrial training.[2] In 1895, shortly before his death, Maples wrote an article criticizing the 'industrial' principle in mission work: he did not answer the legitimate argument that practical training was at least as necessary to the native character as doctrinal instruction, but he very properly opposed the view, which was naturally prevalent among a number of the planters who had by that time become fairly numerous, that the chief end of missions was to train workers for the convenience of the white settlers.[3] Yet, about the same time, Commissioner Johnston was praising the Universities' Mission for providing trained workers to the European community in the Shiré Highlands, and contrasting them with the Livingstonia Mission, which, he alleged, discouraged its natives from entering any service other than its own.[4] There could be no more remarkable illustration of the power of circumstances to prevail over preconceived ideas.

Yet, even if the views of Maples and Johnson on those subjects had not much lasting importance, they are not without interest, for their somewhat unrealistic, other-worldly character helps to explain the attitude adopted by these missionaries on the question of the Arab War.

◦   ◦   ◦

At the beginning of February 1888 Consul O'Neill, writing from Blantyre, informed the Foreign Office that he thought it his duty to accompany the Lakes Company's expedition against Mlozi, and he asked for leave of absence from his post at Mozambique in order that he might go in a private capacity, thus avoiding either implicating the Government in the disturbances or interfering in the consular district of his colleague, Hawes. Great was his astonishment when, a few days later, that colleague angrily protested against the course of action he proposed. Hawes had already been made to realize that his influence with the natives in his consular district was virtually non-existent; now he found that the white men were organizing themselves around O'Neill, whose

[1] R. Laws, *Reminiscences of Livingstonia*, pp. 64–65 (Dr. Laws did not specifically name the Universities' Mission, but it was almost certainly to it that he was referring).

[2] Barnes, op. cit., p. 83.   [3] *Journals and Papers*, pp. 268–75.

[4] F.O. 2/88: Johnston to Kimberley, No. 62, C.A., 30 May 1895.

prestige entirely eclipsed his own. Desperately reasserting himself, he wrote an intemperate letter to O'Neill, accusing him of 'interference' which 'has tended to lessen respect towards me, the constituted authority'. O'Neill, in reply, complained that Hawes had not objected to the renewal of the war when it was first proposed, but added that he would now withdraw from the expedition. He then wrote to the Foreign Office to cancel his application for leave of absence, at the same time expressing a fear that he was carrying his respect for official etiquette to a point where it amounted to moral cowardice. If the company were to adopt Hawes's policy, the result, he maintained, would be disastrous for British interests; and, 'worse than this, little consideration seems to have been given to the condition of the WaNkonde and WaMwamba tribes', who would then be left without a protector.[1]

At the same time an acrimonious correspondence took place between Hawes and John Moir. The main cause of this dispute must be found in the injured feelings of the tired, feverish, and dispirited official, though he doubtless had some grounds for the charge that during the previous fighting John Moir had shown himself altogether too ready to attack any Arab caravan in the belief or on the pretext that it was taking supplies to Mlozi.[2]

Hawes also asked the missionaries for their opinions. The Rev. D. C. Scott, of Blantyre, assured the consul that he quite agreed with his views 'and could not support hostilities undertaken by the African Lakes Company'; but, a week later, Scott called a meeting of the Blantyre staff to discuss the question, and it was decided by a majority of six to two to support the company's efforts, 'the reverend gentleman himself voting with the majority for the renewal of hostilities, and being fully aware at the time of what had transpired between Consul O'Neill and myself'.[3] It may perhaps be suggested, in passing, that this awareness was not an altogether bad reason why Scott should have changed his mind.

The Livingstonia missionaries seem also to have favoured, as a body, the renewal of the struggle. Two of them, Dr. Cross and the Rev. Bain, were with Fotheringham at Mwiniwanda. Dr. Laws

[1] F.O. 84/1901: O'Neill to Salisbury, No. 3, C.A., 10 Feb. 1888 (this dispatch was received at the Foreign Office on 9 Apr., by the same mail as his No. 2, C.A., of 3 Feb. requesting leave of absence: so no action was taken on either).
[2] F.O. 84/1883: Hawes to Salisbury, No. 14, C.A., 10 Feb. 1888, with numerous enclosures; also his No. 5, C.A., Confidential, 28 Jan. 1888.
[3] Hawes's No. 14, C.A., of 1888, loc. cit.

took much the same view of the position as did O'Neill, partly because he had received information that the Arabs, before making their attack on Karonga, had enlisted the support of the Bemba, who would have given armed assistance to Mlozi had not the Angoni made a successful raid upon them before they could carry out the plan.[1] On 20 December 1877 he had written to Hawes, expressing wholehearted approval of the decision to meet force with force.

> Already [he declared] the people round here [Bandawe] are beginning to change their minds with regard to the English being children who could not fight, and if your plan of driving off the Arabs succeeds, a prestige will be gained which may save much future trouble.

> I feel strongly that the struggle in which you are now engaged will, by its results, do much to crush or resuscitate the slave trade, and what help we can render, you are welcome to have.[2]

When John Moir spoke to him about the question of renewing the war, he replied that, of course, the mission itself must remain non-combatant, but, had the positions been reversed, his attitude would have been the same as Moir's.[3] The company had therefore the approval of both the Scottish missions for its policy, and its managers informed the consul that they regarded themselves as the defenders of all the British interests in Nyasaland.

The Universities' Mission, however, dissociated itself entirely from this claim, and Maples, in a letter to Hawes, declared: 'We do not look to the Company for anything beyond bringing our goods up the river.' He was 'utterly out of sympathy' with the attitude of O'Neill and Scott, and complained that 'the principle of "live and let live" certainly does not seem to come into Mr. Bain's creed when "Arabs" are in the question'.[4] He might have added that the same trite maxim did not appear to have a prominent place in the philosophy of the Arabs themselves where either the natives or the white men were concerned. A similar attitude to that of Maples was expressed verbally to Buchanan by W. P. Johnson.[5]

[1] F.O. 84/1833: Hawes to Salisbury, No. 3, C.A., 16 Jan. 1888.
[2] Ibid., enclosure No. 2.
[3] Hawes's No. 14, C.A., of 1888, loc. cit.; enclosure 3: Moir to Hawes, 8 Feb. 1888.
[4] F.O. 84/1883: Maples to Hawes, 19 Mar. 1888. It will be remembered that Bain was the missionary at Mwiniwanda, who joined Fotheringham at Karonga when the troubles began.
[5] F.O. 84/1883: Buchanan to Hawes, No. 15, C.A., 23 Feb. 1888.

Having vehemently but ineffectually delivered his protest, Hawes took the wisest course which was open to him: he availed himself of his leave of absence and returned to England, leaving John Buchanan as acting-consul.

At the end of February Buchanan proceeded to the north end in the *Charles Janson*, and attempted to negotiate a settlement. Calling at Bandawe, he asked Dr. Laws to convene a meeting of the missionaries to define their position. At this meeting, Laws stated that he had hitherto acted in support of the Government, and he desired to continue to act in accordance with its wishes. The meeting accepted this view, and resolved that there ought to be no more fighting except in self-defence.[1] Buchanan then continued his journey to Karonga, and on the morning of 20 March, accompanied by Johnson, he met Mlozi, Kopa-Kopa, and Msalema, 'and shook hands heartily'.[2] He explained that the company intended to renew the war unless a satisfactory settlement was reached, but that he was present in an entirely independent capacity, and that the Government would in no way be responsible for any hostilities which might arise.

This was, in fact, an accurate statement of the attitude of the Foreign Office, although neither Hawes nor Buchanan had yet received any instructions on the subject. Hawes, it is true, was afterwards officially congratulated on the 'courage, prudence, and clear-sightedness' which he had shown during the troubles at the end of 1887;[3] but it was not intended that the Government should allow itself to be drawn, through its representative, into the acceptance of responsibility for warlike operations in so remote a country, and Buchanan was instructed accordingly in May and again in August.[4]

Having made his position clear, the acting-consul bluntly asked the Arabs why they had behaved as they had done. For some time they could make no reply; then Kopa-Kopa made a number of counter-charges against Fotheringham, and against Chief Karonga, whom Fotheringham had taken under his protection. Buchanan offered to bring Fotheringham to answer these accusations, but Mlozi positively refused to meet him. The Arabs had now been forced tacitly to admit that they had no case whatever, so Buchanan

[1] F.O. 84/1883: Buchanan to Hawes, No. 17, C.A., 12 Apr. 1888.
[2] Ibid.   [3] F.O. 84/1883: F.O. to Hawes, 19 May 1888.
[4] F.O. to Buchanan, 18 May 1888; 26 May 1888 (telegraphic); 9 Aug. 1888.

asked them what compensation they were prepared to pay. They replied that they had been so impoverished when the Mwamba looted Mlozi's village that they could offer nothing at all. He then asked them if they were prepared to demolish their stockades and evacuate the Konde country, on condition that all claims for compensation were waived by the company. After some hesitation they agreed. It was arranged that Buchanan should draw up a formal Agreement, providing that they would be allowed two months to complete their evacuation, and that the stockades should be pulled down before he left the north end. The document was to be signed on the following day by Frederick Moir and by the three leading Arabs.

Buchanan and Moir kept their appointment, and waited 'for hours'; but the Arabs did not come. A message was then sent to Mlozi asking for an explanation, and the reply was given that if the English wanted war it was their own fault, and they could have it. Buchanan could do no more. 'It was now evident', he reported, 'no peaceful settlement could be effected other than simply allowing them to remain in their stockaded villages, and thus be a continual menace to all peace-loving and law-abiding people.' He therefore returned to Blantyre.[1]

On his way south he called at the village of Makanjira, the powerful Yao chief on the south-east shore of the lake, to inform him that his neutrality would be respected if the war was renewed. Buchanan spoke the Yao language fluently, but he had no capacity for conciliating an unfriendly audience, and he seems to have warned Makanjira's people that if they did not keep the peace they might have cause to regret it. When he had finished his speech and was returning with Johnson to the steamer, the Yao suddenly rushed upon the two men. Johnson made no resistance, and his attackers were so surprised by this that they did him little harm; but Buchanan fought back angrily, and was stripped and beaten. They were then imprisoned in a small hut until the following evening, and had to pay Makanjira several drums of paint and oil as well as a quantity of cloth in order to secure their release. 'The cloth', declared Buchanan, 'was divided amongst the coast men, and I do not hesitate to say they were entirely responsible for this dastardly act.'

'We have been none too soon in telling him to keep quiet', com-

[1] Buchanan's No. 17, C.A., of 1888, loc. cit.

mented Sir Percy Anderson. 'I am afraid', added Lord Salisbury, 'it will not be of much use': meaning, presumably, that the mischief had been done and that nothing could now prevent matters from drifting from bad to worse.[1]

O'Neill's desire to join in the offensive against Mlozi sprang from his conviction that Mlozi's actions were part of a general upsurge of Arab power in Central Africa, which, by its destructiveness and its intensification of the slave-trade, directly challenged the policy of Britain. In the dispatch in which he sought leave of absence to accompany the Lakes Company's expedition, he declared that:

Never since my arrival in East Africa have there arisen dangers so menacing to British interests in the territories contiguous to Mozambique, or which so imperatively called for the union of all Englishmen here to do their utmost to check. . . . I must record my conviction that a very great increase of the Slave Trade has already taken place, by the depopulation of the country west of Tanganyika. That I have not before reported it . . . is due only to the fact that the slaves carried off have mostly been sent by routes to the Zanzibar coast, and have not reached the coast of Mozambique. It is, however, the Mozambique coast that would receive the greater mass of the slaves, were an increase of the Slave Trade to take place in the Nyassa region.

The only means by which a real check can be given to the devastation of East Central Africa and some protection afforded to the varied interests now created in the country, will be by representation at Zanzibar. Whoever, and wherever, the real authors of these movements may be, it is at Zanzibar their chief agents reside: thence the sinews of war have been furnished: and only at that place therefore can the evil be really nipped. At whose instigation, and with what objects, have the swarms of Arabs that have poured into Central Africa during the past three years, left that place? By whom are they being provided with guns and powder? Residents on the Tanganyika and travellers throughout that district tell us the inrush still continues.[2]

The revival of the slave-trade to which he referred was attributed by Kirk to 'the unsettled state of government on the coast due to German claims and hostile demonstrations in that region'.[3] No

---

[1] F.O. 84/1883: Buchanan to Hawes, No. 18, C.A., 12 Apr. 1888, with minutes; W. P. Johnson, *My African Reminiscences*, pp. 152–6.

[2] F.O. 84/1901: O'Neill to Salisbury, No. 2, Africa, 3 Feb. 1888.

[3] F.O. 84/1851: Memorandum by Kirk, 22 Jan. 1887.

doubt this was largely true, for the Germans had fatally weakened
the Sultan's prestige by their seizure of the country lying behind
a ten-mile coastal strip to which alone they recognized that he had
any claim, and, as Kirk declared, 'the last decided act of his,
undertaken at our request, for the suppression of the slave trade
[was] regarded as a hostile demonstration by Germany'. While
action against slave-caravans near the coast was thus suspended,
the more powerful Arabs in the far interior were stung by their
resentment against the incursion of the Europeans—Belgians as
well as Germans, the Belgians having been the first on the scene—
to consolidate their position by setting themselves up as rulers,
dignifying themselves with the style of Sultans. Kirk's deputy at
Zanzibar, Holmwood, warned the British Government in July
1887 that before settled conditions returned 'we must be prepared
for a combination of the Arabs in the interior against European
progress generally', and that the stations of both the L.M.S. and
the C.M.S. would all be 'in extreme peril'.[1] The agents of the
L.M.S. were, indeed, to owe their lives in the months ahead to the
relations of personal friendship which had grown up in previous
years between themselves and Rumaliza, the leading Arab of
Ujiji, who restrained his followers from injuring them.

No doubt the Arabs throughout East and Central Africa would
all have been highly pleased to see the Lakes Company defeated
and destroyed in its little war against Mlozi. But the actual fighting
was confined to the north end of Lake Nyasa and to those Arabs
who had settled within a few miles of Karonga, and O'Neill himself fully understood the importance of preventing the conflict
from spreading and developing into an 'inter-racial antagonism'
between Arabs and British. In November 1888 he pointed out that
'our quarrel is with Mlozi and his fellow-robbers and slave-hunters
at the North End, *not with Arabs in general or with Islam*'.[2] In the
previous July he had been dismayed to learn that the Sultan,
under British official pressure, had ordered the sequestration of

---

[1] F.O. 84/1853: Holmwood to Foreign Secretary, No. 113, 10 July 1887. A
good comprehensive account of Arab activity throughout East and Central
Africa in 1884 and the following years is given by Dr. Roland Oliver in his
recent book, *The Missionary Factor in East Africa*, chap. 3. Dr. Oliver rightly
emphasizes the importance of the German incursion in stimulating this activity
in the interior (ibid., pp. 97–98, 101–2), but he does not mention the Belgians.

[2] O'Neill to Lugard, 10 Nov. 1888. Quoted from the Lugard Papers by Miss
Margery Perham in chap. 8 of her forthcoming biography of Lord Lugard. The
words in italics were underlined by O'Neill.

any property which Jumbe and other Nyasa Arabs had within the dominions of Zanzibar, as a means of putting pressure upon them to desist from supporting Mlozi; and at his urgent plea the order had been revoked. 'The difficulties of British residents on Nyassa', he explained on that occasion, 'will be augmented by punishment of Arabs who have been friendly or neutral.'[1]

'If Consul O'Neill is now right', commented Anderson in bewilderment, 'all his former sensational reports of a great wave of Arab slave-dealers pressing southward were all wrong.'[2] There was, however, no real contradiction between O'Neill's earlier reports, calling attention to a real danger, and his later plea for a prudent restraint in selecting measures for meeting that danger.

The answer to his question, 'By whom are [the Arabs] being provided with guns and powder?' was contained in a report by Colonel Euan Smith, Consul-General at Zanzibar as successor to Kirk, in June 1888. Euan Smith asserted that between 80,000 and 100,000 firearms passed into Africa through the eastern ports every year, 'and this supply has been going on for years'. Formerly the guns were of inferior quality, inaccurate and soon worn out, but more recently breach-loading rifles and cartridges were being imported in very large quantities, and at extraordinarily low prices —a first-class Snider rifle costing only thirteen shillings.

The trade in arms and ammunition [he explained] is at present entirely in the hands of the British Indian subjects, with this important reservation, that gunpowder is still . . . a strict monopoly of the Sultans of Zanzibar. No one else imports powder. His Highness buys the gunpowder from two German firms here at a contract rate of 13 dollars the 100 lbs. and retails it to the Indians at 30 dollars. . . . It is through these British Indian merchants that the Arabs and chiefs in the interior are supplied with all these arms and ammunition, which having once paid duty on arrival at Zanzibar are re-exported without any account being kept as to the quantities in which or the places whither they are sent. No English powder is as a rule to be obtained in Zanzibar. It is found to be too expensive for this market.[3]

But, however much justification there was for O'Neill's conviction that the ills of Central Africa had their roots in Zanzibar, he was mistaken in drawing the conclusion that much good could be

---

[1] F.O. 84/1908: Euan Smith to Salisbury, No. 179, 19 July 1888, with enclosures. [2] Ibid., minute.
[3] F.O. 84/1907: Euan Smith to Salisbury, No. 154, 28 June 1888.

done by making representations to the Sultan. It was not in the Sultan's power to cut off the supply of arms to the interior, since the importers could adopt the alternative route through the Portuguese port of Ibo. Nor could he achieve much by exercising his influence over the Arabs in the interior, for the prestige on which that influence—such as it had ever been—had formerly depended was rapidly diminishing.[1] Moreover, neither Mlozi nor his associates, Kopa-Kopa and Msalema, had any property in Zanzibar or in the coastal towns, and the Sultan was therefore unable to put pressure upon them by sequestrating their goods.[2] The best that he could do was to send a representative to the interior, to call upon Mlozi, Kopa-Kopa, and Msalema to make peace and pay compensation to the Lakes Company, and to urge the other Arabs to desist from the slave-trade, keep the peace, and use their influence in favour of peace. Urged by Euan Smith, he took this step on 10 August 1888, appointing as 'special commissioner' a certain Ali bin Suroor. After a long interview with this individual, Euan Smith pronounced him to be 'a very apt intelligent man', and reported that he had promised to reach the north end of Nyasa before the end of September.[3]

◇　◇　◇

It was not until the beginning of March 1888 that Fotheringham and his party were relieved by Frederick Moir. Ten weeks had passed, instead of two as John Moir had airily promised, and the white men at Mwiniwanda had exhausted their food, had no cloth with which to buy more, and, as Fotheringham put it, 'were almost *in extremis*'.[4] Karonga was now reoccupied, though the fort had been entirely demolished by the Arabs and was overgrown with grass. On 10 April the war was vigorously renewed by an attack on the village of Mlozi's ally, Msalema, which was on the point of being captured when it was saved by a sally from Kopa-Kopa's. The attack was resumed when this sally had been checked, but in vain. Frederick Moir had been severely wounded in the fighting, and had to return to the south end, leaving Fotheringham in command.

Desultory skirmishing continued until 28 May, when a strong

[1] Ibid.; also F.O. 84/1908: Euan Smith to Salisbury, No. 162, 2 July 1888.
[2] F.O. 84/1908: Euan Smith to Salisbury, No. 179, 19 July 1888.
[3] F.O. 84/1908: Euan Smith to Salisbury, No. 212, 11 Aug. 1888.
[4] Fotheringham, op. cit., pp. 145-6.

party of reinforcements arrived: John Moir with five of his employees and nine volunteers from Natal. With them came Captain F. D. Lugard, D.S.O., of the Norfolk Regiment. Captain Lugard had obtained sick leave from his regiment at Gibraltar at the end of 1887, and had come to Africa in the belief that 'active hard work, rather than rest' was what he needed to regain his health.[1] At Mozambique, Consul O'Neill had told him about the fighting at Karonga and about the expedition which was being prepared, adding, 'You would be a godsend to them.' Lugard therefore set out for Nyasa, and at Katunga he met Sharpe, whose views, he found, were 'almost identical' with O'Neill's. Sharpe offered to join the expedition if it was properly led, but not otherwise. When he reached Mandala, John Moir offered him the command of the expedition; he therefore wrote to Acting-Consul Buchanan for advice.[2] The Blantyre missionaries and two members of the Livingstonia Mission who happened to be present also sent a letter to Buchanan, expressing their 'whole-hearted concurrence' in the call addressed to Lugard by the Lakes Company, and their belief that his presence provided an opportunity 'of lifting the whole expedition into the sympathy and moral support of the whole community'. Buchanan, in reply, stated that although the Government accepted no responsibility for the expedition, he gave his 'strong, hearty approval' to Lugard's going, provided he confined his action to Mlozi, Kopa-Kopa, and Msalema.[3] 'In the last resort,' Lugard afterwards declared, 'I would have gone even without such approval, and at the risk of my commission—so serious did the crisis seem to me.'[4]

Reporting on his own action, Buchanan remarked that, without further instructions, he was in 'a position so awkward and trying as to be almost untenable'. The expedition, as originally planned, 'should never have had any countenance' from him; for,

whilst not wishing to speak derogatorily of that gentleman [John Moir], I trembled at what I thought might be the result of an Expedition whose avowed object was fighting, carried out under his command. Whilst therefore I was powerless to prevent the Expedition from proceeding, I did the next best thing I could do under the circumstances, viz., to

[1] F. D. Lugard, *The Rise of Our East African Empire*, vol. i, pp. 1–2.
[2] Ibid., pp. 18, 42–45.
[3] Two of these letters are reproduced and the others are summarized by Lugard, op. cit., pp. 45–49.   [4] Ibid., p. 50.

approve Captain Lugard's going as commander of the Expedition, as I judged him qualified to keep the Expedition within the limits of legal warfare, and prevent it assuming an aggressive and desultory character, and finally ending in disaster, and further loss of prestige to the English.[1]

The arrival of these reinforcements raised the number of white men to twenty-four, in addition to some 400 natives. The life of the station was vigorously reorganized in the interests of efficiency and health, and at dawn on 15 June, assisted by a force of 190 Tonga who had been brought up by Sharpe on the 6th, an attack was made on Kopa-Kopa's village. The force employed consisted of twenty-three white men and 300 black: Lugard refusing to take the Mwamba because he believed that their presence would be subversive of all discipline, and that they would frustrate the purpose of the assault by a mad rush for loot which would make it impossible for victory to be followed up.[2] The greater part of the force therefore consisted of Tonga. Lugard called them together and warned them that if they seized loot or women, they would be shot: for although Fotheringham and Sharpe protested that such an order could not possibly be enforced, he was determined to prevent atrocities.

The attack was made with the greatest gallantry, but it failed completely. It had not been possible adequately to reconnoitre the stockade, which was found to have been so strongly reinforced that it could not be torn down by the storming party, especially as the majority of the natives, having been deprived of a personal stake in victory, disobeyed the order to charge. Through the loopholes in the stockade a deadly fire was poured into the attackers. Lugard attempted to clamber over, and a bullet passed through both his arms. It was fortunate for him that he received this wound, for had he succeeded in hoisting himself on to the stockade he would, as he afterwards admitted, have been riddled with bullets, and in all probability none of the natives would have followed. The attack had to be called off, and the party made an orderly retreat to Karonga. One white man had been killed, and

[1] F.O. 84/1883: Buchanan to Hawes, No. 26, C.A., Private and Confidential, 20 May 1888.
[2] In 1938 the late G. Wilson recorded that the Nyakyusa (i.e. Mwamba) had nearly a hundred independent chiefs ('The Land Rights of Individuals among the Nyakyusa' (Rhodes–Livingstone Papers, No. 1), p. 6)—a fact not conducive to public order or any kind of civic discipline.

two, including Lugard, seriously wounded. Three of the natives
had also been killed.

Lugard now realized that the enemy stockades were impreg-
nable to anything less than artillery, and John Moir set off to make
arrangements to bring up a seven-pounder. Only a desultory
guerilla warfare was kept up in the months which followed. In
Scotland James Stevenson and other merchants set up a 'Nyassa
Anti-Slavery and Defence Fund' in an attempt to raise £10,000 by
public subscription to finance the struggle against Mlozi and his
associates. This appeal, launched in July or August 1888, was
approved of even by the Universities' Mission,[1] but, although with
his usual generosity Stevenson himself contributed £1,000, the
total amount raised within nine or ten months was only £3,000.[2]

By the end of the year 1888 the garrison had almost sunk into
despair, and many had gone away. 'What can I do?' wrote Lugard
in his diary in December. 'I am pretty well played out, but if I
went, how could I expect the half-dozen sick survivors to stay on
at Karonga's? And if *they* went, and we gave in utterly, the results
would be disastrous indeed. . . . Lake Nyasa would be lost to us—
we should simply be kicked out by the Arabs. God, who defends
the right, prevent this! . . . Only half a dozen white men, and those
all sick, and many of them disheartened, and wanting to go;
natives we can't rely on, and discontented to boot; bad guns, bad
ammunition, no bayonets, no entrenching tools, and so vast an
area to guard, and so powerful an enemy. It is an uphill task!'[3]

On 25 November, two months later than he had promised, Ali
bin Suroor arrived at Karonga. In the following weeks he paid
repeated visits to Mlozi's, and Mlozi found it convenient to pro-
tract the negotiations by giving the impression that he was willing
to evacuate his fortified village and retire peacefully to Senga, as
his opponents demanded. Lugard reluctantly acquiesced in these
time-wasting parleys, for, as he wrote to Euan Smith, 'unwilling
as I was from the first to be fooled from day to day and week to

---

[1] *Central Africa* (the mission's journal), Mar. 1889. 'As a Mission, of course,
we could take no part in action such as is proposed. But as individuals, all must
feel that unless this marauding horde be checked, there can be but little prospect
of Mission work in the country.' It is not clear whether this attitude at headquarters reflected a change of opinion on the part of the missionaries in the field.

[2] This information, based on the Lugard Papers, is taken from chaps. 8 and
9 of Miss Margery Perham's forthcoming biography of Lord Lugard, by kind
permission of the author.   [3] Lugard, op. cit., pp. 135–6.

week by Mlozi, I was the less annoyed as our own defences were very greatly in need of amendment', and as he could not himself launch an attack until the seven-pounder arrived.[1] Finally, on 28 January, Ali bin Suroor went to Mlozi's and did not come back. Lugard sent repeated messages calling upon him to return, but in vain. 'Whether he had been finally won over', wrote Fotheringham, 'or whether he found life at the Arab stockades more agreeable than with us (it was rumoured that he had taken unto himself a couple of wives and was enjoying the sweets of matrimony), are points that have never been cleared up.'[2]

On 20 February 1889 Lugard determined to delay the shelling of the stockades no longer—the gun having arrived on 16 January. The stockades, however, did not offer enough resistance to the shells to cause them to explode and effect a breach. By bursting inside the village they inflicted considerable loss on the enemy, but this was small compensation for their failure to open a way for a storming party. After using the gun a second time, with similar inconclusive results, on 13 March, Lugard decided that he could not afford to remain any longer, and that in any case he could perhaps achieve more by attempting to expedite the dispatch of supplies and reinforcements than by remaining in command of what appeared a forlorn hope. On the 17th he sailed away in the *Ilala*, and Sharpe and three others accompanied him.

When he passed through Zanzibar on his homeward journey he had conversations with Gerald Portal, who was then acting-consul-general, and with Consul Hawes, who was being employed at the Agency there instead of being sent back to Zomba. He told Hawes that John Moir was greatly to blame for the weakness of the garrison at Karonga, having assured him at the time of his departure that twelve Europeans had been engaged as reinforcements and were daily expected at Mandala, whereas when he reached Quilimane the relevant telegrams and correspondence came into his hands and showed that only three had been asked for, only one had been engaged, and that one had absconded in Natal when on the way out.[3]

In his conversation with Portal, he begged that official to urge

[1] F.O. 84/1978: Lugard to Euan Smith, 8 Jan. 1889, enclosed in Hawes to Salisbury, No. 190, 8 Apr. 1889.

[2] Fotheringham, op. cit., p. 226.

[3] F.O. 84/1979: Memorandum by Hawes, 2 June 1889, enclosed in Portal to Salisbury, No. 235, same date.

the Government to press the company to take decided measures to re-establish their authority; but Portal, while agreeing to send home his message, replied that he 'did not think it in the least likely that Her Majesty's Government would take any responsibility in the matter, which was one entirely between the Lakes Company and the native tribes [sic]'. Lugard next asked that Buchanan might be authorized to try to negotiate peace in his capacity as acting-consul, but here again Portal said he 'could hold out no hope to him'. Finally, he suggested that the Sultan be asked to send out another envoy, but Portal reminded him that Euan Smith 'had taken a deal of trouble' in arranging for the dispatch of Ali bin Suroor, with results which were 'hardly such as would seem to warrant a repetition of the experiment'. All Portal could suggest was that Lugard should personally inform the Directors of the Lakes Company of the unsatisfactory state of affairs on Lake Nyasa.

When Anderson read Portal's dispatch, he commented: 'The Company and Captain Lugard are at their wits' end how to get out of the scrape they have got into. Consul Hawes strongly advises that Acting Consul Buchanan should not be compromised.' And Lister added: 'I think we should take the first opportunity of reminding the African Lakes Company that Her Majesty's Government have no responsibility for the acts of Captain Lugard.'[1]

◦ ◦ ◦

After Lugard's departure from Karonga, Fotheringham was once more in command, with six white men to assist him. Every day he sent out bands to patrol the country, destroying the crops of the slavers, and preventing them from obtaining food or other supplies. So the war dragged on, and, as he himself put it, 'the country remained in a chronic state of disorder'.[2]

[1] F.O. 84/1978: Portal to Salisbury, No. 212, 4 May 1889, with minutes.
[2] Fotheringham, op. cit., p. 255.

II

THE BRITISH ASSUMPTION OF
POLITICAL CONTROL

1. *The Development of the Dispute with Portugal*

SOON after taking up his duties as consul at Mozambique, Elton reported that the restrictions which 'a weak and selfish system of fiscalization' imposed on trade had the effect of stimulating the slave-trade, which was highly lucrative, rather than ordinary smuggling: 'for', he declared, 'experience records that the legal trader without papers fares worse, as a smuggler, at the hands of the Portuguese local authorities, than the slave trader does, but without the same chances of profit'.[1] His reports prompted the Foreign Office[2] to raise with the Portuguese Government the question of removing some of the shackles from lawful trade.[3] This action was taken, not because there were any British interests wishing to break into the Portuguese colonial market, but solely for the reason that it was deemed likely to undermine the slave-trade.

By this time, it is true, the Livingstonia Mission was already beginning work on the shores of Lake Nyasa, and it needed regular supplies from Britain. The Portuguese Government had granted a free pass for the *Ilala* and the other equipment and stores which the first party of missionaries took with them, but the general question of transit rights to the interior had not yet been raised— except, indeed, by Livingstone himself, who had vainly urged the Foreign Office to insist that the Portuguese remove the dead hand of mercantilism from the Zambesi, so that it could become a high-way for European commerce with the interior.[4] The Foreign Office

[1] F.O. 84/1411: Elton to Derby, No. 36, S.T., 25 Oct. 1875. Morier, the British ambassador at Lisbon, addressing the Portuguese Foreign Minister, denounced 'a treatment which seems to regard the legitimate trader as the natural foe of the human race'.
[2] As is shown by its minutes on his reports, in F.O. 63/1036.
[3] F.O. 63/1036: Derby to Watson, 22 Mar. 1876.
[4] Coupland, *Kirk on the Zambesi*, pp. 90–94, 144, 264–5. The Portuguese had given Livingstone's expedition special permission to import all its possessions

does not seem to have had the Nyasa missionaries in mind when, on 22 March 1876, it sent its dispatch to the British Chargé d'Affaires in Lisbon instructing him to urge the Portuguese Government to employ not only British naval support but also a more liberal commercial policy in the struggle against the slave-trade.

Less than a week afterwards, however, a certain H. B. Cotterill wrote to it asking for letters of introduction to the authorities of Portuguese East Africa, and also for information about the tariff, which he feared might be prohibitive. He explained that he proposed to set out in May, in company with reinforcements for the Livingstonia Mission, 'for the purpose of attempting to carry out the idea strongly advocated by Dr. Livingstone, of introducing legitimate commerce into the region of Lake Nyassa, and thus counteracting the evil influence of the slavers, who are the only traders in that country'. He was not himself a business man, but a school-teacher, the son of a bishop, and there is no reason to doubt that the motive of his journey was primarily what he stated it to be rather than any hope of self-enrichment. Not only did the Foreign Office comply with his modest request: it also sharpened the point of its previous dispatch to Lisbon by asking for a free pass for his goods. The negotiations on this subject dragged on for the rest of the year.[1] Their eventual outcome was entirely satisfactory to Cotterill, but their main importance lay in the fact that they involved a discussion of the general question of transit to the interior.

To meet an objection raised by the Portuguese, the British Chargé d'Affaires gave an explicit assurance, on 31 May, that the permission which had been requested was only 'applicable to the first attempt on the part of Mr. Cotterill to encourage a commerce among the natives inhabiting the Region of Lake Nyassa, and not, as Your Excellency seemed to suppose, to an indefinite period, or for an unlimited number of voyages'. The Foreign Office approved this Note, and in so doing admitted, by implication, that Portugal's control of the Lower Zambesi gave her a right to benefit financially

---

free of duty, but had been careful to point out that this was an exceptional privilege, not a general rule.

[1] The relevant documents are collected in F.O. 84/1468.

On his return journey to Britain, Cotterill accompanied Elton from the north end of Lake Nyasa, and, after the consul's death, brought back his journal, afterwards editing it for publication.

on any future occasions when British subjects might desire to take
their goods up-river. But to what extent was she thus to benefit?
Was the ordinary Mozambique tariff to be applied, as if Nyasaland was part of the Portuguese possessions? The Foreign Office
would certainly have refused to accept any such interpretation of
the Note of 31 May.[1] It did not, however, take any initiative in
attempting to devise the basis of a permanent arrangement, tolerably satisfactory to both countries.

◇   ◇   ◇

While Britain was seeking free or semi-free access to regions
which she regarded as independent of European rule, Portugal was
making arrangements to monopolize the resources of a large part
of those regions on her own account. Two of her merchants were
given, for a period of thirty years, a concession of the sole right to
place steamers on the rivers Shiré and Zambesi.[2] Since it is not in
the power of any country to bestow what it does not possess, this
grant implied an assertion of Portuguese sovereignty over those
rivers, thus bringing Portuguese authority, for international purposes, up to the south-eastern extremity of the lake.

The British Government did not expressly deny this assertion,
and made no formal protest against the monopoly.[3] In later years,
when the Blantyre Mission and the African Lakes Company were
established in the Shiré Highlands, it vigorously opposed a similar
claim; but for the present it was specially interested only in what
directly concerned Lake Nyasa and its shores. The Portuguese
appear to have realized that the existence of the Livingstonia
Mission made it necessary for them to proceed very cautiously
with regard to the lake itself. Their press threw out hints that it
came within their jurisdiction, and in various maps of their African
possessions the limits of their territory were indicated with an
exceedingly liberal hand. What was perhaps even more significant
—a senior official of their Foreign Office went so far as to express
to the British Chargé d'Affaires his own impression that Lake
Nyasa and its surrounding country formed part of the Province of
Mozambique. All this, however, was very tentative, and fell far
short of a formal claim. The Lisbon Government did not include
Lake Nyasa in its concession, and Corvo, the Portuguese Foreign

---

[1] F.O. 84/1468: Minutes on Jervoise to Derby, No. 23, Consular, 4 June 1876.
[2] F.O. 63/1036: Derby to Jervoise, No. 29, Consular, 16 May 1876.
[3] Ibid.

Minister, denied that the lake's communications with the sea would suffer any interference. Nor did he contest the observation which Jervoise, the British Chargé d'Affaires, 'was careful to introduce more than once' during an interview on 5 July, 'that Lake Nyassa is beyond the territorial jurisdiction of Portugal'. The Foreign Office entirely approved of the firmness shown by its representative, and expressed the view that 'the timely expression of the opinion of Her Majesty's Government in regard to this matter may tend to prevent the occurrence of future complications'. Indeed, T. V. Lister observed privately that 'the pretensions of Portugal to the interior of Africa are ridiculous'.[1]

This contempt for Portugal's 'pretensions' embraced the Shiré country as well as the lake: the only difference was that, in the one case, determination was expressed 'not to permit any interference with the rights of British subjects to the free navigation and trade of Lake Nyassa', whereas, in the other, Britain confined herself to giving some sharply worded advice about the impolicy of granting a monopoly whose effects, by restricting trade, were 'calculated to maintain the country in a state of savagery and barbarism'.

When Corvo received the Note which, though courteously expressed on the whole, embodied these phrases, he not unnaturally commented that it was *un peu dure*.[2] It was, he added, an instance of the rather unpleasant correspondence to which these questions in Africa had unfortunately, and frequently, given rise; and he suggested that such friction might be avoided in future if the two Governments negotiated an agreement on the general question of transit to the lake. This proposal was accepted in Downing Street,[3] and there pigeon-holed.

       o   o   o

Corvo, although a patriotic Portuguese, sensitive about his country's dignity and devoted to its interests, was an enlightened and reforming statesman, whose professed desire for friendship instead of friction with Britain was thoroughly sincere. This was

[1] F.O. 84/1468: Jervoise to Derby, No. 23, Consular, 4 June 1876; with minutes; F.O. 63/1037: J. to D., No. 30, Consular, 5 July 1876, and Derby to Jervoise, No. 41, Consular, 28 July; ibid., Morier to Derby, No. 48, Consular, 18 Oct. 1876.

[2] F.O. 63/1036: Derby to Jervoise, No. 29, Consular, 16 May 1876; F.O. 84/1468: Jervoise to Derby, No. 24, Consular, 4 June 1876, with enclosed copy of Note; F.O. 63/1037: J. to D., No. 30, Consular, 5 July 1876.

[3] F.O. 63/1037: Derby to Jervoise, No. 41, Consular, 28 July 1876.

quickly recognized by R. B. D. (afterwards Sir Robert) Morier,
who took up his duties as British ambassador[1] in Lisbon on 12
August 1876. Burly and jovial, with the grand manner and the
mordant wit of a sophisticated aristocrat, he was distinguished by
the breadth of his outlook and the clarity of his understanding as
well as by his formidable and even domineering personality. It
was he, and not those who nominally directed his actions from
London, who really shaped his country's policy towards South-
East Africa and its hinterland during the next few years. His
general aim was to achieve full co-operation in all African affairs
between Britain and Portugal, in the belief that the interests of
both countries and also of the African tribes were essentially in
harmony, and that the Portuguese, in so far as they failed to per-
ceive that this was so and to act accordingly, were injuring themselves as well as others. Between him and Corvo a close friendship
grew up, rooted in mutual confidence and in harmony of purpose,
so that it amounted to a political partnership. This was all the
more important as Corvo was not only Foreign Minister but
Minister of Marine and of the Colonies as well.

The first task which Morier set himself was to throw open the
Mozambique coast to the commerce of the world, and at the same
time to secure the right of Britain—and equally of any other
nations which might become interested—to pursue her civilizing
activities in the interior, unhindered by the corrupt officialdom of
a degenerate Power. But before he could proceed with it he had to
deal with the inflated claims of that Power to jurisdiction over the
interior of Africa, because those claims were put on record at the
end of a long Note on the subject of the Zambesi–Shiré waterway,
addressed to him by Corvo a few weeks after his arrival.[2] The Note
assured him that the monopoly of steam navigation was intended
solely to make provision for an adequate steamer service on the
two rivers, and that it did not, '*and could not*',[3] include transit to
Lake Nyasa. Not that Portugal admitted that she lacked the right,

[1] Strictly speaking, his status was that of minister, not ambassador, because in
the nineteenth century Britain regarded only a small number of the more important Powers as worthy of embassies, and maintained only legations at such lesser
capitals as Lisbon. But the term 'ambassador' is convenient in the present con-
text, because any reference to 'the minister' without qualification would appear
to mean the Portuguese statesman with whom Morier was negotiating rather
than Morier himself.

[2] F.O. 63/1037: dated 3 Oct. 1876, and enclosed in Morier to Derby, No. 48,
Consular, 18 Oct. 1876.   [3] Underlined by Morier.

in international law, to close the Zambesi to such transit; but, far from wishing to exercise such a right, she was anxious to afford assistance. Then came the concluding passage:

His Majesty's Government is disposed to enter into an agreement with the British Government for regulating the navigation in question, but it considers it to be its duty and its right to assert once more the Sovereignty of the Portuguese Crown over the Rivers Zambesi and Shiré, and over all the territories of Eastern Africa comprised within the limits fixed by the Treaty of the 28th. of July, 1817.

Morier called the attention of the Foreign Office to this passage, not indeed because of the unequivocal claim which it asserted to the Shiré country, but because of what followed: for this could be interpreted to include Lake Nyasa and indeed the whole expanse of territory between the Mozambique coast and the Atlantic. This larger claim was, indeed, tentative and vague; nor was any attempt made to apply it in practice, since, 'except upon the hypothesis that Lake Nyassa is not within Portuguese territory, it is difficult to understand why a monopoly obviously conceded for the navigation of the Portuguese Inland waters should suddenly stop short at a point apparently offering the fairest prospects of trade'. Indeed, the mere use of the word 'transit' implied that Portuguese jurisdiction was as non-existent in the region to which the goods were being conveyed as in that from which they came. Nevertheless, the claim had been put on record, even though unobtrusively, and Morier considered that it should receive 'very serious attention'. Fortunately, what he called 'the over-subtlety of their language' made it possible for Britain to express agreement with the Portuguese Note, at the same time laying down her own interpretation of it. Thus, while in effect refuting the claim, she would avoid being drawn into a controversy at the very moment when there were good hopes of fruitful co-operation between the two countries: unless indeed, the Portuguese denied the correctness of the British interpretation, 'which I altogether doubt their having the courage to do'.

He accordingly asked and was given permission to send to Corvo a Note[1] containing the following passage:

As regards the latter portion of your Excellency's Note, I am

[1] Dated 14 Jan. 1877; enclosed in Morier to Derby, No. 6, S.T., 16 Jan. 1877 (in. F.O. 84/1476).

instructed to inform you that Her Majesty's Government have at present no desire to enter into a discussion respecting the precise limits of the Portuguese territories in Eastern Africa. They have never thrown a doubt respecting the full sovereignty of the Portuguese Crown over the coastal territory between Cape Delgado and the Bay of Lourenço Marques, as defined in Article II of the Treaty of July 28, 1817; but with regard to the vast interior of the African continent, respecting which no Treaties exist, they do not admit that the idea of sovereignty can be dissociated from that of *bona fide* occupation and *de facto* jurisdiction of a continuous and non-intermittent kind.

His insertion of the word 'coastal' was intended to remove an ambiguity latent in the text of the 1817 treaty, which defined Portugal's possessions in East Africa as 'le Territoire compris entre le Cap Delgado et la Baie de Lourence Marques'[1]—for if Portugal maintained that this phrase included an unlimited extent of the interior, while Britain denied that it applied to more than a coastal strip, the argument could go on till the end of time.

Particularly important was the principle which he laid down in the concluding words of his Note. As he remarked some time afterwards:

A very idle and therefore very acrimonious controversy has been and is being carried on as to who was the first white man who struggled up the swamps of the Shiré and sighted with European eyes the waters of the Nyassa. For my part, I believe it to be as certain that the Nyassa was known to the Portuguese in the XVIth. Century as that it was unknown to them in the XIXth., and would have continued unknown to them, but for its rediscovery by Dr. Livingstone.

In my treatment of the question with the Portuguese Government I have therefore always carefully avoided this rock of stumbling, and have urged the objections of Her Majesty's Government to the Portuguese claims on the sole ground of their refusal to recognise sovereignty when dissociated from *bona fide* occupation and the *de facto* continuous exercise of jurisdiction.[2]

And there, for a time, the question of sovereignty was allowed to rest.

Morier now turned his energies to the question of transit dues on the Zambesi. This subject, however, was already under con-

[1] *Br. & For. State Papers*, vol. iv, p. 88.
[2] F.O. 84/1504: Morier to Salisbury, No. 12, S.T., Confidential, 14 May 1878.

sideration by a special commission appointed by the Portuguees Government to report on the Mozambique tariff, and Corvo declined to negotiate upon it until the commission had presented its report. But he courteously offered to inform the commission of any views which Morier might wish to express, and the ambassador seized this opportunity with both hands. He replied that he thought that, even from the Portuguese point of view, the transit charges could scarcely be made too low, 'because the object that should be sought for ought rather to be the collateral advantages from the creation of the route, the establishment of *entrepôts* at Quilimane and elsewhere, the development of the trade of the Zambesi, etc., than the immediate revenue to be derived from the dues'. In no circumstances should the Portuguese rate exceed that adopted by Zanzibar, otherwise merchants would take the overland route to the north end of Nyasa instead of the water route to the south end, and the Portuguese revenue would lose more than it would gain.[1]

This emphasis on the prospect of competition by way of the Zanzibar route was undoubtedly exaggerated, for the expenses of land transport—on the heads of porters, who were usually hard to manage and often untrustworthy—would probably more than absorb whatever might be saved at the customs-house. But it was just at this time that the attempt was being made to construct a road from Dar-es-Salaam to the north end of Lake Nyasa: and Cotterill, writing to Kirk from that lake, was expressing the opinion that 'the land route . . . will prove of great use, especially to the northern parts of the Lake. The opening up of such a route', he continued, 'would likewise benefit the southern parts, for it would raise a competition with the river route and thus perhaps induce the Portuguese to accept a reasonable tariff.' Cotterill added, it is true, that in existing conditions, with the road as yet unbuilt, the route was impracticable for purposes of trade.[2] Nevertheless it was possible for Morier to put forward, with all the sincerity of a confessed 'free-trader to the finger-tips', the argument he used; and not only did Corvo accept it at its face value, but the commission embodied it in their report, which was liberal beyond anything for which Morier had dared to

[1] F.O. 84/1476: Morier to Derby, No. 13, S.T., 1 Mar. 1877, with enclosures.
[2] F.O. 84/1484: Cotterill to Kirk, extract enclosed in Kirk to Derby, No. 78, 5 May 1877.

hope.[1] The report asserted that the first aim of the new policy was to facilitate the development of resources rather than to raise revenue, and pointed out that the annual imports[2] on the Zanzibar coast were worth four times as much as those to the province of Mozambique. It therefore recommended that the tariff should be lowered to a maximum rate of 10 per cent.—about a third of the existing rate—and that transit dues should be only 3 per cent. For this very satisfactory report, which was accepted by the Portuguese Government, the Foreign Office gave most of the credit to Morier, while Morier gave most of it to Corvo.[3]

One important point still remained to be settled in connexion with the transit dues. The commission had not specified the point or points at which goods could be cleared on their way out of Portuguese territory, although it had described the destinations of such goods as including 'the regions which are situated beyond the confluence of the rivers Shiré and Zambesi'. This phrase gave Morier an opportunity to deal with the matter without becoming involved in an argument about the limits of the Portuguese possessions. Carefully avoiding that controversial question, he asked Corvo to establish a customs-house at the confluence of the two rivers, and on 28 September 1878 he was able to inform his Government that the necessary orders to that effect had been sent out.

By that time he had already succeeded, after a great deal of trouble, in obtaining the nullification of the monopoly. On 2 August 1878 it became, as he said, 'dead without possibility of returning to life'. The Zambesi–Shiré now lay open to the commerce of the world in general and of Scotland in particular, and he had good reason when he observed that the cause of Anglo-Portuguese co-operation in Africa 'is at present progressing as favourably as I could wish'.

◇   ◇   ◇

Having triumphantly achieved his first object, the opening up of

[1] F.O. 84/1477: Morier to Derby, No. 39, S.T., Confidential, 11 May 1877. The enclosed report is published in A. & P., 1878, lxvii, pp. 628–38, together with most of Morier's covering dispatch: yet he had stated that it had been given to him *confidentially* by the Portuguese Finance Minister.

[2] The question of imports *into* a territory is, of course, quite different from that of transit *through* that territory; but the distinction seems to be ignored in this part of the report.

[3] F.O. 84/1475: Derby to Morier, No. 39, 4 May 1877; F.O. 84/1476: Morier to Derby, No. 16, S.T., Confidential, 12 Mar. 1877.

Portuguese East Africa and its hinterland to the commerce of the world, Morier pressed on with unabated energy and enthusiasm towards the second. What had been done already was essentially negative: the removal of obstacles to economic advance. The sequel, as he planned it, was to be a programme of positive co-operation: 'to extend across the seas, where local jealousies and petty antagonisms have hitherto been the order of the day, the relations of mutual confidence and exceptional intimacy which have always characterised the intercourse between the two crowns in Europe'.

In January 1879 he sent home a draft treaty[1] which, had it been accepted by both Governments, would have been of profound importance to the future development of South-East Africa. It laid down what he called 'the general principle of the absolute freedom from all restriction of the great waterways connecting the interior of Africa with the civilised world'. Of course, this stipulation applied chiefly to the Zambesi, and Morier attached great importance to it.

I have had to toil and moil for two years [he wrote] to get rid of the trumpery Anahory-Zagury[2] monopoly. As long as Senhor Corvo is minister I am certain that the monopoly will not be resuscitated, but I have no guarantee for the future, as there is no official record which any of my successors could appeal to of the verbal assurances I have received on the subject. Any future minister therefore would be at liberty to revive the monopoly. The Treaty stipulation will secure permanently the freedom we require.

The treaty also provided for joint action by the vessels of the two Powers to suppress the slave-trade: thus securing for the British Navy what Elton had so often vainly sought on its behalf after the one successful co-operative effort of 1875. Further, the Governor-General of Mozambique was to be explicitly entrusted with discretionary power to authorize British cruisers to act independently in Portuguese territorial waters, whenever their commanders could show good reason for the proposed action. Moreover, the colonial authorities of both countries were to be instructed to communicate any information that they might possess concerning

[1] F.O. 84/1537: Morier to Salisbury, No. 6, S.T., 27 Jan. 1879: treaty enclosed.

[2] Messrs. Anahory and Zagury were the merchants who had obtained the monopoly of the steam navigation on the Zambesi and Shiré.

the slave-trade to the authorities of the other Power, who would be under an obligation to act upon it. This provision, Morier explained,

is intended as a gentle irritant to act as a corrective to the normal torpor of Portuguese officialism. For instance, under this Article Dr. Kirk will be able, whenever he obtains the valuable information he so often communicates to Her Majesty's Government, and which is passed on through this Legation to the Portuguese Ministry of Foreign Affairs, where it is invariably consigned to a dusty pigeon-hole, to communicate it directly to the Governor-General of Mozambique, *who will be bound to act upon it*.[1]

In addition to this clause providing for concerted action on the coast the treaty contained another clause concerned with the slave-trade; this was even more ambitious in its conception, though necessarily much less precise in its terms. It dealt not with the maritime slave-trade but with the slave-trade in the interior. Each country was pledged to furnish the other with whatever information on this subject it might obtain, and to give serious consideration to any measure which the other might propose for the purpose of joint action in repressing that trade. The main function of the clause, as indeed of the preceding one, was, in Morier's words, 'to foster the idea of joint action and joint responsibility and *pro tanto* to remove the prevalent idea that we desire to monopolise not only the loaves and fishes but also the philanthropy of South Africa, an article on which this Country [Portugal] piques itself not a little'.

The consideration which made the Portuguese Government willing to acquiesce in these provisions, and also in others which allowed Britain the free use of the harbour of Delagoa Bay for both commercial and military purposes, was Britain's agreement to join with Portugal in building a railway from Lourenço Marques to the Transvaal. The fate of the treaty depended on the willingness of the British Colonial Office to commit itself to this undertaking. In the previous August (1878) that department had itself initiated the whole proceeding by its request to Morier, through the Foreign Office, that he should sound the Portuguese Government as to its willingness to conclude an agreement covering the importation of arms through Delagoa Bay, the regulation of the tariff, and the construction of a railway. The other provisions, notably the slave-

---

[1] The words in italics were underlined by Morier.

trade clauses, had been inserted by the British ambassador himself.
But not only had he obtained the approval of the Foreign Office to
his adoption of this course: he had also been instructed, in terms
which suggested considerable urgency, to 'commence and conduct'
a negotiation on the lines he had suggested and on which his draft
treaty was afterwards based. Now, however, the Colonial Office
proposed to keep those parts of the draft for which it had most use,
and to reject the one provision which powerfully appealed to the
Portuguese: that which referred to the construction of a railway.
It pointed out that there were no funds available for such a purpose
in the Transvaal itself, and no assurance could be given that they
would be forthcoming in Britain. It alleged that Morier had exceeded his instructions by embarking on a formal negotiation, since
all it had originally asked for was that he should ascertain the disposition of the Lisbon Government. Morier tore this accusation to
shreds, and in so doing he could not avoid presenting the actions
of the Colonial Office in a light which made them appear absurdly
unintelligent.[1]

In the following weeks he strove with all his might to save his
treaty. He pointed out that all that he had pledged the British
Government to do was '*to enter into negotiation for the purpose of
taking joint action for the construction of the railway*'; far from
minimizing the difficulties of the undertaking in his discussions
with Corvo, he had stressed them. 'I venture to ask', he added,
'whether, after receiving categorical instructions to commence a
bona fide negotiation, it was possible for me to pledge Her Majesty's
Government to less.'

The advantages of the railway are altogether on our side. The future
existence of the Transvaal depends on its construction. We and not
Portugal have come forward to propose the undertaking. Yet all the
important concessions have to be made by Portugal. The concessions I
have asked for *and obtained* are far in excess of any similar concessions
that to my knowledge have ever been made by one Government to
another. Could I put forward these demands without offering *something*
in return? Could I offer less than the pledge to enter into negotiation for
the purpose of joint action—i.e., the pledge earnestly, conscientiously
and honestly to endeavour to attain by joint means and joint exertions

[1] The earlier history of the negotiations is surveyed, with references to documents, in Morier to Salisbury, No. 11, S.T., 5 Feb. 1879, supplemented by his
No. 15, S.T., 7 Feb. 1879 (both in F.O. 84/1537).

an object of the highest importance to ourselves and of life and death to the inhabitants of our latest annexation [i.e., the Transvaal].[1]

Before the dispatch which contained these arguments reached London, the Foreign Office had informed him by telegraph that it had never meant to convey to him any intention on the part of the British Government to pay for the railway. To this he retorted:

When, in the exact terms of the Colonial Office letter of the 17th August, I put forward as the *first condition* to be agreed to by Portugal that it should 'engage on reasonable terms to bear its legitimate share of the expenditure,' I most undoubtedly stated *by implication* that the party making the proposal would, on their part, engage to bear their legitimate share of such expenditure.[2]

Nevertheless, to remove his Government's objection, he redrafted the relevant clause so as to bind the two Powers to no more than a joint survey of the country over which the proposed railway was to run. The Portuguese, he thought, would accept his modification.[3]

Then came the news of the disaster which had befallen British arms at Isandhlwana on 22 January, when a force of 800 white troops and 500 native auxiliaries had been surrounded by a Zulu horde and cut down to a man. When Morier witnessed the consternation to which this event gave rise in Portugal, he wrote that it 'brought home vividly to my mind the degree to which, willingly or unwillingly, wittingly or unwittingly, we have become credited in the imagination of mankind with the rôle of Suzerain in that unprofitable Continent'. He asked Corvo whether this crisis in the fortunes of South Africa would interfere with the prosecution of the Lourenço Marques treaty; to which Corvo replied that, on the contrary, 'the effect of the news would be to force all the men who had any political stake in the country, and who were not mere adventurers, to rally round the policy of the Government, as the only possible policy in view of the dangers that menaced the existence of the white man in Africa; and that consequently the moment was more than ever favourable for concluding the Treaty, the delay in the negotiation of which he greatly lamented'.[4] To Morier

---

[1] His No. 11, S.T., of 1879. The words in italics were underlined by him.
[2] F.O. 84/1537: Morier to Salisbury, No. 16, S.T., 7 Feb. 1879. Words in italics were underlined by Morier.
[3] F.O. 84/1537: Morier to Salisbury, No. 17, S.T., 7 Feb. 1879.
[4] F.O. 84/1537: Morier to Salisbury, No. 19, S.T., 15 Feb. 1879; cf. (ibid.) his No. 22, S.T., 8 Mar. 1879.

also it seemed that the catastrophe made it even more important than before that Britain should obtain the use of the Delagoa Bay route for her troops and supplies. Lord Salisbury, however, took the opposite view, and himself drafted a telegram, dated 12 March, stating that the railway project had now become impracticable. 'The security of persons and works during construction and after it could not be guaranteed, possibly for many years.'[1] To this Morier promptly replied that 'the importance of securing the military use of the harbour . . . seems to me conclusively established by the very words of your Lordship's telegram'. He entirely agreed that the railway could not be built at once, but that was no reason why the treaty should be abandoned. 'All the objects which, on being named to this post, I was told I ought to endeavour to obtain, I have virtually obtained, and registered in the Draft Treaty. All we have to do is to accept that which is tendered to us.'[2]

At last Morier had his way. On 27 May he arrived back in Lisbon after a visit to London which had lasted several weeks, with authority to sign the treaty on behalf of the British Government. But the delay had been fatal. Corvo told him that the Portuguese Government had been clinging to office in a steadily weakening political position in the hope that it would be able to sign the treaty before its fall, and now its resignation could no longer be postponed. On 30 May Morier telegraphed to the Foreign Office:

The Treaty is signed. The Government have resigned.[3]

He was thus confronted with a further task: to try to persuade the new ministry to ratify a treaty hastily signed by its predecessor on the very day it quitted office. And this task proved beyond his powers. In a private letter to Lord Salisbury[4] he described the men with whom he had now to deal as 'stupid beyond words to describe'. He added, 'As the French phrase runs, "ils abusent du privilège d'être bêtes".' Their supporters, inspired by a chauvinistic hatred of Britain, launched a vehement press campaign against the treaty, in order, 'under the influence of distorted facts and misrepresented data, to produce one of those blind and unreasoning

[1] In F.O. 84/1536.
[2] F.O. 84/1537: Morier to Salisbury, No. 32, S.T., 14 Mar. 1879; F.O. 84/1538: Morier's Memorandum of 4 Apr. 1879.
[3] In F.O. 84/1538.
[4] Dated 26 Sept. 1879. In F.O. 84/1538.

states of public opinion which no amount of rectified facts and corrected data can afterwards dispel'.[1]

The treaty was never ratified. Its loss involved the extinction of the hope that Britain could obtain from Portugal the facilities she required to act effectively against the maritime slave-trade. When Morier was instructed, in February 1880, to make representations about the unwillingness of the Mozambique authorities to co-operate with Consul O'Neill and the British Navy, he replied that although he did not cease 'at all seasons' to make such representations, he must remind his Government that he had always insisted that, 'until this policy of joint action in Portuguese waters was solemnly recorded in a treaty to which we had an international right to appeal, and the due execution of which we had an international right to demand, no amount of urgency and no amount of Notes would be of any practical use whatever'. And he continued:

I know the ways of this Government, and the very pigeon-holes in which they bury my Notes, and how impossible it is even for an active and sympathetic minister such as Senhor Corvo . . . to get anything done out of the common routine. . . . That this Treaty has not yet been ratified, that it now runs every chance of remaining a dead letter, is neither my fault nor that of the Foreign Office.[2] . . . I need not refer to the matter here, except to express my deep regret that it should be just this question of the Slave Trade, to which for so many years the Foreign Office has devoted such unremitting attention, that should be the one the most seriously affected by the complete derangement of all my plans.[3]

The ultra-nationalists of Portugal were more than equalled in their hostility towards Britain by the Portuguese colonists in South-East Africa. There was among them what Consul O'Neill, reporting in 1881, described as 'a party with which the suspicion and distrust of the English Government, as seen through their lights, amounts to a mania'. According to their creed, 'every English mission established in the interior is political in its object;

[1] F.O. 84/1538: Morier to Salisbury, No. 69, S.T., 6 Oct. 1879.
[2] Clearly a hit at the Colonial Office—and probably at the Treasury too, since the Colonial Office *volte face* was due to lack of financial means.
[3] F.O. 84/1563: Morier to Salisbury, No. 5, S.T., 16 Feb. 1880. Cf. Saurin to Salisbury, No. 35, S.T., 28 Mar. 1879, in F.O. 84/1537; also Morier to Salisbury, No. 48, S.T., Confidential, 28 May 1879 (in F.O. 84/1538), in which he shows that, but for British dilatoriness, the treaty could have been passed through the Cortes during the life of the Fontes–Corvo ministry.

every exploring expedition that starts from the coast is playing its
part in the ambitious policy of the English Government, and the
ultimate object of all, in this quarter of the globe, is to oust the
Portuguese from the province of Mozambique. With the holders
of such a belief it is impossible to argue.' The Secretary-General
of the province was a fanatical believer in this doctrine, and his
brother, the judge of Quilimane, hearing that an English mission
station had been raided by a native tribe, exclaimed in public,
'Would to God that they would murder them all!'[1]

The frequent journeys of Elton and O'Neill were regarded with
intense suspicion by such people, who accused them of wishing to
teach the natives to hate and attack the Portuguese.[2] It need
scarcely be remarked that a study of the dispatches of both consuls
shows that there was no foundation whatever for these fears and
slanders. O'Neill, indeed, earnestly desired that the Portuguese
would strengthen their hold upon the coast, over most of which
they had no control whatever—the so-called 'province of Mozambique' being in reality little more than a few unconnected footholds
on the coast, in addition to those on the Zambesi. When Captain
Augusto Castilho was about to assume office as Governor-General
at the end of 1884, he wrote that 'from the windows of his palace
the Governor-General of Mozambique looks over territories
which are absolutely beyond his dominion, although they are but
a few miles distant from the sea-shore';[3] and O'Neill had several
times to report that the stores or vessels of British Indians trading
in his consular district had been plundered by natives, whom the
Portuguese were powerless to bring to justice, so that in the end
he told the Foreign Office that he 'saw it would be no use to make
an official representation'.[4] He believed that, in the eighties, the
failure of the Portuguese to act effectively against slave-exporters
was due to weakness rather than to bad faith; and for this reason,
as well as for the sake of good relations between the two countries,
he wished that they would devote themselves with what vigour they
could command to consolidating their authority and suppressing

[1] F.O. 84/1595: O'Neill to Granville, No. 18, S.T., Confidential, 3 Aug. 1881.
[2] Ibid.; cf. F.O. 84/1616: O'Neill to Granville, No. 22, S.T., Confidential,
25 Apr. 1882.
[3] F.O. 84/1671: Quoted by O'Neill to Granville, No. 62, Africa, Confidential,
26 Dec. 1884. O'Neill described this statement as 'strictly correct'.
[4] F.O. 84/1671: O'Neill to Granville, No. 56, Africa, Confidential, 1 Dec.
1884. Cf. F.O. 84/1616: O'N. to G., No. 12, S.T., Confidential, 20 Feb. 1882.

the slave-trade in the maritime belt to which their claims had long ago been formally recognized, instead of spending their slender resources in an attempt to annex the Nyasa country, an attempt which would bring them into needless and fruitless conflict with Britain.[1]

With the Portuguese colonists, however, the consciousness of weakness merely added to the fear that, if Britain forestalled them in taking control of the interior, she would proceed to expel them from the coast as well. Hence, as O'Neill reported in November 1881, 'the cry . . . that the Portuguese standard be raised on the shores of the Nyassa' was 'strengthening every day'.[2] Moreover, they were not without encouragement from the Government at Lisbon. In December 1878, while Corvo was still Foreign Secretary, Fontes, the Prime Minister, had granted to a personal friend named Captain Paiva d'Andrade a concession of amazing magnitude. A circle with a radius of thirty-six leagues was drawn round Tete—it included Blantyre and most of the Shiré Highlands, but did not quite reach Lake Nyasa—and a similar circle round Zumbo; and the two circles were connected with parallel lines. Andrade was given the exclusive right to mine gold and other metals within this vast area, and also to mine coal in a still larger territory, the hydrographical basin of the Zambesi. This included the whole of Lake Nyasa. Wylde, at the Foreign Office, described the project as 'a most visionary one'; he thought Andrade would learn from painful experience that any scheme on so large a scale 'must inevitably fail and bring ruin on those connected with it', and that 'Africa is not to be opened to commerce or civilised in one generation; it must be a work of time'.[3] This comment on the purely economic aspect of the concession was not, in fact, far from the mark.[4] O'Neill, however, thought that this aspect was sub-

[1] F.O. 84/1640: O'Neill to Granville, No. 4, S.T., Confidential, 12 Feb. 1883.

[2] F.O. 84/1595: O'Neill to Granville, No. 24, S.T., Confidential, 19 Nov. 1881.

[3] F.O. 84/1537: Morier to Salisbury, No. 4, S.T., 27 Jan. 1879, with enclosed decree; F.O. 84/1538: Morier to Salisbury, No. 60, S.T., 28 July 1879, with minute.

[4] Andrade failed to raise the necessary capital, and the concession lapsed, though it was revived in a more modest and realistic form (for which see A. & P., 1890, li, p. 140: O'Neill to Salisbury, 20 Aug. 1888). Some English capitalists were interested in the scheme, and Mackinnon (of the East Africa Company) told Sir Clement Hill (of the Foreign Office) that he had invested £5,000 in it. 'I said', declared Hill, 'it was a scheme which, as likely to bring the Portuguese up to Blantyre, was one we looked on with suspicion. He replied he would try to

ordinate to the political, and that the chief purpose was to stake a claim to territory; in this respect the concession resembled the monopoly of steam navigation on the Zambesi and Shiré which had been conceded in 1875. 'It is easy', he commented, 'to see how short a step has now to be taken to fix the western limit of Portuguese territory at the western shores of the Lake, thereby including the two English[1] mission settlements already formed, and considerably interfering with the prospects and working of any vigorous effort to develop the trade of the entire Lake district'.[2]

It was not, however, until August 1882 that the Portuguese made a definite extension of their rule (as distinct from their claims) in the direction of the lake. The Governor of Quilimane proceeded with an armed force to the Lower Shiré, summoned the chiefs, and 'invited' them to deliver over to his Government 'all the lands now in their power and which by right belonged to the Crown'. The Portuguese flag was hoisted; a solemn proclamation was made; and both banks of the Shiré, as far north as the Ruo, passed under Portuguese rule.[3]

The Foreign Office had been warned, a few months previously, by a telegram from the Agency at Zanzibar, that the Portuguese intended to occupy Blantyre, and had indeed already dispatched a company of soldiers with that object. The report proved to be incorrect, but the attitude of the Foreign Office as expressed in the minutes on the telegram is none the less interesting. Britain, it was stated, had no wish to claim Blantyre for herself, and, provided the Portuguese did not harm British subjects or their property, there did not seem to be any objection to their occupying it if they wished. The date of these comments was November 1881.[4]

A year afterwards, when the Portuguese had advanced their frontier to the Ruo but had, for the time at least, stopped there, their Government made an overture to Britain for recognition of its right to extend its jurisdiction in West Africa north of the line of latitude 8° S., to which it had hitherto been restricted by a

---

get out of it, even at a sacrifice.' F.O. 84/1669: Petre to Granville, No. 115, Africa, 17 Dec. 1884, with minute by Hill.

[1] i.e. Scottish.

[2] F.O. 84/1539: O'Neill to Salisbury, No. 44, S.T., 14 Oct. 1879.

[3] F.O. 84/1616: O'Neill to Granville, No. 62, S.T., Confidential, 30 Nov. 1882.

[4] F.O. 84/1601: Miles to Granville, 15 Nov. 1881, with minutes.

British threat of naval action, a drastic measure judged necessary for the effective suppression of the transatlantic slave-trade. That necessity had now passed away, while the need for some administrative authority on the Congo was becoming increasingly urgent as more traders settled there, not all of them being impeccably law-abiding. Replying to this request, the British Government displayed a candour amounting to insolence in its announcement that, while it was willing to drive a bargain, it had no intention of giving anything away. 'The position of Her Majesty's Government', it declared, 'from their own point of view, is not that of asking concessions as a favour, but of attaching them as a condition.' Portugal's eagerness to establish herself on the Congo was providing the Foreign Office with a lever with which to obtain a final settlement on the Zambesi, and to resuscitate the slave-trade clauses of the defunct Lourenço Marques Treaty. After prolonged diplomatic activity, a treaty was signed on 26 February 1884, recognizing Portugal's territorial claims on the Congo, but providing, among other things, that there should be free navigation on both the Congo and the Zambesi, that Portugal's claims on the Shiré should not extend above the Ruo, and that British naval vessels should be allowed to operate for the suppression of the slave-trade in the territorial waters of Portuguese East Africa.

The treaty, however, was not ratified. The recognition of Portugal's sovereignty on the Congo was unpopular in England, where the Manchester Chamber of Commerce was convinced that, in spite of all safeguards, the genius of Portuguese officialdom would find means of crippling Lancashire's trade with that region, and where the influential Anti-Slavery Society maintained that Portugal could not be trusted to act effectively against the slave-trade.[1] But what finally killed the treaty was the refusal of the German Government to recognize it. Bismarck was determined to assert his country's right to a voice in the future of the Congo, and consequently the whole question had to be reopened at the international conference which, at Bismarck's invitation, met in Berlin in November 1884, and concluded its labours by signing the famous Berlin Act in February 1885.[2]

Meanwhile, at the end of May 1884, instructions had been given

---

[1] The relevant documents are in A. & P., 1884, lvi, pp. 3–119.

[2] S. E. Crowe, *The Berlin West African Conference, 1884–5* (Longmans, London, 1942), pp. 21–33, 101–2.

to George G. Petre, who was now the British ambassador in Lisbon, to remind the Portuguese Government that 'by the recent Congo Treaty the confluence of the River Ruo with the Shiré is fixed as the limit of Portuguese jurisdiction in that direction, and that Her Majesty's Government do not recognise jurisdiction beyond that limit'. This reminder was given in connexion with the strong disposition shown by the Governor of Quilimane[1] to occupy the Makololo country while it was in confusion after the murder of Chipatula. When Petre communicated the message to Bocage, the Portuguese Foreign Minister, the latter retorted with some warmth that the Congo treaty could not be appealed to until it had been ratified.[2] Instructions were indeed sent, though somewhat reluctantly, to restrain the Governor from crossing the Ruo; but they were sent in response to the argument that the best way in which the Portuguese Government could show the solicitude which it professed for the safety of the British missionaries was by refraining from going to their aid.[3] This was very true, for D. C. Scott afterwards told O'Neill that the natives had threatened to attack Blantyre 'and slay all they could' if a European force came up the Shiré.[4] But Bocage was careful to state, at the same time as he complied with Petre's request, that on account of the non-ratification of the treaty he did not recognize the Ruo as the Portuguese frontier; while Petre, acting on his instructions, denied that Portugal had any right to exercise authority beyond it. The negotiations, coinciding as they did with the creation of the Nyasa consulate, had defined Britain's attitude as to the point on the water-route to the interior at which the Portuguese must, if possible, be halted. But they ended in deadlock.

◦   ◦   ◦

In August 1884 the natives of the recently annexed country had risen in revolt against the Portuguese, razing the stockades to the ground and massacring the soldiers and their families. They then

[1] Not for the first time. In the previous year he had proclaimed Chipatula a 'rebel', at the same time announcing that he would not accept responsibility for any injury which the British missions might suffer in the suppression of this 'revolt'. O'Neill's anxiety was aroused, and as a result representations were made at Lisbon, causing instructions to be sent to Mozambique by telegraph, commanding moderation.

[2] F.O. 84/1669: Petre to Granville, No. 60, Africa, 12 June 1884.

[3] Ibid.; also P. to G., telegram of 13 June 1884.

[4] F.O. 84/1671: Scott to O'Neill, 9 July 1884, enclosed in O'Neill to Granville, No. 28, Africa, 5 Sept. 1884.

swarmed southwards, and destroyed the fiscal post at the confluence of the Shiré and the Zambesi. Before the end of the year
the revolt had been crushed and retribution had been inflicted in
a manner which even a Portuguese official admitted to have been
'rather barbarous'; but the customs-house was not rebuilt. It was
therefore impossible for goods in transit to the interior to be
cleared on leaving Portuguese territory, and consequently the
ordinary duties were imposed upon them.[1]

Moreover, the Portuguese authorities began to compel British
subjects on their way to the interior to buy 'tickets of residence' in
the province of Mozambique, and in 1884 John Moir was charged
tax not only upon the profits of the Lakes Company but upon his
private income as well. Thus the Portuguese officials were giving
practical application to their theory that the Nyasa region lay
within the province of Mozambique.[2]

Commenting upon these complaints, Petre suggested that instead of merely protesting on matters of detail and refusing to
recognize Portuguese sovereignty north of the Ruo, Britain should
settle the issue once and for all by declaring that the Shiré Highlands 'are henceforth to be considered as being under the protectorate and jurisdiction of Great Britain'. Lister agreed: 'I am
convinced', he wrote, 'that this will have to be done, and that it
should be done quickly.'[3] The provocations of the Portuguese made
the Foreign Office at first distinctly well-disposed towards the
Lakes Company's application, which was made about this time,
for authority to establish a protectorate.[4]

But the British Government had still no intention of assuming

---

[1] F.O. 84/1671: O'Neill to Granville, No. 25, Africa, 1 Sept. 1884; O'N. to
G., No. 29, Africa, Confidential, 10 Sept. 1884; O'N. to G., No. 48, Africa,
Confidential, 14 Nov. 1884.

[2] F.O. 84/1709: O'Neill to Granville, No. 14, Africa, Confidential, 24 Jan.
1885. In this dispatch O'Neill called attention to Article I of the Berlin Act,
which declared that all imports to tropical Africa, including Nyasaland, should
be completely free of duty, but which nevertheless expressly recognized 'that in
the territories belonging to an independent Sovereign State this principle shall
only be applicable in so far as it is approved by such State'. Thus, within the
boundaries of Portuguese East Africa—whatever those boundaries might be—
the authorities remained free to impose whatever duties they thought fit. O'Neill
suggested that this provision 'gives Portugal the spur to extend her claims as far
as she possibly can and in as short a time as possible', and attributed to this
motive the sale of 'tickets of residence' and similar actions.

[3] F.O. 84/1708: Petre to Granville, No. 22, Africa, 20 Feb. 1885, with minute.

[4] F.O. 84/1708: Minute by Anderson on Petre to Granville, No. 35, Africa,
4 May 1885.

administrative responsibility in Central Africa by its own direct action, and, when it became convinced that the Lakes Company was unequal to the task, it concentrated its attention on securing a reasonable measure of freedom for commerce with the interior. In 1886, scarcely more than a year after he had recommended that Britain declare a protectorate, Petre suggested that she should recognize the territory north of the Zambesi as within Portugal's sphere of influence and outside her own, provided that Portugal would concede by treaty the commercial facilities which the British settlers required. The gain to them would, he urged, be immediate, whereas Portugal could make a reality of her rights of jurisdiction only 'in a dim and distant future'. It is strange to find even the disdainful Lister remarking that this would be a good arrangement, though he doubted the willingness of the German Government and the Cape Government to agree to it.[1] It is stranger still to find Lord Rosebery, who was at this time Foreign Secretary, taking a serious and friendly interest in a Portuguese proposal, made in the following April (1886), that Britain should look with favour on 'the generous efforts of Portugal' to establish a protectorate over Matabeleland. Rosebery promised to refer the matter to the Secretary of State for the Colonies.[2] We hear no more of it, so probably it was quietly killed and buried by the Colonial Office. But it is interesting to note that Britain came very close to recognizing Portugal's claim to a belt of territory stretching from the east coast of Africa to the west, and embracing a vast area south as well as north of the Zambesi.

A new stage in Anglo-Portuguese relations was begun in the following year, 1887, when the Lisbon Government published maps showing the whole Zambesi basin south of the Rovuma river, and including Nyasaland and Matabeleland, as Portuguese territory.[3] They were in a good diplomatic position to make this definite assertion of their claim, for they had recently concluded treaties delimiting their boundaries with the spheres of France and Germany, and both these States had formally recognized Portuguese sovereignty in the belt of territory between Angola and Mozambique: though they had at the same time stated that this

---

[1] F.O. 84/1766: Petre to Rosebery, No. 23, Africa, 2 Apr. 1886, with minute.
[2] F.O. 84/1765: Rosebery to Petre, No. 32, Africa, 22 Apr. 1886.
[3] A. & P., 1890, li, pp. 71–72: Salisbury to Petre, 2 Aug. 1887. The map is reproduced in Sir E. Hertslet's *Map of Africa by Treaty*, vol. ii, facing p. 706.

recognition did not prejudice the rights of 'other Powers'.[1] Clearly the only 'other Power' with such rights was Britain, and Lord Salisbury at once called attention to the fact, and instructed Petre to protest against any claims not founded on effective occupation of the land in question. Great Britain considered, he added, that the Berlin Act had established this principle.[2] To this protest the Portuguese Foreign Minister, Barros Gomes, made a conciliatory reply. But he effectively demolished the British reference to the Berlin Act by showing that the clauses in question referred only to the coasts of Africa, not to the interior.[3]

It is quite clear, however, that Britain's contempt for Portugal's claim to Central Africa was not really due to Portugal's failure to occupy the territory in the past, but rather to her present pitiable lack both of the economic resources and of the able, honest administrators necessary to the effective discharge of such vast responsibilities. If she was allowed to prevent British enterprise, missionary and commercial, from working freely in Nyasaland in the mutual interests of Britain and Africa, she would be incapable of substituting any enterprise of her own, and the result would be stagnation and misrule. As late as 1889 Lister showed his total lack of confidence in Portuguese protestations of philanthropic motives by his comment on a report that the Lisbon Geographical Society—the very body whose intrigues had brought about the recall of Acting-Governor-General Sarmento—had established an Anti-Slavery League with the king as its patron, and had declared, in Petre's words, 'that in supporting the mission inaugurated by Cardinal Lavigerie, Portugal is only carrying out her traditional anti-slavery policy'. 'They have discovered', remarked Lister, 'that the suppression of slavery is the traditional policy of Portugal. They have no sense of the ridiculous.' Lord Salisbury agreed with him.[4]

In March 1887 the Mozambique publication *Africa Oriental* had written as follows in a leading article:

The state of this Province is getting day by day more alarming. We

---

[1] A. & P., 1890, li, pp. 65–71: Petre to Salisbury, 22 June 1887: enclosures.

[2] A. & P., loc. cit., pp. 71–73: Salisbury to Petre, 2 Aug. 1887; de Bunsen to Salisbury, 13 Aug. 1887, with enclosures.

[3] Ibid., pp. 73–77: de Bunsen to Salisbury, 17 Aug. 1887; also 22 Aug., with enclosure. For the clauses themselves (Nos. 34 and 35) see Hertslet, op. cit., vol. ii, pp. 484–5.

[4] F.O. 84/1955: Petre to Salisbury, No. 33, Africa, 28 Mar. 1889: minutes.

have never seen the Province of Mozambique in a more deplorable state than at present. Petty wars and native raids are increasing everywhere—in the north, south, and centre—whilst our resources of men and money are everywhere diminishing. . . .

O'Neill, who had no bitterness or bias against the Portuguese, and who viewed their shortcomings with sorrow rather than with anger, commented that this statement was 'substantially correct'.[1] Such was the reality behind the rhetoric of the excited orators and journalists in Lisbon.

The Portuguese, however, did not rely on words alone to make good their claims in Central Africa. In February 1886 an explorer named Cardoza, or Cardoso, arrived at Mandala after travelling overland to Makanjira's on the south-east shores of the lake. He told Consul Hawes that his purpose was 'purely to gain geographical information'.[2] His journey had, nevertheless, a political aspect. Though he made no treaty with Makanjira,[3] he made one with a sub-chief of Makanjira's called Kwirazia, and the Portuguese Government afterwards expressed the view that this was a document of some importance.[4] Hawes visited Kwirazia's village, and was told that Cardoso had been very short of goods, and, 'as he was unable to give much, he asked him [Kwirazia] to accept a flag and a letter which would secure for him the friendship of all white people. He recommended the chief to take the letter with him when he went on a journey, and to show it to every white man he met. He also told him to hoist the flag at his village to attract the notice of steamers on the Lake, if he wished the friendship of those on board.' The flag had not been formally hoisted in Cardoso's presence, and the contents of the letter had not been explained. Would the consul wait till the letter and flag could be fetched? Kwirazia would gladly part with both for a little calico.[5]

In the year 1888, however, the Portuguese declared that Kwirazia had gone to Ibo of his own accord and had renewed his 'oath

[1] F.O. 84/1846: O'Neill to Salisbury, No. 28, Africa, 3 May 1887, with enclosure.

[2] F.O. 84/1751: Hawes to Rosebery, No. 7, C.A., 13 Feb. 1886.

[3] Barros Gomes admitted this: A. & P., 1890, li, p. 139: Bonham to Salisbury, 19 Sept. 1888, with enclosure.

[4] Ibid., p. 123: Bonham to Salisbury, 20 Aug. 1888, with enclosure.

[5] F.O. 84/1829: Hawes to Salisbury, No. 19, C.A., 22 Apr. 1887.

of vassalage'. A similar compliment, they alleged, had been paid
to the Governor-General of Mozambique, when he was at Quilimane, by a son of Mlauri, who had recently succeeded Ramakukan as paramount chief of the Makololo. The sequel to this
occurred in November (1888), when the Portuguese sent a Dutch
trader named Maas to invite Mlauri to accept the office of
'Capitão Môr', or local administrator. Not only did Mlauri refuse
but when his subjects heard what was afoot they clamoured for
Maas's blood, and the Dutchman was lucky to escape with his
life.[1]

In 1889 the Portuguese redoubled their efforts, supplying chiefs
with liberal quantities of arms and ammunition as well as 'kachaso'
—cheap drink—with promises of more—'thereby obtaining', reported Buchanan, 'promises of friendship and tokens of vassalage,
the meaning of which they [the chiefs] do not in the least understand'.[2] Cardoso returned to the Shiré Highlands at the end of
1888, and in the following April Vice-Consul Ross announced his
arrival at Quilimane, accompanied by the representatives of six
chiefs who had come to swear fealty and accept the flag. 'I was
myself invited to, and attended at, one of these ceremonies', declared Ross, 'and found it to be just the sort of thing anyone in
authority could get an ignorant native to do for a few pieces of
cotton and a gaudy flag.'[3] Between January and September 1889
no fewer than twenty-five chiefs or headmen—some from south of
the Zambesi, but most from the Shiré Highlands and south-east
Nyasa—had made treaties with the Portuguese.[4]

The Universities' Mission, with its base on Likoma and its
steamer paying regular visits to the villages along the south-east
coast of the lake, was well placed to observe this activity. It had not
in the past sought any protection from the British Government,
but it now became so alarmed that its members seem actually to
have taken it upon themselves to distribute Union Jacks to any
chiefs who would accept them, in the hope of forestalling the

[1] A. & P., loc. cit., pp. 113, 125: Bonham to Salisbury, 12 July and 30 Aug.
1888; ibid., p. 165: Buchanan to Salisbury, 21 Nov. 1888; F.O. 84/1883:
Buchanan to Hawes, Nos. 28 and 29, C.A., 5 June 1888; No. 33, C.A., 30 June
1888.

[2] A. & P., loc. cit., p. 195: Buchanan to Salisbury, 23 May 1889, with
enclosure.

[3] F.O. 84/1969: Smith to Salisbury, No. 25, Africa, 29 Apr. 1889: enclosure.

[4] F.O. 84/1969: Churchill to Salisbury, No. 7, Africa, 26 Oct. 1889, with
enclosures.

Portuguese. On 16 August 1889 Bishop Smythies, the head of the mission, reported as follows from Likoma:

I fancy all the leading chiefs here are really dallying with the Portuguese. They of course wish to take our advice as we are their friends, living among them, exchanging salt and cloth for the wood and the simple products they can supply. But then they are harassed terribly by the Magwangwara,[1] and if the Portuguese send guns and powder and presents, what are they to do? There is nothing to correspond with that on our side. They will generally refuse to hoist the flag at our suggestion, because the Magwangwara will punish them if they do. . . . If it was thought well that an English representative should appear on the Lake . . . there would be something tangible; otherwise the first steps are being taken, since I was here last, to make Nyasa a Portuguese Lake.[2] You know their law is to have none but Roman Catholic missionaries.[2]

⟡　⟡　⟡

In January 1888 the Portuguese local authorities found a pretext in the port regulations for seizing a new steamer which the Lakes Company had brought out to operate on the Zambesi and Lower Shiré. They could not release her, they declared, until a promise was given to transfer her to a Portuguese owner. The free navigation of the Zambesi had been ended—and Lisbon had not even been informed. The purpose of this action was obviously to place the British settlers in the Nyasa country in a virtual state of siege.

The Portuguese Government upheld the decision of the Mozambique authorities. Under pressure, however, they abandoned their right to close the Zambesi in practice: but they insisted on maintaining it in principle. Petre was directed by telegraph to state that Britain would never acknowledge such a right.[3]

The next diplomatic clash began in May 1888, when Portugal was asked to permit a quantity of ammunition to be imported by the Lakes Company for use in the war against Mlozi. After much correspondence, the necessary permission was given in July. Then, in August, a further request was made: this time to be allowed to import a quick-firing gun and two light mountain guns. The Portuguese Government was shocked at the suggestion that it

---

[1] i.e. the Gwangwara or eastern Angoni.
[2] U.M.C.A. correspondence: Smythies to W. H. Penney. This quotation has been kindly supplied to me by Mr. P. Rayner.
[3] A. & P., 1890, li, p. 77: O'Neill to Salisbury (tel.), 2 Mar. 1888; ibid., p. 86: O'N. to S., 24 Mar. 1888; ibid., p. 78: Petre to S., 12 Mar. 1888; ibid., p. 85: P. to S., 25 Apr. 1888; ibid., p. 86: S. to P., 3 May 1888.

should permit a foreign company to use artillery within what it insisted on regarding as its own territory. Instead, it offered to settle the dispute with Mlozi, by negotiation if possible, and if necessary by force.[1] At last, on 18 October, Lord Salisbury lost patience, and with his own hand drafted the following telegram to the British Chargé d'Affaires:

Represent to M[inister] F[oreign] A[ffairs] that the recent news from Africa gives ground for the gravest anxiety as to the lives of the Englishmen on Lake Nyassa; that the arms on which their lives depend are now waiting at Quilimane, stopped by the Portuguese authorities: that the Governor-General of Mozambique has advised the RR. [representatives] of the Company to telegraph for permission to import them: that in their cruel refusal to give this permission the Portuguese Government are straining their international rights to the utmost, and that if they persist in it, the responsibility for the permanent effect it will have upon the relations between Great Britain and Portugal must rest with the Government at Lisbon.[2]

The effect was immediate, and the necessary orders were promptly sent to Mozambique.

2. *The Crisis*

In November 1888 H. H. Johnston was appointed consul for Mozambique in succession to O'Neill, whose health had broken down under the strain of his prolonged and devoted labours in that unhealthy climate.[3] Johnston had been vice-consul for two and a half years in the Niger delta, and evidently his exceptional talents had been noticed by Lord Salisbury, who was well informed on African affairs. The Prime Minister interviewed him when he arrived in London in June 1886, and invited him to spend a week-end at Hatfield, where he met Morier—now Sir Robert and ambassador at St. Petersburg—and where the main topic of conversation during his visit was the problems of the Zambesi and of the Arabs in Central Africa. According to Johnston, Salisbury was at this time contemplating the establishment of a British sphere north of the Zambesi, though he had to abandon the project later in the year owing to the steadfast refusal of Goschen, the Chancellor of the Exchequer, to provide the necessary funds.[4]

[1] A. & P., 1890, li, pp. 96–148.   [2] F.O. 84/1901: to Bonham.
[3] He was transferred to the consulate at Leghorn.
[4] Johnston, *The Story of my Life*, pp. 217–30.

In the previous February a treaty with Lobengula, chief of the Matabele, had been negotiated by J. S. Moffat, an official of the Cape Government and, incidentally, a brother-in-law of David Livingstone. It was a treaty of perpetual peace, by which the Matabele despot undertook not to alienate any part of his territory to any foreign Power without the consent of the High Commissioner for South Africa. Thus the first step had been taken towards carrying the frontier of Britain's South African empire northward to the Zambesi. The immediate reason for the negotiation of this treaty lay in the fact that a similar move was about to be made by the Transvaal, which had now recovered its independence as a Boer republic;[1] but Mashonaland, a raiding-ground of the Matabele, lay within the belt of territory claimed by Portugal, and as soon as the Lisbon Government received news of the treaty from their consul at Cape Town they protested.[2] The Anglo-Portuguese controversy was therefore extended from the Nyasa region to the country south of the Zambesi: with this distinction, that whereas in the north the interests which confronted the Portuguese belonged to the United Kingdom, in the south they belonged to Cape Colony.

No such distinction, however, was relevant to the Portuguese, who began to display unprecedented activity. Their two chief agents were Paiva d'Andrade and a Goanese named Manoel Antonio de Sousa, whom O'Neill described as 'the real ruler of the districts of Manica, Barue, and a portion of Quiteve, south of the Zambesi'. Partly as a consequence of his marriage with the negress queen of Barue, de Sousa was in a position to call up seven or eight thousand native irregulars, and he was therefore treated with the most flattering consideration by the Portuguese authorities, who showered presents upon him and paid for the education of his sons at Lisbon. 'Any further operations', wrote O'Neill in August 1888, 'will depend for their success far more upon his irregulars than upon the two or three companies of regular troops that accompany them.'[3] These two men arrived at Lourenço

---

[1] B. Williams, *Cecil Rhodes*, pp. 116–21. The treaty is printed in A. & P., 1890, li, p. 80.

[2] A. & P., loc. cit., p. 87: Petre to Salisbury, 2 May 1888; p. 88: S. to P., 7 May 1888.

[3] Ibid., pp. 140–1: O'Neill to Salisbury, 20 Aug. 1888. De Sousa's marriage is mentioned in F.O. 84/1671: O'Neill to Granville, No. 62, Africa, Confidential, 26 Dec. 1884.

Marques on 6 August, after a visit to Lisbon, and pressed into the interior in the direction of Zumbo.

In November the Governor of Quilimane officially informed Vice-Consul Ross of the departure of another expedition, consisting of 1,200 armed men and 2,000 followers. Its destination was the west coast of Nyasa, where it was to 'assist' the British at Karonga; it was referred to as a *missão civilisadora*. Forwarding this news to the Foreign Office, O'Neill commented that 'the nature of an expedition of over 3,000 men, and carrying 1,200 guns, into a country where our traders and missionaries have been in the habit of moving about unarmed and in twos and threes, is too clear to need explanation'.[1] And on 30 October Barros Gomes frankly mentioned to Petre that he had lately been advised by 'experienced and energetic colonial authorities' to avoid negotiations with Britain, and to bide his time until these expeditions enabled him to present London with a *fait accompli*.[2]

In these circumstances, Petre repeated his advice that Britain should recognize Portuguese jurisdiction in Nyasaland and thus remove the one great obstacle to a settlement.[3] Lord Salisbury, too, had his doubts about the wisdom of continuing to be firm. 'My hopes about the Zambesi are breaking down', he wrote to Lord Knutsford, the Colonial Secretary, on 12 October. 'It is no use declaring a river to be a highway of nations when there is only one fathom of water in it—and not always that.'[4] But a month later he had renewed his determination, perhaps under the stimulus of the open Portuguese challenge. He told Petre, by telegraph, that 'it is necessary to keep our full claim on record: but there is no use in discussing it, until we have an opportunity of enforcing it'.[5] Here is clear documentary proof that Johnston was right in stating that he wished to establish a protectorate over Nyasaland; and the word 'opportunity' probably means 'finance'. This message was sent in reply to one by Petre,[6] asking: 'Would it not be advisable

---

[1] A. & P., loc. cit., p. 159: O'Neill to Salisbury, 8 Nov. 1888. By 'unarmed' he can only mean 'without a large armed following'.

[2] Ibid., p. 152: Petre to Salisbury, 31 Oct. 1888; cf. p. 154: Salisbury to Petre, 14 Nov. 1888.

[3] Ibid., p. 152: Petre to Salisbury, 30 Oct. 1888.

[4] Lady Gwendolen Cecil quotes this letter in her *Life of Robert, Marquis of Salisbury*, vol. iv, p. 241.

[5] F.O. 84/1901: sent as tel. No. 21 of 20 Nov. 1888.

[6] F.O. 84/1901: No. 25, Africa, 19 Nov. 1888. (Salisbury's drafts are scribbled on the backs of two different copies of the decipher of this telegram.)

that I should make it clear to the Portuguese Government that whatever may be the result of the expedition to the western district of Lake Nyassa, we shall not recognise, except by agreement, any Portuguese jurisdiction over districts where British settlements are at present situated?' As an afterthought, the Prime Minister drafted a second telegram[1] which was, in effect, a negative answer—although the first had begun with the words: 'Yes—if the Minister gives you any opportunity of saying so.' But the second ran as follows: 'The time has not arrived for making such a declaration. It would certainly become known and would irritate the Chauvinists without really alarming the Govt.' Probably Salisbury's two telegrams, taken together—and both were sent—should be interpreted to mean that he was at that time powerless to take any action, but that he hoped that public indignation would be sufficiently roused by the reports of the Portuguese advance to enable him to wring from the Treasury the funds needed to administer and police the desired protectorate.

Several months passed before the new consul proceeded to his post. On 2 February he officially asked to be instructed to proceed up the Zambesi in the following May and June, to report confidentially 'on the exact condition and extent of Portuguese rule in the vicinity of that river'. He said that if circumstances were favourable he might proceed as far as Zumbo; but he did not express any intention of visiting Nyasaland, nor did he suggest that he should be authorized to make any treaties with the natives. 'I need scarcely say', he added, 'I would do nothing foolish or rash and would modify my plans on the spot if I felt they were likely to cause serious trouble and embarrassment to H.M. Government. I also trust in this as in other matters to work easily with the Portuguese, who are usually most kind-hearted, hospitable folk, easily won over by a little flattery and the lengthy compliments of their own language.'[2]

Lord Salisbury approved. Johnston made his arrangements to sail for Africa, sent his luggage to the docks, and went to the Foreign Office to say farewell to the officials. Sir Villiers Lister, merely as a matter of course, asked Salisbury if he would like to speak to the departing consul. Great was the astonishment of Lister and Johnston when Salisbury remarked that the idea had

[1] Sent as telegram No. 22, 21 Nov.
[2] F.O. 84/1969: Johnston to Salisbury, Confidential, 2 Feb. 1889.

occurred to him that Johnston should go to Lisbon to try to negotiate 'an understanding about frontiers which would keep the Portuguese out of the Shiré Highlands and Central Zambesia'.[1] Johnston accepted the suggestion, and began the negotiations with the greatest eagerness. His task was not to conclude a treaty but to reach a preliminary agreement on the basis of which a treaty could afterwards be drawn up.[2] Johnston interpreted his instructions in a liberal sense. His chief aim was to build an empire, not to safeguard Blantyre. Since Barros Gomes stubbornly insisted that the Portuguese boundary must include the Shiré Highlands and the southern half of Lake Nyasa, he acquiesced, on condition that Portugal accepted a limitation of her territory to the west. In a private letter to Lister, he explained fully what was in his mind, pointing out that the Nyasa region was dependent for its communications with the outside world on transit rights through Portuguese territory, and that even if such rights were formally secured in a treaty, 'we should know by this time how our enterprises in foreign territory can be hampered and restricted by a jealous spiteful little Power like Portugal. No', he continued,

let us keep open a belt of free *British* (not *neutral*—God forbid— schemes of neutralisation are the most hopeless solutions that despairing statesmen could devise) territory, Sphere of influence, or whatever you like to call it, so that it be coloured pink, between Tanganyika and the Zambesi. . . . Fortunately the Portuguese think we are very much in earnest about this and are prepared to concede this interruption of their band [across Africa] on condition of getting the South, South-East, and South west of Nyasa and the Zambesi as far as the Loangwa (just beyond Zumbo, no farther in fact than they at present go).

It was, he urged, far more important to safeguard the right of the Cape colonists to expand northwards beyond the Zambesi as far as Tanganyika than to keep the Portuguese out of Blantyre. Besides, he had asked for treaty recognition of absolute religious freedom for all Christian denominations throughout Portuguese East Africa, of free navigation on the Zambesi, of free transit, of the right to import war material 'under reasonable conditions', and of an Anglo-Portuguese commercial treaty establishing in

[1] Johnston, *The Story of My Life*, p. 231. Johnston attributes the words quoted to Lord Salisbury.

[2] His instructions are in F.O. 84/1968: F.O. to Johnston, 16 Mar. 1889.

perpetuity a moderate tariff for Portuguese East Africa. Barros Gomes, however, had asked for a 3 per cent. transit due, and a restriction of religious freedom and of the commercial treaty to a period of fifteen years and to the regions which Britain was now for the first time recognizing as Portuguese territory, instead of extending them for all future time to the whole Mozambique province. But Johnston brushed aside these matters as mere points of detail, and gaily remarked to Lister that 'if the missionaries felt they could not evangelise on Portuguese territory, why, they could move over to Western Nyassa where they could be as British as they please'.[1]

Petre, in forwarding Johnston's memorandum which contained the bases of the proposed treaty, declared that he thought the consul had been 'eminently successful'; and even Lister thought 'it would be a great pity to reject it in order to please one very shaky Co. and a few Missionaries', at the same time reminding Lord Salisbury that the Portuguese had an expedition on the spot and another on its way, led by an explorer of some distinction, Major Serpa Pinto. These expeditions would have both the company and the missionaries at their mercy, especially as Britain had made no treaties with the natives enabling her to claim the territory.[2]

Arriving back in London on 22 April, Johnston at once renewed his pressure for the acceptance of his proposals. His arguments were concerned entirely with the material interests of his own fellow countrymen, to the complete exclusion of spiritual and philanthropic considerations.

The sentiments of our missionaries in the Shire district [he wrote] are not the only element for consideration in an arrangement with Portugal. There are also the interests and expectations of the numerous British subjects who have just obtained or are awaiting concessions from the Portuguese Government for the opening up of the mining and

---

[1] F.O. 84/1969: Johnston to Lister, 5 Apr. 1889. He described his diplomatic methods in equally lighthearted terms: 'I smile widely on an average for 8 hours a day, so that I have lost all control over the muscles at the corners of my mouth. I extol everything Portuguese—the sky, the public gardens, the local opera, the hotels, the wines, the recent realistic fiction, the Colonial Administration, the language, the history, the army, navy, and police, and anything else Lusitanian on which my opinion is asked. I also paint Lord Salisbury as a raging lion where the least little tiny bit of British interests is concerned. The joint effect of these two phases seems to have made a good impression on the Portuguese.'

[2] F.O. 84/1965: Petre to Salisbury, No. 39, Africa, 9 Apr. 1889, with minute.

agricultural wealth of the Sofala territories south of the Zambesi, and whose prospects of commercial success will be seriously jeopardised if we fail to come to terms with Portugal for the settlement of our respective spheres of political influence in South-East Africa.[1]

He was himself given the task of winning the Scottish ecclesiastical authorities to his way of thinking. Very reluctantly, the Free Church accepted the arrangement, which did not seriously injure them since Bandawe lay north of the proposed frontier, and therefore within the British sphere.[2] But the Established Church refused to move an inch. Mr. W. P. Livingstone has published, in his biography of Hetherwick, an account of what took place, and there is no apparent reason to question its substantial accuracy.

In the offices of the Church [he writes] Johnston met a large company of dour-looking men. With plausible tongue he endeavoured to persuade them to accept the Portuguese terms. They sat with faces like granite. That night Dr. Archibald Scott, of St. George's, Edinburgh, the Convener of the Foreign Mission Committee, wrote to Lord Balfour of Burleigh informing him definitely that they would have nothing to do with Johnston's treaty.

Next day Lord Balfour sat down beside the Prime Minister in the House of Lords. 'My Lord,' he said, 'my Scottish friends don't like the Portuguese terms.' 'Neither do I,' was the reply. 'I don't want your Scottish friends to accept them. I want the Portuguese to know that I, too, have a strong public opinion behind me, and I am sending their Government a warning that they must not go too far.' The hint was taken. The campaign in Scotland was intensified. Representative meetings were held in the principal towns, and a memorial signed by 11,000 ministers and elders was taken to London and presented to Lord Salisbury. 'My Lord,' said Dr. Scott, 'this is the voice of Scotland.'[3]

◦   ◦   ◦

On 27 May 1889, two or three weeks after the rejection of his agreement with Portugal, Johnston was informed that the course of events at Mozambique rendered it essential that he should at once proceed to his post. He therefore sailed on the 31st.[4] During the five weeks since his return from Lisbon, two new factors of the

---

[1] F.O. 84/1969: Johnston to Salisbury, 22 Apr. 1889.
[2] Mins., F.C. of S. For. Miss. Comm., 14 May 1889.
[3] W. P. Livingstone, *A Prince of Missionaries*, pp. 51–52.
[4] F.O. 84/1968: F.O. to Johnston, 27 May 1889; F.O. 84/1969: Johnston to Salisbury, Confidential, 30 May 1889.

greatest importance had entered into the situation. One of these was his meeting with Cecil Rhodes.

Rhodes, though not yet thirty-six years old, had already achieved remarkable things. The son of an English vicar, he had gone out to Natal in 1870, at the age of seventeen, because his father hoped that an open-air life would strengthen his anaemic constitution. In the following year he had left Natal, and, taking his belongings in an ox-cart, had made the laborious 400-mile journey to the recently opened diamond field at Kimberley. Thus began a commercial career of such extraordinary achievement that by 1888 he had secured a monopoly not only of Kimberley diamonds but of Witwatersrand gold, and probably even he himself did not know exactly how rich he had become. But for Rhodes wealth was not the end but the beginning. Realistic business-man though he was, he was first and foremost a patriotic visionary, a man who profoundly believed that he had a mission in life, which was to extend British civilization as widely as possible throughout the world. He did not, indeed, wish to add to the powers of the Colonial Office in London: the empire which he envisaged was confederate and decentralized. He had become much more of a South African than an Englishman, and his strong Boer sympathies made him at first rather suspect at home. Nevertheless, his belief that British civilization—with which he associated the United States—would prove the salvation of world order was the motivating force behind his whole career; and though he could be cynical, callous, and thoroughly disagreeable, though his ideals were tarnished by his too-frequent experience of the base side of human nature, yet that belief remained the master-influence in his life, to which all personal ambitions were subordinate.[1]

It was Rhodes who prompted and nerved a sceptical High Commissioner to make the treaty of February 1888 with Lobengula, and he lost no time in following up this advantage by obtaining from that despot a concession of all mining rights in Matabeleland, together with authority to exclude from it the numerous rival concession-hunters whose activities threatened the country with political disruption. Having secured this historic 'Rudd Concession'—so named after C. D. Rudd, Rhodes's friend and business associate, who had conducted the negotiations with Lobengula—Rhodes proceeded to England to obtain from the Government a

[1] Williams, *Cecil Rhodes*, chaps. i–ix.

charter empowering him to administer the territory. He arrived in March 1889.[1]

While in England he met Captain Lugard, who had returned from the Arab War, and who outlined to him a scheme for the suppression of the slave-trade in Nyasaland. An armed trading-steamer should be maintained on the lake and used to attack slave dhows, to convey troops and stores, and, when not otherwise required, to engage in trade in order partly to defray the cost of its upkeep. There should also be a force of native police, with a nucleus of officers and men from the Indian army. The head-quarters of this force should be on the Nyasa–Tanganyika plateau.

Rhodes was impressed by this scheme, and offered Lugard £20,000, plus a further £9,000 a year, if he would put it into operation. Nyasaland would thus be included within the sphere of the new Chartered Company.[2] An essential part of the project was the securing by Rhodes's Company of a controlling interest in the Lakes Company; but the latter, while agreeing in principle, pro-crastinated, and when Rhodes returned to South Africa later in the year the plan seemed to have broken down, and Lugard heard no more about it.[3]

It must have been in connexion with this scheme that Rhodes first decided to employ the services of the consul for Mozambique, whom he met at a party, probably in the second or third week of May.[4] Johnston was five years younger than Rhodes, and fired with the same ardour in the cause of the British Empire. He relates in his autobiography that they spent the whole night, during and after the party, in eager conversation, and that before they

[1] Williams, *Cecil Rhodes*, pp. 121–30. The Charter was published in the *London Gazette*, 20 Dec. 1889; it is reproduced in Eybers, *Select Constitutional Documents Illustrating South African History*, as an appendix.

[2] The terms of the Charter did not fix any northward limit to the Company's field of operations, which were defined in Clause 1 with studied vagueness as follows: 'The principal field of the operations of the British South Africa Com-pany shall be the region of South Africa lying immediately to the north of British Bechuanaland, and to the north and west of the South African Republic, and to the west of the Portuguese Dominions.'

[3] Lugard, *The Rise of Our East African Empire*, pp. 158–9, 203–7.

[4] Johnston describes this meeting and its sequel in *The Story of My Life*, pp. 234–42. It must have taken place several days before he sailed for Africa on the 31st, for a good deal happened in the interval (ibid., 239–42); and it was presumably later than 4 May, when he wrote to Lister deploring that the Chindé had become known before his arrangement with Portugal could be foisted on the Church of Scotland. (The letter is in F.O. 84/1969.)

separated Rhodes gave him a cheque to cover the expenses of the journey which, as already mentioned, he had been planning to make to the Zambesi valley. Since the travelling expenses of consuls were normally paid by the Government, it may be presumed that the cheque was not intended to defray the ordinary cost of travel. Its purpose was almost certainly to enable him to pay for presents, to be given to the chiefs in the country between the Zambesi and Lakes Nyasa and Tanganyika, in exchange for their acceptance of treaties which would bring Central Africa within the British 'sphere of influence' and exclude it from the Portuguese.

Rhodes and those who were associated with him in seeking a charter were interested in land and mineral concessions as well as in the extension of British political authority, and several years afterwards Johnston told the Foreign Office that 'the gentlemen now forming the Directorate of the British South Africa Company' had consulted him 'as early as the spring of 1889' about the course to be taken in obtaining concessions north of the Zambesi.[1] But when he first mentioned to the Foreign Office the subject of treaty-making, in a confidential dispatch written on 27 May, his language was exceedingly cautious and tentative. He merely asked 'whether it would be convenient to Her Majesty's Government if I concluded preliminary Treaties with the Native Chiefs, of a character not necessarily committing the British Government to actually granting British protection, but still forestalling and precluding any subsequent attempts on the part of Portuguese emissaries to bring the same districts by Treaty under Portuguese sovereignty'. The treaties, he explained, would be confidential, and could be repudiated by the Government if it found them 'inconvenient or inopportune'.[2]

Lord Salisbury and Sir Percy Anderson were prepared to authorize him to proceed as he proposed, for on the day after his first meeting with Rhodes he had gone to the Foreign Office and told them something of the plans which he had been discussing. Until that time they had known almost nothing of the great South African capitalist, but they now understood that they need no longer be deterred by lack of money from asserting British interests

---

[1] F.O. 84/2197: Johnston to Rosebery, No. 40, C.A., Confidential, 18 Oct. 1892.
[2] The dispatch is in F.O. 84/1969. The minutes show that Johnston had not previously made this proposal in conversation.

in the face of the Portuguese threat, since, if Nyasaland was definitely claimed for Britain, Rhodes would finance Lugard to establish British rule.

There was a further and almost equally important reason why Salisbury should be prepared to take Nyasaland under British protection. At the beginning of May the British public had been made aware of the existence of the Chinde mouth of the Zambesi, where there was a much greater depth of water than at any of the other mouths of the delta.[1] Thus it would be possible to enter the Zambesi by way of the Chinde, and to steam up the Shiré as far as Katunga, without ever setting foot on Portuguese territory. Chinde provided a means of escape from the Portuguese stranglehold at Quilimane. If Central Africa became British, the Portuguese would no longer have it in their power seriously to impede its development.

⌐   ⌐   ⌐

Johnston arrived at Mozambique on 9 July 1889. 'This is not a bad sort of place on the whole', he wrote to Wylde. 'The Portuguese are a very inferior lot, but they are civil and leave me alone.'[2] At dawn on 28 July H.M.S. *Stork*, which drew 10 feet 6 inches of water, conveyed him up the Chinde to the main channel of the Zambesi, 'without hitch or stoppage', thus confirming the report of its navigability.[3]

Before leaving Mozambique he asked the Governor-General to give him a letter of recommendation to the Portuguese officers he might meet in the course of his journey. This was given, and he informed the Governor-General of his cordial appreciation of this kindness. With remarkable effrontery, since his purpose was to forestall the Portuguese in the annexation of the Shiré Highlands, he expressed the hope that on his return he would be 'able to acquaint your Excellency with a favourable result'. Barros Gomes published Johnston's letters in the newspaper *O Dia* on 18 December 1889, together with an article which he inspired and perhaps actually wrote. In this article, Johnston was described as 'a slippery individual, mellifluous and insinuating', who repaid the friendly assistance of the Portuguese authorities by encouraging the Mako-

---

[1] F.O. 84/1969: Johnston to Lister, 4 May 1889. For an account of the discovery of the Chindé see D. J. Rankin, *The Zambesi Basin and Nyassaland*, chap. xiii (where there is also a map of the Zambesi delta).

[2] F.O. 84/1969: Johnston to Wylde, 21 July 1889.

[3] A. & P., 1890, li, pp. 204–5: Johnston to Salisbury, 4 Aug. 1889.

lolo to resist the advance of Serpa Pinto's expedition, which was 'engaged in a peaceful and conciliatory mission'. Petre at once spoke to Barros Gomes, complaining that he saw no ground for these reproaches, and that if the Governor-General's letter was used at all it could only be used on Portuguese territory, and had no relevance whatever to Johnston's activities when he passed beyond Portuguese jurisdiction.[1] The Foreign Office showed its contempt for what Sir Philip Currie called an 'absurd charge'[2] by reproducing the whole article in a Blue Book. Johnston was certainly not guilty of actual bad faith, but it was not to his credit that he was quite so sweet and bland to the Portuguese at the very time when he was setting out to thwart their most cherished aspirations.

Arriving at the Ruo early in August, he reported that Serpa Pinto's expedition had reached the country south of that river and was rumoured to be about to press on. He therefore resolved that if, in spite of Makololo hostility, Serpa Pinto attempted to march into the Blantyre district, he would, 'in the last extremity', declare a British protectorate. But unless he was driven to do this, he would keep secret the treaties which he was about to make, leaving the open declaration of a British sphere of influence or protectorate to his Government's initiative.

With its recently increased resources [he wrote], the African Lakes Co. will soon be in a position to successfully maintain order in the southern Nyasa territories, especially if strengthened by a charter from Her Majesty's Government.[3]

Shortly afterwards he had an interview with Serpa Pinto, who received him with great courtesy and asked him to reason with the Makololo to allow the Portuguese expedition, whose purposes were purely scientific, to pass through their country without bloodshed. He replied that he saw no hope of the Makololo allowing the Portuguese force—which consisted chiefly of Zulus—to pass; and he stressed the danger to British subjects resident in the Shiré Highlands, and consequently to Anglo-Portuguese relations, if fighting should occur. In the course of further conversation 'the "Scientific" fiction gradually disappeared and gave place to a frank intention of extending Portuguese influence northward to Lake Bangweolo

---

[1] A. & P., 1890, li, pp. 255–7: Petre to Salisbury, 19 Dec. 1889, with enclosure.
[2] F.O. 84/1966: Petre to Salisbury, No. 180, Africa, 19 Dec. 1889: minute.
[3] F.O. 84/1969: Johnston to Salisbury, No. 8, Africa, Confidential, 9 Aug. 1889.

and westward across the Continent. In fact the old "continuous band" revived again in his ambitious plans.'[1]

Johnston parted from Serpa Pinto under the impression that the Portuguese commander had abandoned all intention of invading the Makololo country, and would proceed northwards by way of Mount Mlanje and Lake Shirwa. The consul then went on to Katunga, where he met Buchanan. The latter had already been asked for advice by Mlauri, Ramakukan's successor as paramount chief of the Makololo, as to what action should be taken in face of the Portuguese advance. He had at once called a meeting of representatives of British interests in the Shiré Highlands, and a document had been drawn up protesting 'most strongly' against any invasion of the Makololo country, and declaring that such action would be not only 'absolutely uncalled for' but a serious danger to the lives and property of British subjects.[2] This protest, dated 12 August,[3] was answered by a Portuguese counter-protest dated 20 August, in which the four white officers in charge of the expedition denounced 'the manoeuvres and intrigues of the English at Blantyre, who have wished to persuade the people that we wish to make war on them'. Serpa Pinto also sent Buchanan a letter in which he emphasized the 'purely scientific' character of his expedition, adding: 'If I take with me some armed Zulus, it is in order that the work of the mission [i.e. the expedition] shall not be hindered by ignorant people. . . . I cannot consent that a negro chief should wish to dispute the passage with me. . . . If, on my entry into Makololo territory, I am attacked, I shall immediately take the offensive and shall finish off at once the constant cause of disturbance on this part of the Shiré.'[4]

This reply was the more remarkable because Buchanan, in forwarding the Blantyre protest, had intimated in a covering letter, dated 19 August, 'that the Makololo country and Shiré Hills,

---

[1] F.O. 84/1969: Johnston to Salisbury, No. 9, Africa, 26 Aug. 1889.

[2] A. & P., 1890, li, pp. 215–16: Buchanan to Salisbury, 19 Aug. 1889, with enclosures. The protest was signed by Buchanan as acting-consul, by his brother David on behalf of the Buchanan firm, by D. C. Scott and John Moir, and by E. H. Sharrer, a British subject of German origins who had recently entered the country, and who afterwards not only became a substantial planter but competed with the Lakes Company in the steam navigation of the Lower Shiré and Zambesi.

[3] The date is given wrongly in A. & P. For the original see F.O. 84/1942.

[4] F.O. 84/1942: Buchanan to Salisbury, No. 30, C.A., Confidential, 10 Sept. 1889, with enclosures.

commencing at the Ruo river, had been placed under the protection of Her Majesty'.[1] The declaration of a British protectorate was almost certainly made on Johnston's instructions, for it was he who at about the same time directed the acting-consul to conclude treaties with the Makololo chiefs.[2]

The formal assumption of British suzerainty was hailed with rejoicing at Blantyre. 'This month', wrote one of the missionaries to his Committee, 'there has dawned a new life upon this land. British protection was what we had hardly dared to hope for; the utmost we had been taught to expect was that we would not be driven out of the country by the Portuguese. . . . Nothing could exceed the heartiness with which we welcome what has been done.' A later report declared that after some speech-making at a meeting held at Blantyre on 10 October, 'the meeting rose and lustily sang "Rule Britannia".'[3]

This exultation was a little premature. The Portuguese expedition remained south of the Ruo, determined to advance and awaiting reinforcements, and early in September fighting occurred between its forces and some of the Makololo: an event which would in more civilized countries be described as a 'frontier incident'.[4] Buchanan was in an exceedingly difficult position, with a growing Portuguese force, whose numbers in the end were said to number 4,000, threatening to cross the Ruo, and the Makololo who had accepted British protection looking to him to make that protection a reality.

Unlike the other Makololo rulers, Mlauri, the paramount chief, showed considerable reluctance to put his mark on a treaty and accept a British flag. Buchanan at first attributed this to what he called 'a superstitious fear'; but he afterwards claimed to have discovered that it 'was largely owing to the erroneous idea that the English and Portuguese had compacted together to divide his country, and that while he might be receiving a flag at the hands of the British Consul, it might afterwards turn out to be the Portuguese flag he had received'.[5] However that may be, the treaty

---

[1] A. & P., loc. cit., p. 215.

[2] F.O. 84/1969: Johnston to Salisbury, No. 9, Africa, 26 Aug. 1889.

[3] These letters are quoted by Horace Waller in his pamphlet, *Nyassaland: Great Britain's Case against Portugal*, pp. 36–38.

[4] A. & P., 1890, li, pp. 235–6: Buchanan to Salisbury, 17 Dec. 1890, with enclosure.

[5] Ibid., pp. 237, 241: Buchanan to Salisbury, 25 Sept. and 7 Oct., 1889.

was signed, after a fashion, on 24 September. John Moir and another witness testified on oath that they had faithfully interpreted its terms in the native language: it contained the following remarkable statement:

I, John Buchanan, Her Majesty's Acting Consul for Nyassa, do hereby swear that Mlauli, here present, superstitiously afraid of putting his hand to this paper, has authorized me, in the presence of Katunga and Masea, Makololo Chiefs, and of a great number of his people, and of all the undersigned witnesses, to make the above mark on his behalf.[1]

On 7 October Buchanan reported that 'Mlauli[2] is acting in a most friendly manner, and assisting us most loyally'. At the same time, however, he added that 'he is easily influenced by evil counsel';[3] and within a week he received bad news. Instead of hoisting the Union Jack at a safe distance from the Portuguese, where they could see it, but could not easily molest it, he left it flying night and day, unprotected, immediately opposite their encampment. Naturally, the Portuguese sent some Zulus to pull it down. Mlauri was utterly disillusioned, accused Buchanan of having cheated him, refused to accept another flag in place of the one which had been stolen, and declared: 'My heart is sore. I want to go to war against them. I shall not wait for a letter. No, I want to proceed hence because I am tired of waiting. I do not hoe. No; and what shall I eat? They [the Portuguese] are hoeing.' As the anger of Mlauri and his followers rose, Buchanan's ability to restrain and guide them declined; and, gathering his forces, Mlauri sent them into battle against the Portuguese. They were repulsed with heavy loss.[4]

The Portuguese then sent messenger after messenger to the Makololo chiefs, calling upon them to give up the British flags they had received and acknowledge themselves to be vassals of the king of Portugal. The chiefs refused, and Buchanan advised them to retreat northwards rather than surrender. He also wrote to Serpa Pinto on 10 December, warning him that if he attacked them because of their loyalty to the Queen, he would 'have to answer

---

[1] A. & P., 1890, li, pp. 219–20: Buchanan to Salisbury, 30 Sept. 1889, with enclosure No. 1.

[2] i.e. Mlauri. The 'l' and 'r' are interchangeable.

[3] A. & P., loc. cit., pp. 240–1: Buchanan to Salisbury, 7 Oct. 1889.

[4] Ibid., pp. 280–7: Buchanan to Salisbury, 8 Nov. 1889, with enclosures; B. to S., 11 Nov. 1889.

for it at no very distant date'.[1] About this time, Serpa Pinto himself returned to Mozambique, where his arrival on Christmas Day was reported by William A. Churchill, whom Johnston had appointed acting-consul.[2] Churchill learnt from him in conversation that the expedition would proceed to Katunga—the port of Blantyre, at the foot of the Murchison Cataracts—and would fortify and garrison it. This news was sent to London by telegraph.[3]

Lord Salisbury had been watching these developments with close attention. The War Office cordially favoured plans formed by the South Africa Company for sending an armed expedition to the Zambesi and another overland from the south.[4] The Cabinet had decided, on 23 December, to send a naval force to occupy the island of Mozambique if the Portuguese Government refused to undertake to keep its forces south of the Ruo.[5] Four days later, the Prime Minister was struck down by a serious attack of influenza, but he insisted on keeping the negotiations in his own hands, and dictated from his bed the series of telegrams which culminated, on 11 January 1890, in a formal ultimatum to the Portuguese Government. That Government had no choice but to accept: but its acceptance was followed immediately by its fall, and Petre reported that public feeling was exasperated to an extent that he had never before witnessed in Portugal. He could only compare the mob's hatred of Britain with the anti-German feeling in France after the war of 1870.[6]

If [he wrote] Her Majesty's Naval forces had already wrested from Portugal the island of Madeira, or her Indian possessions, or had occupied her East African ports, the clamour could not have been louder or the abuse heaped upon Great Britain by the press and public more virulent than they have been. . . . In point of fact, at the present moment all foreign Governments, with the exception perhaps of Italy and Belgium, are lauded to the skies at our expense, and their representatives here have been serenaded by applauding crowds of students and military and naval cadets.

---

[1] F.O. 84/1942: Buchanan to Salisbury, No. 47, C.A., Confidential, 11 Dec. 1889, with enclosure.

[2] A. & P., 1890, li, p. 259; Churchill to Salisbury, 25 Dec. 1889 (telegraphic).

[3] Ibid., p. 271: Churchill to Salisbury, 4 Jan. 1890. Cf. his dispatch No. 21, Africa, 29 Dec. 1889, in F.O. 84/1969.

[4] Cawston Papers, vol. i, Weatherley to Cawston, 20 Dec. 1889 (copy).

[5] Cecil, Life of Salisbury, vol. iv, pp. 262-3.

[6] F.O. 84/2042: Petre to Salisbury, 13 Jan. 1890; P. to S., No. 16, Africa, 16 Jan. 1890.

A considerable time necessarily elapsed between the issuing of the ultimatum and its effects on the Shiré. On 1 January a force of 600 Zulus had advanced to Katunga, and the British flag had been hauled down. Soon afterwards they went to Masea's, capturing his people but not the chief himself; and Buchanan reported that some of the atrocities perpetrated at this time were 'a disgrace to any civilised nation'. The acting-consul expressed the conviction that,

were we to meet the Portuguese by active resistance, and raise the natives against them, we could drive them out of the country. Such a course, however, I presume, would not be approved of by your Lordship, and I have therefore decided to submit under protest, unless they actually proceed to haul down the British flag, and hoist the Portuguese flag, at Blantyre: a proceeding which I will not say I should not actively resist, and which I fear few British subjects here would submit to.[1]

On 8 February, however, an order reached Katunga commanding the Portuguese to withdraw below the Ruo, and it was promptly obeyed.[2] From behind their frontier they showed their resentment by protesting against the action of Buchanan in rehoisting the British flag at Chiromo on the north (or British) bank of the Ruo, and in burning down the insanitary grass huts which they had erected during their occupation. Their protest was couched in terms which not even the twentieth-century Kremlin could well surpass: it accused Buchanan of having displayed 'the most complete and wanton breach of the most elementary principles of public law, both national and international, and the clearest neglect of the articles in Treaties amongst civilized nations'; and continued:

I[3] PROTEST energetically in the name of His Majesty the King of Portugal, Don Carlos I; in the name of all Portuguese subjects and citizens, in the name of the Law of peoples, of Treaties of International Law, in the name of the glorious banner of the Quinas, before the constituted authorities of all nations, against the insolent outrage and subversive act of the Consul of Her Britannic Majesty and his followers, lately perpetrated on the Lower Shiré.

So far as Britain was concerned, such language could only

[1] F.O. 84/2021: Buchanan to Salisbury, No. 2, C.A., 5 Jan. 1890.
[2] F.O. 84/2021: Buchanan to Salisbury, No. 9, C.A., 26 Feb. 1890.
[3] Major Machado, Governor of Quilimane.

spice with a little humour a somewhat tedious and unpleasant episode.[1]

☙ ☙ ☙

After meeting Buchanan at Katunga and instructing him to make treaties with the Makololo chiefs, Johnston proceeded to Blantyre, to which place he was conveyed with more speed than dignity on the back of a wild mare which had been lent him by John Moir.[2] His impressions of Blantyre were enthusiastically favourable. In his report[3] he described it as 'a pleasing English Arcadia, set in the middle of harsh African savagery'; 'a place of roses and geraniums, pink-cheeked English children, large-uddered cattle and laying hens'. 'No one', he added, 'who has known Blantyre of late years and the industrious energetic people who reside there can wonder at the pride which the Scotch feel in its creation, or the tenacity with which they cling to the hope of its being governed by the British.'

On his way up the Shiré, Johnston had gone ashore while the steamer was taking in wood for fuel, and, quite by accident, met and became acquainted with Alfred Sharpe, the solicitor-hunter who had helped in the fighting in the vicinity of Karonga.[4] Johnston was at once impressed—as Lugard had been[5]—by the character and capacity of this matter-of-fact English gentleman, and engaged his services. From Blantyre he sent Sharpe due westwards, with instructions to proceed to the River Luangwa and follow its course as far as its confluence with the Zambesi, making treaties as he went. Sharpe had been intending to shoot big game in those regions, and he undertook to perform the journey at his own expense, Johnston merely placing at his disposal a sum not exceeding £100, to be distributed among the chiefs in the form of presents.[6]

---

[1] F.O. 84/2021: Buchanan to Salisbury, No. 16, C.A., Confidential, 15 Apr. 1890, with enclosures; F.O. 84/2051: Johnston to Salisbury, No. 13, Africa, 16 Mar. 1890, with enclosures, and with Anderson's minute: 'The Protest is worth reading.'

[2] Johnston, *The Story of My Life*, p. 257.

[3] F.O. 84/2051: enclosed in Johnston to Salisbury, No. 14, Africa, 17th Mar. 1890.

[4] Johnston, *The Story of My Life*, pp. 254–6.

[5] Lugard described him (*The Rise of Our East African Empire*, vol. i, p. 43) as 'one whose whole demeanour proclaimed him at once a thorough gentleman, and a practical, shrewd, common-sense man'.

[6] F.O. 84/1969: Johnston to Salisbury, No. 9, Africa, 26 Aug. 1889.

The consul then continued his journey to Mponda's, at the south end of Lake Nyasa, and was relieved to receive assurances from that chief that no treaty had been made with the Portuguese. On the contrary, Mponda professed great friendship for the British. At the same time he hesitated to make a treaty with Johnston, and said he wished to think the matter over. Johnston therefore went on his way to Kota-Kota, on the west coast of the lake, to negotiate with Jumbe.[1] Soon afterwards, when W. P. Johnson passed by, Mponda, who was evidently in doubt as to whether he should be contemptuous or alarmed, asked the missionary: 'Who is this little man, that comes and talks with authority?'[2]

Johnston found that Jumbe, while professing neutrality in the war at the north end of the lake, 'had of late rendered that neutrality very benevolent towards the Arabs, who were undoubtedly obtaining supplies of ammunition and other warlike materials from his country'. But, rightly or wrongly, he attributed this unfriendly attitude to 'certain foolish actions' on the part of the Lakes Company's officials. In any case, Jumbe was powerful enough to be a dangerous enemy and a useful friend, and Johnston was determined to conciliate him. This task was made easier by a letter from his nominal overlord, the Sultan of Zanzibar. Moreover, he happened to be very ill, and Johnston tactfully showed much solicitude in nursing him during his fever, giving him, as 'medicine', a bottle of Chartreuse, which he relished exceedingly. So, as soon as he was sufficiently well, Johnston made two treaties with him: one on behalf of the Government, securing political control of his country to the Queen's duly authorized representative; the other on behalf of the Lakes Company, promising him a subsidy of 750 rupees quarterly so long as he fulfilled his treaty obligations to the Government and imposed no dues or taxes on any British subjects who might settle in his dominions.[3] 'We give the Jumbe this money just to get a footing and pay our way', explained Moir in conversation with W. P. Johnson.[4]

Leaving Kota-Kota, Johnston sailed to Bandawe, where he spent four days. He described it as 'another Blantyre in its civilisation and comfort, but unfortunately not in its climate, which is

[1] F.O. 84/1969: Johnston to Salisbury, No. 10, Africa, 18 Sept. 1889.

[2] W. P. Johnson, *My African Reminiscences*, p. 202.

[3] F.O. 84/1969: Johnston to Salisbury, 16 Oct. 1889, with enclosures; *The Story of My Life*, pp. 260–5.

[4] Quoted by Barnes, *Johnson of Nyasaland*, p. 88.

not particularly healthy'. 'Bandawe', he declared, 'with its little colony of five Europeans, its large school of native children, its dependent villages of friendly natives, and its general air of brisk industry and cheerful comfort, is one of the most creditable and agreeable results of British Missionary enterprise which ever gladdened the eyes of a traveller, weary with the monotonous savagery of the African wilds. Here one feels in touch with Europe.' Of Dr. Laws he wrote in the following terms:

This man, with his fifteen years of whole-hearted devotion to Nyasaland, and his energy of doing good which has made him learn to make bricks himself in order that he may teach others, which has led him to become a practical carpenter, joiner, printer, photographer, farrier, boatbuilder, engineer and druggist, so that he might induct his once-savage pupils into these arts and trades; which has made him study medicine and surgery to heal the bodies, and sufficient theology to instruct the minds, of these Africans, about whom he never speaks with silly sentiment and gush, but whose faults, failings, and capabilities he appraises with calm common sense—Dr. Laws with these qualities of truly Christian self-devotion should justly be regarded as the greatest man who has yet appeared in Nyasaland.[1]

Coming as it did from one who loved to boast of his agnosticism, this was praise indeed.

During his stay at Bandawe, Johnston made treaties with twenty-three Tonga chiefs;[2] then he proceeded to Karonga to undertake the difficult task of ending the Arab War. Here, as in his dealings with Jumbe, he was helped by a letter from the Sultan of Zanzibar. But Mlozi and his colleagues were extremely suspicious, and refused to come out to meet him; so, having proclaimed a truce, he took his life in his hands and visited them within their stockades. The negotiations were far from easy, but he was determined to succeed, and on 22 October 1889, at the end of a week of strenuous activity, a treaty was signed by the Arab leaders and by the representatives of the company. This ceremony, which took place at a little wood between Karonga and the Arabs' stockades, was followed by much solemn handshaking, and by prolonged prayers —on the part of the Arabs—'that Allah would help them to keep the treaty and let an unbroken peace henceforth reign between

[1] F.O. 84/2051: enclosed in Johnston to Salisbury, No. 14, Africa, 17 Mar. 1890.
[2] F.O. 84/1969: Johnston to Salisbury, 16 Oct. 1889, with enclosures.

them and "the people of the Queen". . . . A bullock was killed (the loud sighs of its death agony and gurgling of its spouting veins coming in as a curious second to the Arabs' prayers, and being the only sounds which accompanied the intoning of their guttural Arabic phrases) and its meat was divided among the wild-looking savages who represented the body-guards of white men and Arabs. Then, with the sweetest compliments and most graceful phrases which the Swahili tongue with its Arabic intermixture can frame, the Arabs bade us adieu and we severally returned to our towns, where for two days a continual firing of guns, feasting, and dancing, was kept up.' Three days after the signing of peace there were further ceremonies, with exchanges of presents and 'polite but vapid compliments'; on each side a spear was broken, the broken fragments were exchanged, 'and the day ended in a riot of noisy friendship which was most fatiguing'. Such was Johnston's account of the conclusion of the Arab War.[1]

The terms of the treaty represented no substantial concession by either side. All claims to compensation were waived, and the Arabs were to be allowed to remain within their fortified stockades, except that either Msalema or Kopa-Kopa, both of whose villages were within three miles of the Stevenson Road, must remove his settlement within twelve months. The Wankonde survivors were to be at liberty to return to the places from which they had been driven, and were not to be molested in future. Any further disputes between the Arabs and the company were to be referred to a duly authorized representative of the Crown, whose decision would be final and binding.

These terms were a bitter disappointment to Captain Lugard.[2] He knew very well that Mlozi's most solemn undertakings were valueless from the moment when they ceased accurately to represent Mlozi's own interests, and that there could be no real and enduring peace until these Arabs had been expelled from the country. But Johnston had countered any such criticisms in advance. Although the Arabs had been reduced to 'eating rats, leather and roots, besides being scourged by a terrible outbreak of smallpox', the British, for their part, had almost reached their last

---

[1] F.O. 84/1969: Johnston to Salisbury, 26 Oct. 1889, with enclosed copy of treaty. Also, F.O. 84/2051: enclosure in Johnston to Salisbury, No. 14, Africa, 17 Mar. 1890.

[2] For his criticisms see *The Rise of Our East African Empire*, vol. i, pp. 161, 164–5.

cartridge. Neither side was strong enough to force its will upon the other, and both sides desperately needed peace. Fotheringham, who had borne the burden and heat of the day from beginning to end, called the settlement 'a triumph' for the consul.[1] Further, as Johnston remarked in a strikingly accurate forecast of the course of events:

The Arabs of North Nyasaland have had a most severe lesson, they have lost nearly all their property in ivory which they had amassed, their prestige and credit with the natives is gone, and I do not think that they will attempt to tackle us again; at any rate, not for several years, and by that time if we are not in a position to deal with them effectually we should have no right to arrogate to ourselves the position of rulers in Nyasaland.[2]

From the north end of Nyasa Johnston took a north-westerly course to the south end of Lake Rukwa, where he decided not to linger. He described the vicinity of Rukwa as 'a terrestrial hell', on account of its extreme heat and lack of water; 'under these conditions', he remarked, 'I thought we might well leave Rukwa to German enterprise'.[3] Ascending the Nyasa–Tanganyika plateau, he proceeded to the south-east corner of Lake Tanganyika, making treaties on the way, and bringing much-needed supplies to the missionaries at Fwambo, who had for several months been cut off from the outside world by the blocking of both the Zanzibar and the Nyasa routes.

On 26 November he arrived at Niamkolo, and there made the acquaintance of Swann, who conveyed him in a sailing-boat along the south coast of the lake to Cameron Bay. Thence he travelled inland to within a short distance of Lake Mweru, 'being everywhere well received (after a little explanation) by Arabs and natives. Indeed', he declared, 'the Arabs were exceedingly good to me, and I could never have accomplished what I did without their help. They were very generous in supplying me with food. All spoke in terms of the greatest respect of Her Majesty the Queen, and repeatedly assured me that they would submissively obey her orders and "sit down" under her rule, but would never, never tolerate the domination of "other kinds of white men".'[4]

[1] Fotheringham, *Adventures in Nyassaland*, p. 298.
[2] Report of 17 Mar. 1890, loc. cit.
[3] F.O. 84/2051: Johnston to Salisbury, No. 6, Africa, 1 Feb. 1890.
[4] Ibid.

What was their motive? Respect for the Sultan of Zanzibar had doubtless some genuine influence with them, but it would never have led them to act in a manner contrary to their own interests. They must, therefore, have been suiting their own convenience by seeking to ingratiate themselves with the British consul. They had had a long acquaintance with the agents of the London Missionary Society, who, while openly condemning the slave-trade, scrupulously refrained from actively interfering with it. The Germans and Belgians, on the contrary, were doing their utmost to put it down with a strong hand. The Arabs probably imagined that the British Government would act in the same way as the British missionaries, and that its authority would, in effect, serve as a bulwark against those other Europeans who, in its absence, would occupy the country and hang every slave-trader they could catch. Moreover, Johnston was at this time exceedingly well-disposed towards the Arabs, whom he thought Britain could use as fellow workers in the task of civilizing Central Africa. The real enemies of peace-loving native peoples were not the Arabs, he alleged, but such native marauders as the Angoni and the Bemba, and he recommended that, if possible, the help of the Arabs should be enlisted for the purpose of 'subduing and taming' these warrior tribes, whom he described as 'irrational, bloodthirsty wild-beasts'. He even made light of the crimes of Mlozi and his allies, who, he airily remarked, 'were not . . . much wickeder than we have been in many of our acquirements of territory'. But his model Arab was Jumbe, who, he believed, had almost entirely abandoned the slave-trade because it was more profitable to keep the people on the land, producing 'the magnificent crops of rice . . . which is famed far and wide in Nyasaland, and of which he sells quantities to the passing caravans'.[1] This may well have been substantially true; and indeed it would seem that even Mlozi, if left to his own devices, would eventually have had to set a limit to the devastation and depopulation of the country which he was making his own.

The best commentary on Johnston's early hopes in connexion with the Arabs is provided by his own riper experience. On the last day of December 1895 he wrote thus to Rhodes:

We have now completely smashed the Arabs in the North Nyasa District. In fact I think I am right in saying that there is not an Arab left in that part of the Territory, and every one of their stockades is

[1] Report of 17 Mar. 1890, loc. cit.

destroyed. . . . The Awemba raids were, in my opinion, directly due to
the instigation and co-operation of the Arabs under Mlozi, and will
probably cease of themselves now that Mlozi is hanged.

. . . Within the Protectorate we have waged war against the Yaos and
Arabs because they are (1) Not natives of the country, (2) They are
rival aspirants with us to be the rulers of the country, (3) and because
they are recalcitrant to all compliance with elementary regulations providing for peace and quiet and undisturbed commerce.[1]

With the Angoni and the Bemba, on the other hand, he had never
come into conflict, and the purpose of his letter to Rhodes was to
urge his conviction that a policy of friendship with the Bemba
would have a very good chance of succeeding in the future.

Receiving word that Portuguese action on the Shiré was moving
towards a climax, Johnston hastened back from Tanganyika.
Calling at Kota-Kota, he was given two fine tusks of ivory as a
personal present from Jumbe to the Queen. When he reached the
village of Mponda he found that two Portuguese agents had
arrived there during his absence, accompanied by three French
priests, whom he assumed—erroneously, it seems—to have come
for purposes which were primarily political rather than religious.[2]

[1] Rhodes Papers, Groote Schuur, 26, 14: Johnston to Rhodes, 31 Dec. 1895.

[2] His assumption seems to have been shared by the Scottish missionaries and
the agents of the Lakes Company, who received them with coldness and uncon-
cealed dislike. And, in fact, it was the Portuguese Government which had taken
the initiative in causing them to be sent out. It had suggested to Cardinal Lavigerie, the founder of the missionary order of White Fathers to which they
belonged, that it would itself bear all the costs of sending a mission to Nyasaland, and an agreement to this effect had been signed in June 1889. Serpa Pinto
seems virtually to have admitted (to a Belgian journalist) that the Portuguese
motive in sponsoring the mission to southern Nyasaland was primarily political
(Cawston Papers, vol. ii: Kirk to Cawston, 6 May 1890). But this does not prove
that the Frenchmen themselves were conscious that they were being made use
of for the secular purposes of Portugal. They are said to have been greatly surprised, on their arrival in December, to find that her claim to their mission-
field was in dispute with Britain: their surprise was probably genuine, for they
showed the sincerity of their own intentions by remaining at Mponda's long
after their Portuguese companions had departed. It was not until June 1891 that
they withdrew to the Tanganyika region. During their sojourn of eighteen
months they were denied all opportunities of teaching their doctrine to the
people, for Mponda was a convert to Islam, and kept them continuously under
his personal surveillance. Their presence under these conditions was of some use
to him, since they treated the wounds of his followers after his frequent slave-
raids. (Henri Pineau, Evêque roi des brigands (Pères Blancs, Quebec and Montreal,
1944), pp. 62–64. For the career of Cardinal Lavigerie and the work of his
missionaries see R. Oliver, The Missionary Factor in East Africa, pp. 45–49,
51–52, 117–19, 164–5.)

He observed with amused satisfaction that his Portuguese rivals and their French associates were being treated by Mponda with disfavour and contempt. 'They were not allowed', he wrote, 'to hoist the Portuguese flag, and were practically prisoners in their own hired compound. Mponda, having reflected since my former visit on the relative advantages of a Portuguese or English alliance, and not liking the Portuguese on nearer acquaintance, had decided to make a treaty with us and accept our flag.... After signing this treaty he proceeded to hoist the British flag on his beach, just in front of the house where the Portuguese were residing. The latter surveyed the scene through their binoculars, but made no attempt to interfere.'[1]

Proceeding to Blantyre, he found that most of the Makololo chiefs were living there, having acted upon Buchanan's advice to withdraw from their own country in the face of the Portuguese advance. The Portuguese stopped his boat on its way down the Shiré, but he extricated himself with the greatest of ease: as he put it, 'the "Governor of the Shire" "se confondit en excuses".' He arrived at Mozambique on 30 January, having accomplished the journey from Tanganyika in the record time of six weeks.

૦ ૦ ૦

After being sent to the country west of Nyasa in August 1889, Sharpe had concluded a number of treaties, but had for some reason returned without going nearly as far as the Luangwa. In the middle of March 1890 he set out on a second expedition, at Johnston's request.

He had to travel through thick grass 8 or 10 feet high, in constant rain, and with his carriers so demoralized and ill that they would, he said, 'lie down and howl in a morning when told to take up their loads'. In all probability their demoralization was caused by a quite understandable dread of the spears of the Angoni warriors, into whose country they were being required to advance in accordance with some bargain between the white traveller and their chiefs.

On 28 March he reached the village of Mpeseni, the Angoni chief who dominated the area of which Fort Jameson is now the centre. But Mpeseni kept him waiting till 4 April before granting him an interview, and even then the result was disappointing. The chief was friendly, 'but Treaties he would not touch, nor the flag'. He could see no valid reason why he should grant special privileges to Sharpe and those whom Sharpe represented, since

[1] His No. 6 of 1 Feb. 1890, loc. cit.

he had no need to invoke their protection against his neighbours
—it was, on the contrary, his Chewa neighbours who needed to be
protected against him. 'He is under the impression', his frustrated
visitor complained, 'that he is the most powerful monarch in the
world, except possibly Mombera; and the suggestion that it would
be a good thing for him to have (in case of a future war) so powerful
a friend as the Queen, created great amusement.'

In reality Sharpe had good cause to be pleased rather than
annoyed by this independent attitude, for he was not the first conces-
sion-hunter to approach Mpeseni. A Portuguese lieutenant named
Solla, accompanied by a German land-speculator named Wiese,
had arrived before him, and would undoubtedly have established
a prior claim to both political and economic control of the country
had Mpeseni been willing to dispose of his rights to anyone.

Leaving Mpeseni's, Sharpe continued his journey to the
Luangwa. The whole country through which he passed had, he
found, been stripped of its population, for the first half of the distance by the Angoni, and for the second half by the Portuguese
half-castes whose headquarters were at Zumbo. Matakenya, by far
the most important of these half-castes, dominated and terrorized
a huge region, and, since the inhabitants did not dare to call their
canoes or even their food their own, there was little treaty-making
to be done amongst them. Two insignificant chiefs who did sign
treaties expressed great fear lest Matakenya should hear of it. So
all that Sharpe could do was to 'make a liberal display of the
English flag' wherever he went. When he found it necessary to
turn back at a point about 29° 48′ E., he hoisted the flag, fired a
salute, 'and formally declared the whole country west of the
Loangwa and N[orth] of [the] Zambesi to be under British protection'. He had not been authorized to make any such declaration,
but he made it so that it might be 'noticed or disregarded at home,
as may be convenient'. He arrived back at Lake Nyasa on 5 June.[1]

Within a few weeks, however, he was again on the march. This
time his destination was Katanga, or Garenganze as it was then
usually called. Rhodes and Johnston were both anxious to acquire
Katanga, which was already famous for its wealth in copper, and
when they met in 1889 they agreed to send a certain Keppel Stier
as their agent to negotiate a treaty with Msidi (or Msiri), its chief.

[1] F.O. 84/2052: Sharpe to Johnston, written at various times between 26 Mar.
1890 and the following June.

But when Johnston reached Quilimane he decided, for reasons unknown, that Stier was unsuitable for the work, and dismissed him: an action which received Rhodes's approval.[1] In the spring of 1890 the London Directors of the South Africa Company obtained Rhodes's agreement to sending out Joseph Thomson, the famous explorer, to proceed to Katanga on their behalf to make treaties with Msidi and with the chiefs whose country his route would cross.[2] It appears that on his way out Thomson met Johnston at Cape Town, for Johnston, on arriving in London in June, referred to him as 'a terribly obstinate man' who 'would not take my advice as to the route he should follow—nor would he listen any more to Rhodes. We gave up advising him', Johnston added, 'because he is after all such a wily and successful traveller that he is pretty sure to pull through all difficulties if left to himself.'[3] But Johnston himself was 'a terribly obstinate man'—and a 'wily' one as well. It may have been as a result of his disagreement with Thomson that he sent instructions to Sharpe, in whom he had unbounded confidence, to set out for Katanga. However it came about, it was not until Thomson and Sharpe actually met in Nyasaland that either learned that the other had been entrusted with a mission to Msidi.

When I came here [Thomson explained to Rhodes, in a letter written at Kota-Kota on 8 August[4]], I was under the impression that I was the sole representative of the B.S.A.C[ompany]. Conceive my surprise on finding it otherwise. Mr. Sharpe. . . . I found installed under the B.S.A.C. as Commissioner for Nyassa[5] at so much per year, and with

---

[1] F.O. 2/55: Johnston to Rhodes, 8 Oct. 1893, enclosed in Johnston to Rosebery, No. 53, C.A., Confidential, 8 Oct. 1893.

[2] Cawston Papers, vol. ii, Cawston to Rhodes, 14 Mar. 1890; Thomson to Cawston, 30 Mar. 1890.

[3] Cawston Papers, vol. ii, Johnston to Cawston, 16 June 1890. The disagreement about the route is explained by some remarks of Thomson's in his letter to Rhodes from Kota-Kota, dated 8 Aug. 1890 (Rhodes Papers, Charters, Bundle 3A, 29): 'Here I am in 2 months from the Cape ready to start inland for Bangweolo. . . . Happily none of Johnston's dire predictions have been fulfilled, and I daily thank the Lord that I went neither by Bechuanaland nor overland from Mozambique—a proceeding that would have landed me at Msiri's sometime next year after suffering all the dangers and hardships of the wet season.' Presumably Johnston's fear was that the Portuguese would make it impossible for Thomson to reach Nyasaland at all—and Sharpe was already there.

[4] Rhodes Papers, loc. cit.

[5] It is impossible to say what was the precise truth behind this statement. Clearly, however, Thomson's resentment against Johnston led him to exaggerate a good deal.

such and such work to do. In that capacity I found him back at the Lake after an extremely plucky journey to the Loangwa and preparing to proceed to Msiri's and Moero—whither I also had been directed to go in my instructions. In fact we have come up the Lake together, he to proceed from Karonga. All this I need hardly say has been the work of Mr. H. H. Johnston, and Mr. Sharpe, who is a very superior and capital fellow, was very much surprised to learn that his appointment was unknown at Kimberley when I left there. He was puzzled what to do, and I could not help him under the circumstances. I could only express my opinion that perhaps his best course was to carry out Mr. Johnston's orders—but that as he was to be paid by the Company, he had better communicate direct to you and get the situation cleared up. I need hardly say that I would consider it a favour if you will write and tell me what my position is to be in relation to Mr. Sharpe.

So both men set out for Msidi's, but by different routes. Thomson travelled westwards from Kota-Kota to the Luapula, south of Lake Bangweulu, and proceeded as far as the upper Kafue. But he was unable to reach his destination, and returned to Kota-Kota, broken in health, by way of the Luangwa and Mpeseni's. He claimed, however, to have travelled more than 1,250 miles between his departure from and his arrival at the Nyasa coast; of this distance, more than 900 miles lay across country never previously traversed by a European. And, although he had failed in his main purpose, he had made treaties with various chiefs in what is now the Central Province of Northern Rhodesia.[1] 'Over an area of about 40,000 square miles', he reported, 'the entire political, trading and mineral rights have been acquired at a very small present expense and few future liabilities.' He was sure that at least three-quarters of this area was 'capital agricultural and pastoral land', and even healthier than Blantyre. And he—a geologist, it may be remarked—had not the least doubt that the whole plateau was rich in gold.[2]

[1] In a memorandum dated 17 Oct. 1894 (in F.O. 2/67), Johnston urged the Foreign Office to recognize as much of the contents of these treaties as was legally admissible. The fact that certain parts might have to be rejected was no sufficient reason for non-recognition of other parts; but in this connexion Johnston remarked that 'the Thomson Treaties were most absurdly worded.' J. E. Stephenson, who was sent to the Hook of the Kafue in 1899 as an official in the North Eastern Rhodesia Administration, made some caustic remarks about the Thomson treaties in his book, Chirupula's Tale (Bles, London, 1937), p. 26.

[2] Lengthy extracts from his report are printed in the B.S.A. Company's Report of the Company's Proceedings, 1889–92, pp. 34–37.

Sharpe set out from Karonga, and went by way of Tanganyika to Lake Mweru, arriving at Kazembe's, near its south-eastern shore, at the end of September 1890. Kazembe, who was the most powerful native chief Sharpe had yet seen in Africa, was friendly, and agreed to sign a treaty accepting British protection and granting mineral concessions to the Chartered Company. Another important chief, named Nsama, whose territory of Itawa lay north of Kazembe's, did likewise. But although Sharpe was more successful than Thomson in that he was able to reach Msidi's, in November, he was quite unable to allay the suspicions of that shrewd old despot, who had taken heed of a warning given him by F. S. Arnot, the notable missionary, against signing papers submitted to him by Europeans, as by so doing he would be giving away his country. Sharpe thought for a time that his party, which was weak in numbers, would be attacked by order of the enraged chief—a cruel savage whose stockade was decorated with the decomposing heads of his victims. But Msidi contented himself with bidding the intruder be gone by the way he had come, and by no other, lest he spy out the country.[1] In the bitterness of his frustration Sharpe seems to have wished it were in his power to resort to force, so perhaps it would be unjust to contrast with his peaceful departure the action taken by a Belgian expedition (under an English officer, Captain Stairs) a year later, when Msidi was shot dead for persisting in his refusal to place his country under European rule.[2]

Even if Sharpe had been able to obtain Msidi's consent to a treaty, Katanga could not have become British territory. It lay within the boundaries of the Congo Free State, as defined by the Belgian authorities in a declaration issued on 1 August 1885; and Britain, which had formally recognized the existence of that 'state' in the previous December, had made no protest.[3] Her tacit acquiescence is not surprising, since at that time she was in no way interested in Katanga, and the South Africa Company did not yet exist. But in 1890 Sir Percy Anderson, speaking for the Foreign Office, made it clear to the Company that it was now too late for Britain to challenge the Belgian monarch's claim to Katanga, or

---

[1] F.O. 84/2114: Sharpe's report to Johnston, written at various times between 8 Sept. 1890 and 21 Feb. 1891, enclosed in Johnston to Salisbury, Confidential, 3 May 1891.

[2] Johnston's report of the affair, as related to him by Stairs himself, is in his No. 36, Confidential, 12 Oct. 1892, in F.O. 84/2197.

[3] Hertslet, vol. ii, pp. 552–3, 573.

to allow the Company to press its interests there as if that claim did not exist.[1]

But the treaties made by Thomson and Sharpe, together with Johnston's own, secured for Britain a belt of territory enveloping what was to become known as North Eastern Rhodesia. It was of no practical consequence that Mpeseni had refused to sign a treaty, and that the Bemba had never even been visited by a white man—for their lands lay within that circular belt, and would sooner or later be absorbed.

◦   ◦   ◦

Johnston was not content to stop at the south end of Tanganyika. He desired earnestly to establish a corridor of British territory north of that lake, to link the new acquisitions, and Cape Colony which lay behind them, with Uganda on the route to Egypt. So, when he was at the south end of Tanganyika in the course of his treaty-making expedition, he asked Swann to undertake for him the task of negotiating the cession to Britain, by the native chiefs, of the Rusizi valley, and thus securing the much-longed-for corridor to the north.[2] After his return to Mozambique, he sent Swann a packet of printed treaty-forms, which reached Tanganyika in July 1890. Swann had given Johnston no promise to do more than convey him or his representative around the lake in one of the Society's vessels, and he now wrote to him privately, pointing out that all official communications must be sent to the secretary of the Tanganyika District Committee, and that he had no authority to make use of the forms without definite instructions from the consul himself and from the Directors of the mission, to whom he asked Johnston to write.[3]

Johnston, however, knew very well the non-political character of the mission; he realized that to write to its authorities either in London or on the lake would be to invite a refusal. He therefore wrote again to Swann, privately, forbidding him to show his handwriting to anyone, and insisting: 'The North End is the highway to the Equatorial regions, and the Germans have despatched Emin Pasha to take it over and so close the door to Britain. *Go at once.* I ask you because there is no one else who can assist me in this crisis, and I trust your connection with the L.M.S. will prove no

---

[1] Cawston Papers, vol. ii; Cawston to Rhodes, 20 June 1890.
[2] Johnston, *The Story of My Life*, p. 275.
[3] L.M.S., C.A., 8.1.C: Swann to Thompson, 2 Aug. 1890.

hindrance. I will see your Directors about it, as I am going home to England.'[1]

Swann therefore asked his colleagues to support him in his decision to respond to the call; but they refused, and entirely dissociated themselves from his proposed course of action.[2] He was not deterred by this refusal. 'I considered', he told his Directors, 'the interests at stake warranted me in *sacrificing discipline*. . . . If I have erred, it has been that the people for whom I have laid out my life may be benefited; and whatever your verdict may be, I shall always feel the London M. Society have raised a monument on Tanganyika that is worthy of the illustrious Livingstone, viz: the British Ensign.'[3] He was anxious, moreover, that the Society should not be content to remain confined to the south end of the lake, and if it was to plant an offshoot in the north end, this would be much more easily done if the territory was British than if it was German. Certainly it was not self-interest that led him to take up the work, for he refused a generous honorarium offered in respect of it, and proudly informed Johnston 'that L.M.S. men are "*not to be hired*"'.[4]

Proceeding to Ujiji, he met Rumaliza, who spoke to him with much bitterness about the treatment accorded by Stanley and white men in general to Arabs who had helped them on their journeys, instead of closing the route to the interior against them. But, having thus relieved his feelings, he referred in the warmest terms to the memory of Livingstone, and showed himself as friendly as ever towards Swann. Swann had been accompanied by Frederick Moir, who had come for purposes of trade, and Rumaliza readily accepted his assurance that Moir could pay for whatever ivory he bought, and handed over nearly £1,000 worth on credit. At this time, with the route to the Zanzibar coast blocked by the Germans, the Ujiji Arabs were at a loss to know what to do with their ivory, and the Lakes Company had a wonderful opportunity to become almost its sole exporters: an opportunity which they completely lacked the capacity, and apparently also the will, to seize.[5]

---

[1] Quoted in Swann's report to Thompson, loc. cit.
[2] L.M.S., C.A., 8.1.D: Carson to Thompson, 2 Aug. 1890.
[3] Swann's report, loc. cit.
[4] L.M.S., C.A., 8.5.A: Swann to Thompson, Jan. 1892. The words in italics were underlined by Swann.
[5] Details are given, with scathing comments, in Sharpe to Johnston, 26

Rumaliza was eager to work with the British politically as well as commercially, as Swann found on the following evening, when they met with no one else present. 'I told him everything that had been done', Swann reported: 'that Ujiji was in German territory and the west coast Belgian. He said, "Give me the flag of England and I will hoist it here today."' On being told that this was no longer possible, but that the north end of the lake was as yet unappropriated by any European Power, he not only authorized but urged Swann to go there and take it for the Queen. 'Tell the natives your errand', he said, 'give them your flag, and tell them I send you.'

So Swann left Ujiji and sailed to the north end, where he made friends with the simple folk by organizing canoe races by the children,[1] obtained the signatures of the chiefs to his treaties, 'and endeavoured to prepare the way for those who bear the best Treaty, that of the Gospel'. Then he hastened back to Niamkolo, whence he forwarded the precious documents to Johnston at his London home.

His Directors read his long report of these proceedings with mixed feelings. Replying to it on their behalf, R. W. Thompson told him that 'as men and Englishmen' they were gratified, and congratulated him. As a Society, however, they were bound to disapprove. 'The policy of the Society through all the years of its history has been one of non-intervention in any political matters. This policy has been justified by frequent experience, and every departure from it on the part of the Society's agents has proved a source of trouble. . . . Moreover, we believe it to be not only the more expedient, but also the only right, course for a Missionary Society to take.' Nevertheless, while disapproving of his action, they saw no grounds for any severe censure of it, nor any reason to doubt the disinterestedness of his motives.

'Consul Johnston', added Thompson, 'has not fulfilled his promise to you by making any explanations to us. He has not come near this House since his arrival in England.'[2]

ᴖ   ᴖ   ᴖ

It was not only the north end of Tanganyika which was in dispute between Germany and Britain, for the Germans also claimed

Dec. 1890, enclosed in Johnston to Salisbury, Confidential, 6 May 1891 (in F.O. 84/2114).

[1] In his book, *Fighting the Slave-Hunters*, he gives a delightful account of how he managed this: pp. 218–20.

[2] L.M.S., Southern, outgoing: Thompson to Swann, 13 Dec. 1890.

the northern part of Lake Nyasa and the country south of Tanganyika. The Foreign Office appears to have sorrowfully reconciled itself to acquiescence: this seems to be implied in Anderson's comments on the treaties made with chiefs on the northern and north-western shores of Nyasa, and forwarded by Johnston with his account of the settlement of the Arab War:

The Treaties with chiefs seem to be all in the German hinterland; and it is a curious commentary on the German claims that the fighting at Karonga's, and the settlement in which the Germans had not, and could not have had, any part, are all concerned with the hinterland.

It is consequently a question whether we should tell the Germans of this settlement.

'Not necessary', replied Lord Salisbury.[1]

But when Johnston, on 30 January 1890, sent home a long telegram announcing his arrival that day in Mozambique and summarizing the achievements of his journey, the Foreign Office promptly replied, by telegraph, that his action was entirely approved so far as it was concerned with territory south of the parallel of 11° south latitude: north of that parallel, however, Britain was not free to take any action without German approval, because of an agreement made by the two Governments in the previous summer. His treaties would therefore be invalidated by that promise, and he was instructed to make no public statement about them.[2]

To this, Johnston answered as follows:

Will observe scrupulous secrecy about Tanganyika arrangements, but desire [to] impress on your Lordship that it is chiefly the magnificent country between [the] South end of Tanganyika and [the] eleventh parallel that is worth having for health and mineral wealth. My journey has convinced me of this, but [I] suspected it before, and [I was] therefore at first indifferent as to Southern Nyassa, but [the] value of [the] Shire Highlands [is] now enhanced since [the] discovery [of the] navigability [of the] Chinde. But [the] Tanganyika plateau [is the] finest country in all Africa, and already strangely anglicised.[3]

Whether or not Johnston could have his wish depended on the general character of the agreement eventually reached between Britain and Germany on the whole question of East Africa's politi-

[1] F.O. 84/1969: Johnston to Salisbury, 26 Oct. 1889: minutes.
[2] F.O. 84/2050: F.O. to Johnston, No. 4, 31 Jan. 1890.
[3] This and Johnston's telegram of 30 Jan. are both recorded in F.O. 84/2051: Johnston to Salisbury, No. 6, Africa, 1 Feb. 1890.

cal future. Since Britain's relations with France and Russia were
far from cordial, Britain was obliged to avoid friction with Germany, and to cultivate her goodwill by making concessions to
which Germany was in no way entitled. The Duke of Abercorn,
chairman of the South Africa Company's Board of Directors,
watched Lord Salisbury's moves with an anxious eye. 'The policy
of the Government', he wrote to his colleague, Cawston, on 23
March 1890, 'is that of extreme friendliness to Germany for the
exclusion of other nations, and this policy will have to be carried
out by us'. A fortnight later he was more outspoken:

You know *how anxious* Lord Salisbury is to please the German
Government, and in fact has been giving way to them as regards African
policy and delimitation of territory. . . . He must be watched, and I hope
he is not playing a fast and loose game with us and our possessions.
There is no doubt some arrangement with Germany, probably on
account of European policy. But if no protest is made against Germany
running up to the Congo frontier, which they are anxious to do, it will
look very like as if our Government were quietly and silently backing up
this policy.[1]

In the end, the cession of Heligoland enabled the British
Government to secure most of the Nyasa–Tanganyika plateau, as
well as a protectorate over the island of Zanzibar and the withdrawal
of the Germans from Witu, on the coast of what is now Kenya.[2]
The Anglo-German Agreement was signed in Berlin on 1 July.[3] By
its terms, the north end of Nyasa was recognized as part of German
East Africa, although its inhabitants had for long been under the
influence of Fotheringham and his assistant, Nicoll, the agents of
the Lakes Company at Karonga, and had joined forces with them
during the fighting against Mlozi. The Livingstonia Mission,
moreover, regarded the north end as part of its mission-field, and
its committee in Scotland went so far as to write to Sir Percy
Anderson, complaining bitterly against this provision and asking
that the question should be reopened. Anderson, of course, replied
that this was impossible.[4]

The German part of the Nyasa coast stopped at the River
Songwe, a considerable distance north of Karonga. From the

[1] Cawston Papers, vol. ii: Abercorn to Cawston, 29 Mar. and 5 Apr. 1890.
The words in italics were underlined by Abercorn.
[2] Cecil, *Life of Salisbury*, vol. iv, chap. 10.
[3] The Agreement, together with a small number of relevant dispatches, is
printed in A. & P., 1890, li, pp. 15–31. It is also in Hertslet, vol. iii, pp. 899–906.
[4] Mins., F.C. of S. For. Miss. Comm., 22 July 1890.

Songwe the frontier ran to the south-east of Tanganyika, following approximately the line of the Stevenson Road, though that 'road' itself was included in the British sphere.

The north end of Tanganyika, however, was secured by Germany. Whether or not it would have been otherwise had Swann's treaties reached England a few months earlier it is impossible to say: they were made at the end of July and the beginning of August, and did not reach London until December. They were then communicated to the Foreign Office by Johnston. 'This', commented Anderson, 'is the proceeding respecting which we have had the warm remonstrances from the London Missionary Society, and may have a still warmer one from the Germans.'[1]

The conclusion of a treaty with Portugal proved a more difficult matter than the arrangement with Germany. The Portuguese Government, indeed, realized that it would have to come to terms: Lord Salisbury's ultimatum had made it plain that they could no longer cherish the slightest hope of obtaining British recognition of their full claim. On 20 August 1890 a convention was signed, defining the boundaries between Portuguese East Africa and the British territories in the interior.[2] The Portuguese secured the country south of the Rovuma and east of Nyasa as far as the line of latitude 13° 30′ South; thence the boundary ran south-eastwards from the Nyasa coast, crossed Lake Chiuta, followed the eastern shore of Lake Shirwa, and ran due south to the Ruo, which it followed to its confluence with the Shiré. Thence a line was drawn on the map to a point on the Zambesi half-way between Tete and the Kebrabasa Rapids. The country north of this line, and north of the Zambesi above the point where it terminated, was British, except for a semicircle north of Zumbo whose radius was a mere ten miles.

South of the Zambesi the boundary ran due south from the western extremity of the Zumbo semicircle as far as the 16th parallel of south latitude, which it followed to its intersection with the 31st degree of east longitude. Thence it ran eastward and southward to the River Mazoe where that river is intersected by the 33rd degree of east longitude. From this point it continued due south to the parallel of latitude 18° 30′ South; then west to a tribu-

[1] F.O. 84/2052: Johnston to Salisbury, 5 Dec. 1890, with minutes. The treaties are enclosed.   [2] A. & P., 1890-1, lvii, pp. 588-96.

tary of the Sabi called the Masheke, following these rivers to the confluence of the Sabi and the Lunte, from which point it took a straight course to the Transvaal frontier.

On 25 July Johnston wrote to Rhodes from London begging him to accept the agreement. He had already, he said, sent two telegrams in the same sense. 'It is the best thing that can be done', he urged. 'And unless this Portuguese difficulty is first settled, the Government will not do anything towards consolidating our influence and interests over Trans-Zambesian Africa. . . . For Heaven's sake, let us get the Portuguese question settled somehow and quickly, so that we may set to work and administer British Central Africa before a hundred bogus claims and interloping Companies are started to contest with you the exclusive rights to mine and govern.'[1]

A month previously Johnston had written a confidential dispatch urging that the time was past when any hope could reasonably be placed in the policy which had found expression in his visit to Lisbon in 1889: that is, 'the policy of working East Africa through and with the Portuguese'. 'Moreover', he had declared, 'I return from Moçambique utterly disgusted with the simulacrum of Portuguese rule which would attempt to shut up or restrict the development of these rich provinces in a manner typically Turkish or Chinese. . . . I should be inclined to circumscribe their rights to the smallest possible dimensions and to recommend that any infringement on their part of our rights be punished by their gradual exclusion from East Africa.' But Lord Salisbury had given a decidedly unfavourable reception to this dispatch.[2] He was, as Johnston afterwards put it in a letter to Rhodes, 'in one of his cold fits'. He had to consider not only the feelings of the Portuguese but the attitude of other Powers, and he had also to take account of the serious concern felt by Queen Victoria lest the Portuguese monarchy should be overthrown as a result of too sharp a national humiliation at the hands of Britain.[3] So Johnston drew the

---

[1] Rhodes Papers, Charters, 3A, 18: dated 25 July 1890.

[2] The dispatch, dated 28 June 1890, is in F.O. 84/2052; Johnston's letter to Rhodes mentioning Salisbury's reception of it is in Rhodes Papers, Charters, 3A, 52, dated 13 Oct. 1890.

[3] 'He [Rhodes] will need guiding by [those] acquainted with European politics. These Portuguese questions cannot be treated as if they were colonial. They involve among other things the existence of monarchical government in the Iberian peninsula.' Kirk to Cawston, 13 Jan. 1891 (Cawston Papers, vol. iii).

conclusion, expressed in his plea to Rhodes, that nothing would be gained by pressing for a more favourable territorial settlement, and that delay could do nothing but harm to British interests.

Rhodes, however, was infuriated by the treaty. He abused Johnston for supporting it, and even threatened to withdraw from the South Africa Company because his fellow Directors were less bellicose than himself.[1] 'I am afraid', wrote the Duke of Abercorn on 16 August, 'that Rhodes's views on action as regards Portugal cannot be entertained by the Government. A settlement must be arrived at. It is an Imperial question, not a South African one entirely. Rhodes only looks upon it in the latter light.'[2] Three days later, the day before the Agreement was actually signed, Abercorn's impression was confirmed by a letter from the Foreign Office written by Sir Philip Currie:

It is a pity that Rhodes is so exacting, but it is now too late to draw back. . . . I am quite unable to understand Rhodes's policy, unless he proposes to make war on Portugal, seize her territories, and occupy her ports. The arrangement we have proposed is a vast improvement on the present state of things, and the utmost that there is any chance of obtaining without the use of force. It is not probable that Her Majesty's Government would sanction the Company engaging in hostilities with a European Power, and they are likely to have enough on their hands in dealing with Lobengula and the other colored [sic] potentates with whom they have relations.[3]

'Rhodes', remarked Abercorn, 'is I fancy a little bit of an autocrat, and he does not consider that in dealing with Portugal's claims the Government have a line of policy to pursue, which I conclude must also be acceptable to Germany as well as this country.'[4] And on 25 September he remarked that he had received a letter from Lord Salisbury, who 'apparently has had enough of Rhodes'.

By that time, however, the treaty had come before the Cortes for ratification, and had been given such a cold reception that the

[1] This is fairly clearly implied by Abercorn in a letter to Cawston dated 29 Sept. (Cawston Papers, vol. ii), containing the sentence: 'Rhodes sends off very fiery telegrams, but I trust he really has no intention of severing himself from our Company, as this would be disastrous; but I have pointed out to Lord Salisbury that his wishes should be listened to, as he is a man of great influence, power and knowledge.' [2] To Cawston. Cawston Papers, vol. ii.

[3] Ibid., Currie to Cawston, 19 Aug. 1890.

[4] Ibid., to Cawston; date missing, probably early Sept. (1890).

Foreign Minister resigned, followed a day later by the rest of the Cabinet.[1] Salisbury therefore sent a telegram to Petre, on 21 September, instructing him to inform the Portuguese Government unofficially that if that Cortes did not at once ratify the agreement, the British Government would act as if they had rejected it. 'It is impossible', he declared, 'for Great Britain to remain bound, while Portugal is not bound, by the Convention.'[2]

On 23 September Rhodes wrote to Sir Philip Currie at the Foreign Office to make his position plain. 'Now that the Portuguese Ministry has resigned', he urged, 'I hope you will drop this wretched treaty, under which we get nothing and give away a great deal. . . . You have given away Manika. My people are now occupying and out of it *they will not go*, and further they will not be ruled by a half-caste Portugee and I hope you will draw Lord Salisbury's attention to this fact.' He went on to denounce Portuguese ill treatment of the natives, and then declared:

It is to a nation of this kind that you are for no valid reason giving away half of Africa. . . . The Portuguese have proved that they can neither govern whites or blacks. I should like to ask you are you going to use English soldiers to force our people to accept Portuguese rule in a country where there is not a single Portugee, why the whole thing is ridiculous. . . . What single advantage did you obtain? Is it that Portuguese half-castes agreed not to drive your people out of Blantyre where they had been for fifteen years? Or is it that you got a free Zambesi? Why you always had that. South of the Zambesi you certainly obtained nothing for me. I can hold my own against the Portuguese.[3]

The non-ratification of the Convention was followed by the negotiation, as an interim measure, of a *modus vivendi* between Britain and Portugal, concluded on 14 November 1890. This provided that 'neither Power will make Treaties, accept Protectorates, or exercise any act of sovereignty within the spheres of influence assigned to the other party by the said Convention. But neither Power will thereby be held to prejudice any question whatever which may arise as to the said territorial limits in the course of the ulterior negotiations.'[4] Lord Salisbury, however, made it clear that while this understanding would be binding on the Government,

---

[1] A. & P., 1890-1, lvii, pp. 601-3: Petre to Salisbury, 16 Sept. 1890, with enclosure, and 17 Sept. 1890; pp. 606-7: P. to S. 18 Sept. 1890.
[2] A. & P., 1890-1, lvii, p. 603: Salisbury to Petre, 21 Sept. 1890.
[3] Rhodes Papers, Charters, 3A, 63: Rhodes to Currie, 23 Sept. 1890.
[4] A. & P., 1890-1, lvii, pp. 613-14.

he was not going to try to enforce it if it were violated by Rhodes. 'It is the business of the Portuguese to protect their own territory', he told the Queen.[1]

While this *modus vivendi* was being negotiated, Rhodes sent some of his 'Pioneers' into Manica, and, on the very day after it was signed, their leader, Major Forbes, arrested Paiva d'Andrade and Manoel Antonio de Souza, who were themselves attempting to occupy Manica on behalf of Portugal. The sequence of events was explained to the Foreign Office by Cawston as follows:

On the 18th October we received the following telegram from Kimberley: 'Since the refusal of the treaty by the Cortes, Rhodes has given instructions to effectually occupy Manica.' Our representative received his instructions to go to Manica long before the 20th August [the date on which the treaty was signed], but no steps were taken by the Company to occupy the country until by the breaking up of the Cortes [on 15th October] it was inferred that the agreement did not exist. . . .[2]

Five days before Forbes arrested the Portuguese leaders, the following telegram had been sent to Rhodes by his agent, Dr. Rutherfoord Harris, in the name of the Directors in London:

Our impression is, Government acquiesce in [the] occupation of Manica but dare not say so. We advise you to occupy, secure as many concessions as possible: you should strengthen the Government hand in case of new agreements. Send all the evidence you can against Portugal's claims.[3]

In fact, the Government drew a distinction between obtaining concessions from native chiefs in territory which the treaty had assigned to Portugal and setting up an administration in such territory; it approved the former but not the latter.[4] In the event, the Foreign Office, deluged with Portuguese protests, administered a rebuke which Abercorn described as 'wild', though he admitted that 'no doubt Rhodes rather exceeded his limits of action'.[5]

Whether or not Lord Salisbury had any secret sympathy with the filibustering activities of Rhodes, his attitude to Portugal had certainly stiffened by the end of the year 1890. How exasperated

---

[1] Cecil, *Life of Salisbury*, vol. iv, p. 269.
[2] Cawston Papers, vol. iii; dated 7 Dec. 1890 (Copy).
[3] Rhodes Papers, Charters, 3A, 66; dated 10 Nov.
[4] As Cawston explained to Hawksley on 6 Nov. (Copy in Cawston Papers, vol. ii).
[5] Ibid., vol. iii: Abercorn to Cawston, 30 Dec. 1890.

he had become is shown by the tone of a private letter to Petre, written on 24 December, in which he declared that the Portuguese were in 'a fool's Paradise' if they imagined that Britain would accept less than she had obtained by the treaty of 20 August, and added, 'I think your language should be stiff and uncompromising'. If the Portuguese did not adopt a reasonable attitude, especially in granting facilities for communications across their dominions, 'they must expect much more rigorous terms in the delimitation of frontier than those of August 20th'.[1]

The Prime Minister was not content with words alone. Knowing that an ounce of pressure applied locally was worth a pound applied at Lisbon, he arranged for the navy to send out two gunboats to operate on the Zambesi and Lower Shiré, to protect British interests from Portuguese interference, and vindicate by their presence the right of free navigation on the waterway. More than a year after their arrival, Johnston reported from Nyasaland that

the presence of the two gunboats on the Zambesi has been and is the chiefest means of preserving peace with the Portuguese. The Portuguese officials in the Zambesi district are utterly indifferent to orders from home or from their superior officers at Moçambique. They are only restrained from continuing that arbitrary and illegal interference with British political and commercial interests (which nearly provoked a conflict between the two nations in 1889–90 and '91) by the pressure of the two British gunboats on the Zambesi–Shire. These gunboats therefore cannot be removed, unless it is intended to abandon all British interests in Central Africa.[2]

Although the Manica incident gave rise to prolonged recriminations, the Portuguese eventually came to realize that a treaty would have to be made in a manner satisfactory to British requirements. So, on 11 June 1891, a new Convention was signed, the Cortes having quietly approved its bases on the previous day.[3] Britain secured the Manica plateau, which the South Africa Company coveted for the sake of its gold, and Portugal was given, as compensation, a large tract of territory north of the Zambesi and west of the Shiré. The British Protectorate in the Shiré valley was

[1] Quoted in Cecil, *Life of Salisbury*, vol. iv, pp. 270–1.
[2] F.O. 84/2197: Johnston to Salisbury, No. 2, 12 Feb. 1892.
[3] A. & P., 1890–1, lvii, p. 906: Petre to Salisbury, 11 and 12 June 1891; ibid., pp. 625–9.

somewhat enlarged by the addition of a strip of land extending some miles down the right bank of the river below its confluence with the Ruo, and bounded on the west by the watershed between the Shiré and the Zambesi. Freedom of navigation on these rivers was recognized, as it had been in the previous Convention and in the *modus vivendi*; and, as the necessary complement of this provision, Britain obtained for ninety-nine years a lease of a piece of land at the Chinde mouth for the construction of warehouses and the transhipment of goods on their way into or out of the British territory in the interior. In return for the Chinde concession Britain leased to Portugal on similar terms a similar area of land at Leopard Bay, on the south-west shore of Lake Nyasa: the rents of the two concessions cancelling each other out.[1]

Thus Britain's long dispute with Portugal was at last brought to an end. But her political involvement in the Nyasa–Tanganyika country had only just begun.

---

[1] The detailed agreements concerning the Chinde and Leopard Bay concessions, like the demarcation of the frontier, were necessarily made locally at a later date. The Chinde agreement was signed on 19 Sept. 1891 (F.O. 84/2115: Sharpe to Salisbury, 6 Nov. 1891), and the Leopard Bay agreement on the following 29 Dec. (F.O. 84/2114: Johnston to Salisbury, No. 28, C.A., 30 Dec. 1891). Clause 12 of the latter document stated that the validity of the agreement was 'entirely dependent on the full execution' by the Portuguese Government of the undertakings it had made by the terms of the former.

Ten years later, by an agreement dated 12 Jan. 1901, Portugal exchanged the Leopard Bay concession for a similar one at Rhoades Bay, farther south (Hertslet, vol. iii, p. 1071).

III

THE ESTABLISHMENT OF BRITISH
CENTRAL AFRICA

1. *Two Companies and a Consul*

WHEN John Buchanan declared the Makololo country to
be under British protection, his sole purpose was to commit his Government to taking action against Portugal if
her representatives led their forces across the Ruo. Similarly, when,
in May 1890, Sharpe saluted the British flag and 'formally declared the whole country west of the Loangwa and north of the
Zambesi to be under British protection', he was merely putting a
claim on record, and did not mean that he saw any immediate
prospect of protecting the miserable inhabitants from the raids of
Matakenya. Indeed, on reading his report, Lord Salisbury commented: 'It is rather comical that all this should have been declared to be under our influence.' The term 'protection', in fact,
meant no more than the exclusion of other European Powers.

Nevertheless, by the very act of denying to others the right to
annex south-central Africa, Britain necessarily assumed a certain
amount of responsibility for its future. It had now become her
duty to see that slave-raiding was brought to an end, and that the
white men who were arriving in growing numbers were not
allowed to violate civilized standards of conduct in their dealings
with the natives and with one another. However reluctant she
might be to face the fact, she was now under an obligation to
provide some kind of administration and police for her 'sphere of
influence' north of the Zambesi.

Since there was no possibility that this obligation would at once
be accepted by the Treasury and the House of Commons, the
South Africa Company assumed the financial burden of making
British political control effective north of the Zambesi. Sir John
Kirk, who seems to have assumed that the Company—in which he
held shares—ought to be concerned solely with its own interests as
a commercial undertaking, complained that this commitment was

'money thrown away', and thought the whole British sphere north of the Zambesi should be handed over to the Portuguese in exchange for territory in the south;[1] and had the Company not been devoted to northward expansion as an imperial ideal even more than as a business venture, it might have recognized the worldly wisdom of his advice.

But although its charter did not prescribe any northern boundary to its sphere of operations, it had no clear mandate to extend its control beyond the Zambesi; moreover, its own energies were fully occupied in laying the foundations of what was to become Southern Rhodesia. It therefore entered into an arrangement with the African Lakes Company, which already had some sort of organization throughout Nyasaland and along the Stevenson Road, and had for several years been ambitious to assume the functions of a Chartered Company in its own right. The South Africa Company bought Lakes Company shares to the value of £20,000, as a preliminary to the absorption of that company; it also agreed to provide a sum not exceeding £9,000 a year, from 1 January 1890, 'for the purpose of maintaining law and order north of the Zambesi, and for the protection of mission stations'.[2]

The interval between the declaration of a protectorate in 1889 and the creation of an administration in 1891 was employed by certain concession-hunters, of doubtful antecedents, to obtain from native chiefs extensive grants of land and mineral rights. The most important were E. C. Sharrer, a German who had become a naturalized British subject, and who had been declared bankrupt in the British court at Zanzibar, and L. P. Bowler, the agent of a German who had interests in the Transvaal. When Joseph Thomson was passing through Quilimane in June 1890, he wrote to George Cawston, one of the Directors of the South Africa Company, that

the irrepressible L. P. Bowler arrived here with several men and a huge quantity of goods etc.—including the sections of a boat—in the same steamer as myself and bound also for the Lake. There are many stories as to his objects, more or less near the truth, but whatever they are they mean mischief. . . . Bowler says that Rankin [the discoverer of the Chinde, but a distinctly 'shady' character] is going to join him.

---

[1] Cawston Papers, vol. iii: Kirk to Cawston, 13 Jan. 1891; cf. vol. ii, 8 Nov. 1890.
[2] B.S.A. Co.: *Directors' Report and Accounts*, 31 Mar. 1891, p. 16.

There is a German on the Lake at present named Sharer [*sic*] who is buying right and left. These facts point to the importance of hurrying on the negotiations for a final settlement . . . with the African Lakes Company so as to get your charter extended to put you in a position to deal with all these cases, otherwise you may soon find that there are a good many other people to deal with who will doubtless be sufficiently unscrupulous in putting forth their real or imaginary claims.[1]

A fortnight before these words were written Consul Johnston had arrived in London on leave of absence, to recover from illness caused by the strain and hardship of his hurried journey to the interior of Africa; and on 12 July he wrote to Cawston confidentially as follows:

Disagreeable news has arrived about Bowler's intentions to establish himself on Nyasa. To safeguard your interests you and the Lakes Company should buy up all the land and territorial and mining rights everywhere, especially in [the] Shire Highlands, along [the] course of [the] Shire above [the] Ruo and from Matope to Mponda's (you have already got Monkey Bay) and *all the west coast of Nyasa* from Monkey Bay up to Karonga (you have already got the north end beyond Karonga). But especially buy up all the southern part. If Bowler chooses to go east of Nyasa, let him.

Can you have the substance of this telegraphed out to some competent person in the Lakes Company's employ in those regions? Better concert matters with Ewing [the secretary of the Lakes Company]. But move quickly, *please*.[2]

Thus prompted, the Directors requested Ewing to send to his company's representatives in Nyasaland a cable in code as follows:

Buy all lands west Nyassa Shire Highlands Upper Shire same manner as you purchased land north Nyassa under Johnston's direction. Fred Moir should do this. Expenses B.S.A.C.[3]

But it is fairly clear that the Directors of the Lakes Company, regardless of the controlling interest which the Chartered Company had acquired in their affairs, had set themselves with Scottish dourness to pursue their own course in their own way. Little or nothing was done to comply with the request, but a year later Sharpe found that Frederick Moir was obtaining what purported

---

[1] Cawston Papers, vol. iv: letter dated 22 June [1890].
[2] Ibid., vol. ii.
[3] Rhodes Papers, Charters, 3A, 30: Weatherley to Ewing, 16 July 1890. Cf. below, p. 177.

to be sales of land on behalf of the Lakes Company alone, and was making absurdly small payments in return. Makandanji, for example, was alleged to have disposed of his entire country for £5 or £6; so was Liwonde. 'These two', wrote Sharpe, 'F. M. had the cheek to send to Buchanan to verify and register, but both Makandanji and Liwonde disclaimed any intention of selling their countries.'[1]

It is, indeed, hard to see what the Lakes Company did in return for the £13,500 which they received during the eighteen months when they were supposed to be administering Nyasaland. Johnston became increasingly impatient and exasperated, and he plied Cawston with letters. 'What I feel *earnestly*', he wrote on 18 July, 'is that the matter should soon be brought to a decisive issue; that you should make up your minds speedily as to your willingness and power [i.e. financial ability] to administer British Central Africa, and then apply to the Government for powers to do so. But there must be no one horse business. *The Glasgow Board are not capable of administering British Central Africa.*'[2] And, barely three weeks later, he returned to the charge:

Now, are you going to let Nyasaland slip through your hands? It looks like it. After all our worry and trouble in making arrangements with Germany and Portugal, we shall find nearly all the soil of Nyasaland bought up by Scharrer and Bowler and others of that sort. And this mainly because you are content to leave the management of these parts in the hands of the Glasgow people.

'Why don't you make haste and swallow up, absorb, digest, deglute the African Lakes Company?' he demanded on 8 October; and on the 13th he fired a full broadside:

... I won't hold any more converse with the South Africa Company in any way whatever till you have completely absorbed the African Lakes Company and have stepped into its shoes. As long as from scruples of over-kindly good nature or from the dread of spending money you allow the A.L. Co. to maintain an independent existence, you have no claim to be consulted or considered in Nyasaland matters. I judge the A.L. Co. utterly unfitted to be entrusted with governing powers, so unless and until the South Africa Company has swallowed it up and has

---

[1] F.O. 84/2114: Sharpe to Johnston, 3 June 1891, enclosed in Johnston to Salisbury, No. 6, C.A., 7 July 1891.
[2] Italicized words underlined by Johnston.

sat in its place and calls to me from Nyasaland 'Here I am, where once the A.L. Co. was' I shall devote my attention wholly to seeing in what way this country [i.e. Nyasaland] can be rescued from anarchy and its affairs controlled by the Imperial Government.

I have written a long letter to the Duke of Abercorn, which I have authorised His Grace to lay before the Board; I am writing to-day a long letter to Rhodes in answer to one I received from him this morning; this closes the matter as far as I am concerned.

As long as there exists in any shape or form such an association as the A.L. Co. I will discuss with you the new pieces at the theatre, the chances of the Government at the next election, the Trans-Siberian railway, or any becoming topic of conversation *except* Africa between the 4th and 37th degrees of South latitude.[1]

The negotiations between the two companies, however, lasted not months but years. Kirk, who tried to act, as he put it, 'as a sort of intermediary' in the spring of 1892, reached the conclusion that the Lakes Company was 'playing a foolish game'. 'I am quite tired of them', he wrote, 'for there is no finality in anything they do.' But the reluctance was not entirely on the part of the Lakes Company, and, according to Kirk, there had been 'a want of tact shown on both sides'. The Duke of Abercorn was probably expressing the general sentiment of his colleagues on the Board of the Chartered Company when he wrote, in November 1890: 'I suppose we must submit to a necessity and the amalgamation must take place, together with the admission to our Board of a Director of the Lakes Company. It is most distasteful to have all our doings made known to one of that lot.'[2]

At last, on 4 August 1893, an agreement providing for the voluntary liquidation of the Lakes Company was signed and sealed. The more important concessions which, at various times between 1885 and 1891, it had acquired from native chiefs were transferred to the Chartered Company, which thus became proprietor of the soil both over the entire area of the Nyasaland Protectorate north of the River Rukuru—some $2\frac{3}{4}$ million acres—and over a further $1\frac{1}{2}$ million acres in the region of the Stevenson Road, west of the Protectorate. It also acquired from the Lakes Company the exclusive mineral rights in Marimba (Jumbe's country), in Central and Southern Angoniland, and in the countries of Mwasi Kazungu and of Undi, important chiefs of the Chewa tribe dwelling along the

---

[1] These letters are in the Cawston Papers, vol. ii.   [2] Ibid.

watershed west of Lake Nyasa.[1] In Central (but not Southern) Angoniland, and in Mwasi Kazungu's country, these rights were accompanied by rights of pre-emption.

The Lakes Company's trading functions and assets were not, however, taken over by the South Africa Company. They passed to a new Scottish association, the African Lakes Trading Corporation Limited, which soon afterwards shortened its name by dropping the word 'Trading'. Frederick Moir became its secretary, and his brother John was dismissed, being succeeded as manager by the incomparably more efficient and sensible Fotheringham. Thus reorganized, and disposing of a capital of £150,000, the Corporation settled down to a prosperous and useful existence as a purely business concern. Its interests were agricultural as well as commercial, for it inherited from the Lakes Company some 40,000 acres of land.[2]

Johnston, who had by this time formed the habit of describing the Lakes Company, in his private letters to the South Africa Company, as 'the Vampire', derided this agreement, summarizing it as follows:

(a). That you give back to the Vampire all that it has which is worth having, that is to say, all its steamers, its plant, and the 999 shares hitherto held by the British South Africa Company. (b). That while the Lakes Company affects to hand over to you its landed possessions out here, you in turn agree to hand back to it the cream of the said

[1] And thus being partly in Nyasaland and partly in Northern Rhodesia. Part of Undi's tribe also found itself situated within Portuguese East Africa—as did part of the southern Angoni ruled by Chikusi.

[2] I am greatly indebted to Sir Dougal Malcolm for providing me with copies of the relevant Certificates of Claim and of the Agreements of 1890, 1893, and 1895, and of the 'General Disposition and Assignation', dated 10 Apr. 1895.

The allocation of the Lakes Company's land between the South Africa Company and the Lakes Corporation was made by an amending Agreement dated 3 Apr. 1895. The land acquired by the Corporation was situated as follows (figures in acres): Karonga, 6,000; Fife, 6,000; Kituta (Abercorn), 6,000; Mandala (Blantyre), about 5,500; Angoniland (Chikusi's), 5,000; Matope, 3,000; Leopard Bay, 2,000; Chiwara, 2,000; Mweru, 2,000; Liwonde, 1,500; also a relatively small estate of unspecified extent at Katunga, and eight plots of land in Chiromo township, besides 35 acres in various small holdings (10 at Deep Bay, 4 at Fort Johnston, &c.).

The South Africa Company acquired from the Lakes Company, in addition to the vast tracts mentioned in the text, some 20,000 acres in the vicinity of Matope, 840 acres in Mlanje (Namonde's), 500 acres at Mandala, and a dozen plots of land in Chiromo township.

Besides all this, a further 4,200 acres on Mlanje had been owned by the Lakes Company: this was sold to John Moir.

landed possessions, viz. 2,500 acres round each one of their stations. This is simply ridiculous.[1]

Subsequent experience was, in fact, to show that there was scant economic advantage to be had from the Chartered Company's acquisitions, impressive though they were in appearance. But even if the price was high, the transaction put an end at last to the Lakes Company as a factor in the political affairs of Central Africa.

Arrangements for the effective administration of Nyasaland had not, however, remained in suspense until this business agreement was completed. Having withdrawn from its fairly definite understanding with Lugard without even troubling to notify him of the fact, the South Africa Company had turned to Johnston instead. On 3 November 1890 Cawston wrote to him that the question of administration was being 'continually' discussed by the Chartered Company's Board, and disclosed unofficially that 'the general feeling is to ask if you would care to accept the appointment from us'. If Johnston's answer was favourable he would bring the matter before the Board at its next meeting. What was contemplated was to entrust Johnston with the £9,000 a year which were at that time being paid to the Lakes Company, and a larger sum 'if good cause shewn'.

Johnston promptly replied that his answer must depend on the attitude of Lord Salisbury and the Foreign Office, because he did not intend to abandon his position in the consular service. He would willingly accept the offer, provided that he could 'induce the Foreign Office to allow me to be a sort of Consul General for South-East Africa and (temporarily) an Administrator for the B.S.A. Company in Trans-Zambesian Africa. . . . But, if the Foreign Office cannot be got to come to some arrangement by which I can serve two masters, why I must continue to serve the first one.' He assured Cawston that, even if he remained at Mozambique as consul, he would accord the Company's administration 'the same willing support and assistance as you have met with at my hands from the day of your Company's birth, and will meet with as long as you remain an Imperial factor'.

A few days later, after discussions at the Foreign Office, he informed Cawston that Lord Salisbury thought 'that it was highly

[1] B.S.A. Co. Papers, Cape Town: Johnston to Secretary of the B.S.A. Co., 23 July 1893.

unadvisable that I or any one should take up that post while administrative powers [north of the Zambesi] remained unconferred on the Company, and that inasmuch as it might be some time before that happened, and matters out there required speedy and effective control, I had better prepare myself to return to south-east Africa as soon as possible to resume my Consular work on a somewhat more extended scale'.

The stumbling-block was what the Duke of Abercorn described as 'Scotch jealousies and cussedness': that is, not only the independent attitude of the Lakes Company, but also the determination of the Scottish missions not to be placed, if they could help it, under the rule of the South Africa Company. Consequently Abercorn and his colleagues began to favour the idea of separating Nyasaland from the Company's sphere, and of paying the annual subsidy of £9,000 to the Government on condition that it accepted the territory as a direct imperial responsibility.[1] The idea was discussed with Currie and Anderson, of the Foreign Office, and on 17 December Anderson wrote privately to Cawston:

I have been thinking over our yesterday's conversation, and am disposed to think that the question of administration is a serious obstacle to your pecuniary arrangements with the Lakes Company, as, put it how you may, you are giving £9,000 a year for the maintenance of law and order, which cannot be so used by the recipient.

On the other hand, it might be employed to useful purpose by the real administering body, the Government, who might not find it easy to get a grant from the House of Commons.

If you should be disposed to follow this train of thought and would see your way to working it into a proposal, I am disposed to think that Lord Salisbury should have the chance of considering it: what his view might be I of course could not at present say.[2]

By this time Johnston had been told unofficially that Lord Salisbury had decided to send him out to Nyasaland with the status of Commissioner, and that he would have an assistant. But no arrangement had been made to provide him with the first requirement of all government, an armed force to make his authority effective; and although he pleaded that without some force at his disposal he and his assistant would be as impotent as Hawes had been—'two lone men giving out a *vox et praeterea nihil*'—he had

---

[1] Cawston Papers, vol. ii: Abercorn to Cawston, 30 Nov. 1890.
[2] Cawston Papers, vol. ii.

to be told that it had been as much as the Foreign Office could do to extract from the Treasury the funds necessary for the two salaries, and that it would be hopeless to press for more.[1] If, then, his administration was not to be a tragi-comedy, he must have a subsidy from the South Africa Company. But he himself insisted that it would be utterly inconsistent with the dignity of Government that its representative should be little more than a puppet in the hands of the Chartered Company, compelled to dance to its piping because it possessed the power of the purse.[2]

In these circumstances, what was necessary was an arrangement by which the Company would provide the Government with the funds necessary to maintain an armed force, but would leave it with complete freedom of action. Early in February 1891, when Rhodes was in London, Johnston 'had three hours' talk with him and settled everything—or I should say settled the main lines of our understanding. . . . I got him to put the basis of the arrangement in writing and took it to the Foreign Office this morning [9 February]. Except in one little point, not of cardinal importance, it (the arrangement) answered Lord Salisbury's views (so Currie told me).'[3]

According to this scheme, as Johnston himself expounded it in a letter to Currie, the British territory north of the Zambesi was to be divided into two parts, one of which would include all four missions and would be administered by the Government, while the other part would be administered by the Company. The Government's sphere, bounded on the south and south-east by the Portuguese frontier, was to extend westwards from Lake Nyasa as far as the watershed between the Lake and the Congo; and, north of latitude 10° S., its boundary would leave the watershed and follow a line parallel to the Stevenson Road, so as to include the south end of Lake Tanganyika and most of the Nyasa–Tanganyika plateau.

Within this sphere the South Africa Company would not interfere in any way. 'If its servants traded or mined within the limits of Nyasaland in such portions of land as the Company may have already bought, they would do so as private individuals subject to the same conditions as other traders or miners.'

[1] F.O. 84/2052: Johnston to Barrington, 15 Dec. 1890; F.O. 84/2050: Anderson to Johnston, 22 Dec. 1890.   [2] Johnston to Barrington, loc. cit.
[3] Cawston Papers, vol. iii: Johnston to Cawston, 9 Feb. 1891.

Moreover, although the British territories[1] west of Nyasaland would be 'directly developed and "exploited" by the South Africa Company, and be brought within the scope of its Charter', yet 'the political control of these lands will be considered to be vested solely in Her Majesty's Commissioner for Nyasaland, who will also exercise such supervision over the doings of the Company's employés, and over all "foreigners",[2] as may be necessary to the maintenance of peace and order'. He would also have control over the Company's armed forces north of the Zambesi, employing them wherever he pleased, and being authorized to concentrate them all, if he chose, in Nyasaland. The Company would spend £10,000 a year on their maintenance and for purposes of general administration: no part of this sum—which was in lieu of the subsidy of £9,000 formerly paid to the Lakes Company—was to be spent 'on purely commercial matters'. The Commissioner would 'have absolutely nothing to do' with the Company's commercial expenditure, nor would he have any control over its trading agents—provided, of course, they did not infringe his regulations. Such agents, when residing within the imperially-administered territory, would be as much liable to taxation as anyone else.[3]

A few days after this proposal was submitted to the Foreign Office, Johnston was formally given his appointment 'to be Her Majesty's Commissioner and Consul-General to the Territories under British influence to the north of the Zambesi'.[4] About the same time the agreement between the Government and the Company was made definitive. The Charter was to extend north of the Zambesi as far as German East Africa and the Congo Free State; Nyasaland was excluded, but its boundary was to follow the Nyasa–Congo watershed all the way northwards to the German frontier, so that the Nyasa–Tanganyika plateau was assigned to the Company's sphere. The provisions about the annual subsidy and the Commissioner's political control over the Company's sphere were to last until 1 January 1894, and after that day the arrange-

---

[1] Strictly speaking, they were not British at all, and should be called (as Johnston called them in the letter referred to) 'territories within the British sphere of influence'; but this is excessively cumbrous, and 'British-influenced territories' would be misleading. Nor could they be called 'British-protected' (notwithstanding Sharpe's treaties and declaration) until 1924.

[2] i.e. non-Africans, including British.

[3] F.O. 84/2114: Johnston to Currie, 9 Feb. 1891.

[4] F.O. 84/2113: F.O. to Johnston, 14 Feb. 1891.

ment was renewable, at the discretion of the Government, for a further period not exceeding two years.[1]

Some weeks later, on 24 March, Johnston was provided with his instructions.[2] He was to retain the Mozambique consulate as well as his new post, leaving a vice-consul in charge when he was absent on account of his administrative duties. It is extraordinary that the position of administrator in a vast, inchoate, anarchic dependency should have been in effect regarded as a part-time appointment; but the idea was his own,[3] and is not by any means the only example of his exuberant over-optimism.

In the Nyassa districts [the instructions declared] your duty will be to supervise the organisation of the administration of justice as regards foreigners (under which heading British subjects are, for this purpose, included); to consolidate the protectorate of Her Majesty over the native chiefs; to advise those chiefs on their external relations with each other and with foreigners, not interfering unduly with their internal administration; to secure peace and order; and by every legitimate means in your power, to check the slave trade.

He was to observe scrupulously the provisions of the Berlin Act (1885) and of the Brussels Act (1890)—the two great international agreements regulating European activity in tropical Africa. For the rest, the conditions under which he was to work were approximately those he had himself set forth in his letter of 9 February.

On 14 May 1891 the Foreign Office issued a formal notification, which was published in the *London Gazette* on the following day, that 'under and by virtue of Agreements with the native Chiefs, and by other lawful means, the territories in Africa, hereinafter referred to as the Nyasaland Districts, are under the Protectorate of Her Majesty the Queen'.[4] The Nyasaland Protectorate thus received its birth certificate.

2. *The Establishment of Order*

On his way out to Nyasaland to take up his new duties, Johnston paused at Chinde to secure the British concession there 'before the

---

[1] C. 7637 (A. & P., 1895), pp. 1–2. The Foreign Office availed itself of this provision, in a letter to the Company dated 8 Dec. 1893. The letter stated that 'the arrangement will be renewed subject to any agreement which may hereafter be arrived at with the Company as to its modification'.

[2] F.O. 84/2113: F.O. to Johnston, 24 Mar. 1891.

[3] F.O. 84/2052: Memorandum on the administration of Nyasaland (Confidential), dated 7 Oct. 1890.

[4] Printed in Hertslet, *The Map of Africa by Treaty*, vol. i, p. 286.

rush of speculation and land-grabbers should come'. Since a provision in the law of Portuguese East Africa gave squatters on unoccupied land a prescriptive right, over other applicants, of legal tenure, he marked off 400 metres of river frontage behind which lay nearly all the good building ground on the south bank of the river, and, in his own words, 'endeavoured to accentuate this "squatting" by hurrying the naval authorities and the Lakes Company into the erection of stores and houses'. The local Portuguese authorities, he remarked, 'are very unwilling to give us anything, but when we have once taken hold are equally loth to turn us out'. His tactics were successful. True, the agreement obtained from the Portuguese Commissioner a few weeks later brought only some 10 hectares (25 acres) within the concession, instead of the 100 hectares which had been asked; but the water frontage of 400 metres remained unchanged, and the Portuguese had no objection to granting an 'extra concession' of about 50 hectares (125 acres) immediately behind—that is, inland from—the other, provided that this additional area should not enjoy exemption from their customs duties. After what Johnston called 'the usual delays' this further grant was made in 1893. The British could not reasonably expect more favourable treatment: the concession proper was quite large enough for the erection of bonded stores for goods which were in transit, free of duty, to British-protected territory, and there was no justification for expecting that the exemption from duty should be extended to goods not in transit, but intended for consumption by the growing British community who worked at Chinde itself, and to whom the 'extra concession' was assigned as private living-space.[1]

The concession proper was almost cut into two fairly equal parts by a tidal swamp which extended southwards from the river, covering some 4 or 5 acres and reducing the area suitable for building to about 20 acres. By August 1892 the Nyasaland Ad-

[1] F.O. 84/2114: Johnston to Salisbury, No. 3, C.A., 28 June 1891; No. 4, C.A., 7 July 1891; No. 5, C.A., 7 July 1891; F.O. 84/2115: Sharpe to Salisbury, 6 Nov. 1891; F.O. 2/54: Johnston to Rosebery, No. 19, C.A., 3 June 1893; No. 29, C.A., 19 Aug. 1893, with minutes.

'We *must* have this "extra concession"', Johnston explained, in his dispatch of 3 June 1893. 'If we do not obtain it . . . the land will be bought up for a trifle by Dutch and German speculators (the Portuguese will not sell to the English); drinking and gambling saloons will be established just behind the British Concession, and the English who form seven-eighths of the white population at Tshinde will have no control over the planning of the future township.'

ministration had built a bridge across the inlet, drained part of the marsh, embanked the shore, surrounded the whole concession by a fence, and employed a competent surveyor to lay out the eastern and slightly larger part in plots and roads: all at a cost to itself of five hundred precious pounds. The largest plot, 7,300 square yards in extent, was sub-let to the Admiralty;[1] the others, of varying size, to the African Lakes Company and the various missions and private individuals with interests in the interior; a few were providently kept back to be assigned when new needs arose. West of the tidal swamp the Administration retained the land for its own use: for a post office, powder magazine, and other purposes.

There was keen and indeed acrimonious competition for the plots which were sub-let, and a busy little settlement of corrugated-iron buildings sprang up and flourished until a few years after the First World War, when the completion of a railway from southern Nyasaland to the port of Beira made the water-route obsolete and deprived Chinde of its value.[2]

On 16 July 1891 Johnston reported his arrival at Chiromo, the confluence of the Ruo and the Shiré: a place which was soon to become the most important port of entry for goods being conveyed into the Protectorate. There he remained for several weeks, and it was not until 10 September that he reached Zomba and made it his administrative headquarters. From the time of his landing at Chiromo, however, he considered that his administration of British Central Africa had begun, and he set himself to bring order out of chaos with extraordinary energy and ability, though with such scanty resources that he afterwards referred to Nyasaland as 'this Cinderella among the Protectorates'.[3]

The name 'British Central Africa' was chosen by himself in preference to the only alternatives which presented themselves: 'Livingstonia', which had already been appropriated by the Free Church Mission, and 'Northern Zambesia', which 'had a cold,

[1] For use in maintaining its gunboats on the Zambesi and Lower Shiré.

[2] F.O. 84/2197: Johnston to Salisbury, No. 9, C.A., 4 Mar. 1892; No. 11, C.A., of 10 Mar. 1892; Johnston to Rosebery, No. 29, C.A., 18 Aug. 1892; Johnston's memorandum of 17 Oct. 1892, accompanied by a detailed map of the concession prepared by the surveyor; also F.O. 2/66: Johnston to Rosebery, No. 2, C.A., of 12 Jan. 1894.

For a good description of Chinde in the middle nineties see R. C. F. Maugham, *Africa as I have known it*, pp. 24–36.

[3] Johnston, *British Central Africa*, Dedication.

repellent sound about it, in its cold, neutral statement of a geographical fact: moreover, it might have been taken exception to
by Portugal, who claims quite as much of the northern Zambesi
basin as we do'. The time had not yet come, apparently, when the
name 'Rhodesia' would suggest itself for anything more important
than an outpost on Lake Mweru. Since 'it is convenient in a
general way that in "short titles" the greater [in this case the
entire British sphere of influence north of the Zambesi, covered by
the term "British Central Africa"] should contain the less', he had
a very strong whim in favour of calling Nyasaland 'the British
Central Africa Protectorate'; and the Foreign Office let him have
his way, Lord Salisbury observing: 'I have no objection whatever
to the name. It is cumbersome, but not nearly so cumbersome as
the "short titles" of Acts of Parliament. The region it indicates is
anywhere but in the centre of Africa: but that again is a British
habit. The Middle Temple is not in the middle.'[1]

The first condition of effective administration was internal
peace, and this could not be secured until the Yao chiefs learnt
from hard experience that the fruits of disturbing it would in future
prove bitter to themselves. Only four or five months before Johnston's arrival, Makanjira, who possessed five of the eleven dhows
known to be on Lake Nyasa, had conveyed nearly a thousand men
to Leopard Bay, where Kazembe, notwithstanding a British treaty,
had joined forces with him to make a sudden overwhelming on-
slaught on a chief named Pemba, whose town lay a few miles to
the south. After hard fighting the surviving defenders had been
overwhelmed and enslaved, and thus Makanjira established his
power on the western as well as the eastern side of the lake.[2]
Farther south there had been fighting from time to time for the
previous two years between Mponda and Chikusi's Angoni, and

[1] F.O. 84/2197: Johnston to Salisbury, No. 19, C.A., 11 May 1892, with
minutes.

The change of name from 'the Nyasaland Districts' to 'the British Central
Africa Protectorate' was announced in the *London Gazette* of 24 Feb. 1893.
(Hertslet, op. cit., vol. i, p. 287.)

The justification for this rather ponderous nomenclature ceased to exist when
the Company's 'sphere' and the Protectorate ceased to be governed as a single
administrative unit, and the Protectorate was therefore renamed 'Nyasaland' by
Order in Council in 1907.

[2] F.O. 84/2115: Buchanan to Salisbury, No. 16, C.A., 7 Apr. 1891; also his
No. 21 of 10 June 1891, with enclosed letter from Rev. A. C. Murray, dated
27 Mar. 1891; also his No. 27 of 17 July 1891.

in the Shiré Highlands there was a continuing widespread selling of people in small numbers to traders who wished to make up caravans for export.[1]

Kawinga, by what seemed an agreeable contrast, had withdrawn his refusal to have any dealings with the British representative, and had made friendly overtures, in response to which Buchanan visited him in his mountain stronghold of Chikala, in June 1891, and obtained his assent to a treaty allowing British subjects free access to his country, agreeing that the Queen's representative should decide finally all disputes between his 'subjects' and them, and undertaking not to make any agreement with any foreign Power (that is, Portugal) without the Queen's consent. A further clause bound him and all his subordinates to take no further part in the slave-trade. On the day after Buchanan's departure he called a meeting of all his people, 'and', according to Buchanan, 'informed them of all that had taken place during my visit, specially emphasising his having bound himself and them to give over slavery'.[2] The acting-consul was well satisfied with the results of this visit, for, without taking at its face value the promise that slave-trading would entirely cease, he hoped that 'as our connection with him grows, and our influence increases, he will gradually abandon this illicit trade for less exciting but legitimate commerce'.

Buchanan himself recognized, however, that, as he put it, 'something more than moral suasion is needed to instil into the mind of the African the inviolability of his neighbour person'; and he had expressed the opinion that a British gunboat on the lake was 'an absolute necessity'.[3] Returning south in the Lakes Company's steamer *Domira*[4] from a visit to Mlozi in March 1891, he had encountered a canoe crossing the lake with slaves, and had been obliged to decide whether or not to interfere. 'As Acting British Consul,' he explained,

a report of my action in the matter would be circulated far and wide,

---

[1] F.O. 84/2115: Buchanan to Salisbury, No. 17, 20 Apr. 1891.

[2] F.O. 84/2115: Buchanan to Salisbury, No. 23 of 11 June and No. 24 of 20 June 1891. One may wonder how Buchanan knew what happened on the day after his own departure; it is possible that Dr. Henry Scott, of the Blantyre Mission, who accompanied him to Kawinga's, remained there somewhat longer and, on returning, gave him the information.

[3] F.O. 84/2115: Buchanan to Salisbury, No. 17, 20 Apr. 1891.

[4] The *Domira* was a larger vessel than the *Ilala*; it had been placed on Lake Nyasa not long before this incident.

and as slavery must sooner or later be put down, I felt it incumbent upon me to let the attitude of the British towards it be clearly known, and therefore, after the strictest enquiry into the case, ordered the slaves to be put on board the *Domira*, where I declared them free. I cautioned the native in charge of them that should he be caught in a repetition of this act he should forfeit his canoe and be severely dealt with.

It is my intention to hand over these slaves to one or other of the Missions to be taught and cared for.

While fully recognising the difficulties attendant upon indiscriminate interference with slave caravans, as Acting British Consul I could not see how I could have acted otherwise in the present instance.

He therefore asked for Foreign Office approval. But the prudent Anderson did not wish to be impaled on either horn of the dilemma, and, with Lord Salisbury's assent, avoided it by merely giving a general approval to his recent actions as a whole.[1]

When Johnston arrived in the following July he brought with him what he called a 'police force', such being the term that had been used in the agreement with the Chartered Company, providing for the creation of the force. In reality it was a tiny army, consisting of seventy-one Indian soldiers (of whom about forty were Sikhs) supported by a few Zanzibaris. These troops were under the command of Captain Cecil Maguire, with whom Johnston had become acquainted through his brother, Rochfort Maguire, who was Rhodes's private secretary. Johnston and Maguire at once proceeded vigorously and enthusiastically to do their best 'to make our protectorate a reality to the unfortunate mass of people who are robbed, raided, and carried into captivity to satisfy the greed and lust of bloodshed prevailing among a few chieftains of the Yao race'.[2]

The sequel was one little war after another. The first blow was struck against Chikumbu, who lived on the southern slope of Mount Mlanje and had begun to make attacks on European coffee-planters; the second subdued Mponda, and was accompanied by the establishment of Fort Johnston[3] close to the point at which the Shiré flows out of Lake Nyasa; the third drove Makanjira out

---

[1] F.O. 84/2115: Buchanan to Salisbury, No. 15, C.A., 31 Mar. 1891, with minutes.

[2] F.O. 84/2114: Johnston to Salisbury, 24–29 Nov. 1891.

[3] The Commissioner explained that it was 'half in fun' that Maguire named it after him.

of his village and made him take refuge some distance away from the lake shore until the British, who were operating from the *Domira*, had withdrawn. Before returning to Zomba after this conflict with Makanjira, Johnston and Maguire visited Kazembe and obtained from him without a struggle an undertaking to desist from slave-trading. By the end of November 1891 the Administration had gained considerable prestige and appeared to be well on the way to obtaining general acceptance of its supremacy throughout the southern half of the Protectorate.[1]

At this time, only some five months after Buchanan's visit to Chikala, Johnston deemed it necessary to send Maguire with a small force of Indian troops, and accompanied by Buchanan himself, to chastise Kawinga for renewed slave-raiding. The attack was only partially successful, but it so far served its purpose that Kawinga asked for terms. He was told that he must make a new treaty, accepting the sovereignty of the Queen and agreeing that his people should pay taxes to the Administration and buy licences for their guns; moreover, he must renounce slave-trading and witch-hunting. He replied that he was willing to put his mark on a treaty of peace, and he even sent ivory and cattle to pay for his gun-licences; but he was, in Johnston's words, 'quite frank and outspoken' in his determination to continue to sell slaves. Why he should have been so obstinate on this point in the face of armed force, after having been so complaisant so short a time previously when negotiating with the powerless Buchanan, is a question on which conjecture is neither assisted nor arrested by any known facts or even by any contemporary statement of opinion. Perhaps, in June, he had heard some rumour that a formidable British army was approaching, and by November he realized how small and how far from invincible that army really was. However that may be, the struggle was not at that time renewed against him, Johnston being of necessity content to make a separate peace with his sub-chiefs in the hope of detaching them from his control.[2]

---

[1] Writing from Blantyre on 15 Nov. Bishop Smythies, the head of the Universities' Mission, expressed complete approval of Johnston's action against Mponda and Makanjira, and added, 'As I came down the river [Shiré] I was hailed by Li[w]ondi, a considerable chief, who wanted to know how he was to avoid war. I explained that the English were determined to stop the slave trade. An Arab who was with him seemed very uncomfortable.' Quoted in *Central Africa*, Feb. 1892.

[2] F.O. 84/2114: Johnston to Salisbury, No. 25, C.A., 10 Dec. 1891.

By this time Johnston had obtained treaty recognition of British sovereignty not only from all the other Yao chiefs with whom he had been at war, and from Kazembe whom he had easily been able to overawe, but also from a number of other Yao, who declared in their treaties:

We make over without reserve to Her Majesty's Government the mineral rights of our country, the collection of customs duties and revenue from foreigners, complete jurisdiction over all foreigners, and in return for the protection afforded by the police force of the British Central Africa Administration we agree to pay that Administration an annual tax to be computed at the rate of 6s. per house, or the value of 6s. in foodstuffs or marketable produce.

In addition, two of them, Zarafi and Makandanji, ceded to the Queen the proprietary rights over some thirty-six square miles of 'waste lands' lying immediately west of the Upper Shiré. Likewise, Mponda's treaty provided for the cession of Cape Maclear; the purpose of this latter acquisition was to make it easier for Johnston to settle the claims of the Livingstonia Mission, which, he remarked, had been settled there for fifteen years 'without much other right than possession'. He stated that Mponda 'readily granted' it, which may well have been true, since Mponda's people do not appear at any previous time to have wanted the peninsula for their own use.

On Mlanje the Crown's acquisitions were more extensive. The defeat of Chikumbu had been complete, and he had been forced to make way for another chief, who was required to cede the land-title to the entire area over which he ruled. Additional lands on Mlanje had been acquired in the previous year by the diplomacy of Buchanan; besides which the whole upper plateau, being completely unoccupied, was claimed for the Crown in the absence of any counter-claim, native or other. The total area of Crown land on Mlanje was thus about 173,000 acres, 38,000 acres being upland and the remainder lying on the southern and western slopes.

In general, however, proprietary rights to the soil remained, in the eyes of British law, with the Yao chiefs;[1] though Johnston conveniently forgot this fact when he excised the Leopard Bay Concession out of Kazembe's country and gave it (as leasehold, it is true) to the Portuguese.

[1] Ibid., with enclosed treaties. For the Crown's claims on Mlanje see F.O. 84/2197: Johnston to Salisbury, No. 39, C.A., 13 Oct. 1892.

The chiefs on their side, or at least some of them, were to be paid an annual subsidy by the Administration. Mponda fared best with £100 a year, together with 5 per cent. of the profits of working any minerals that might be found in his territory. Zarafi and Makandanji received £50 a year each; but they, it seems, were expected, in view of this subsidy, to refrain from levying any taxes on their own account.[1]

The negotiation of treaties which conferred 'sovereignty' upon the Crown was in accordance with instructions given to Johnston by the Foreign Office, which feared that international difficulties might arise if the subjects of foreign Powers complained to their Governments against the imposition of British duties in a territory over which the precise extent of British authority was undefined. 'To set any such disputes at rest', he was told, 'it is highly desirable that powers of government should be explicitly conferred by the Chiefs within the sphere.'[2]

Before receiving this dispatch, and indeed before it was drafted, Johnston had himself reached a similar opinion; while, by going farther and obtaining for the governing authority, whenever possible, a title to the actual ownership of the soil, he was simply carrying out what he had urged upon the Chartered Company several months before his appointment as Commissioner.[3] As soon as he reached Chiromo he obtained an act of cession of the strip of land west of the Shiré and south of the Ruo confluence, conceded by Portugal under the terms of the new treaty.

As this land [he explained] was threatened with a rush of land-grabbers and speculators immediately the contents of the Portuguese treaty became known, I thought it better to take prompt advantage of a suggestion made by the Chiefs themselves (on the occasion of my hoisting the British flag in their country on July 15th. last) to the effect that they should 'give' the whole of their country to the Queen, who would make the best use of it and 'keep bad white men out.' Practically speaking the Chiefs have given their country to the Crown willingly and gratuitously, but I have nevertheless made them a return present in cloth equal to about £15 in value.[4]

---

[1] The treaty with Mponda, § 4, appears to leave that chief the power to tax his subjects if he liked. If this was what Johnston really intended, it was at variance with his general policy.

[2] F.O. 84/2113: F.O. to Johnston, No. 17, 14 Aug. 1891.

[3] See above, p. 175.

[4] F.O. 84/2114: Johnston to Salisbury, No. 10, C.A., 21 July 1891.

By this transfer the Crown acquired not only sovereign political authority but also the land ownership of the entire area, which Johnston estimated to be more than a million acres in extent, and which he valued a year later at about £14,000.[1]

In the Makololo country the chiefs, with two exceptions, did not give up the title to the soil, and Johnston did not state whether or not he ever asked for it. But he did after a few months secure a cession of sovereign rights, 'including all mineral and mining rights', on the understanding that if any minerals were worked in the country the chiefs would be paid such a percentage of the net profit 'as may seem to Her Majesty's Representative fair and just'.[2] Over most of the southern part of the Protectorate, from the Lower Shiré as far north as Kazembe's, the Crown had now acquired sovereign rights in place of its far more limited rights under the earlier treaties which had made it the protecting Power. The logical sequel would have been formal annexation, for a region which was subject to the Queen's sovereign control must, one would think, be part of her dominions. Neither then nor at any subsequent date, however, did formal annexation take place. The people of Nyasaland have not become British subjects, but have remained 'British protected persons'. The territory could hardly be proclaimed a Crown Colony while its Administration was financially dependent on a subsidy from a Chartered Company, and when in due course that dependence ceased, there probably seemed no practical reason why *vis inertiae* should be disturbed for the sake of a legal technicality which made no difference to the conduct of affairs.

The northern part of the Protectorate, unlike the southern, was not likely to be the scene of disputes with European traders about the Administration's authority to administer; it consequently mattered little whether or not deeds of cession were obtained. Nice distinctions between treaties of protection and treaties of submission could not, it seems, be drawn by the natives themselves, and Johnston and the Foreign Office cared little for them. This was clearly shown when, in 1894, eighteen Tonga chiefs ceded their sovereign and also their territorial rights, and when

[1] F.O. 84/2197: Johnston to Rosebery, No. 38, C.A., 13 Oct. 1892.
[2] F.O. 84/2197: Johnston to Salisbury, No. 10, C.A., 7 Mar. 1892, with enclosed treaties; also his No. 22, C.A., 22 June 1892, enclosing additional treaties.

doing so admitted that they had imagined that they had already done it when they had put their marks on treaties of protection. On that occasion Johnston remarked that all the other chiefs in the Protectorate had already conferred their rights of sovereignty upon the Queen.[1] He qualified this remark with only the casual observation, 'as far as I know', and it did not occur to anyone in the Foreign Office to inquire when the Queen had been thus favoured by Makanjira, or Matapwiri, or Mombera, or Mlozi, to name only the more obvious recalcitrants.

Beyond the Protectorate, in the Company's sphere, one and only one chief had ceded his sovereign rights. This was Mkula, successor to Nsama, the ruler of Itawa who had made a treaty with Sharpe in 1890. Nsama had been killed in 1891 by the followers of an Arab named Abdallah-bin-Suleiman, who had captured his town after besieging it for three months in order to enslave his people. In 1892, when Sharpe was passing through Itawa a second time, Mkula and his adherents were in dread that a similar fate was being prepared for them, and therefore, at Sharpe's suggestion, Mkula ceded all that he had to the Queen, 'for the purpose'—so ran the declaration to which he put his mark—'and in the hope that Her Majesty the Queen may establish a government in the said countries, and protect me and my subjects from war and pillage, and enable us to live in peace and security'. In return, Sharpe sent a warning to Abdallah that any attack on Mkula would be an attack on the Queen of England. In effect, the transaction carried the implication that a chief who accepted British 'protection', as Nsama had done, could not in fact expect the British to protect him unless he also accepted their sovereignty. The Queen would protect territory which was her very own, and its African inhabitants, but she would not bestir herself on behalf of chiefs who were merely, in the parlance of more recent years, her satellites.

But Mkula's territory was some hundreds of miles from the boundary of the Nyasaland Protectorate, for which alone the British Government had accepted administrative responsibility. Hence the following comments were exchanged in the Foreign Office:

SIR CLEMENT HILL: Are we to take any notice of the treaty with Mkula? See end of Sharpe's report.

[1] F.O. 2/66: Johnston to Kimberley, No. 27, C.A., 14 Mar. 1894, with enclosed treaty. (This treaty is here reproduced facing p. 1.)

SIR PERCY ANDERSON: Is it necessary to do anything? Will not Johnston make use of it?

HILL: I meant, should we approve it?

ANDERSON: I think we had better leave it alone.[1]

           *   *   *

Appended to each of the treaties by which Zarafi, Liwonde, and other Yao chiefs ceded sovereign rights to the Queen was a solemn declaration, signed by Johnston himself, that 'the fore-going document has been carefully and exactly translated to the signatories in the Kiswahili and Tshi-Yao languages'. Since the tidy European concept of sovereignty has no counterpart in tribal customary law, it is probable that no amount of interpreting could have made the chiefs, with their profoundly different cultural background and mode of thought, appreciate the precise signifi-cance of what they were doing; nevertheless, it is hard to believe that they completely failed to realize that the general effect of their action was to bind them to submit to the Queen's authority as represented by her Commissioner and Consul-General. But the sanctity of treaties was no part of their creed, and it is unlikely that they ever intended to be a hair's breadth more submissive than necessity or at least prudence might require.

No sooner had Maguire been killed in an ill-fated second attack on Makanjira, made in December 1891, than Zarafi was in arms, and a force sent against him in the following February was de-feated with the loss of six Indians, three Zanzibaris, and the only piece of artillery at that time in the country. With ten of the Indians killed and a further eight incapacitated, Johnston faced an alarming military situation at a time when the administrative difficulties and burdens which beset him were almost overwhelm-ing. He lacked the assistance of the three men on whom he had chiefly relied: Maguire had fallen in armed combat, Sharpe was in England on leave, and Buchanan had been compelled by illness to return to Scotland for a holiday. Until late in 1892, when an accountant sent out to assist him arrived at Zomba, any accounting that was done at all had to be done by himself. River communica-tions were unsatisfactory—'we have had no mails for two months', he reported on one occasion—and the white settlers did not dis-guise the outraged hostility which he aroused in them by his

---

[1] F.O. 2/54: Johnston to Rosebery, No. 3, C.A., 2 Jan. 1893, with enclosures and minutes.

refusal sufficiently to appease their land-hunger at the expense of the natives. 'This time', he afterwards wrote, 'may be taken as the nadir of our fortunes.'

In June Captain C. E. Johnson arrived to take over Maguire's command, and he brought a few Sikhs as reinforcements. But the force was still much too small to meet the full demands of the situation. When Liwonde revolted in February 1893 the men available were barely sufficient to subdue him, and for three days during the campaign the Commissioner himself, with Sharpe, two officials of the Administration, and a few native African troops, was surrounded by his warriors and in deadly danger.

Soon after the suppression of Liwonde a hundred fresh Sikhs arrived from India, but not long after their arrival the survivors of the original contingent returned home, having completed the two-year period of service for which they had volunteered. The Moslems among them had been only partially satisfactory, and from this time on the Indian contingent was composed entirely of Sikhs, for whom Johnston could find no praise sufficiently high. They were, however, made the nucleus of a growing force of African native troops, consisting at first of Makua from Portuguese East Africa, but afterwards of Tonga and later of Yao from the Protectorate itself.[1]

Makanjira, after his triumph over the British in December 1891, had crossed the lake and driven out his former ally, Kazembe, so that his hold upon both sides of the lake was more firmly established than it had been before the Administration began. Johnston did not feel able to suppress him without a substantial increase in the number of Sikhs, and appealed to Rhodes to provide the necessary finance. Rhodes responded by making available a special fund of £10,000,[2] and, in consequence, a second contingent of 100 Sikhs arrived from India within a few months of the first.

These land forces were supported by two gunboats, placed on Lake Nyasa by the Admiralty. Johnston, immediately after his arrival at Chiromo in 1891, had reiterated the plea of Hawes and of Buchanan for one gunboat, at the same time suggesting that at

---

[1] Manganja were recruited as 'police' in the early days, and were of some value as auxiliaries. They hated their Yao enemies, but were of limited value in hard fighting.

[2] Not all of this was in fact spent. The balance, amounting to £4,850, was repaid. F.O. 2/88: Johnston to Kimberley, No. 77, C.A., 10 June 1895, with minutes.

some later date a second might be sent out to do similar work on Tanganyika. Nothing more was heard of this latter suggestion, but in July 1892 he was told of arrangements to place on Lake Nyasa not one gunboat but two, and to provide a light-draught steamer for Government purposes on the Upper Shiré. It was probably the only occasion on which Johnston received more than he asked, and it would be interesting to know how it happened. Had the Foreign Office asked the Admiralty for three vessels in the hope of getting one as a compromise? Or is the explanation to be found in the remark of Lugard—who had little faith in the panacea of sending out gunboats to the lake—that it was politically easier to spend £100,000 or even £200,000 on the suppression of the slave-trade if the sum was included in the naval estimates than to obtain £20,000 for the same purpose if the money was to be spent on the maintenance of an adequate land force?[1] Whatever the reason, the vessels were duly sent out; they reached Chinde in sections in October 1892, and by the middle of 1893 they were in service.

With its increased military force thus supported on the lake, the Administration now disposed for the first time of sufficient armed strength to meet its commitments, and Captain Johnson was able to embark upon his main campaign. Using the Lakes Company's steamers *Domira* and *Ilala* as troop-carriers, and accompanied by the Commissioner and Sharpe, he proceeded first to the west coast to the relief of Jumbe, who was hard pressed by an ally of Makanjira's named Chiwaura. After withstanding a bombardment by seven-pounders, Chiwaura's village was taken by storm, and the chief himself was shot down as he fled. Hundreds of slaves were released, the defences were levelled, and then the little army proceeded by land and lake to Makanjira's. On 19 November 1893, after a five-hour battle to which the Admiralty gunboats contributed their fire, the issue was decided.

Five Arab slavers were captured, but as they were not the main criminals but 'poor fellows left in charge of the slaves', they were very leniently dealt with. It was believed that about half the slaves were driven away by their masters, but 205 were freed. These were interrogated, and it was found that nearly all had come from the valleys of the Luangwa and the Upper Luapula. About three-quarters had been sold to the Arabs by their chiefs or previous

---

[1] *The Rise of Our East African Empire*, vol. i, p. 164, n. 1.

owners, and the others had by one means or another been kid-
napped. They had been warned that they must never allow themselves to fall into the hands of the British, who would certainly
murder them; but in case the British should nevertheless liberate
and question them, they had been taught the routine answers
which it was usual to inculcate into slaves being conveyed on the
dhows off the east coast of Africa: thus, to the first presumed
question, 'Are you a slave?' the answer was 'No'; and to the
second presumed question, 'Then what are you?' the answer was
'A seaman'. When Johnston asked some of the women if they knew
what a seaman was, they replied that it was a way of getting cloth.

'I would call attention to the fact', he reported, 'that the Portuguese Flag was carried in front of this caravan, and that one of the
Arabs in it was furnished with a Portuguese passport.'[1]

In this campaign against Makanjira, including the capture of
Chiwaura's, the British captured 58 barrels of powder, 96 guns,
and one of Makanjira's two cannon, besides 47 tusks of ivory,
25 bales of cloth, and much rice and other food. The proceeds of
the ivory were in part added to the 'Makanjira fund'—the special
financial grant made by Rhodes for the purpose of the campaign—
and in part divided among the Europeans and Sikhs who had
stormed Chiwaura's.[2]

Makanjira himself still refused to make peace, and took refuge
in Portuguese territory. So, to prevent his returning and rebuilding
his power, Johnston ordered the destruction of 'every single town'
in his country, except those occupied by the adherents of Kumbasani, his kinswoman and rival, whom Johnston recognized as
successor to his authority.

But the most important step towards the permanent pacification
of the country was the erection of a fort, named after Captain
Maguire, and situated close to the place where he had fallen. The
establishment of forts at key positions had been from the beginning
a part of the Commissioner's programme for introducing stability
and order in the country, though necessarily the implementing of
it could proceed only as sufficient men and munitions became
available. The forts were square or rectangular in shape, with sides
about 200 yards long, and were enclosed by an earthwork and
ditch with perhaps a thorn entanglement outside. They usually

[1] F.O. 2/55: Johnston to Rosebery, No. 63, C.A., 9 Dec. 1893.
[2] Ibid.

had a watch-tower from which the surrounding country could be surveyed and the approach of an enemy observed. As far as possible they were provided with artillery, but the handful of soldiers who formed the garrison could hardly have defended so long a perimeter if they had not been supported by some partially-trained native auxiliaries.

Despite all adversity Makanjira remained unbroken in spirit, and became a rallying-point for other Yao chiefs who were growing desperate in the awareness that unless they could destroy the Administration they would have to abandon their predatory way of life. Assisted by Zarafi and Makandanji (who was Zarafi's father-in-law), he led a force of 2,000 men against Fort Maguire in January 1894, burst into the adjoining native settlement, and succeeded in setting part of it on fire and in murdering Kumbasani. Captain Edwards, who was in charge of the fort and soon afterwards succeeded Johnson in the chief command, was able to extinguish the fire and, after two hours' hard fighting, to drive off the attackers. Most of Makanjira's headmen now submitted, and for a time it was believed that he himself was about to do so too, for he kept the Administration in play with lengthy negotiations, and even sent in some ivory as a token of sincerity. Instead of surrendering, however, he re-established himself in a valley surrounded by hills, just within British territory, and located about forty miles south-east of Fort Maguire; thence he resumed his raids.

The culminating and decisive campaigns against the Yao were fought in 1895. According to Johnston, a league was formed between Kawinga, Zarafi, and Matapwiri with the object of sweeping the Shiré Highlands completely clear of the British; but if this was so the three chiefs made remarkably little attempt to concert their efforts, and although a son of Zarafi's and some of his fighting men assisted Kawinga when he launched a determined attack on the British settlements at the beginning of the year,[1] the Administration was able to postpone the struggle against Zarafi until its forces had not only inflicted a decisive defeat on Kawinga but had conquered and captured Matapwiri as well.

[1] The attack was described by Sharpe, who was Acting-Commissioner at the time, as 'a most determined affair; the greatest effort, I think, that has ever yet been made by the Yaos'. F.O. 2/88: Sharpe to Kimberley, No. 19, C.A., 14 Feb. 1895; also his No. 20, C.A., 28 Feb. 1895.

Although Matapwiri's own stronghold was situated on the British side of the boundary, on the south-east of Mount Mlanje, most of his lands lay on the Portuguese side; and early in 1893 Johnston had complained that

at the present moment, when it is all we can do to keep the slave-trading chiefs of the eastern Yaos at bay, the Portuguese are sending large quantities of *good* guns and ammunition to Matapwiri.... They have just made Matapwiri a 'Capitão Môr', and sent him a Colonel's uniform to wear. Matapwiri is one of the biggest slave raiders out here. He regularly raids our territory between Zomba, Tshiradzulu and Mlanje about once a month; I mean that he sends out bands of armed men to kidnap people and rob small caravans on the road, either those of the Blantyre Mission, or Buchanan Brothers, or the Administration. I have sent Matapwiri remonstrances as many as his raids, but he pays no heed.

A stiff remonstrance at Lisbon had merely been countered with the assertion that Matapwiri resided on Portuguese territory; and Johnston, owing both to the proximity of the boundary and to the difficulty of the terrain, was for a time content to curb Matapwiri and other robber chiefs in that vicinity by building Forts Lister and Anderson to control the routes north and south of Mount Mlanje.[1]

By the beginning of 1894, however, Matapwiri had completely alienated the Portuguese by kidnapping and selling some of the people belonging to a Jesuit mission on their side of the border, and before that year was out the Portuguese Government was requesting the British ambassador to convey its thanks to the Administration for having rendered timely aid to the mission when it was in serious danger owing to Matapwiri's hostility.[2]

In September 1895 Matapwiri was forced to surrender unconditionally, and at the end of October Major Edwards, as he had now become, delivered his attack on Zarafi's almost inaccessible stronghold of Mangoche, about fifteen miles south-east of Fort Johnston. The complete success which attended this attack was largely due to Kawinga's action in supplying two excellent guides, 'from the double motive', according to Johnston, 'of wishing to see Zarafi

---

[1] F.O. 84/2197: Johnston to Rosebery, No. 41, C.A., 19 Oct. 1892; F.O. 2/54: Johnston to Anderson, 23 Mar. 1893, and to Rosebery, No. 15, 10 Apr. 1893; F.O. 2/53: F.O. to Johnston, No. 50, 10 Aug. 1893.

[2] F.O. 2/66: Johnston to Kimberley, No. 12, C.A., 24 Jan. 1894; F.O. 2/65: F.O. to Sharpe, No. 60, 15 Nov. 1894.

soundly thrashed (to console himself for his own defeat) and of winning my favour to the extent of allowing him to return' from the place of safety to which he had fled. Nevertheless there was much severe fighting before victory was secured, and casualties on the British side would have been very serious had it not been for the tribesmen's habitual mistake in firing high—so that in a number of cases the bullets went harmlessly through the turbans of the Sikhs.

On his return from accompanying this expedition, Johnston received from Mponda a message, 'couched in very insolent language', calling upon him to withdraw all Europeans from the country. At the same time he received a deputation from those of Mponda's people who were on good terms with the Administration, pleading that on account of their friendliness towards the British they were harried by Mponda night after night, and that numbers of them were being murdered or carried off to be sold as slaves. Mponda himself had withdrawn to a place in the hills about ten miles west of Fort Johnston, and it was thence that he hurled his defiance at the British, in the evident assurance that by the time they received it they would have sustained defeat at the hands of Zarafi. Finding, however, that they had been victorious and were about to proceed against him, he surrendered without firing a shot. But, as Edwards pointed out in his report, 'although there was no fighting in the Mponda expedition, yet the effect was none the less crushing to the slave trade in British Central Africa'. Three hundred and seventy-nine slaves were released and formed into a free settlement at Fort Johnston. The captured war material amounted to 112 guns and 270 lb. of gunpowder.

Then, in November, Edwards struck a decisive blow against Makanjira. 'The valley in which Makanjira was settled', he wrote,

was about twelve miles long by eight broad, and contained about 8,000 huts, divided amongst many villages. Many of the houses were built in the coast style, and there was evidence everywhere of the existence of a large Arab and coast population. A great many slave sticks were found in the villages, several of them covered with blood. The population could not have been less than 25,000, and probably much more. The 17th. and 18th. November were employed in destroying all the huts.[1]

One hundred and sixty slaves were freed, and the number would

[1] A. & P., 1896, lviii: Edwards's Report to Johnston, 27 Dec. 1895 (C.8013); also Johnston's Report to Salisbury, 13 Nov. 1895 (C.7925).

have been much greater had not all the Arabs and coast men residing there decamped out of British territory as soon as they heard of Zarafi's defeat. Although Makanjira himself once again found sanctuary on the safe side of the frontier, he was so much impoverished by the loss of captured ivory, as well as of powder and guns, that it was impossible for him to find means of renewing the struggle, since, as Johnston put it, 'even the Portuguese will not supply gunpowder gratis'.[1]

The Yao had been subdued at last. Thenceforth the only outlet for their fighting energies was in the armed forces of their British rulers, and by the beginning of 1897 there were already providing the most efficient and reliable soldiers that could be recruited anywhere in the Protectorate.[2]

In retrospect their subjugation may appear inevitable, when the resources at their disposal are compared with those of Imperial Britain at the summit of her grandeur; yet when it is remembered how slender were the means actually available to the Commissioner, it becomes clear that the final outcome was due not only to the superior equipment and military prowess of the Administration's forces but also to the complete inability of the Yao to combine in a single-minded effort to batter down the new régime in the weakness of its infancy. Another factor, to which Johnston himself repeatedly called attention in his dispatches, was the disposition of the original inhabitants, the majority of the population, to withhold support from their Yao overlords, and indeed to welcome the British as a liberating Power.[3]

◦   ◦   ◦

The judicial powers of the Commissioner were defined by the 'Africa Order in Council, 1889', a long and important document issued on 22 October of that year.[4] This Order provided for the administration of justice by 'consular courts' in 'local jurisdictions'

[1] Rhodes Papers, Groote Schuur, 14: Johnston to Rhodes, 23 Nov. 1895.

[2] Sharpe's Report on the British Central Africa Protectorate for the year 1896–7 (C.8438), p. 12.

[3] The most important reports on the pacification of the country were published as Blue Books: A. & P., 1892, lxxiv (C.6699); 1893–4, lxxxv (C.7031); 1896, lviii (C.7925, C.8013). A detailed narrative of the fighting, including many conflicts not mentioned in the above summary, is contained in Johnston's *British Central Africa*, which also includes many interesting photographs. The account given here is intended to supplement rather than to summarize the much fuller one in that book.

[4] The *London Gazette*, 1889, pp. 5557–5600. The Order was modified in 1893.

created by a Secretary of State; and Lord Salisbury, in his capacity as Foreign Secretary, constituted the whole 'British Sphere North of the Zambesi' as such a 'local jurisdiction'.[1] It was not, indeed, necessary or usual that the magistrates in these so-called 'consular courts' should hold the rank of consul or even of vice-consul, but their appointment had in each case to be approved by the Secretary of State, from whom they received their magistrates' commissions. They had wide powers of judging British subjects in both civil and criminal cases, but there was some ambiguity as to whether or not the Order in Council applied to the natives, who were not British subjects but 'British-protected persons'. The opinion of the Foreign Office was stated by W. E. Davidson, who advised the Africa Department on points of law, when he wrote that Johnston 'does not exercise jurisdiction under the Africa O/C over the natives; he exercises it because they like it and have by implication requested him to do so'.[2] But Johnston appears to have been under a different impression. This is hardly surprising, since Sharpe, his legal adviser, as late as 1894 thought that it provided sufficient authority for the deportation of Chief Kazembe 'to such place as the Secretary of State may direct'. In reply to Sharpe's dispatch reporting that as Acting-Commissioner he had signed a warrant for this purpose, Sir Percy Anderson caused the following telegram to be sent:

Natives of the Protectorate are not justiciable under [the] Africa Order in Council and cannot be deported under its provisions. They should be dealt with according to native law as maintenance of peace and order may require.[3]

In circumstances where an uncertainty of this magnitude could exist, it was inevitable that the sphere within which magistrates concerned themselves with native litigation should be completely undefined. They simply brought natives before their courts when it seemed necessary; but, being very busy men, they were anxious to keep the number of cases which they had to consider as small as possible. According to Johnston the position which existed in 1896, at the end of his period of administration, was as follows:

In reality the native courts are practically held by British magistrates

[1] F.O. 84/2197: Johnston to Rosebery, No. 35, C.A., 11 Oct. 1892: minutes.
[2] F.O. 2/55: Johnston to Rosebery, No. 57, C.A., 18 Oct. 1893: minute.
[3] F.O. 2/69: F.O. to Sharpe, Tel. No. 9, 25 June 1894; in reply to Sharpe to Kimberley, No. 32, C.A. 20 Apr. 1894 (in F.O. 2/66).

in the name of the local chief or as his representative. . . . Still, in some districts, native chiefs are encouraged to settle all minor cases themselves, and the natives are not allowed to go to the European magistrate except where the native chief cannot be relied on for fairness. No native chief or British magistrate, however, is allowed to carry out a death sentence on a native without first referring the case to the Commissioner, and obtaining his sanction to the verdict and sentence.[1]

In cases where there were road robberies or kidnapping for the slave-trade, it was impossible to catch the individual criminal, so the Administration proceeded against the local chief, who, having no very large number of subjects, was fairly certain to know who had committed the crime, and in all probability was himself directly responsible.[2]

In connexion with the administration of justice in respect of natives it is of interest, if not strictly relevant, to observe that in December 1891 Johnston instructed Vice-Consul Ross of Quilimane to uphold the interests of Zanzibaris in Portuguese courts of law—on the ground that since Zanzibar had now become a British Protectorate its natives enjoyed 'the full protection of Her Britannic Majesty's representatives abroad, to the same extent as if they were British subjects'. The Africa Department was somewhat perplexed by the news of Johnston's action, and decided neither to approve nor disapprove it: the question was 'rather a large one'.[3]

       ↄ   ↄ   ↄ

The success of the Administration depended in large measure on the quality of the men who assisted the Commissioner in the laborious pioneer work of building it up. Foremost among them was Alfred Sharpe, of whom it has been said, probably not without reason, that his legal training, 'added to his mature and well-balanced judgement, saved Johnston from many a pitfall'.[4] Sharpe was not endowed with Johnston's rare brilliance of mind, but he was energetic, level-headed, and reliable. The two men had the greatest affection and respect for each other. At first Sharpe's status was that of vice-consul—he was appointed in March 1891—but three years later he was promoted to the rank of consul. During Johnston's two absences from the Protectorate, first to transact

[1] Johnston, *British Central Africa*, p. 114.
[2] F.O. 2/68: Sharpe to Hill, 29 Nov. 1894.
[3] F.O. 84/2114: Johnston to Salisbury, No. 24, C.A., 7 Dec. 1891, with minutes.
[4] R. C. F. Maugham: *Africa as I have known it*, p. 20.

public business with Rhodes in Cape Town and afterwards on leave in England, Sharpe was left in charge of the administration, and in 1896 he was appointed Commissioner and Consul-General when Johnston relinquished the post.

After Sharpe and 'my right-hand man, Maguire', the man whose services Johnston valued most highly was John Buchanan. Buchanan, now a C.M.G., accepted the position of unpaid[1] vice-consul, and placed most of his private business in the hands of his younger brothers in order to devote himself more fully to his official duties. He was, Johnston reported,

indispensable at this early stage of our Administration, where a number of new faces appearing on the scene and displacing the old familiar representatives of the British Government is apt to cause dismay and mistrust among the natives unless they see the old and new régimes linked together by their known friend and counsellor, Buchanan. . . . From his knowledge of the Yao language and the excellent influence he has gained over these most provoking, quarrelsome, turbulent Yao chiefs, Mr. Buchanan is almost the most useful member of my Administration. . . . His services in the way of organising the collection of customs and revenue, and the regular and secure transmission of mails, have been really valuable.[2]

The salaries of Johnston and Sharpe were paid by the Treasury, but it was useless to apply to that source for remuneration for any of the additional officials who were required. Nor could the Chartered Company's subsidy, which was assigned to the maintenance of the police force, be drawn upon habitually for the support of the civil administration, though it is true that Johnston expected the European officer in charge of the police to perform the duties of a magistrate. Yet the Administration would have been almost impotent, and its 'police actions' of little avail, without suitable officials to represent it in the various localities over which it was trying to build up its control: and the salaries of these men had to be paid out of local revenue. Johnston was therefore obliged to proceed gradually in making his appointments, 'a due regard

---

[1] i.e. unpaid by the Home Government, in his consular capacity. He was paid £350 a year from the Nyasaland revenue for his work as magistrate and local official.

[2] F.O. 84/2114: Johnston to Salisbury, No. 18, C.A., 20 Nov. 1891, and No. 23, C.A., 5 Dec. 1891; F.O. 84/2197: No. 15, 29 Mar. 1892. The terms of Buchanan's appointment are stated in F.O. 84/2196: F.O. to Johnston, No. 9, 24 Feb. 1892.

being had to the principle of the adage which recommends us to cut our coat according to our cloth'. It was significant that the designation he gave them was that of 'Collector of Revenues and Resident'—'Collector' for short. But although their most urgent duty was necessarily to secure the revenues out of which they had themselves to be supported, they had much else to do as well; he reported that

they perform multiple and useful functions which most colonial officials would consider too onerous in their conjunction. They collect taxes and revenue, superintend postal affairs, do a little engineering, road making, surveying, and building, and advise the native chiefs in all matters affecting the welfare of the people.

In addition, the most trusted among them were commissioned as magistrates. They were what we should now call district officers.

They were employed at a salary of £350 a year or less,[1] in a climate which took the lives or ruined the health of a large proportion of them, and on the understanding that their appointments gave them no claim as servants of the Imperial Government. They were, as Johnston said, 'what may be called "the uncovenanted civil service" of Nyasaland'; yet, as far as one is able to judge from his dispatches and from a very candid letter of Sharpe's, the men he secured were usually of real worth.

It is true that they were bitterly complained against by the Blantyre Mission, but as that mission pursued a constant vendetta against the Administration and all its works, its opinions can scarcely be regarded as impartial. Its animus against the Administration was attributed by Johnston to resentment against being placed under any kind of civil government, secular authority being a check upon ecclesiastical;[2] it was probably motivated also by profound personal distrust of Johnston, both as one of the ungodly and as the man who had proposed to let Portugal take control of the Shiré Highlands. The leader of its attacks was Alexander Hetherwick, who set himself up as the champion of the natives against

---

[1] Their housing was, indeed, paid for out of the Company's money, and Johnston was emphatic about the need to see that it was of good quality. 'If you have a number of white men out in a climate like this and do not properly house them, they die. That is the long and the short of it. . . . If I have been a little extravagant in house-building, I have housed my employés well, and the result is that the amount of sickness amongst the very large [sic] staff of the Administration has been exceptionally small.' Johnston to Canning, 10 Mar. 1894. Copy in F.O. 2/66.   [2] Cf. above, p. 42.

the oppression of a cruel Government, which he accused of 'raiding for taxes' whenever it adopted punitive measures against robbers and slave-hunters, including even Makanjira.[1] On one occasion, when Hetherwick was able to point to a genuine case of culpable slackness—though not of deliberate oppression—on the part of a Collector, he refused to co-operate by bringing the matter to court as Sharpe asked him to do, declaring that it was not for him to act as Public Prosecutor, and that he preferred to complain to his Church's Foreign Mission Committee.

Johnston related that when the mission heard that one of his officials had built a small grass hut in the 'bush', to serve as a hunting lodge, it could draw only one conclusion: 'What did Mr. M—— want a house for in the "bush"? Why, to keep a harem, of course.' On another occasion the same official was conveying a petty chief as a prisoner from Mount Mlanje to Chiromo, and the chief asked permission to bring two of his wives. So, when they passed through Blantyre on their way, 'a cry was immediately raised by the mission, "M—— travels about the country with women in his train!"' There was scarcely a man in the service of the Administration who was not plagued by gossip of this kind. When the Church of Scotland's Foreign Mission Committee made a formal complaint to the Foreign Office, which duly forwarded it to Johnston, the Commissioner wrote to its Convener asking that the charges should be substantiated. He does not seem to have received any reply.

Passing through Nyasaland in 1892, Carson, a lay member of the L.M.S., had conversations with both Johnston and Hetherwick, and also with the missionaries at Bandawe and at Likoma, with whom Johnston's relations were, on the whole, very friendly. Carson was an honest and intelligent man; in so far as he was predisposed towards either side, it was naturally in favour of his fellow missionaries. The conclusion he reached was that although the charges brought against the Administration might not be entirely baseless, they were being exaggerated in a spirit of quibbling and partisanship; and this is probably as near the truth as it is possible to penetrate.

Johnston and Sharpe were themselves well satisfied with their subordinates, and staunchly supported them against all attacks.

[1] This charge is ridiculous, if only because the cost of the campaigns far exceeded the total tax revenue.

Writing privately to Johnston, Sharpe remarked: 'Among our B.C.A.A. men we really have some worthy men, and all together, we have a *good lot*; some of course are poor.' Forwarding this letter to Anderson, Johnston added a tribute of his own: 'Take them all round, I doubt whether a finer lot of fellows could be got together, and willing to do such excellent work for such very low pay.'[1]

Three of them—Richard Crawshay, John Nicoll, and John Kydd —had been among the defenders of Karonga against Mlozi. A number of them, including Nicoll and Kydd, were former employees of the Lakes Company. Hugh C. Marshall, the first of the Collectors to be appointed, had been stationed at Chiromo in 1890 by Buchanan as 'police officer', and was retained there by Johnston with the new function of collecting customs on imports to the Protectorate. A. J. Swann resigned from the L.M.S. in 1893, after prolonged heart-searching, to serve the Administration. Their numbers increased steadily: there were only about half a dozen of them at the end of 1891, but five years later there were twenty-seven—twelve Collectors and fifteen Assistant Collectors.

In October 1892 Johnston announced that he had divided the whole Protectorate into four districts: Lower Shiré, South Nyasaland, West Nyasaland, and North Nyasaland. To these he added two districts in the Company's sphere: Tanganyika, including the south and south-west coasts of that lake and also the Nyasa–Tanganyika plateau, and Mweru, which, with a grand gesture, embraced the Bemba country as well as the country around Lakes Mweru and Bangweulu. 'These districts', he remarked, 'should be continuous and not have any gaps between their boundaries', but he was expressing a distant aspiration rather than an achieved reality. The Foreign Office tried to introduce greater definiteness into these arrangements by drawing the boundary between West and North Nyasaland along the line of latitude 10° 30' S.: for all that Johnston had said on the subject it might have lain almost

[1] F.O. 2/68: Johnston to Anderson, 13 Nov. 1894, and enclosed letter from Sharpe to Johnston, 16 Sept. 1894.

For the controversy with the Blantyre Mission see (among much other correspondence) F.O. 84/2197: Johnston to Salisbury, No. 24, C.A., 7 July 1892; ibid., J. to S., No. 27, C.A., 22 July 1892; ibid., J. to Rosebery, No. 32, C.A., 19 Sept. 1892, with minutes; F.O. 2/54: J. to R., No. 1, C.A., 1 Jan. 1893; ibid., J. to Lister, 4 June 1893, with enclosures; F.O. 2/56: Sharpe to Rosebery, No. 1, 24 Apr. 1893, with enclosures; F.O. 2/68: Sharpe to Hill, 29 Nov. 1894, with enclosures; Mins., C. of S. For. Miss. Comm., 28 Feb. 1893: letter from Hetherwick, dated 4 Oct. 1892; L.M.S., C.A., 8.6.A: Carson to Thompson, 12 Aug. 1892.

anywhere. Its exact location mattered little. The real ruler of North Nyasaland was Mlozi, and we have it from Mr. C. A. Cardew, who joined the Administration at the end of 1894, that although at that date there were five stations north of Zomba (at Mpimbi, Liwonde, Fort Johnston, Kota-Kota, and Deep Bay), the Collectors there 'had little influence beyond their rear neighbourhood. The stations were mere footholds to be extended later under more peaceful conditions.' By 1896, however, the twelve districts into which the Protectorate had by then been divided were, for the most part, real administrative units under the fairly effective control of their Collectors.[1]

The growth of the central Administration proceeded in the same steady though modest way as the extension of control over the districts. At first Johnston had to be his own secretary and accountant, and the burden was particularly oppressive during Sharpe's absence on leave from September 1891 to the following February. Early in 1892, however, an accountant arrived from England, and from then on it became possible to give the necessary constant attention to the ever-pressing problem of finance. By 1896 the Administration had a chief accountant, three other accountants, and a local auditor, as well as a storekeeper with two assistants, one of them a European and the other a native. It was not until January 1893 that Johnston obtained the assistance of a private secretary: but in the following year this official became Secretary to the Administration, and by 1896 had acquired an Assistant Secretary and two clerks, the nucleus of the Nyasaland Secretariat.[2]

From time to time Johnston pressed the Foreign Office to send him a barrister, who would reside at Blantyre—not Zomba—with the status of 'legal vice-consul' and the duty of establishing among the growing number of settlers 'a more regular, methodical and complete administration of justice'. The man chosen must have 'the making in him of the Chief Justice of a colony. Anything less than that is not worth sending.' By holding courts at Blantyre he

---

[1] F.O. 84/2114: Johnston to Salisbury, No. 12, C.A., 29 July 1891, and No. 23, C.A., 5 Dec. 1891; F.O. 84/2196: F.O. to Johnston, No. 36, 8 June 1892; F.O. 84/2197: J. to S., No. 15, 29 Mar. 1892, and No. 35, C.A., 11 Oct. 1892; F.O. 2/53: F.O. to J., No. 15, 23 Feb. 1893; ibid., Davidson to J., 7 June 1893; F.O. 2/54: J. to Davidson, 10 May 1893 and 24 Aug. 1893; F.O. 2/65: F.O. to J., No. 10, 9 Feb. 1894, and No. 14, 14 Feb. 1894; C. A. Cardew, 'Nyasaland in 1894–5', in the *Nyasaland Journal*, vol. i, No. 1, Jan. 1948, p. 52.

[2] Johnston, *British Central Africa*, pp. 107, 115, 152.

would release Sharpe for urgently needed work in the northern part of the Protectorate and in the Company's sphere; he would also be Johnston's legal adviser, would exercise a general supervision over the administration of justice throughout British Central Africa, and would 'advise our magistrates, review their decisions, and tell them when they are making fools of themselves'. But the Foreign Office found it impossible to grant this request because the necessary salary could not be obtained from the Treasury, and it was far from certain whether the local revenues would cover it.[1] In these first years of British political control, justice must of necessity have been administered in a somewhat amateurish way, but it is impossible to determine how far, if at all, its essential interests suffered. Johnston's own dispatches and semi-official letters are almost the only available evidence. Writing to Anderson in March 1893 he remarked in passing that 'in the middle of this barbarism I feel that we cannot be too fastidiously correct in our legal procedure', and the probability seems to be that he and his officials usually lived up to this aspiration as far as their legal competence and their physical endurance permitted.

The range of activities with which the Administration could even attempt to cope was necessarily limited. Education remained entirely in the hands of the missions. To a large extent the same was true of health, for although a doctor joined the staff in 1892 his work was mainly administrative rather than medical: he was at first 'assistant collector and medical officer'—in that order—at Fort Johnston, and afterwards he was employed as a magistrate in the Company's sphere. It was not until 1895 that the position of Medical Officer to the Administration came into being, though by the following year its holder had acquired the status of Principal Medical Officer, with two junior colleagues.

[1] F.O. 84/2197: Johnston to Salisbury, No. 15, 29 Mar. 1892; F.O. 84/2196: F.O. to Johnston, 8 June 1892; F.O. 2/54: Johnston to Davidson, 10 May 1893; F.O. 2/53: Davidson to Johnston, 7 June 1893; F.O. 2/54: Johnston to Davidson, 24 Aug. 1893; to this last letter there is a minute, dated 19 July 1894, in which Davidson remarks:
'Since he [Johnston] has returned to this country I have seen him and explained the matter to him verbally. He seems to have made arrangements which are, at any rate for the present, fairly satisfactory to him, and there is no need for any further action in the matter, either official or private.'
The position in 1896, according to Johnston's *British Central Africa* (p. 152) was that the Administration now included 'a Judicial Officer at Blantyre, who is at the head of the Judicial Establishment'. So Johnston had his way in the end.

There were, however, two constructive tasks not directly administrative in character to which all possible energy and resources were devoted. One was to make a thorough survey of the Shiré country, and particularly of the boundaries of European estates: for this purpose Johnston in 1892 engaged two qualified surveyors from Natal. The other was to open up the Shiré Highlands and to link them to the river at Chiromo and Katunga by means of roads capable of carrying wheeled traffic, in place of the rough tracks which had hitherto served the Lakes Company. Road-making was the chief duty of Captain B. L. Sclater, an officer of the Royal Engineers who served with the Administration during the first two years of its existence—although, like everyone else, Sclater had to turn his hand to many tasks. In 1896 the Administration included a Superintendent of Public Works, with a European assistant and six Indian artisans; a Superintendent of Roadmaking, with two Assistant Superintendents; and a First Surveyor, who was a European, with three Indian surveyors seconded by the Government of India.

⸱   ⸱   ⸱

Preoccupied though he was by his task in the Shiré country, Johnston never forgot that the territory for which he was responsible extended far to the north and west. But, being completely without the means to make his authority effective throughout so large an area, he was obliged at first to ignore the slave-raiding perpetrated by the powerful Bemba tribe who dominated the Nyasa–Tanganyika plateau, to leave the Angoni to their own devices, and to be very cautious in his relations with the Arabs. Provided that the line of communications with the south end of Tanganyika was not endangered, his Administration would avert its attention from the misdeeds of the inhabitants. Johnston even made a virtue of necessity by declaring that

'subjugation' is an ugly word to use in connection with British enterprise in British Central Africa. We do not come here necessarily to subjugate; we come to protect and instruct: so long as no native tribe attacks us or the natives under our immediate administration we do not attempt to interfere too much with its own internal dissensions or evil practices.[1]

One Government station, it is true, was set up in the Company's

[1] F.O. 2/55: Johnston to Rosebery, No. 56, C.A. , 17 Oct. 1893.

sphere at the very beginning of the Administration's existence, but there was a special reason for founding it. The boundary with the Congo Free State was not yet settled, and Johnston was much worried lest an important part of the country brought within the British sphere by treaty with the native chiefs in 1890 should be lost through unchecked encroachments by the agents of King Leopold—'that old fox of the Belgians', as he called him. He therefore sent an agent to reside at the north-eastern corner of Lake Mweru, and, doubtless for reasons of prestige, named the post 'Rhodesia'. It could and did serve in later years as a base from which to extend effective British administrative authority, but when first created it was much too weak to fulfil more than its primary purpose as a symbol of British determination to prevent the absorption of the country by the Congo State.

Fortunately the Arabs, on their side, had no wish to engage in a life-and-death struggle with the Administration if they could help it. When Buchanan visited Mlozi in March 1891 he found him 'fully prepared to maintain that he is the best behaved Arab in Nyassaland', and stoutly denying that he was continuing to take any part in the slave-trade, although Buchanan himself had no doubt that he was lying, and that he had by no means abandoned his intention 'to play the role of Sultan of Nkonde'.[1] He had recently married a daughter of Jumbe, and there seemed some slight hope that Jumbe's influence combined with the chastisement he had received from the Lakes Company would guide him into more settled and useful ways.

But any influence that there may have been was exercised in the reverse direction, for early in 1892 the Commissioner received a message from Jumbe stating that, while he himself would always remain loyal to the Queen and refrain from slave-trading, some of his captains thought otherwise, and in his old age his control over them was weakening. They saw Mlozi, Makanjira, and others gaining great profit by sending slave-caravans to the coast, and asked, 'Why should we not do the same? Who is this Englishman who tries to stop us?' He therefore warned Johnston 'that the Arabs on the Lake do not like you, and they say that after Ramadhan they will unite and drive you from Nyasa, because you are trying to stop slave-caravans and because you threaten to destroy their dhows'. Johnston received a similar warning, through

[1] F.O. 84/2115: Buchanan to Salisbury, No. 14, 29 Mar. 1891.

Fotheringham, from a professedly friendly Arab at Karonga, and spies whom he maintained at the *barazas* or courts of the chief Arabs reported to the same effect.[1]

It appears that Johnston paid heed to these warnings, recognizing that for the time being he had more than enough to do to suppress the slave-trade in the southern part of the Protectorate, and that he must of necessity turn a blind eye to the misdeeds of the Arabs in the north. When Sharpe visited Karonga in the following August, and discussed affairs with Msalema and another of Mlozi's headmen—Mlozi himself being absent with Kopa-Kopa in Senga—he received complaints of provocative behaviour by the Lakes Company's representative at Karonga,[2] and of an attempt by Dr. Cross of Livingstonia to start a mission school just outside Mlozi's town: but they did not voice any grievances against the Administration itself. The interview with Sharpe was 'friendly', and they repeatedly assured him that they had no desire for war with the British, but wished 'to live quietly and carry on their trade peacefully'.

Equal complaisance was shown to Sharpe by the Arabs of the more remote interior, when, after leaving Karonga, he visited them in the course of a journey to the south end of Tanganyika and to the country around Lake Mweru. He spent two days with Abdallah-bin-Suleiman, who only a year previously had destroyed the town of Nsama, with whom Sharpe had made a treaty on his previous journey through the country, in 1890. The murder of Nsama and the enslavement of many of his people did not, however, prevent Abdallah from receiving the vice-consul cordially, assuring him that he bore no ill will towards the British; and Sharpe on his side deemed it futile to broach the subject of the slave-trade. In the course of conversation he reported,

Abdallah said to me: 'I'll govern the country for you, and you can give me a salary.' This seems to be the idea now general among the Arabs in Central Africa, that they should get a salary and have a free hand. As the Arabs are themselves the only really serious disturbers of the peace in Itawa, it would suit them well.[3]

A similar arrangement had been suggested by Mlozi at his inter-

[1] F.O. 84/2197: Johnston to Salisbury, No. 7, C.A., Confidential, 20 Feb. 1892. [2] At that time a certain White.
[3] F.O. 2/54: Sharpe to Johnston, 17 Dec. 1892, enclosed in Johnston to Rosebery, No. 3, C.A., 2 Jan. 1893.

view with Buchanan in March 1891: he had referred to Jumbe's subsidy as a precedent applicable to himself.

Indeed, as the position of the Arabs in Central Africa became increasingly endangered by the activities of the Germans to the east and of the Belgians to the west, they must have been all the more ready to welcome the desire of the British authorities to avoid a quarrel with them. Before the end of 1894 Rumaliza, his power shattered by the Belgians, was seeking permission—which was refused him—to settle in British territory.[1]

On the east coast, however, the Germans at Kilwa as well as the Portuguese at Quilimane were willing to supply Arab caravans with as many guns and as much gunpowder as their ivory could buy, and the slavers on British territory seldom lacked arms or ammunition. At Johnston's request representations were made at Berlin and Lisbon, and in reply assurances were given that telegraphic instructions had been sent out to the local authorities to cut off these supplies;[2] the supplies nevertheless remained as easily obtainable as before.[3] Johnston was hardly in a morally strong position to complain, as he did, that the Brussels Act was being infringed, for he himself, when preparing to begin his administration, had made the amazing assertion that the slave-trade in the Shiré Highlands and on the Nyasa–Tanganyika plateau was 'absolutely non-existent', and that he therefore saw no reason why he should not permit the importation of gunpowder in order that the revenue might profit from the collection of duty. This suggestion had been treated by Anderson with the contempt it deserved, and he had been directed not only to declare the whole Shiré province 'infected by the slave trade' but to prohibit the sale of firearms in any part of the territory he administered.[4] When he complained that peaceable natives should not be left without the

---

[1] F.O. 2/68: Johnston to Kimberley, 19 Nov. 1894, enclosing Marshall to Johnston, 7 Aug. 1894: Sharpe to Kimberley, No. 101, C.A., 21 Nov. 1894.

[2] F.O. 84/2198: Johnston to Salisbury (tel.), 21 Mar. 1892; F.O. to Johnston, tel. No. 8, Africa, 9 May 1892.

[3] F.O. 84/2197: Johnston to Salisbury, No. 34, C.A., 7 Sept. 1892; F.O. 84/2198: J. to S., tel. of 12 Dec. 1892.

[4] F.O. 84/2114: Johnston to Salisbury, No. 1, 11–13 June 1891, with Anderson's minute; F.O. to Johnston, No. 34, 12 Nov. 1891; F.O. 84/2197: Johnston to Salisbury, No. 17, C.A., 31 Mar. 1892. The word 'province' seems to have been used simply as a geographical expression: there was no provincial administrative authority intermediate between the Commissioner and the district Collector.

means of self-defence while their Yao and Arab enemies were able to obtain guns and powder from across the border, Lord Salisbury expressed the opinion that when the Brussels Act referred to 'regions infected by the slave trade', it must be interpreted to mean 'the regions or districts in which the camps or settlements of the slave-traders are situated', and not those in which slave-raids were being carried on. 'That', he observed, 'would be an absurd definition, and would deprive these poor natives of their last hope of resistance'.[1] Johnston was informed accordingly.[2] It may or may not have been wise to give him this discretion, but Salisbury's motives in giving it were above question, and by the time he received it he was so deeply involved in his struggle against the slave-trade that he was unlikely to see any advantage in conniving at the purchase of arms by those who were engaged in that trade.

In the course of the next year there were repeated complaints that British Central Africa was being 'flooded' with powder from the coast, but diplomatic representations met with denials and even counter-charges, until at last Lord Rosebery—Salisbury's successor for a time at the Foreign Office—exclaimed: 'I am extremely weary of this eternal pot-and-kettle controversy about the importation of arms and powder. Each nation conscientiously believes that the other is a sort of explosive pimp. I suppose the secret to lie in the old query *Quis custodiet ipsos custodes*? But for the present I presume we can only go on forwarding the old fly-blown complaints to each other.'[3] Anderson interpreted this as a directive to refrain from further action.[4] Eventually, indeed, it occurred to him that as British Central Africa, except for the Shiré province, had never been declared 'infected', the Brussels Act was not technically infringed at all (however much violence was done to its spirit) when the Germans connived at the introduction of powder. He pointed this out to Johnston, who was constrained to agree,[5] and (five weeks later!) asked him if there was any objection to extending the area so declared. Johnston replied that there was none:

[1] F.O. 84/2197: Johnston to Salisbury, No. 18, C.A., 10 May 1892, with minutes.
[2] F.O. 84/2196: F.O. to Johnston, No. 44, 14 July 1892.
[3] F.O. 2/55: Johnston to Rosebery, No. 45, C.A., 14 Sept. 1893: minutes.
[4] F.O. 2/66: Johnston to Kimberley, No. 27, C.A., 14 Mar. 1894: minutes.
[5] F.O. 2/66: Sharpe to Kimberley, No. 34, C.A., 26 Apr. 1894: minutes. Johnston was at this time in England and could be consulted at the Foreign Office.

'Extent of district infected with slave trade = All British Central Africa.'[1] An appropriate proclamation was therefore issued.[2]

By this time, however, the British authorities had come to place most of their confidence in self-help; for, although it was obviously impossible to exercise the necessary surveillance over the whole frontier without employing far more men than the available finances could support, the evil could be very largely reduced by plugging the worst leaks. Not much could be smuggled by river past Port Herald and Chiromo, and the overland routes round Mlanje were controlled by Forts Lister and Anderson. Thus, although smuggling into the Shiré province was still possible and was more or less actively carried on, the chief need was to control the ferries across Lake Nyasa, to prevent the westward movement of powder and the eastward movement of slaves.

The slave-route from Rifu (Kazembe's) to Makanjira's seems to have been blocked effectively by the establishment of Fort Maguire; but Makanjira's defeat was followed within a few months by a revival of slave-trading at Kota-Kota, a development which Jumbe seems to have been genuinely unable to prevent. Major Edwards, who was now the senior officer in command of the troops, was therefore sent by Sharpe, acting as Commissioner during Johnston's absence in England, to visit Kota-Kota in one of the lake gunboats. About this time Jumbe died, and although his successor was installed with due solemnity a few weeks later, the opportunity was taken to place the affairs of the Marimba district under the general supervision of a British Resident, who assumed control over the ferry to the Portuguese shore.[3]

[1] F.O. 2/66: Sharpe to Kimberley, No. 39, C.A., 11 June 1894: minutes.
[2] F.O. 2/67: Sharpe to Kimberley, No. 80, C.A., 10 Oct. 1894.
[3] F.O. 2/66: Sharpe to Kimberley, No. 37, C.A., 9 May 1894; Sharpe to Hill, 24 May 1894; F.O. 2/67: Nicoll to Johnston, 16 July 1894; Edwards to Johnston, 17 July 1894; Sharpe to Kimberley, No. 56, C.A., 18 July 1894; No. 62, C.A., 2 Aug. 1894; and No. 71, C.A., 20 Sept. 1894; F.O. 2/68: Nicoll to Johnston, 23 Sept. 1894.
Nicoll was the official placed in charge of Kota-Kota. In his letter of 23 Sept. he gave an eyewitness account of the installation of Mwinyi Heri, the son of the late Jumbe's immediate predecessor, as the new Jumbe. After relating how the Vizier, brother of the late Jumbe, placed upon Mwinyi Heri first a beautiful Muscat shawl, then a gorgeously worked cap, and finally a white turban, all to the accompaniment of Moslem prayers, Nicoll continued:
'The robing ceremony over, the Jumbe had to listen to a long and pointed harangue delivered by the Vizier, who having hold of Jumbe's left ear took pains by sundry smart twitches to emphasise the different points. . . .
'After the Vizier had finished his address a younger brother of the late Jumbe

It was, however, at or near Deep Bay, much farther to the north, that powder was landed in large quantities from German territory. The German authorities had a strong financial inducement to promote this traffic: with them the temptation was not merely, as it had been for Johnston, the revenue to be obtained from customs duties, but the entire proceeds of a Government monopoly. The difficulty was made worse by the presence of a large German expedition, which had arrived in 1892 under the command of Major Hermann von Wissmann, a distinguished but neurotic explorer who now bore the title of Imperial Commissioner for German East Africa. It had come by the Zambesi–Shiré route, for the purpose of conveying to Lake Nyasa the sections of a large steamer, which was to operate for the suppression of the slave-trade, and which was named after Wissmann himself. Johnston, in accordance with instructions from home, had done his best to be helpful and hospitable to the officers who led it, but he found most of them unreasonable in their demands upon him and utterly ungrateful, while towards the natives they were mean and over-bearing. About the end of 1892 Wissmann had departed with the greater part of the expedition to the north end of Lake Nyasa, to establish German authority in the country north of the Songwe boundary, and the task of launching the steamer had been left in the hands of his second-in-command, Baron von Eltz. Eltz was a man with whom friendly relations were possible, and in February 1893, when Johnston was besieged by Liwonde's men on the bank of the Upper Shiré, he brought timely relief with a force of his Sudanese troops. But the departure of Wissmann with his more offensive subordinates did not mean that Johnston was able to forget them. They showed off their power to the natives on the British side of the Songwe, aweing them into making lavish 'presents' of food, telling them that the British were mere traders, and forcing a number of Tonga to work for them. Since the ferry

and of the Vizier seized the right ear and shouted into it, "Che Seyed, Mwinyi". The spectators shouted the same Salute. The Vizier then proclaimed Mwinyi Heri Sultan of Marimba and Jumbe of Kotakota, adding that anyone hereafter found guilty of addressing the Jumbe by his former name—Mwinyi Heri—should be fined to the amount of forty dollars.

'I was then urged to speak to the Sultan and headmen in the name of the Serkal. I did so very briefly and handed to Jumbe a gift from H.M. Commissioner and Consul General.

'Next morning I took my Sikh guard down and saluted Jumbe, who afterwards retired to a six days' seclusion.'

between Deep Bay and their own harbour of Amelia Bay was being used regularly for the transport of slaves, they complained that the British were failing to carry out their obligations under the Brussels Act. Johnston therefore decided that the time had come when he must establish a British post in the northern part of the Protectorate, and dispatched Crawshay to Deep Bay to take nominal charge of the 'North Nyasa District', but with his immediate responsibilities limited to watching the ferry and keeping an eye on the Germans.

After a few months at his post Crawshay reported that his policy towards the actual inhabitants of his district, Arabs as well as Africans, 'has been absolutely one of "Laissez-faire"'. It could not have been otherwise, since the force he commanded consisted only of three Sikhs and half a dozen Makua. Nevertheless he was able to put a fairly effective stop to the use of the ferry for the export of slaves, since it was impossible for an eastward-bound caravan to assemble at the lake shore and embark on dhows without word arriving in time for him to intercept it: Mlozi and his associates were therefore obliged to use the overland route round the north end, where they ran a serious risk of falling into the hands of the Germans. With slaves accumulating in their strongholds they openly threatened, towards the end of 1893, to force the ferry open to the slave-trade by armed assault; but they changed their mind when Crawshay built a fort, augmented its garrison by training some of the local natives as auxiliaries, and protected it with some pieces of artillery which, together with a few additional Sikhs, Johnston sent up to him. For the time being they reconciled themselves to using the ferry under Crawshay's supervision: thus they could dispose of their ivory provided that they paid the prescribed export duty and could find means of transporting it to the sea-coast.[1] When Sharpe visited Karonga early in 1894 and had an interview there with Mlozi and Kopa-Kopa, he was able to report that 'the interview, on their part, consisted mostly in repeated assertions that they desired above all things peace, that they wished to use the Deep Bay ferry under Mr. Crawshay's

[1] 'I look upon ivory and the slave trade as inseparable practically (until there is some means of direct and cheap transport from Nyasa to the sea); but as things are now, we shall be able to prevent the transport of slaves by dhow across the Lake. How Caravans will arrange for the transport of their ivory from the east side of Nyasa to the sea-coast, I do not know, but that will be their affair.' Sharpe to Johnston, 17 Sept. 1894 (in F.O. 2/68).

supervision, that they were willing to pay the duties, and would refrain from the slave trade'.

It was not slave-caravans moving eastward but powder-caravans moving westward which presented the main challenge to Crawshay's authority. Had he attempted to block the path of one of the larger Arab parties, he and his few men would have been annihilated. He therefore contented himself by charging duty, and requiring it to be paid in powder, thereby reducing the amount imported by one-tenth; the Arabs were willing enough to make this payment, nor did their conscience shrink from permitting them to sign a declaration that they would not use what was left to them for any harmful purpose.[1]

By the time that Crawshay had built his fort and was strong enough to ban the importation of powder completely, the *Hermann von Wissmann* was in operation on the lake. Placed there for the declared purpose of combating the slave-trade, she was employed during the greater part of 1894 in conveying powder—not indeed to British territory, since complaints on that score would have been difficult to answer—but to the German shore just north of the Songwe river, across which it was taken soon after being landed. Since representations, made both locally and at Berlin, achieved no result, Acting-Commissioner Sharpe decided that the Administration must incur the expense of establishing a post near the mouth of the Songwe, and thus stop the remaining important leak by which powder came into British territory. By the end of 1894 the post was finished. And by that time, too, Sharpe had received and carried out the belated instruction to issue a formal proclamation banning the importation of firearms and powder all along the frontier except at Chiromo, where such importation was strictly controlled in accordance with the detailed provisions of the Brussels Act.[2]

⚬   ⚬   ⚬

[1] F.O. 2/54: Johnston to Rosebery, No. 32, C.A., 24 Aug. 1893, enclosing Crawshay to Johnston, 30 June 1893; F.O. 2/55: Johnston to Rosebery, No. 56, C.A., 17 Oct. 1893, enclosing Crawshay to Johnston, 23 Sept. 1893; Johnston to Rosebery, No. 68, C.A., 16 Dec. 1893; Johnston to Anderson, 16 Dec. 1893, enclosing Crawshay to Johnston, 17 Oct. 1893; F.O. 2/66: Johnston to Kimberley, No. 12, C.A., 24 Jan. 1894, enclosing Crawshay to Johnston, 28 Oct. 1893; Johnston to Canning [Secretary to the B.S.A. Co.], 10 Mar. 1894; Johnston to Kimberley, No. 27, C.A., 14 Mar. 1894, enclosing Sharpe to Johnston of same date.

[2] F.O. 2/66: Sharpe to Kimberley, No. 33, C.A., 21 Apr. 1894; No. 37, C.A., 9 May 1894; Sharpe to Hill, 24 May 1894; F.O. 2/67: Sharpe to Kimberley,

The activities of Wissmann were not limited to the immediate vicinity of Lake Nyasa. He led an expedition across the Nyasa–Tanganyika plateau, engaging in several conflicts with the natives as he progressed, and in particular putting to flight 5,000 Bemba who, he said, had attacked his camp on 7 July 1893; he then wrote to Johnston pointing out that he could not lawfully pursue the Bemba across the British border, and asking that the British themselves should take some action to prevent them from making annual slave-raids into German territory. Johnston was at this time in no position to add the Bemba to his other enemies, yet it was essential that he should keep open the line of communication with Lake Tanganyika, and concern himself with the safety of the British missionaries and of the Lakes Company's men, whom the Bemba might decide to attack as a measure of retaliation. The anxiety aroused by Wissmann's doings prompted him to send Marshall with a small escort of Sikhs to build a fort at Abercorn, near the Lakes Company's depot of Kituta, a few miles from Lake Tanganyika, on the road from Karonga; and Marshall was able to establish sufficient contact and understanding with the Bemba to restore peace to the Nyasa–Tanganyika plateau.

A few weeks after the engagement of 7 July, Wissmann handed over his command to von Eltz and returned to Germany—but not before he had gone into Itawa in search of big game, and had destroyed a native village there after its inhabitants—so he alleged —had fired upon him. To complete Johnston's exasperation, Wissmann remarked that the village lay north of latitude 8° 30' S., so that it was not in British territory but within the boundary of the Congo Free State. Johnston retorted that its actual position was south of that line, and that, moreover, it was not Wissmann's business to presume to lay down where the boundary between British and Belgian territory should run. King Leopold had, indeed, staked his claim to the 8° 30' line in 1885, and Britain had not contested it; but Johnston and Sharpe were both exceedingly anxious that the final territorial settlement with the Congo State should give the boundary a northward slant between the north end of Lake Mweru and the Tanganyika shore, so that the route round

No. 60, C.A., 30 July 1894; Sharpe to Hill, 8 Aug. 1894; Johnston to Anderson, 15 Aug. 1894; Sharpe to Kimberley, No. 80, C.A., 10 Oct. 1894; Johnston to Kimberley, 15 Oct. 1894.

the north end of the intervening Mweru salt swamp would be kept within the British sphere.

Pending a settlement between Governments, Johnston had on his own responsibility made a provisional arrangement with Captain Jacques, the Congo State's representative in the Tanganyika region, that each would respect as the boundary a line running from the north end of Mweru to Cape Akalunga on Lake Tanganyika; this arrangement was made permanent by a formal agreement between the two Governments concluded on 12 May 1894.[1]

◇　◇　◇

In 1894, although the great majority of the Sikhs were still employed in the southern part of the Protectorate, the Arabs were beginning to find the pressure of the British authorities an intolerable hindrance to their chief business in life. Their powder supply was being stopped, their slaves were being released, and the Government stations were becoming rallying-points for the native population. By the end of the year there were five stations or sub-stations in the Company's sphere, in addition to Deep Bay and the Songwe post in the northern part of the Protectorate: Abercorn and Rhodesia were the most important, and two of the others, Sumbu and Kaputa, were on the route between them. Sumbu was on the south-west coast of Lake Tanganyika, and Kaputa was a village on the northern limit of the Mweru salt swamp—its inhabitants specializing in salt-making and buying food from people who dwelt in more fertile regions. The fifth, Mputa, was on the shore of Lake Mweru close to Rhodesia. When Sharpe had visited Mputa in 1892 he had found that its inhabitants, salt-makers like the Kaputa people, had recently been driven out by Abdallah-bin-Suleiman, and that this same Arab magnate exacted a tribute (paid in salt) from other villages, including Kaputa.[2] Two years later the natives were finding security at both places under the protection of a British official, and Mkula, who had now adopted his father's name of Nsama, was gathering together the scattered survivors of his people in a fortified village, whose defence was assisted by four

[1] F.O. 2/54: Johnston to Rosebery, No. 40, C.A., 31 Aug. 1893, enclosing Wissmann to Johnston, 14 July 1893; F.O. 2/55: Johnston to Rosebery, No. 45, C.A., 14 Sept. 1893; No. 48, C.A., 25 Sept. 1893, with enclosures; No. 56, C.A., 17 Oct. 1893, with enclosures; and No. 63a, C.A., 31 Oct. 1893. The text of the Agreement of 12 May 1894 is in Hertslet, vol. ii, p. 578.

[2] F.O. 2/54: Sharpe to Johnston, 17 Dec. 1892, enclosed in Johnston to Rosebery, No. 3, C.A., 2 Jan. 1893.

African soldiers lent by the Collector at Rhodesia. The latter reported in July (1894) that 'the people really seem to appreciate the security now afforded to them. . . . I am hopeful myself that Itawa will once more become a flourishing country as it was of old, and that its population will rapidly increase up to a certain extent; but allowance will have to be made for the great number of women and children exported from the country', as a result of which the adult males numbered fully 40 per cent. of the whole population.[1]

The situation at Sumbu differed from that at Mputa and Kaputa. Sumbu was the village of an Arab named Teleka, and the official who resided there had, as Sharpe put it, been sent 'as much to be "in evidence" as for any other purpose'. Without quarrelling with the Arabs, he was able to watch and report on their doings, and to acquire influence among the surrounding people. The station was useful also as a depot for stores destined for Mweru.[2] Although Marshall, the Collector at Abercorn whose 'district' included Sumbu, assured Johnston in August that Sharpe had been 'most emphatic in his warnings against provoking the Arabs', he reported in the same letter that towards the end of the previous year all the Arabs from Mpata (Mlozi's) to Itawa had simultaneously begun to strengthen their defences.[3] He did not, indeed, regard this action as anything more than a natural response to the Administration's own policy of strongly fortifying its stations, and it is probably true that the Arabs had not yet made up their minds to initiate hostilities.[4] Yet they must have been realizing with increasing conviction that their way of life could not survive the consolidation of British rule. As early as March 1894 Johnston remarked that they were all 'glowering at us now, and we cannot afford to withdraw a single Sikh or recall a gun'.[5]

By July 1895 the attitude of Mlozi had become so truculent that Johnston paid a special visit to Karonga to try to persuade him to keep the peace according to the treaty of 1889. But Mlozi refused

[1] F.O. 2/68: Watson to Johnston, 8 July 1894, enclosed in Johnston to Kimberley, 19 Nov. 1894.
[2] F.O. 2/66: Sharpe to Hill, 24 May 1894.
[3] F.O. 2/68: Marshall to Johnston, 7 Aug. 1894, enclosed in Johnston to Kimberley, 19 Nov. 1894.
[4] The chastened attitude shown by Mlozi when Sharpe visited him early in 1894 is evidence that at that time he, at least, shrank from plunging into war.
[5] F.O. 2/66: Johnston to Canning, 10 Mar. 1894.

to come to an interview, and sent the Commissioner a threatening letter, in the course of which he announced: 'The British have closed my route to the coast: very well, I will close their road to Tanganyika.' In the following months he obliged the Administration with further evidence of his hostile intentions, seizing and severely flogging a British lay missionary, and openly boasting that he would make war upon the British when the rainy season came to hamper their operations. Johnston was thus given every inducement to strike first.

It was essential to a decisive victory that the Arabs should not be allowed to escape to the interior, and it was therefore necessary to take them by surprise. This could be achieved only if the whole expedition could be conveyed to Karonga in a single journey; but the *Domira* was by itself quite insufficient for this purpose, and the gunboats could provide accommodation for only about fifteen men each. It was now that for the first time Johnston had reason to be pleased that the *Hermann von Wissmann* was in operation on Lake Nyasa. Her captain readily agreed to co-operate, not even asking for any financial profit on the journey.

The expedition, led by Major Edwards and accompanied by Johnston himself, left Fort Johnston on 24 November. Having arrived at Karonga, it made a carefully planned night advance upon the stockaded villages of Kopa-Kopa and Msalema, and began to bombard them soon after dawn on the morning of 2 December. The defenders were able to retreat to Mlozi's, but the evacuation of the two outposts enabled the attacking force to surround the main town and cut off all possibility of escape. After enduring a heavy bombardment, Mlozi asked for conditions of peace. Johnston replied that if he surrendered, his life and the lives of the other Arabs would be spared, but no further promise could be made. He decided to continue the struggle. The bombardment was resumed: the Arabs in desperation made a furious sortie: the Sikhs drove them back to the stockade, seized the chance to scramble over it, and mastered the town. Mlozi, wounded in the head by a shell-splinter, was detected in a hiding-place underneath his house. A council of Wankonde chiefs, held under Johnston's superintendence, found him guilty of the murder of native hostages, and without more ado he was hanged.

The destruction of Mlozi's power was the last and the most important of Johnston's many conflicts with the disturbers of the peace.[1] The rule of law was now at last tolerably secure throughout the Protectorate, and its extension across the Company's sphere, southwards from the Stevenson Road as far as the Portuguese border, was achieved with surprisingly little difficulty in the years immediately following.[2]

3. Lines of Policy

In appointing officials, setting up forts and customs posts, building roads, and making other administrative decisions, Johnston could do as he pleased,[3] provided he did not incur expense which he could not defray out of his revenue, and provided also that he could satisfy the Foreign Office that there was no justification for the complaints presented to it from time to time by the Blantyre Mission and by various traders and planters. Yet the control exercised over him by the Foreign Office was not without importance. He had to obtain from it a magistrate's warrant for every official to whom he wished to entrust the hearing of court cases, and this involved delay and inconvenience, not all of it necessary. He also required its approval for all his legislative acts: thus the general lines of his policy could be, and were, carefully watched and closely controlled—all the more so because, as Lord Salisbury remarked, 'Johnston does not minimise any discretion given to him'.

Johnston's legislative authority was derived from a provision of the Africa Order in Council, 1889, which empowered consuls to make regulations, known as Queen's Regulations, to promote 'peace, order, and good government', to enforce the observance of treaties, and in certain other specified cases. But when he issued regulations laying down customs duties, and proposed to make any breach of them an offence under the Order in Council, there was much heart-searching at the Africa Department of the Foreign Office. Could any of the specific purposes stated in the Order be said to include the raising of a customs revenue? The uncertainty

[1] In all, the number of slaves released by the British between 1891 and 1896 was 2,561: *British Central Africa*, p. 149.

[2] C. Gouldsbury and H. Sheane, *The Great Plateau of Northern Rhodesia* (Edward Arnold, London, 1911), pp. 40–43; H. M. Hole, *The Making of Rhodesia* (Macmillan, London, 1926), pp. 387–90.

[3] Hence it is impossible in most cases to state precisely when a Collector was appointed to, or took up his duties at, a particular post, since Johnston saw no need to report on such matters unless there was some special reason for doing so.

was removed in 1893 by a new Africa Order in Council, which amended that of 1889. 'I don't say', Davidson explained, 'that it is clear that the Regulations are *not* "Queen's Regulations" even under the existing Order in Council, but rather that there is no doubt that they will be Queen's Regulations under a new Order in Council which has been drafted, amongst other things, to remove this very doubt which now exists.'[1]

The Berlin Act of 1885, adopted by the Powers of Europe, great and small, and by the United States, had decreed complete freedom of importation throughout a vast region which included the whole of the Protectorate and a wide strip of territory extending across the Company's sphere from the German border as far south as the watershed between Lake Tanganyika and the Zambesi. Thus the entire area over which Johnston's Administration was able to exercise any degree of authority fell within the free trade zone, and had there been no modification of the Berlin Act his work would have been rendered impossible through lack of revenue. Fortunately this was foreseen by the hard-headed Sir John Kirk, who served as British delegate at the Brussels Conference in 1890.[2] Kirk was able to obtain acceptance of an Agreement supplementary to the Brussels Act[3] and due to come into force on the same date, whereby a revenue duty of 5 per cent. could be imposed on all imports into the free zone, except machinery, agricultural implements, and materials for constructing railways, tramways, or roads, all of which must still be admitted duty free. A specially high duty of 10 per cent. was permitted on such firearms as it was lawful, under the provisions of the Brussels Act, to import.

Johnston would have liked to start levying the permitted duties as soon as he could make arrangements to collect them, but the Foreign Office forbade him to do so until the Brussels Act was ratified. Ratification was delayed by hesitancy on the part of France, and the Act did not come into operation until 2 April 1892. Hence, during the first nine months of his rule, Johnston's revenue was limited to what he could raise by the imposition of

[1] F.O. 2/54: Johnston to Rosebery, No. 12, C.A., 31 Mar. 1893: minutes. Cf. minutes on No. 30, C.A., 18 Aug. 1892, in F.O. 84/2197.

[2] Cawston Papers, vol. ii: Kirk to Cawston, 3 Nov. 1890; Cawston to Kirk, 12 Nov. 1890; Kirk to Cawston, 15 Nov. 1890.

[3] Printed in Hertslet, *The Map of Africa by Treaty*, vol. ii, pp. 518–19. The Agreement was between Britain, Germany, and Italy and was dated 22 Dec. 1890.

an export duty on ivory and by the sale of various licences.[1] But when he argued that it was unfair to invoke the unratified Act to prevent him from admitting guns and powder into regions 'infected by the slave trade', without permitting him on his side to invoke it to levy the duties which he urgently required, his logic made no impression upon the more scrupulous—and, it must be acknowledged, less harassed—Sir Percy Anderson.[2]

In reviewing Johnston's regulations the Foreign Office was less concerned with the appropriateness of the policy they embodied than with their strict legality and, above all, with the possibility that they might give offence to foreigners. Hence the effects of its control were sometimes rather unfortunate. For example, in March 1893 Johnston issued a circular informing the European settlers that debts owed to them by natives could not in future be recovered in the consular courts; his intention was 'to obviate serious troubles which were arising from the usurious practices of the Lakes Company and other traders, practices with which I had become only too conversant on the west coast of Africa'. According to Davidson, however, the circular had the effect of depriving British subjects of their lawful rights, and he was therefore required to withdraw it. Again, when he proposed a maximum penalty of £100 for smuggling, Anderson exclaimed: 'What should we say of this [regulation] if it were made by Portugal? The penalty is absurdly excessive.' Johnston must be told that 'threats of excessive punishments' would 'lead to grave difficulties with Foreign Powers', and, at Lord Salisbury's own behest, the figure was reduced to £10. It was in vain that Johnston argued that such a fine, unaccompanied by imprisonment or even by confiscation of the smuggled goods, would be an insufficient deterrent to the evading of the larger licence-payments or of the heavy export duties on large consignments of ivory.

On the whole, however, the control exercised over Johnston's

[1] At first the export duty on ivory was 1s. a pound, but in Mar. 1892 Johnston reduced it to 6d. a pound on the smaller tusks and 9d. on the larger. The licences were: (1) a gun licence of 4s. a year; (2) to hunt big game, £25 a year (this, unlike the first, concerned only Europeans); (3) to import alcohol, 2s. 6d. for each importation; (4) to sell alcohol (to non-Africans only) on fixed premises, £10, or on a 'perambulating licence', £100; (5) to trade (this concerned only non-Africans), £10. Stamp duties, ranging from 1d. on a cheque to a maximum of 10s., were introduced in 1895.

[2] F.O. 84/2114: Johnston to Salisbury, No. 15, C.A., Confidential, 31 Aug. 1891, with minutes; F.O. to J., 12 Nov. 1891.

decrees was beneficial in its results. On at least one occasion a regulation was amended in the interests of humaneness and common sense: whereas Johnston had proposed that any hut on which the prescribed native tax had not been paid should be forfeit to the Administration the day after the tax fell due, the Foreign Office made provision for giving the defaulter two months' grace. And, on the principle that the right hand of any governing authority ought to be informed of what the left is doing, it was well that the Foreign Office should ask the Colonial Office whether the hut tax regulations would be admissible in African Protectorates under the latter's administration, and that the Post Office should be invited to comment on regulations concerning the mail service. Most important of all, the need for Foreign Office approval was salutary as the only existing check on what would otherwise have been, however well intended, a personal autocracy.[1]

In all his constructive labours Johnston was inspired and driven forward by the vision of a multiracial society which would be harmoniously interdependent, each race contributing of its best to the common good of all. On the general subject of European settlement in Africa, he held that south of the Zambesi, as also north of the Sahara, the majority of the population would eventually consist of pure-blooded white people—a view which, in those days, had not yet become manifestly inconsistent with rationality—but in the tropical heart of the continent European settlement must always be limited to the mountains and high plateaux, so that it could never take place on a large scale. This did not mean, however, that Central Africa should simply be left to the Africans, because the latter were too backward to be capable of unaided progress, and he was disposed to think that their backwardness was not merely cultural but biological, so that he doubted whether they could ever attain 'equal humanity' with peoples more advanced than themselves, unless they were 'dashed with the blood of a superior race'. Europeans were not suitable for this role of blood-donor: they were 'too superior' to the Africans for miscegenation to produce desirable results. An intermediate element was required, and was admirably supplied by the peoples

[1] It was not until 1907 that Executive and Legislative Councils were created to advise the Governor (as the Commissioner and Consul-General had become, in consequence of the transfer of the territory from the Foreign to the Colonial Office in 1904).

of Asia. True, the Arabs who were already present in the country were not Asiatics of the right kind: Johnston's initial hopes in that quarter had sunk so low by the beginning of 1893 that he declared that 'if it rested with us [the Administration] to express a wish and see it fulfilled, we should all of us immediately desire that every Arab might disappear from Central Africa'.[1] For the right kind of Asiatic it was necessary to look to India, whose people had much to contribute both by setting the natives a good example as cultivators and by engaging in small-scale trade. 'I have come to the conclusion', he wrote in 1895, 'that we shall confer a great benefit on India in inducing the stream of its emigrants to set their faces in this direction, and we shall confer an even greater benefit on British Central Africa by locating Indian families in these territories to a prudent and reasonable extent.'[2]

His idea was, in short, that the territory he administered, like the rest of tropical Africa, 'must be ruled by whites, developed by Indians, and worked by blacks'.[3] It never occurred to him—at least, during the Central African phase of his career—to ponder on what would happen if the Indians ever aspired to the role of the whites, and the Africans to equal citizenship and equal economic opportunity with both. A later generation, which has quite enough to do to work out a satisfactory relationship between European and African, has reason to be profoundly thankful that its problems have not—as yet—been complicated even further by the presence of such a large Indian community as Johnston desired to foster, and such as actually exists in Kenya and Natal.[4]

The opinion he held about the function and status appropriate to each of the three races was, of course, an expression of the kind of attitude against which the wrath of the non-European peoples has arisen with irresistible power scarcely more than half a century afterwards. But in Johnston's own mind it was not associated with any idea of racial privilege and repression. Being unable to see into the more distant future and the conflicts of interest which it

[1] F.O. 2/54: Johnston to Rosebery, No. 6, C.A., Confidential, 31 Jan. 1893.
[2] F.O. 2/88: Johnston to Kimberley, No. 68, C.A., 1 June 1895. Also F.O. 2/68: Johnston to Kimberley, 17 Nov. 1894; The Times, 7 Nov. 1894 (report of a speech by Johnston to the Liverpool Chamber of Commerce); British Central Africa, pp. 408, 472.
[3] F.O. 2/55: Johnston to Anderson, 10 Oct. 1893.
[4] The smallness of the Indian population of Nyasaland in recent years should not, however, be exaggerated. The Indians are already more numerous than the Europeans, and are multiplying with characteristic rapidity.

would bring—not as a result of the failure of British rule, but as a result of its very success in bringing the native peoples towards greater maturity, self-confidence, and self-respect—he was able to dwell with sincere enthusiasm on the harmony of interests which, in the more immediate future that he saw before him, would bind the three races into a co-operative whole. The idea found expression in his adoption of the symbolic colours black, white, and yellow—the last-mentioned being supposed to represent the Indian element—to be used on every possible occasion, in season and out of season. He wore a hatband of black, white, and yellow; he wrote his dispatches on notepaper edged with the same colours; the cover of his book, *British Central Africa*, and the flyleaf of his autobiography are similarly adorned. He even had a black, white, and yellow border put round the flags used in the Company's sphere, until he was rescued from this peculiar folly by Rhodes himself, who said to him, 'Please take it down and use a plain Jack. We cannot be too English.'[1]

Since, in actual fact, the 'yellow' element in the population remained comparatively unimportant—apart from the Sikh soldiers, most of whom were not permanent immigrants—the real practical test of his policy was the encounter of black and white.

The majority of the native population, as distinct from the minority who fought in defence of their vested interest in the slave-trade, welcomed the Administration as the bringer of a security hitherto unknown, and were glad to settle wherever its protection was assured, especially in the immediate vicinity of its forts.[2] In the southernmost extremity of the Protectorate, the strip of land on the west bank of the Shiré below Chiromo, numerous fugitives from what Johnston called 'the exorbitant taxation and forced labour of the unwise régime instituted by the Portuguese officials' had already settled even before the British Administration was formed.[3]

[1] A friend who has read this passage in typescript objects that Johnston's views were really rather less doctrinaire than it suggests: that too much emphasis has been given to their 'cold functionalism' and too little to the fiery enthusiasm with which Johnston cherished his ideal of interracial harmony and co-operation.

[2] 'All the people of Mañanja or A-nyanja stock (the real natives of the country) are settling in numbers round the European Stations, feeling at last that there is some part of Nyasaland where they will be tolerably safe from further slave raids.' F.O. 2/66: Johnston to Kimberley, No. 12, C.A., 24 Jan. 1894.

[3] F.O. 84/2114: Johnston to Salisbury, No. 11, C.A., 28 July 1891.

But the Administration's duty as protector did not end with the repression of armed violence committed by Yao and Arabs. It extended also to the restraining of over-acquisitiveness on the part of European planters and traders, and with them Johnston's relations were on the whole far from happy. Rough and impecunious settlers resented the control of this seemingly effeminate little man, who must needs have a white table-cloth, cut glass, and silver cutlery when he dined in the bush,[1] and whose officials, it was once alleged, had 'three yards of the Grace of God pinned to their coat-tails'.[2] Towards the restraints of law and towards the native population they had the attitude usual among pioneers or 'frontiersmen', and they drank whisky in such quantities that Johnston called it 'the bane of the Shire Highlands'. Johnston seems genuinely to have done his best to treat them with friendliness and to uphold what he believed to be their legitimate interests, but when their claims conflicted with native interests he tried to be impartial, and they therefore thought he was against them. He insisted that individual European employers should not themselves administer what they regarded as justice to the Africans who worked for them: all such matters must be decided by the Administration, which must try to hold the scales of justice even.[3] His was an 'imperial', theirs a 'colonial' point of view.

The most important matter that he had to settle was the mass of land claims advanced by Europeans. On 18 July 1891, only two days after his arrival at Chiromo as Commissioner, he put a stop to further speculation by issuing a circular declaring that no further purchases or leases of land from natives of British Central Africa would be recognized unless they received his sanction. The circular also stated that full particulars of all claims already acquired must be sent to him for investigation.[4]

During the two years which followed he was busy from time to time with the intricate and laborious task of examining and

---

[1] He took a certain pride in this, publishing in his *British Central Africa* a little photograph of 'my table in the bush'.

[2] F. M. Withers, 'Nyasaland in 1895–6', in the *Nyasaland Journal*, vol. 2, No. 1 (Jan. 1949), p. 27. Cf. his quotation from the *Central African Planter* of 1896: 'It is rumoured that Sir Harry Johnston will not return, and so far we have not heard anyone deplore the possible contingency. If the rumour proves correct we also hope that it will mean the end of the present autocratic form of government, and the beginning of a new régime.'

[3] F.O. 2/55: Johnston to Rosebery, No. 57, C.A., 18 Oct. 1893.

[4] F.O. 84/2197: Johnston to Rosebery, No. 43, C.A., 19 Nov. 1892: enclosure.

reaching decisions upon these claims. Many of them were extravagant enough to provoke his derision. Those who made them had
usually arrived in Nyasaland 'rich only in aspirations', and with a
small stock of calico and powder and a few cheap guns 'have induced some heedless young Chief or silly old savage to put his mark
on a paper conferring vast territories and sovereign rights on the
needy pioneer'. A certain Henry Brown, formerly an agent of the
Lakes Company, had asked a sub-chief in the Mlanje district to
sell him land, and when the sub-chief refused, pointing out that
the chief himself had already transferred the whole region to the
Crown, Brown replied, 'All right, I only want leave to plant coffee
and build a little house; you take this present gratis, and this
letter; that is all.' The note which he handed over, signed by himself, purported to certify that the sub-chief and the latter's brother
had agreed to sell him a vaguely defined but most desirable estate;
it was dated six months or so before the time when Brown had
first arrived in the country, in order that it should appear to give
him a claim prior to that of the Crown. The Lakes Company itself
put forward a claim to about 140,000 acres of first-class land,
together with what the 'agreement' defined as 'all mining rights,
fisheries, game preserves, taxes, tolls, duties, and privileges, of
whatever sort or kind', including specifically a fortnight's unpaid
labour each year from all able-bodied males resident there, this
corvée being 'in consideration of the protection the Company will
afford us'.[1] In return it had made payment consisting of two
muzzle-loaders and some calico, the total value according to Johnston's estimate being £2. 13s. The alleged vendors were men with
little authority, and the real chiefs had in fact ceded the land to
the Crown five and a half months previously. The Blantyre Mission, not to be outdone by the children of this world, laid claim
to the whole upper plateau of Mlanje, 'because', they declared,
'one of our missionaries was the first white man to ascend the
mountain'.

Of course none of these claims could be sanctioned. Yet Johnston granted to Brown, 'not wishing to be too hard on him', a site
of 15 acres in fee-simple and a lease of 300 acres for twenty-one
years at a rent of a penny an acre; and he presented to the Blantyre
Mission some 20 acres on the healthy Mlanje uplands so that they

---

[1] The date of the 'agreement' (of which Johnston enclosed a copy in his No.
39, C.A., 13 Oct. 1892—in F.O. 84/2197) was 31 Jan. 1891.

could erect a sanatorium. In the same spirit he rewarded claimants for being 'reasonable' and 'meeting him half-way', assigning to them a dozen or two acres to which they had not even a squatter's right.

But however great his desire to encourage enterprise by British immigrants and at the same time to placate vociferous pioneers, he emphatically declared that his main objects were:

firstly, to protect the rights of the natives, to see that their villages and plantations are not disturbed, and that sufficient space is left for their expansion; secondly, to discourage land speculation; and, thirdly, to secure the rights of the Crown in such a way that the Crown shall profit by the development of this country, and find in its landed property a source of revenue which may enable it to further develop the resources of British Central Africa.

He had no doubt that when the first of these objects had been fully secured there would still be plenty of land left for European settlement. Large tracts were completely empty, owing to the slave-raids,[1] and the coming of peace would enable them to be cultivated. He realized that the native population would grow by natural increase, but he probably did not imagine how rapid this growth would be, and it was of course impossible for him to foresee that hundreds of thousands of Alomwe from Portuguese East Africa would cross the border and settle in the Shiré Highlands, so that by the end of the Second World War they would constitute more than 40 per cent. of the entire population of the Southern Province, which would by that time be supporting, on an average, rather more than eighty-nine people per square mile.[2] And there was probably a further reason for his mistaken belief that there was plenty of land which the Africans did not require for their own use: he seems not to have been sufficiently aware of the tribes- men's dependence upon freedom of access to new sites for their villages when the old ones had become too offensive to the nostrils

---

[1] Visiting Mount Mlanje towards the end of 1894, Sharpe found no popula- tion between there and Zomba, although the slopes of Mlanje itself were well populated. (F.O. 2/68: Sharpe to Kimberley, No. 96, C.A., 6 Nov. 1894.) And Mr. Cardew recalls that about that same date there was 'not a single village on the east side of the Upper Shiré from Liwonde's village . . . to the Lake', because of Zarafi's slave-raids (the *Nyasaland Journal*, loc. cit., p. 52). Cf. above, p. 74.

[2] Lord Hailey, *Native Administration in the British African Territories* (H.M.S.O., 1950), part ii, pp. 24, 47–48.

to be habitable, and to fresh land for their gardens when their wasteful primitive methods of agriculture had exhausted the soil previously cultivated. In so far as he considered at all the problem presented by this misuse of the land, he thought that the best remedy would be provided by the instructive example which would be set to the natives by settlers whose methods were more efficient. 'There is room and to spare for everybody in this fertile land', he wrote, 'if only it is cultivated as it is in India.'

From his contemptuous references to those who would have liked to take away the inhabitants' means of subsistence in order to create a rural proletariat economically dependent on themselves, it is clear that Johnston had no wish to make life easier for the white immigrants by herding all who would not work for them into crowded and eroded 'Native Reserves'; but the evil consequences of setting aside for communal subsistence agriculture those areas which were least desired by European purchasers of estates had not yet been made painfully evident elsewhere, and, if Johnston's policy had gone forward in later years, its fruits would have been no sweeter in Nyasaland than they have been in the Union of South Africa and in the Kikuyu Reserves in Kenya. He himself created a small Native Reserve in the vicinity of Chiromo; others would presumably have followed as European settlement became thicker and was reinforced by Indian settlement.

By 'safeguarding native rights' he meant forbidding white men to acquire land on which native villages or gardens already existed, 'unless the consent of all the natives interested in such villages or gardens can be freely obtained'—whatever that might mean—and unless he himself was satisfied that their real interests would not suffer if they in fact chose to give such consent.

Sometimes, however, land which was thickly populated had, as he put it, 'so to speak, been bought "over the heads" of the people by a bargain between the Chief and the purchaser'. Here, he declared, 'I have (usually) insisted that the native occupants should remain in undisturbed possession of their land and villages, and have only allowed the purchaser to make use of waste land'. Because of the restrictions which he imposed on the use of such land he valued it, for the purpose of determining what he would recognize as a fair purchase price, at a penny an acre, or only one-third the usual amount. Nevertheless the position of the occupants was merely that of legally protected squatters on private estates, and time was to show that the protection of the law was far less valuable and permanent than he had intended.[1]

In deciding whether or not a purchase was valid, he tacitly assumed that an independent chief had the right to exercise a prerogative unknown to native customary law—that of alienating land in perpetuity.[2] But he seems genuinely to have regarded it as essential that the chief should have known what he was doing when he scrawled his squiggle on the deed of cession. Thus he rejected the claims of the Lakes Company in the Tonga country on the ground that 'they were entirely repudiated by the Chiefs, who were not aware at the time what they were granting'; whereas he sanctioned that company's claims to the whole country from the River Rukuru northwards to the German border,[3] because 'the Deeds conferring this territory on the Company are perfectly valid, having been repeatedly confirmed by the vendors in the presence of Acting Consul Buchanan and myself'.

He insisted, moreover, that the chief who sold the land must have been the real ruler of the country and not merely some sub-chief. Further, the purchaser must have given what Johnston considered a fair price, and there were few cases in which he did not demand that the price be increased, or, alternatively, that the size of the estate be reduced—often drastically. Of 'squatters' he said some rather hard things; on the other hand, if they had really started to clear the ground and plant crops he never turned them

[1] The social problem which developed out of this part of Johnston's land settlement was examined with thoroughness and candour by Sir Sidney Abrahams in the Land Report which he prepared in 1946 (Govt. Printer, Zomba). In accordance with the recommendations of this report, the Nyasaland Government has bought some 300,000 acres, nearly a third of the total land formerly alienated in the Southern Province, for systematic resettlement by squatters. This purchase has cost about £190,000. (Information kindly supplied by the Chief Secretary of the Nyasaland Government.)

[2] 'There is no absolute ownership of land by the individual, but this is regarded as belonging to the community, and a portion is allotted to the individual for his personal use by the head of the particular community to which he belongs or to which he obtains admission. The individual's right to the land continues only so long as he is in personal occupation and remains a member of the community by which it was allotted to him.' *Report of the Commission appointed to Enquire into the Occupation of Land in the Nyasaland Protectorate* (Govt. Printer, Zomba, 1921), p. 5.

[3] This 'North Nyasa Estate' was afterwards transferred to the South Africa Company.

In 1895 Johnston expressed the hope that it might be possible to modify the terms of this extravagant grant, in the interests of the Administration; but it was then too late. F.O. 2/88: Johnston to Kimberley, No. 74, C.A., 10 June 1895.

out. And if he thought that a man whose claims were rather shaky was likely to do useful service in developing the country, he would count it heavily in the applicant's favour.

Did he, however, require the claims of the Crown itself to pass the tests by which he judged those of its subjects? Before the end of 1893 he reported that, throughout the Shiré valley and Highlands, he had acquired for the Crown the whole of the land which was not alienated to settlers or included in the Chiromo Reserve, with the inevitable exception of the unsettled regions (or 'no man's land', as he called it) north-east of Zomba, and the further exception of parts of the Blantyre and Zomba districts, in which he had been content to obtain for the Crown a right of pre-emption. He informed the Foreign Office that due payment had been made to the chiefs concerned, except in the cases of Yao forced to submit after taking up arms against the Administration; but he did not state the amount paid, or where it came from, and no one in Downing Street thought of asking him to do so.[1] It is also far from certain that he did not sometimes—for example, in the cases of most of the Makololo—quietly assume that a land title had been granted by a treaty which in fact conferred only political sovereignty.

A really confident judgement upon his methods of obtaining these Crown lands is unattainable, since his own reports are our only source of information. But it is fairly clear that he sincerely regarded the interests of the Crown as being identical with those of the tribesmen: it was for their good that the Administration should be in a position to prevent their chiefs from selling to European settlers land which they needed for their own use; it was for their good, too, that it should increase its revenue by leasing (and rarely, if ever, selling) such land as they did not need to Europeans who were prepared to pay an economic rent.

The rights which Johnston secured for the Crown extended even to the lands of the settlers, for in every case when a deed (or 'Certificate of Claim',[2] as it was called) was being granted for an

[1] He mentioned to Rhodes (in a letter dated 7 June 1893—in the B.S.A. Co. Papers, Cape Town) that the Treasury had spent £2,500 'in presents to natives and purchase of land'. If the vendors received anything more than this total amount, it must almost certainly have come from his own private resources.

[2] Johnston had no legal authority, in his capacity as Consul-General, to issue land titles. When investigating land claims he was acting in his capacity as Commissioner, empowered in a general way to inquire, regulate, and administer. (Minute on Johnston to Rosebery, No. 39, C.A., 13 Oct. 1892.) In a 'certificate of claim' he declared the claim 'to be established and to be recognized as legal

estate, Johnston reserved to the Crown the right to build roads, railways, or other communications across it without compensation, and also the right to control the water supply. Sometimes mineral rights were reserved as well; if not, provision was made for the payment of a royalty of 5 or 10 per cent.

It was only in the southern part of the Protectorate, particularly the Shiré Highlands, that there was any rush for land by planters. Seventeen individuals or partnerships received estates there— some of them more than one estate—not counting the Lakes Company, the South Africa Company, or the various missions. It is interesting to note that an estate of unspecified extent was also acquired by a certain chief named Kumtaja, who had obtained it partly by inheritance and partly by purchase. Johnston described Kumtaja as 'an intelligent educated native who deserved, I thought, much encouragement at our hands, because in his efforts to march with the times he had started as a brick-maker and coffee-planter and in consequence had gone bankrupt'. Johnston placed considerable hopes in the emergence of Africans such as this, who would obtain land in private ownership and cultivate it for profit instead of mere subsistence; but the experience of Kumtaja himself was not encouraging to others, and private ownership of land by Africans in Nyasaland has never yet developed to any significant extent.

Farther north, in the part of the Protectorate lying west of Lake Nyasa, there were a few land claims by the missions, but no others except those of the South Africa Company and the Lakes Company, with their vast North Nyasa estate, their extensive rights of pre-emption, and their even more extensive mineral rights.

Writing to Rhodes in May 1893 Johnston summarized his land settlement in the Protectorate as follows: about one-fifth belonged to the Chartered Company (as heir of the Lakes Company), and a further fifth was in the hands of the various planters and missions; another fifth belonged to the Crown, and the remaining two-fifths were owned by the natives, 'subject to the provision that they cannot part with their land without the consent of H.M. Government'.[1] But this neat summary compares oddly with the figures given in the report of the Land Commission of 1920, which showed

and valid by the Government of Her Britannic Majesty' under specified conditions. Technically such a document was not a title to land, but in fact it was virtually so.

[1] F.O. 2/54: Johnston to Rhodes, 3 May 1893, enclosed in Johnston to Rosebery, No. 17, C.A., 3 May 1893.

that the total land alienated under Johnston's certificates of claim, including the holdings of the South Africa Company, was 3,705,255 acres, while the total land area of the Protectorate was 25,161,924 acres: the proportion was therefore one-seventh instead of two-fifths, and there is no reason to conjecture that several million acres alienated in the 1890's had been relinquished by their owners before 1920.[1]

To the west of the Protectorate the Chartered Company claimed that throughout its sphere as far west as the Kafue it was entitled, by virtue of the Sharpe–Thomson treaties, to exclusive mining, commercial, and manufacturing rights. Clearly these rights could not be recognized without modification, at least in respect of the northern part of the territory, which lay within the free trade zone defined by the Berlin Act. As a general principle, too, the Foreign Office looked with disfavour on such claims to exclusive privileges, and so indeed did Johnston himself. On the whole, however, Johnston was the advocate rather than the critic of the South Africa Company's claims within its own sphere,[2] because, according to his reckoning, it had spent between £6,000 and £7,000 in securing them, and a further £10,000 'in commencing the development of the Territories over which these claims extend', besides the even larger sums devoted to the financing of his 'police force' and to buying up the claims of the Lakes Company. He was 'certain', he declared, that the Company 'will not wish to exercise any

---

[1] The report (Govt. Printer, Zomba, 1921) showed that during the intervening period a further 139,472 acres had been alienated in freehold, besides 118,504 acres granted on lease (usually for seven years).

In more recent years there has been a great reduction in the alienated area, which was diminished by more than two-thirds at a single stroke when the South Africa Company renounced its title to ownership of the land (though not of the mineral rights) in the North Nyasa district. See also above, p. 233, n. 1.

[2] Within the Protectorate itself Johnston showed little if any bias in favour of the Company. He rejected a claim which it made, jointly with the Lakes Company, to certain lands in the West Shiré district, on the ground that the vendors were persons with no authority to sell them. He himself, it is true, confessed to Anderson (letter of 23 Mar. 1893, in F.O. 2/54) that his impartiality towards the Company was a matter of necessity rather than of choice: 'If I swerve from this policy in the least I should immediately have creatures like Sharrer down on me. . . . Under the watchful eyes of the [Blantyre] Mission and Sharrer I have done nothing to advance the Company's interests within the Protectorate.' Nevertheless it seems fair to say that his only real bias was in favour of whatever agency happened to be carrying the responsibilities of government: in the Protectorate, the Crown, and in the Company's sphere, the Company.

unfair monopolies within this large area, and in all matters connected with their estates and rights in British Central Africa they
have always up to the present time desired me, as their representative, to show the utmost liberality and encouragement to all well-
conducted pioneers who may wish to open up the territories over
which the Chartered Company claims these exclusive privileges'.
Eventually, in November 1894, the Foreign Office agreed[1] to
sanction the claims, in so far as they were consistent with the terms
of the Berlin Act and also of the Company's own charter, which
forbade it to set up or grant any monopoly of trade, with the
important reservation that 'monopolies' should not be deemed to
include arrangements concerning banking, public works, or patents
and copyrights.

But these rights, extensive as they were, did not include the
ownership of the soil: this was obtained by the Company only in
one area, the vicinity of the Stevenson Road, where three vast
estates were transferred to it by the Lakes Company. Apart from
these estates the only lands outside the Protectorate which Johnston confirmed in European ownership were those claimed by the
London Missionary Society and by their Roman Catholic rivals,
the White Fathers. To the one remaining set of claims he was
bitterly opposed. They were put forward by Karl Wiese, the German who had been at Mpeseni's at the time of Sharpe's fruitless
visit there in 1890, and were based on concessions alleged to have
been obtained from Mpeseni himself and a number of other chiefs.
According to Johnston, Sharpe's journeys had furnished 'many
proofs that Wiese was little else than a slave-trader', who employed
armed natives to raid the country 'right and left' for slaves to work
plantations which the Portuguese had granted him in return
for his political services. Johnston was so anxious to prove the
claims invalid that he even resorted to the argument that Mpeseni
was not a genuine paramount chief but was 'merely a Zulu raider',
and it was not without reason that Anderson accused him of
'special pleading'. Soon afterwards, however, he discovered an
incomparably better argument in the fact that the alleged concession bore no mark made by Mpeseni himself or by any of his
sub-chiefs; instead, it had been signed 'at my [Mpeseni's] request'
by Lieutenant Solla, Wiese's Portuguese companion.

[1] By clause 5 of the general Agreement between the Company and the British
Government—for which see below, pp. 263–4.

'I look upon Wiese as a very dangerous man', declared Johnston. 'He is utterly unscrupulous'. The Portuguese had granted to him for twenty-five years 'the bulk of the land between Quilimane and the Shiré and the Ruo', and 'in order to attract the ivory trade of Nyasaland in his direction he is selling guns and powder under some figment or another to those Yaos who bring him ivory'. At the same time he appeared to be 'doing his very best to Germanise these prazos', and was in high favour with the German Government. That such a man should become lord of several thousand square miles of British territory was abhorrent to him. But the claims survived his criticisms, and it was in vain that the South Africa Company tried to buy them out. Eventually, however, an arrangement was made between Wiese and the Company for the creation of a new company, which would take over the concessions, and in which the South Africa Company would have a substantial interest. This new company, the North Charterland Exploration Company, became the proprietor of lands which, even after the excision of a native reserve in 1924, were still more than 4,000,000 acres in extent. In attempting to take control of this huge domain it roused the Angoni to revolt in December 1897; their subjugation two months later was followed by the creation of the township of Fort Jameson, which became the centre of a fairly important area of white settlement.

The acceptance of Wiese's claims was almost the only case in which Johnston's decisions concerning the land settlement were overridden by the Foreign Office. The only serious objection which could justifiably have been raised would have been that they were over-generous to the European planters at the expense of the natives; but this was certainly not evident at the time, and no one yet doubted that the settlement of Europeans on uncultivated land could prove other than wholly beneficial to the surrounding villagers. It is fair to assume that the main lines of Johnston's land policy would have received the approval of Livingstone himself. Sir Percy Anderson's comment was scarcely an exaggeration: 'Johnston', he wrote, 'has shown extraordinary industry and ability, and, as far as it is possible at present to judge, seems to have placed the question on a just and sound basis'.[1]

ᴏ   ᴏ   ᴏ

[1] Johnston's land policy is set forth in his dispatch to the Foreign Secretary, No. 39, C.A., 13 Oct. 1892, in F.O. 84/2197; and the details of the settlement,

The labourers who cultivated the estates of the European planters were not, for the most part, local villagers. As early as January 1893 Johnston reported that the Angoni from Chikusi's country supplied 'nearly all' of them; four years later, and only a few months after Chikusi himself[1] had been overthrown and put to death by a British punitive expedition, the number of Angoni working for wages in the Shiré Highlands was estimated by Sharpe at 'something like 5,000'. Nor were the Angoni the only migrant labourers. An even longer journey was made in search of work by Tonga from the vicinity of Bandawe. Both they and the Angoni, it appears, were found much more satisfactory as workers than the local natives, probably for reasons similar to those given by the Committee on Emigrant Labour of 1935, which declared that

it seems to be the universal experience that the African labourer, regarded purely as a machine to get work done in the shortest time, works far better away from his home and country than in it. Family obligations, the necessity for attending every village function, visiting funerals, weddings or the like, have still a strong hold on the worker who is working in the vicinity of his home. He will continually be taking

together with a discussion of the Chartered Company's claims to exclusive privileges in its own sphere, are contained in the memorandum enclosed in his No. 55, C.A., 14 Oct. 1893, in F.O. 2/55. A map of the Shiré Highlands, scale ¼ in. to the mile, in colour, showing the land settlement there, is printed in A. & P., 1896, lviii, C. 8254. The circular of 18 July 1891 is enclosed in No. 43, C.A., 19 Nov. 1892, in F.O. 84/2197. Various matters connected with the land settlement are discussed in F.O. 2/54: Johnston to Anderson, 21 Jan. 1893, and in F.O. 2/88: No. 72, C.A., 7 June 1895. There is a good short account in *British Central Africa*, pp. 112–13.

The particularly troublesome claims of the Central Africa Company to a great tract of land west of the Shiré—claims not discussed here for reasons of space— are dealt with in F.O. 2/54: No. 5, C.A., 5 Jan. 1893, with enclosures and minutes, and No. 6, C.A., Confidential, 31 Jan. 1893; also F.O. 2/56: telegram of 22 July 1893; F.O. 2/66: Johnston's Memorandum of 18 June 1894; F.O. 2/68: Johnston to Anderson, 15 Nov. 1894; F.O. 2/88: No. 78, C.A., 15 June 1895, with minutes.

The claims of Karl Wiese are discussed in F.O. 84/2197: No. 16, C.A., 31 Mar. 1892, with the enclosed memorandum; F.O. 2/54: Johnston to Anderson, 23 Mar. 1893, with confidential enclosure; F.O. 2/66: No. 23, C.A., 3 Mar. 1894, with enclosures and minutes, and No. 29, C.A., 23 Mar. 1894, with enclosures and minutes; for the sequel see H. M. Hole, *The Making of Rhodesia*, pp. 387–90; and for the extent of land involved see the Pim Report (*Report of the Commission Appointed to Enquire into the Financial and Economic Position of Northern Rhodesia*—Colonial No. 145), pp. 15 and 58, and the *Rhodesia-Nyasaland Royal Commission Report* (Cmd. 5949), p.37.

[1] Not the Chikusi who was visited by Hawes, but his successor.

'off days'. . . . Further, at the period of the year when the planters require most labour, local natives are busy in their own gardens.[1]

The growth of the labour supply kept pace with the growth of the planters' demand, especially as the Administration's road-building achievements made possible the use of ox-drawn wagons instead of scores of human carriers on the most frequented routes.[2] Wages therefore remained low. A native worker was lucky if he received three shillings a month in calico or cash in addition to his food. The planters could argue with much justification that their employees were so inefficient and work-shy that even these low wages were a very adequate return for the services received; nevertheless Johnston very properly deemed it necessary to interfere when natives from time to time complained to his magistrates that after they had worked three months or more they had been discharged by their employers with little or no pay, on the ground that they had incurred fines, or on no ground at all. In January 1894 he declared that 'as the one hope of this country lies in Plantation work, and in the cultivation of coffee, tobacco, sugar, etc., for which cheap negro labour is necessary, it is before all things essential that this labour should now be placed under proper Regulations'.

The draft regulations which he then proposed, and which he provisionally began to enforce from 1 February, were revised by the Foreign Office in consultation with him when he was in London during the summer of the same year. In their revised form they received the Secretary of State's assent in October, and were put into operation early in 1895.

They forbade the employment of natives for periods of longer than one month except under a written contract, made in the presence of a magistrate and signed by him, and bearing a revenue stamp costing a shilling (paid by the employer). The period of service under a single written contract must not exceed twelve months. At the end of it the worker was to receive from the magistrate a ticket of discharge, which enabled him either to enter into a new contract (with his former employer, or with a different one) or to return home.

If his home was not in the same administrative district as his

---

[1] *Report of Committee Appointed to Enquire into Emigrant Labour, 1935* (Govt. Printer, Zomba, 1936), p. 20.
[2] F.O. 2/54: Johnston to Anderson, 20 June 1893.

place of work, his employer must pay him 'conduct-money' at the time of his discharge, and the rate was fixed at 2s. for the first hundred miles and a further 1s. 6d. for each additional hundred. Both wages and 'conduct-money' must be paid in the magistrate's presence, a safeguard of the native's interests which would scarcely have been administratively practicable but for the custom, accepted under the regulations, of making a single payment at the end of the term of service.

The employer was required to provide all his native workers—including those not employed under written contract—with adequate food, shelter, sanitary arrangements, medicine, and (if procurable) medical attendance. If a native died during service, any property he had with him and whatever wages were due to him at the time of his death must be handed over to the magistrate, who was to forward them to the man's heirs under native law.

The employers at first resented this Government 'interference', but they soon became reconciled to it, and even began to realize that the enforcement of reasonable safeguards for their labourers was in their own best interests.[1]

⌀ ⌀ ⌀

If the natives were to receive protection from the Administration, it seemed to Johnston only fair that they should render in return some contribution to its support. Unless they did so, there could be no hope of solvency. 'The salvation of this country' (British Central Africa), he wrote, 'will be the taxation of the native within moderate bounds.' But the introduction of a native tax was viewed with some misgiving by the Foreign Office, which sanctioned it only on the clear understanding that it would be withdrawn if it gave rise to serious discontent, and as late as March 1894 Johnston told the secretary of the South Africa Company that 'really the principle of taxation barely exists on sufferance from H.M. Government'. Whatever his personal inclinations may have been, he had no choice but to proceed cautiously.

---

[1] F.O. 2/54: Johnston to Rosebery, No. 6, C.A., Confidential, 31 Jan. 1893; F.O. 2/66: Johnston to Kimberley, No. 3, C.A., 12 Jan. 1894; and Sharpe to K., No. 37, C.A., 9 May 1894; F.O. 2/65: F.O. to Sharpe, No. 54, 22 Oct. 1894; C.8438, pp. 7 and 11; F. M. Withers, 'Nyasaland in 1895–6', in the *Nyasaland Journal*, vol. ii, No. 1 (Jan. 1949), pp. 18–20. Mr. Withers states that 'food was not given to workers on less than a three months' contract, nor was it given to locals'. If this is true, there must have been laxity in enforcing the regulations, for No. 11 was perfectly unambiguous on this point.

His method of introducing the tax in the first months of his administration was to make liability to it one of the conditions which a chief had to accept on behalf of his people when he accepted British sovereignty. Acceptance was voluntary, except in the cases of chiefs who were forced to submit after having gone to war with the Administration. 'In ordinary cases', Johnston reported, 'I have held this language to the chiefs':

If you are unable to govern and protect your own countries properly, and we are obliged to station our police in your lands, either at your own request or to keep order where you cannot, then you must give up your sovereign rights to the Queen, and must contribute a reasonable sum towards the expense of governing the country. If, on the other hand, you do not wish to cede your sovereign rights nor to pay taxes to the Administration: very well, then, you need not; but you must, in that case, rule your own country wisely and well, must keep the peace with your neighbours, and protect yourself if attacked; and you must lend no countenance to the Slave Trade.

This argument, rendered impressive by the initial victories of Maguire and his Indian 'police', sufficed to make taxpayers of the Makololo.

The 'reasonable sum' which he expected annually was a poll tax of 6s. a head, which, he claimed, was a modest demand when compared with the taxes in force elsewhere, for instance, the 14s. a hut levied in Bechuanaland. But it was equal to rather more than the entire cash wages which an African labourer could earn in two months, and was, therefore, an excessively heavy burden. And although he reported that the tax had been collected without difficulty in the first year, he admitted that the amount actually charged had been not more than 1s. per head instead of the nominal 6s., 'since we take payment in produce more than in money and do not press for the full tax'. In 1893, by his own decision, the tax was reduced to 3s., a figure which genuinely deserved his description of 'reasonable'. This was, however, only one of the changes which were made by the formal tax regulations which he then introduced for the first time. The regulations made the tax payable on each hut instead of on each adult male, and, more important, they made it compulsory instead of semi-optional within 'that portion of British Central Africa which is subject to taxation': a phrase which referred only to the Shiré valley and Highlands, since the collection of the tax was necessarily limited to the area over which the Administration had the means to enforce its authority.

In the more northerly part of the Protectorate taxation remained optional for some years longer, and in fact none of the tribes chose to pay. When, towards the end of 1893, the Tonga asked for a European magistrate to be sent to reside among them, Johnston told them that their request would be granted on condition that they agreed to pay taxes to defray the cost of the official's salary. 'After some consideration', he reported, 'they have decided for the present that they do not wish to pay taxes; I have therefore informed them that in this case they must endeavour to get on as well as they can without a Resident European Magistrate.'

It was not until after the destruction of Mlozi's power that the tax was made compulsory throughout the Protectorate, except in Northern Angoniland. The reason for this exception was explained by Johnston in a letter to the Livingstonia Mission: the Angoni, he said, had shown themselves capable of managing their own affairs without giving the Administration any trouble or putting it to any expense.[1] In this state of virtual independence they continued until April 1904, when, at Dr. Laws's suggestion, Sir Alfred Sharpe, Johnston's successor, visited them and invited them to accept British jurisdiction. They were not subjected either to military pressure or to the threat of it, and the issues were explained to them with frankness and tact. 'I was surprised', wrote Sharpe to the Doctor, 'to find the Chiefs already quite prepared and ready, if not even glad, to accept the new condition of affairs: this is undoubtedly largely due to the influence exercised by your people.'[2]

The extension of the taxable area beyond the Protectorate to the Company's sphere—North Eastern Rhodesia as it became—did not take place until 1901.

When the area under taxation was extended to include the northern part of the Protectorate, the revenue from the native tax was almost doubled—even though the migrant workers from the north had already been brought into the net by the regulations of 1893, which made liable to tax all Africans residing in the south, whether or not they had permanent homes there.

In the early days, when everything was being improvised, the

---

[1] The letter is printed in Elmslie, *Among the Wild Ngoni*, pp. 294–5.
[2] W. P. Livingstone, *Laws of Livingstonia*, pp. 314–16.

collection of the tax was entrusted to the chiefs themselves, and 'in return for the trouble', Johnston explained,

I pay each chief a certain stipend, which usually amounts to about ten per cent of the revenue he has collected, and this stipend is paid him on condition that he exacts no other tax from the people for himself— he deriving his subsistence mainly from tribal lands set apart for his use. In this way the people are saved from the irregular and often exorbitant contributions levied on them by the chiefs; on the other hand, the chief now touches with certainty the £40, £50, or £60 a year (a great sum in his eyes) which may be his percentage on the taxes gathered in.

It is not at all clear from this statement how Johnston ensured that the chiefs did not in fact retain in their own hands a larger proportion of what they collected than the percentage to which he thought them entitled. Nor does it appear that he was acting upon any theoretical preference for indirect rule: it seems rather that he merely wished both to minimize the burdens of his overworked officials and to avoid giving offence to those chiefs who were not hostile to British authority. Hence it is scarcely surprising to find that the employment of the chiefs as tax-collectors, like their option to retain sovereignty in their own hands, did not outlast the Administration's inability to end it. In his report for the year 1896–7 Sharpe stated that:

The natives are beginning to fully understand the value of a tax receipt. They are grasping the fact that the possession of it frees them from the oppression of their Chiefs. During the past year there has been a marked diminution of the autocratic power formerly held by native Chiefs throughout the Protectorate

—a statement which, incidentally, implies that its author considered that the diminution of chiefly power was desirable for its own sake.

This was a very reasonable point of view, since it is no insult to the African as such to hold that a fairly well-educated European official is much better qualified to rule efficiently and well than a chief nurtured in superstitious ignorance. But it failed to take account of the importance to any community, however backward, of maintaining some continuity of tradition and some organic link between Government and governed. From 1912 onwards, therefore, the Nyasaland Administration moved by gradual and cautious steps towards the arrangements eventually embodied in the Native Authority and Native Courts Ordinances of 1933, which were designed to employ to the full the traditional native organizations for all purposes of local government. In Northern Rhodesia similar ordinances, representing a similar culmination of a similar reversal of policy, were passed in 1936.[1]

4. The Breach with Rhodes and the Separation of the Territories

When Johnston formed his Administration in 1891 there were, as far as he could calculate, 57 Europeans in British Central Africa. Five years later there were more than 300 in the Protectorate alone, and about another 45 in the Company's sphere. Since there was probably little change in the number of missionaries, the influx was presumably composed almost entirely of officials, planters, traders, and big-game hunters. The amount of land under cultivation by Europeans—as distinct from the much larger areas under their ownership—had increased in the same period from 1,600 acres to 5,700. The total trade had increased in value from about £40,000 in 1891 to over £100,000 in the year ending in March 1896. Coffee was giving good promise as an economic crop; about 320 tons were exported in 1896, and much of it fetched high prices in the London market.[2]

The number of British cargo-steamers on the Zambesi and Lower Shiré had risen from two to fifteen,[2] and from 1893 onwards Chinde was brought into satisfactory communication with the outside world by a regular and efficient steamship service to Zanzibar, provided by Rennie & Sons' Aberdeen line and the German East Africa line, whereas at first it had received only

---

[1] Hailey, op. cit., part ii, pp. 25–27, 83. The sources for the earlier period are as follows: F.O. 84/2114: Johnston to Salisbury, No. 25, C.A., 10 Dec. 1891; F.O. 84/2197: J. to S., No. 11, C.A., 10 Mar. 1892; F.O. 84/2196: F.O. to J., No. 35, 4 June 1892, and No. 63, 21 Sept. 1892; F.O. 84/2198: F.O. to J., tel. No. 18, 21 Sept. 1892; J. to Rosebery, tel. No. 16, 25 Aug. 1892; F.O. 84/2197: J. to R., No. 32, 6 Sept. 1892; F.O. 2/54: J. to R., No. 21, C.A., 12 June 1893; F.O. 2/65: F.O. to J., No. 21, 1 May 1894; F.O. 2/66: J. to Canning, 10 Mar. 1894, and to Kimberley, No. 27, C.A., 14 Mar. 1894; C.8438, pp. 7–8; Gouldsbury and Sheane, op. cit., p. 44.

[2] The figures are from *British Central Africa*, pp. 146–51. This promise was not in fact fulfilled, and Nyasaland has for many years exported no coffee at all. Its main exports are now tobacco and tea.

occasional and reluctant visits from the ships of the two Cape lines, the Union and the Castle. By 1893, too, an efficient mail service had been organized, though it involved the Administration in an annual loss of £400 or £500.[1] Until the end of Johnston's period of office, it is true, the link with Britain by telegraph stopped at Mozambique, and telegrams exchanged by the Commissioner and the Foreign Office had to be conveyed between Zomba and Mozambique by land, river, and sea, so that it took them about a month to travel—almost half as long as it took the ordinary dispatches. But it was Rhodes's intention that a telegraph should run across the continent all the way from the Cape to Cairo, and the route lay through British Central Africa. Although it was never completed—the African Trans-Continental Telegraph Company, launched with high hopes as a subsidiary of the Chartered Company in December 1892, went into voluntary liquidation in December 1911—the telegraph had by 1902 been carried from Salisbury in Southern Rhodesia through Portuguese territory *via* Tete to Blantyre and Zomba, thence to Fort Johnston, and by way of the Nyasa shore and the Stevenson Road to Abercorn and the German territory beyond; while a link between Chiromo and Chinde was provided by a Portuguese line.[2]

Johnston took a natural pride in such developments, and he considered that in helping to promote them he was serving the vital long-term needs of Britain herself. 'A prudent nation', he remarked in a private letter to Davidson, 'must prepare for itself new markets and new fields of enterprise to take the place of those which are now shut to its commerce or are self-supporting.'[3] He had also a more urgent and immediate interest in the Protectorate's economic growth, because it brought with it a growing customs and licence revenue. In the fourteen months which ended on 31 March 1893 the total revenue from local sources (including £700 of native tax) was £4,820,[4] but by March of the following year he thought he could count on an annual revenue of £9,000, 'with signs of a

[1] F.O. 2/54: Johnston to Anderson, 23 Mar. 1893 and 20 June 1893; also various dispatches in F.O. 2/53, 54, 65, and 66.

[2] B.S.A. Co., Annual Reports; H. M. Hole, *The Making of Rhodesia*, pp. 383–4; Gouldsbury and Sheane, op. cit., p. 45. The B.C.A. Administration's role in the construction is reported upon in various dispatches and telegrams in F.O. 2/66–69.

[3] F.O. 2/54: Johnston to Davidson, 24 Aug. 1893.

[4] F.O. 2/55: Johnston to Rosebery, No. 60, C.A., 21 Oct. 1893.

steady increase',[1] and in the financial year which ended in 1896 the amount actually collected exceeded £22,000.[2]

But, despite his best efforts to govern economically and to increase his Administration's resources, his expenditure grew more rapidly than his revenue. In his first financial year, which began on 1 February 1891, the South Africa Company had given him, in addition to the 'police subsidy' of £10,000, a further £5,000 'to meet the extra cost of introducing Indian troops, and of opening up stations in the northern part of our sphere'; he thus received £15,000 to cover the expenses which he had to incur before his Administration could be set up, together with those of the first six months of its existence. Nor was this the whole of the financial assistance furnished him by the Company: it also carried out an obligation it had accepted as part of its agreement with the Foreign Office, to make arrangements with the Lakes Company under which he should be empowered to use, free of charge, for administrative purposes, that company's steamers on Lake Nyasa, 'with due precautions against unreasonable interference with their employment for the Company's trade'. He complained, it is true, that the Lakes Company kept their co-operation to a minimum and 'thwarted him at every turn', so that he was at his wits' end to get his goods transported; but this was in no way the fault of the South Africa Company, and the arrangement saved him considerable expense. Even though he had only a few hundred pounds of local revenue with which to supplement the subsidy, it is not surprising that he ended the year with a balance of over £2,000. A year later, however, he had an overdraft on the South Africa Company of almost £5,600; but at the same time he declared that he 'confidently hoped' that after a further year this would be 'diminished considerably'.[3] Nevertheless, at the end of the third year he had to confess to the Company that instead it had increased to £20,000, and that as matters stood it must continue to increase 'at the rate of about £1,458 a month'.[4]

Among the causes of this over-spending, he explained, the attempted suppression of the slave-trade ranked 'chiefly and mainly above all others'. He therefore continued: 'You may

[1] F.O. 2/66: Johnston to Canning (Confidential), 10 Mar. 1894. The native tax for 1893 had brought in £1,640.
[2] *British Central Africa*, p. 150.
[3] F.O. 2/55: Johnston to Rosebery, No. 60, C.A., 21 Oct. 1893.
[4] F.O. 2/66: Johnston to Canning, 10 Mar. 1894.

naturally ask why I embarked on such an expensive undertaking as a crusade against the Slave Trade when I had only some average £15,000 a year to spend. In reply I can only say that I did not knowingly embark on such a crusade, but it has been forced on me, and that my one effort has been to keep it within reasonable limits, consistent with the protection of friendly natives . . . and with . . . security for life and property for Europeans.' This did not mean that Johnston was at heart indifferent to the slave-trade —he made his feelings and opinions on that subject clear enough on numerous occasions, including passages of this same letter— but rather that he had not made a wild attempt to suppress it everywhere at once, and that when the struggle with the Yao began he had no idea how widespread and protracted, and therefore expensive, it was going to prove. As he put it, 'the thing has grown insensibly'. Each step made it imperative to take the next.

Quite apart from the slave-trade, there was other expenditure which Johnston charged to the Company because he found it indispensable yet had no other means of meeting it. This included the housing of his officials—among them a vice-consul at Chinde— and his road-building programme in the Shiré Highlands. 'You have paid', he told the Company, 'for every single building [used by the Administration] in this country with the sole exception of the Vice-Consulate at Blantyre . . . and the Residency at Zomba.' On road-making he had spent some £5,000 or £6,000. 'Why? Because we are compelled to open up communications. . . . But although these roads were to a certain extent matters of military necessity and useful for Administration waggon traffic, still the people who have benefited to the greatest extent are the European planters and missionaries who have not contributed one penny towards their construction and who raise a fearful howl if a flood sweeps away a bridge.'

In all, he had spent about £55,000 of the Company's money, not including the £20,000 which he owed them, and of this expenditure only about £12,000 had been devoted to the Company's own sphere. (Part of this £12,000, he mentioned, had gone to 'the strengthening of certain treaties by the making of additional payments to Chiefs'.)

He not only admitted to the Company but vigorously represented to the Foreign Office that this situation was grossly unfair. In a private letter to Anderson, dated 23 March 1893, he had taken up the subject. 'And yet', he asked, 'what am I to do? If I remove the police force from Nyasaland to the Company's sphere the whole country would be swamped at once by the descent of the slave-trading Yaos. Yet if the British South Africa Company are to get any return for their money, it is only by the vigorous development of the magnificent territories lying westward and northward of the Protectorate. To develop these at present there is no money, although I still, at the risk of a deficit, keep up our station on Lake Mweru.'[1]

It is uncertain at what date either Rhodes himself or the Directors in London began to show signs of dissatisfaction at the manner in which their money was being spent. In October 1892 he had told the Foreign Office that the Company had not 'as yet' made any complaint. 'No doubt', he had then explained, 'the Directors of this Company are convinced, like myself, that no good can be done with British Central Africa until Nyasaland is first made into a secure and prosperous base of operations. . . . So they raise no objection when I employ all their officials except one and all their police except thirty within the boundaries of Nyasaland.'[2] And in his letter to Anderson in the following March he went further:

At the present moment I am, so to speak, crying out for an auditor. I have not had a single word from the British South Africa Company about the accounts sent in for 1891–92. Sooner than meet with what is no doubt a kindly tolerance on their part, I would like to have every detail most searchingly gone into, so that it might be clearly established that every penny of the money has been honestly and properly spent.

He knew well that this state of affairs could not continue much longer, and admitted that he would have 'a great weight off my shoulders and a constant carking care removed' if his finances were placed under Treasury control in return for a subsidy for the Protectorate, so that the Company's money could be used solely for its own possessions to the west.[3]

Already, indeed, his relations with Rhodes were much less harmonious than he cared to admit. He had asked for the Company's subsidy to be increased by £5,000 a year, but Rhodes had learnt that in his land settlement he had not yet sanctioned the

[1] F.O. 2/54: Johnston to Anderson, 23 Mar. 1893.
[2] F.O. 84/2197: Johnston to Rosebery, No. 41, C.A., 19 Oct. 1892.
[3] F.O. 2/54: Johnston to Anderson, 23 Mar. 1893.

claims of the African Lakes Company (which were to be transferred to the South Africa Company), whereas he had sanctioned almost all other claims within the Protectorate.[1] Rhodes did not object to the grants already made, because their recipients were resident in the country and were spending money on its development; but he demanded that in future only the Chartered Company should have the right to obtain concessions of land or mineral rights in the Protectorate, and that when Johnston sanctioned the claims of the Lakes Company the grants should be made 'as large as possible'. Outside the Protectorate, in the Chartered Company's territory, Rhodes would tolerate no claims whatever except the Company's own. 'Therefore', he warned Johnston, 'should you be applied to for recognition of any concessions in the Chartered Sphere outside the Nyasa Protectorate you must boldly and plainly say no.' On these conditions he was prepared to agree to pay the increased subsidy for which Johnston had asked.[2]

In April Johnston visited him in Cape Town and discussed the whole matter, and on 3 May he put his signature on Johnston's draft of what they hoped would be the basis of a new agreement between the Company and the home Government.[3] The annual subsidy was to be increased by £7,500—a figure which had been arrived at by adding to the £5,000 previously discussed the sum of £2,500, in lieu of the payment hitherto made by the Company to the Lakes Company for providing the Administration with free water transport. With his usual over-optimism, Johnston had miscalculated the cost of this service; experience soon showed him that it would be about three times the £2,500 which he had thought adequate.[4] The total increase in the subsidy to £17,500 a year was therefore more apparent than real. In return, the Crown was to transfer to the Company all its land and all its rights of preemption in the Protectorate. (The question of land rights to the west of the Protectorate was ambiguously glossed over.)[5] The

[1] B.S.A. Co. Papers, Cape Town: Rhodes to Johnston, 4 Apr. 1893. It is a fact, whatever the reason, that all the certificates of claim issued to the Lakes Company were issued between 18 and 27 Sept. in that year.

[2] Ibid.

[3] F.O. 2/54: Johnston to Rosebery, No. 17, C.A., 3 May 1893, with enclosures.

[4] F.O. 2/66: Johnston to Canning, 10 Mar. 1894.

[5] In a postscript Johnston wrote: 'I have not touched on the Company's rights of pre-emption and land and mining claims in the sphere *outside* the Protectorate because such rights and claims are supported in almost all parts by valid documents and are, I take it, admitted by H.M. Government.' This took

Company, however, would derive no immediate profit from these land rights, which it would use to finance the development of the country.

Johnston could not consent to such a transfer without reservation, but his reservations proved acceptable to Rhodes. They were:

That as regards lands now *owned* by the Crown, such portions of them shall be reserved as Crown property as constitute the sites and surrounding grounds (garden, etc.) of existing Crown buildings. Further, that when and if in future the Imperial Government shall require sites of moderate dimensions for naval, military, or consular purposes from out of the estates now belonging to it, those sites shall be granted to the Crown free, by the Chartered Company.

That in exercising the Crown's right of pre-emption by taking up land (purchasing) from the natives, a fair price shall be paid to the natives, the judge of the fairness to be H.M. Commissioner and Consul General; and that no land shall be taken from the natives with their villages and plantations on it (even if the Chief wishes to sell) against the general wishes of the native inhabitants; this question however to be finally decided also by appeal to the Commissioner and Consul General.

Finally, Johnston asked and Rhodes agreed that the increased subsidy should be guaranteed for a five-year period, instead of the three years specified in the agreement of 1891; further, there would be no objection to the Commissioner's spending up to £10,000 a year on the Protectorate alone.

On his return to Nyasaland Johnston wrote again to Anderson, urging that the Government should decide quickly either to accept the agreement or to furnish a subsidy of its own. 'The Government', he declared, 'must be *honest*.'

In this world you get nothing for nothing. Already, no doubt, you think the £10,000 a year subsidy of the B.S.A. Co. dearly purchased by the lien which it gives them over British Central Africa. Well, you have only the — — —[1] Treasury to thank for the awkwardness of the situation. Had not this odious, short-sighted, soulless miser in 1890–91

no account of the claims of Wiese (which Johnston himself refused to recognize), or of the London Missionary Society and the White Fathers (which were of relatively small importance).

[1] You can fill up these blanks with expressions of bitter abuse which I cannot trust myself to write. (Note by Johnston.)

refused resolutely to entertain the idea of a subsidy[1] to start the new protectorate, you would not have had to appeal, as a last chance of saving the country for Great Britain, to the generosity of a Chartered Company.

I, personally, am quite indifferent as to who provides the money, . . . provided that there is enough, and that British Central Africa is administered by the Imperial Government, as it is at present. The South Africa Company have behaved splendidly (I think) but I am not in any way pledged to support their interests. I have told them all along that all I cared about was the Britannising of the country: they have said, 'that is all *we* care about.' So they cannot blame me if the Britannising of the country is done by the Government direct. Personally I think they are singularly disinterested and patriotic in their procedure in British Central Africa. . . .

However, if the Government can devise and the — — — Treasury will allow them to execute a better way of finding the funds necessary to 'run' the Protectorate, for such time as it may need financial support, than the bargain with the South Africa Company, by all means let us embark on this way. . . . On the other hand, if the Treasury are not going to find the money, it seems to me the only plan is to make a fair bargain with the Company to do so, and let this be so fair a bargain that it does not have to be hidden under phrases of doubtful meaning, or diplomatically denied in Parliament by the Under Secretary of State for Foreign Affairs. Money, I am afraid, I must have. You can't levy customs duties without building customs houses, can you?

✧ ✧ ✧

The proposals of 3 May were drafted into a formal agreement after consultations between the Foreign Office and the Colonial Office.[2] This document took the form of an amended version of the agreement of 1891. It repeated the provision in the earlier agreement that the Commissioner should be empowered to use the Lakes Company's steamers free of charge: this was a misunderstanding due to the fact that when setting out the proposals Johnston had forgotten to mention that he had verbally agreed to abandon this provision in exchange for an annual payment of £2,500, and Rhodes had not noticed the omission. It bound the Chartered Company to contribute £17,500 a year for a period of ten years—not, as suggested in the proposals, for a minimum of five; and, more serious, it stipulated that the whole of this sum was to be assigned to the service of the Protectorate, and that in addition 'all expenses connected with the field of the Chartered

---

[1] Which I know you again and again put forward. (Note by Johnston.)
[2] There is a copy of the draft agreement in the B.S.A. Co. Papers, Cape Town.

Company's Administration shall be defrayed by the Company, either by a fixed annual payment or by liquidation of accounts rendered by the Commissioner'. Finally, it made the Company liable to such taxation as the Commissioner, with the approval of the home Government, might think proper to impose.

This draft was sent to Dr. Rutherfoord Harris, the Company's Cape Town secretary. On receiving it, Harris sent an urgent telegram to Rhodes, who was at Durban.[1] 'It is a pure mockery', he declared, 'and as [Rochfort] Maguire says we really get nothing and are at H.H.'s mercy. I think he must have written privately, and hope you will at once notify him by letter that the entire £7,500 is at once stopped, as [the] agreement is so utterly in opposition to what was agreed here as to render any chance of accord from your point of view impossible.'

When in due course a copy of this document came before him, Sir Percy Anderson suggested as a possible reason for it 'that Harris, and perhaps somebody else behind him, disliked the agreement, thought Johnston was getting too much influence with Rhodes, and made mischief in this way'.[2] In view of the reference to Maguire, who was in London, Sir Philip Currie saw him and came back with the information that 'he said Rhodes's letter was quite unjustifiable and ought to be withdrawn'. Since the letter to which he alluded had been sent to Johnston as the direct consequence of Harris's telegram, it may be assumed that Maguire dissociated himself from that as well.

Rhodes had written to Johnston at once, on 16 September 1893, as soon as he received Harris's telegram of the same date. He had

[1] This telegram and Rhodes's letter of the same date (16 Sept. 1893) are quoted in full in Johnston's letter to Rhodes of 8 Oct. 1893, enclosed in Johnston to Rosebery, No. 52, C.A., Confidential, 8 Oct. 1893.

[2] Minute on Johnston's No. 52, C.A., 8 Oct. 1893. Astonishing as it is, Anderson seems to have been genuinely convinced that the draft agreement accorded closely with the Rhodes–Johnston proposals of 3 May. In this minute he informed the Foreign Secretary (Lord Rosebery) that he had not previously understood that, according to those proposals, only £10,000 of the £17,500 could be spent on the Protectorate. Yet there is no ambiguity in the relevant paragraph of the proposals. Anderson was a busy man and might perhaps be excused such a mistake, but the draftsmen who produced the document ought to have known what they were doing.

Anderson was right, however, in his suspicion that there was 'somebody else behind' Harris. The Company's Cape Town correspondence shows that Harris's antipathy towards Johnston was assiduously encouraged by a lawyer named Michel, who examined in microscopic detail both the draft agreement and all Johnston's activities, real or imagined, for the purpose of finding fault.

not yet seen the draft agreement for himself. Enclosing the telegram, he declared that it 'speaks for itself', and continued:

I have, of course, stopped at once your extra amount, and shall arrange as soon as possible to spend the whole of our subsidy north of the Zambesi in our own Territories by someone in whom I can place confidence.

What I feel deeply is your disloyalty, though it was not altogether unexpected. Your conduct for some time past led me to feel that you were not worthy of my complete confidence, but I thought, as it appears erroneously, after your visit to Cape Town, that you meant to act in the future loyally to myself.

It is clear you must have written privately, and in a perfectly different style, to the basis arranged between us at Cape Town.

I have at once instructed Harris to at once reduce to old basis of supply, pending transference of expenditure to our own Territories or re-consideration of position by Foreign Office. They clearly must have been misinformed by you.

Subsequent study of the draft agreement did not lead him to a more moderate attitude. He described as 'impudent' and 'absurd' the clause giving Johnston power to tax the Company in its own territory without its own approval, and regarded the whole draft as a scheme by Johnston to aggrandize his own personal position. In comparison with this objection his other complaints became merely incidental. It was only in passing that he remarked that 'of course' the Company had not intended the subsidy of £17,500 to be spent exclusively on the Protectorate, and he gave the Foreign Office credit for having 'meant well' in its handling of the land question, even though it had not conceded his demand that all claims other than his Company's to land in the Company's sphere should be disallowed regardless of their legal merit. It was against the alleged pretensions of Johnston that he fulminated. 'I am not going', he told Harris, 'to create with my funds an independent King Johnston over the Zambesi.' 'I . . . quite agree', chimed in Harris, 'that he has deposed King Moir in order that King Johnston might reign.' According to Rhodes, the position was that

Up to the present he has been a servant of the Home Government in the Protectorate and a servant of ours in the Sphere north of the Zambesi. In the proposed agreement I see he tried to get the Sphere added to the Protectorate and to be independent of us in both. We understood the agreement to be that the Protectorate should be added to the Sphere and that he should be under us in both. The difficulty is that he is an imperial officer, but still we will see what they [the Foreign Office] say to my demands.[1]

Apart from the taxation clause, there was in fact nothing in the draft agreement which altered the relationship between the Commissioner and the Company. This was in accordance with the proposals of 3 May, in which Rhodes had acknowledged that he was quite content that in both the Protectorate and the Company's sphere the administration should 'remain under the direction of the Foreign Office in exactly the conditions set forth in the Instructions issued to me [Johnston] on taking up my appointment'. Thus, in response to the promptings of Harris, Rhodes wittingly or unwittingly repudiated in October the arrangement to which he had put his signature in May.

Whereas Johnston was anxious that the unseemly abuse to which Rhodes had subjected him should not become a matter of public gossip, and that all knowledge of the matter should be kept within the circle of the Foreign Office and the Company, Rhodes expressed contempt of Johnston to all and sundry, ridiculing his physique as well as vilifying his character.[2] Johnston on his side preserved an attitude of dignity and moderation, though in December he told Harris that he was 'increasingly of opinion that a further personal connection between myself and the Company is rendered difficult'.[3]

On 8 October he replied at length to Rhodes's letter of 16 September. He began with an indignant and unqualified denial of the charge of 'disloyalty', but continued:

Before I proceed farther with my letter I want to control the very natural resentment I feel towards you by detailing the reasons which should make me more tolerant of temper or even insult from you than from almost any other person in the world.

I have often told you, though I dare say you have classed it with a good deal of the cant and humbug you hear, that I had but one religion, and that was the extension and development of the British Empire. I almost hesitate to make this statement, because anything approaching sentimentality grates on you and has a false ring in the hearing of most

[1] B.S.A. Co. Papers, Cape Town: Telegrams exchanged by Rhodes and Harris, 16 Oct. 1893.
[2] B.S.A. Co. Papers, Cape Town: Johnston to Harris, 26 Nov. 1893.
[3] Ibid., 9 Dec. 1893.

people; but I have to start with this premise in order to explain why I feel so deeply indebted towards you and so bound by gratitude to make every allowance for the imperfections of temper from which you, no more than any other healthy, vigorous human being, are free.

I believe, from such sources of knowledge as are at my disposal, that you have been the direct means of saving for the British Empire all the territories stretching between the north of the Transvaal and the Basin of the Congo, in addition to having given a valuable impetus to the growing idea among the British people that we should not abandon our control over the destinies of Egypt, but that we should rather seek to open up a continuous chain of Empire from the Cape to Cairo. This last expression, 'From the Cape to Cairo,' though often credited to you, is of my invention, and was one of the first phrases I uttered on the earliest occasion of my meeting you in 1889 which attracted your attention.[1]

After recalling at some length Rhodes's part in bringing the territories north of the Zambesi under British control, he went on to pay lavish tribute to Rhodes's generosity 'as a paymaster', but at the same time he thought it well to point out that his gratitude was not for any favours of a private character bestowed on him personally, for there had been none. 'I have never', he declared—and it must have been the simple truth, for Rhodes obviously knew the facts—'received any emolument or gift from you or your Company, of any kind, and the very offer of such has never been made to me.' His co-operation with them had been 'in the support of an idea, without the hope of personal gain of any kind whatever'.

He now came to the subject of the several occasions on which his relations with Rhodes had been strained. The first such occasion was in 1890, when Rhodes had written him 'a very intemperate letter' about his share in the making of the abortive Anglo-Portuguese Convention.[2] The second arose shortly afterwards, 'over this matter of what should be Protectorate and what Sphere of Influence'.

If I am not assuming too high a rôle [he explained] I may say that I acted as go-between between yourself and the Foreign Office. The Foreign Office may have been somewhat cautious in their views and you

[1] I used it in a Review article and on a little map privately printed for me by Bartholomew Brothers, showing what has since become an established fact, viz. the extension from South Africa upwards to the Egyptian Soudan and Egypt. (Note by Johnston.)

[2] In this letter Rhodes had accused him of 'desertion'. His reply is in the Rhodes Papers, Charters, 3A, No. 52; it is dated 13 Oct. 1890.

may have been rather extreme in yours—I know for myself that at that time I held this opinion privately, that it would be better either to turn the whole thing into a Protectorate, or place the whole of it under the Company's Charter—but a compromise had to be arrived at. In attempting to suggest a basis for this compromise I was again subjected to a good deal of intemperate language on your part, and once or twice accused of 'treachery,' which meant, I suppose, that I had failed to act according to your opinion as an uncompromising partisan of the British South Africa Company. My main object throughout was to arrive at *a* settlement which would enable me to begin work as soon as possible. Nevertheless, this little trouble soon passed over. The Foreign Office, to a certain extent, accepted your views regarding the definition of the Protectorate, and we parted to engage in our respective tasks with as strong a feeling of personal friendship as ever.

Again, however, and for no earthly cause on my part, a feeling of distrust sprang up in your mind at the end of 1892. You were galled by the ingratitude displayed by most of the Missionaries, traders and planters in the Protectorate, and justly hurt by the offensive things they said of you and of your policy. Acting always on the opinion that I was playing a double game, and was not to be trusted, you felt and expressed the opinion that this agitation against any possible extension of the Company's rule over Nyasaland was inspired by myself, and not a feeling emanating quite independently from the settlers in and around the Shire Highlands. You proposed a meeting with me at the coast in which we could have a frank discussion of this matter and arrive at a thoroughly satisfactory settlement. You and your Directors in sending me these communications relative to this meeting appear to have been under the delusion that Zomba was within a few days' reach by telegram of London, and not more than a month by the Postal Route. As it happened, the letters and telegrams which announced to me that you would be at Tshinde by a certain date and that you wished to meet me reached me just within a fortnight of that date. On the very same day on which they arrived, and while I was debating whether it was possible for me to reach Tshinde in time to see you, or whether I should make that long journey fruitlessly, arrived the news from Captain Johnson that he had met with a serious repulse at the hands of some slave traders, and that the whole Upper Shire was in revolt,[1] the 'Domira' in the hands of the enemy, boats captured, people killed, and all communication with Fort Johnston and the regions beyond cut off. At that time we had exactly 40 Sikhs and a handful of Makua, perhaps 20 or 30, to defend all British Central Africa. It was a crisis in our affairs when for me to have left the scene and gone to the coast would have exposed the whole

---

[1] This was the Liwonde rising. See above, pp. 195, 216.

Protectorate to the gravest disaster and would have brought down on me the charge of personal cowardice. In fact I do not think I took five minutes to consider whether I was to go up country to the seat of war or down to Tshinde to meet you. I packed a few things and started the next morning for the Upper Shire, but to save you disappointment I sat up till within a few hours of the time of starting writing you a very, very long private letter which I despatched by my Oriental clerk, whom I believed to be a trustworthy person, to be delivered to you at Quelimane or Tshinde. My clerk was misled by information which he received, and instead of waiting for you at Tshinde, passed on to Quelimane, just missing your steamer, in fact delivering the letter to Mr. Ross[1] on the same day that your steamer had left Quelimane. Nevertheless, although you heard pretty correct rumours from Mr. King, my Agent at Tshinde, as to the state of affairs up country, you gave me no credit for ordinary civility or common sense and at once proceeded to write me a bitter and almost rude letter.

Replying to this I bore in mind the circumstances of disappointment under which it was written. Although absolutely exhausted by the physical fatigues and mental anxieties of this trying campaign on the Upper Shire in the height of the rainy season, I had barely concluded it than I went with the greatest speed possible with horses, boats, porters and steamers from Zomba to Cape Town, and met you there to hold the desired interview.

The only acknowledgement of the efforts I had made to both meet your views and carry out my duty were accusations of disloyalty, untrustworthiness, &c., &c., all the more difficult to answer because made to me in your own house. Still, whilst defending myself temperately, I forbore to take offence, because you seemed so anxious all the time to arrive at a fair and even generous settlement, and also because I quite realised that the position as regards your Company within the Protectorate was at that time an unjust one, and that even from the point of view of a business man you were right in protesting that your money should be spent in developing a part of British Central Africa where you were not allowed to hold any interests. So that after several rather brisk conversations in which I kept nothing of my true opinions hidden from you, but always made it a *sine qua non* that Imperial control and supremacy over British Central Africa should be maintained (a position which you never once disputed)[2] a basis of agreement was arrived at,

[1] Vice-consul at Quilimane.

[2] Throughout all these conversations you frequently assured me (1) that you were satisfied with the way in which I was developing these countries, and (2) that you had no objection whatever to the control of the Foreign Office exercised over me and, through me, over the affairs of British Central Africa. (Note by Johnston.)

and drawn up by me in the office of the British South Africa Company, and signed by you the same day.

He then compared this document with the draft agreement prepared in Downing Street, and made the extraordinary blunder of asserting that he could see no important difference between the two. Such an assertion could only confirm Rhodes in his belief that Johnston had sabotaged the proposals of 3 May, whereas the accusation that he 'must have' done so, by private letters to the Foreign Office, is completely disproved by the text of his letter to Anderson, already quoted.[1] It was with good reason that he called for a candid apology as the condition of his having anything further to do with the Company after his return to England on prolonged leave of absence in the following spring.

In the closing paragraphs of his letter he turned to the crucial issue of the subsidy.

Perhaps, however, at this crisis when I am just about to start on the biggest campaign against the slave trade we have ever undertaken here, I might have let your letter pass for a while had it not been that you cut me to the ground by a single blow by threatening to stop the supply of funds.

When I drew up my letter to you of the 3rd. May I distinctly said to you: 'These are my opinions, but I cannot guarantee that they will be the opinions of the Foreign Office. I have not even been directly authorised by the Foreign Office to come and treat with you on these matters at all. You, however, wish me to commence a forward movement throughout the interior of British Central Africa, especially in the Lake Regions about the Luapula. I am as anxious as you to go ahead, but it will require a larger subsidy per annum than £10,000. You offer me this increase of subsidy, which I think sufficient; but supposing the Foreign Office rejects our proposals, and yet I have engaged men, bought goods and ordered boats to carry on this movement, where shall I be?' You replied to me: 'I will tell you what I will do in any case—I will guarantee you £17,500 for one year, starting from the 1st. April, therefore you may go ahead without fear.' Later on, and quite unsolicited by me, you were much concerned at the difficulties in the way of crushing the slave trade and pacifying Nyasaland by our inability to completely conquer Makanjira and the chiefs allied with him. You very rightly observed that we could only do him a certain amount of damage by peppering him from the gun-boats on the Lake, but he could always keep our border in a state of disquiet and oblige us to lock up in our

[1] Above, pp. 251–2.

forts near his country expensive garrisons. You were also distressed at the thought that the remains of Captain Maguire and those who perished with him were used by Makanjira as trophies to decorate his stockade. You therefore abruptly offered me £10,000 as a fund against which to draw for the special purpose of entirely conquering Makanjira's country, and of attempting the removal and burial of Captain Maguire's remains and those of the other persons assassinated. I did not accept straight off, because I thought the offer too extraordinarily generous to be real; but you gave me practical proof of your sincerity by going to the Bank, and informing the said Bank that you had authorised me to draw Bills on you for a certain fund to the extent of £10,000. I then telegraphed for 100 more Sikhs from India, and I made arrangements for obtaining 300 or 400 Makua from Moçambique; I have also embarked on other expenditure, all with the one aim in view of completely conquering Makanjira's country. . . . You, now, having authorised me to embark on all this expenditure, coolly threaten to leave me bankrupt.

. . . .

As regards the £10,000 (or rather the permission to spend up to £10,000 in the campaign against Makanjira) I must hold you as a man of honour to your word, because I have gone too far forward now to retreat. The new Indians are already in the country and all preparations have been made to carry the campaign to a successful conclusion.

Apart from drawing on the Makanjira fund, he would, he declared, try so to limit his administrative expenses as to balance his budget with the old subsidy of £10,000. The economies would be made chiefly in the Company's sphere, from which he said he would recall all the officials and police.

On reflection, however, he decided to postpone such ruinous economies at least until 31 March 1894. For the financial year ending on that date he would insist on his right to spend up to the full £17,500, in accordance with Rhodes's verbal promise.[1] In giving a direct refusal to Harris's demands for immediate retrenchment, he probably assumed that Rhodes could not afford the political embarrassment of dishonouring his drafts. If so, his conjecture was sound, for Rhodes, while bidding Harris 'pay not a penny more than £10,000 a year', admitted that he did not 'want scandals of drafts of Her Majesty's Commissioner in Nyasaland being dishonoured' at the very time when Johnston was fighting Makanjira.[2]

---

[1] B.S.A. Co. Papers, Cape Town: Johnston to Harris, 9 Dec. 1893; Johnston to Canning, 10 Dec. 1893.

[2] B.S.A. Co. Papers, Cape Town: Telegrams exchanged by Rhodes and Harris, 16 Oct. 1893.

It had become perfectly clear before Johnston went home on leave in 1894 that even the subsidy of £17,500 would have fallen far short of his needs. In December 1893 he wrote a long dispatch to the Foreign Office, defining the problem on which the Government must give a decision. Unless the money he required could be supplied him from one source or another, he must abandon his attempt to suppress the slave-trade and to check the importation of guns and powder. If this were done 'we might live here in perfect peace with the Arabs, the Yaos and the other slave-trading people with whom our quarrels have lain since the commencement of an active opposition to the slave trade'. The half-dozen stations in the Protectorate which had been established primarily as defensive positions and military bases rather than as administrative and fiscal posts—Deep Bay, Fort Johnston, Liwonde, Chiradzulu, and Forts Anderson and Lister—must all be closed, and the military expenditure must be brought back within the £10,000 a year provided by the Company. Half of the reduced force which could still be maintained would be stationed 'at one or two points in the northern part of British Central Africa where the British South Africa Company has special interests at stake'; the other half, retained in the south, would be used only for the protection of planters, traders, and missionaries. There would still be the two gunboats on the lake, but, now that they were there, the limitations of their usefulness could be seen. Apart from the fact that they could not be everywhere on the lake at once, they could not attack the dhows and canoes of the slave-traders unless there was an effective land force to co-operate with them: otherwise 'the missionaries and traders on the Lake shore would infallibly be massacred and their property seized by the indignant dhow owners'. Finally, nothing that could be done on the lake itself could prevent the slavers from taking their victims by land round the southern coast; and 'these routes can only be stopped by the employment of a police force at least as large as that which we at present possess'—a force at double its old strength because of the reinforcements brought in for the campaign against Makanjira.

If the disastrous consequences of retrenchment were to be avoided, he must be able to spend about £35,000 a year. Estimating his revenue at little more than £7,000, he therefore put his need of outside help at £28,000 a year 'for some years to come'—and even this did not include his own salary, or Sharpe's. He suggested that the only fair solution of the difficulty was that the British Government should provide £16,000 a year, leaving the Company to contribute the remaining £12,000.[1]

In the following March he sent a final plea to the Directors in London. If he had to reduce his forces for the sake of his finances, the only possible way to save the British in Central Africa from massacre or expulsion would be 'to make a public proclamation that we now permitted the slave trade and were very sorry for what we had done in the past. We might then', he added sarcastically, 'raise a large revenue by levying an export tax on slaves. To avoid a little bother and trouble the Arabs would gladly pay this.' Consequently 'you must hold on until the Nation realises its duties or calmly agrees to the non-recognition of them'.[2]

In the summer, when Johnston was in London, the outcome of many discussions and memoranda was as favourable as he could reasonably have hoped. It is not clear precisely when or why the Treasury agreed to assume financial control over the Protectorate, but a succession of small concessions had impelled it in that direction. First it had paid the salary of a consul accredited to the Nyasa chiefs, then it had paid those of a Consul-General and of a vice-consul to assist him. It had built the Zomba Residency at the request of Hawes, and spent £1,000 on repairing it at the request of Johnston. It had provided £1,200 to compensate the Makololo for their losses during the Portuguese invasion in 1889–90, and £2,500 for 'presents' to chiefs and the purchase of land. It had granted many hundreds of pounds to finance the journeys undertaken from time to time by Johnston and Sharpe, though this admittedly counted as ordinary consular expenditure; more important, it had allowed the War Office to supply the Administration free of charge, and at a cost of £9,200, with the nine-pounder and seven-pounder guns, the rifles, and the very large quantities of ammunition required by his 'police'. It had contributed £1,100 to compensate the Lakes Company and its employees for damage and casualties sustained aboard the *Domira* at the hands of Makanjira's people. Its maintenance of the Nyasa gunboats, even though until 1895 they were under Admiralty and not Administration control, was at any rate expenditure on Central Africa. From Johnston's point of view, this accumulation of miscellaneous contributions

[1] F.O. 2/55: Johnston to Rosebery, No. 68, C.A., 16 Dec. 1893.
[2] F.O. 2/66: Johnston to Canning, 10 Mar. 1894.

was naturally less conspicuous than, for example, the Treasury's refusal to defray the cost of court houses, or of land surveys in the Shiré Highlands. Yet Johnston himself reckoned that from 1891 to the end of March 1893 the Treasury had spent about £24,297 on the country under his administration, not counting naval expenditure; whereas the Chartered Company's total contribution for the same period was about £30,000. 'Perhaps', he confessed to Rhodes when giving these figures, 'to be perfectly just, I have been a little ungrateful towards the Government in my complaints about "no money".'[1] By the end of 1893 the Treasury was finding these repeated requests for specific payments so annoying that it took the initiative in offering a fixed annual grant on condition that nothing more would be asked from it.[2] Imperceptibly, over a period of ten years, the thin end of the wedge had been inserted, and Johnston's task during the following summer was to drive it home. Lastly, the attitude not only of the Treasury but of the Cabinet must have been influenced by the contemporary parallel issue of Uganda. It was in vain that Sir William Harcourt, the Chancellor of the Exchequer, sighed about 'the natural fruits of jingoism'.[3]

The effect of the new arrangements was to make the Administration of the Protectorate responsible to the home Government for its expenditure, as well as for its general policy. Thenceforth the Commissioner was to be spared the embarrassment of being 'the servant of two masters'. At the same time, and as the appropriate accompaniment of this change, Rhodes carried out his intention of withdrawing his Company's sphere from Johnston's control. An agreement between the Company and the Foreign Office, signed by Rhodes and Anderson on 24 November 1894, provided that the Commissioner should relinquish administrative control over the country west of the Protectorate not later than 30 June 1895, and that the Company's subsidy should cease at the end of that year. The tangled financial situation would be sorted out by the joint efforts of the Company's accountants and those of the Foreign Office, 'on the basis that the Company is liable only for the annual police contribution of £10,000, for £5,000 given in 1891 for expenses in connection with raising and organising the police force,

[1] B.S.A. Co. Papers, Cape Town: Johnston to Rhodes, 7 June 1893.
[2] F.O. 2/53: F.O. to Johnston, No. 84, 14 Nov. 1893.
[3] Minute on Johnston to Canning, loc. cit.

for expenditure in connection with steam transport on the lake for administrative purposes, and for amounts which can be shown to have been expended for the benefit of, or on account of, the Chartered territory as distinct from the Protectorate'; and as much of the £10,000 'Makanjira fund' as had not been spent on the operations against Makanjira should be repaid to Rhodes by the Treasury.[1]

In accordance with this agreement, Major Forbes, whom Rhodes had appointed Administrator of the Company's territory, arrived at Zomba on 23 June 1895, and spent a few days there as Johnston's guest. Their relations were friendly, and Johnston reported that he had done everything in his power to assist Forbes and 'enable him to take up his duties without any breach of continuity'.[2]

From this date the separate existence of Northern Rhodesia may be said to have begun. But it was not until 1900 that the administration of the part of it lying east of the Kafue was placed on an organized basis by the North Eastern Rhodesia Order in Council; separate arrangements had already been made for the rest of the territory in the previous year by the North Western Rhodesia Order in Council, which concerned a region unaffected by any kind of European penetration from the east, and brought within the orbit of the Chartered Company entirely as a result of missionary and commercial influences reaching northward from the Cape.[3] And it was not until 1899 that North Eastern Rhodesia acquired a capital on its own soil, at Fort Jameson: before that date the Administrator lived at Blantyre, in a house which had been built for the telegraph company. Until 1909 the British Government's general supervision of the Company's rule in North Eastern Rhodesia was exercised by the Commissioner for the Protectorate, and it was only the approaching unification of Northern Rhodesia (completed in 1911) that caused this function to be transferred to the High Commissioner for South Africa, who already exercised it in North Western Rhodesia. A continuing link of even greater importance was provided by an arrangement by which the armed forces of the Protectorate were made available for service in North Eastern Rhodesia in return for an annual subsidy by the Company.

---

[1] C.7637 (A. & P. 1895), pp. 3–4. Cf. Johnston to Kimberley, No. 77, C.A., 10 June 1895, with minutes.
[2] F.O. 2/88: Johnston to Kimberley, No. 83, C.A., 25 June 1895.
[3] The story is told in detail by H. M. Hole in *The Passing of the Black Kings*.

It was a force from Nyasaland which crushed Mpeseni's Angoni in 1898. In 1903 the Company informed its shareholders that it wished to end the arrangement, because it believed that it could itself provide a more efficient protection at less cost; but the Government was reluctant to acquiesce, and it was not until 31 March 1911 that this last political tie with the Protectorate was cut.

APPENDIXES

1. *Johnston to Anderson, Private, 21 January 1893*[1]

[Extract]

I am always worrying myself by thinking that you at the Foreign Office must, from all you hear, believe me to be a very combative and quarrelsome person, because I constantly seem to be having a conflict with somebody; and no doubt a good many of my decisions and actions are deeply resented by those against whom I am upholding the law. As a matter of fact, a more peace-loving being than myself never entered Africa. At the same time, with every wish to get on well with all people of all colours out here, there are some times when I am obliged to take up a stand against law-breakers.

You can well understand that in a newly administered country like this it is very hard for the Europeans who have hitherto been a law unto themselves to understand that they must now submit to authority. There is also an absurdly mean spirit in some of the new comers which actuates them to endeavour to evade paying money if they can possibly outwit the Administration.

Take this case in point:—A party of English sportsmen arrived here last June to shoot Big Game in Nyasaland. I afforded them all the facilities I could under the Brussels Act for passing their sporting guns and ammunition; I let them use our Administration stores at Tshiromo for storing their superfluous baggage; and my agents everywhere did what they were able to facilitate their movements. I acted thus, not because I sympathised with the purpose of their visit (because I detest this sort of sportsmen whose one ambition is to make their camps wherever they go a vast butcher's shop, and who recklessly slay with vulgar ostentation every horned beast or large cat they come across), but because I knew that if I was not very civil to them they would abuse me and my Administration in the columns of the 'Field'. However, I had it pointed out to these hunters that if they intended to shoot Rhinoceros or Elephant they must take out a Big Game Licence, costing £25. They replied to my agents that 'they would see about it.' Nevertheless, for the past seven months they have been scouring the country for elephants and have succeeded in shooting several near the west bank of the Upper Shire, on British territory, bien entendu. Now, in so doing they have

[1] In F.O. 2/54.

deliberately broken one of our Regulations. . . . The result of this will be that probably when they return within the reach of one of our collectors of Revenue proceedings will have to be taken against them for breach of this Regulation. This will lead to all manner of unpleasantness, no doubt, and the sportsmen in question (who are all of them exceptionally wealthy men: the leader of the band is a certain Captain Weatherley) will go home abusing the unfortunate B.C.A.A., and saying that it has made the country unbearable for decent sportsmen. Well, what am I to do? Those persons in this country . . . who are what may be called resident elephant hunters, have to take out a yearly licence, costing £25: and they are already asking how it is that I exact this so rigidly from them and yet allow this Weatherley to go about the country shooting elephants and take no measures to bring him to book.

Then again here is a typical instance of another kind of lawlessness which breaks out from time to time, chiefly in the African Lakes Company: One of the Lakes Company's agents at Matope quarrels with his table-boy or steward because the tinned fish is served up cold. He whacks the boy and the boy runs away to the neighbouring village, where his parents live. The irate agent demands his surrender, but in the meantime the boy has run off to Blantyre to lay his complaint before the Lakes Company's Manager. The Agent then raids the village with his station-men, carries off numbers of fowls, and such cloth and brass wire and other goods as his followers can lay hands on, ties up for 3 days the boy's mother, father, and some other relative, beats them all three, and only releases them when the boy himself returns with a message of conciliation from the Company's Manager at Blantyre. Instead, however, of letting the matter stop there, the boy himself is tied up and further punished for daring to carry his complaint to the Manager. This occurs at a place within 29 miles of where I am writing. Yet probably I shall be deemed very harsh by the Lakes Company for taking any notice of it, although I need hardly say I have had to make it a Court case.

Here is another instance which may amuse you to read:—In last October a native Chief on Mount Mlanje, who has always behaved very well to the English, and is a very decent fellow, trudged 60 miles to see me, and complained bitterly against the conduct of a wild Irishman named Bradshaw, a coffee planter in that district. This Bradshaw had cast his eyes on one of the Chief's wives, and had 'ordered' the said Chief to send the woman to his house. The Chief refused, whereupon Bradshaw uttered the most terrible threats of what he would do to him, how he would tie him up, burn his town down, etc. Captain Sclater was sent over by me to investigate the matter, and although Bradshaw denied having made these threats, there was ample evidence to show that he had used the words attributed to him, whilst he himself admitted having attempted to obtain the chief's wife. There was, however, no very good case for trial, but to reassure the Chief, Captain Sclater said in the course of the investigation that he was to pay no heed to such threats uttered on the part of white men, because if Mr. Bradshaw had really done what he threatened to do he would be himself liable 'to be tied up' and imprisoned. Bradshaw considered himself insulted by his name being associated with the idea of imprisonment, and called upon Sclater, who was then sitting as a magistrate, to withdraw his words. He of course declined to do so, and the matter ended there for the time. But Bradshaw by dint of brooding over the subject fancied himself to be a very injured person, and resolved that he was either to obtain the withdrawal of the terms used by Captain Sclater or fight a duel with him. He first applied to me. I reviewed the whole case, informed him that I thought Captain Sclater justified in using the language attributed to him, and that I could take no further steps in the matter. Bradshaw therefore followed Captain Sclater persistently about and finally called on him with witnesses to tell him that he was 'a cad and a coward.' He also said that he hoped he would go into the adjoining coffee plantation 'and give him satisfaction.' This case I tried myself, and fined Mr. Bradshaw £5 for contempt of court and inciting to a breach of the Peace.[1]

Then there are the disappointed land claimants whose land claims have been shown to be absolute bosh without documentary proof, or who are denied the hundred thousand acres they pretend to have bought for a few trade guns. These people are particularly lively in their denunciations of the tyranny of the Administration, and so on. Again, there are other land-holders who are proceeding to treat the natives, living on native reserves within their estates, as their serfs: these also are very indignant because I assert the right of the native to work for whom he will, or not to work at all unless he chooses.

The great point that I try to bear in mind is to be without resentment as far as possible: not to refrain from asking a man to dinner this week because he may have abused me heartily the week before. When I leave this country for pleasanter scenes, I think the general impression left on my memory will be that I never had a more disagreeable lot of people to deal with in my life than these missionaries, planters, and traders of Nyasaland. But still, as long as I remain here I shall try to do the best I can to advance their interests in a legitimate way, because they are all of them aiding in the development of the country, and, no doubt, in

---

[1] This annoyance had been going on for a matter of two months and a half. Sclater was very anxious to try the *argumentum ad hominem*, but as he holds a Magistrate's Commission I told him I could not allow that. (Note by Johnston.)

time will be succeeded by a more agreeable set of people, as the attractions of the country become better known.

2. *Johnston to Anderson, 23 March 1893*[1]

[*Extract*]

Dear Sir Percy,

Thanks for your letters of December 14th and 27th. I only received them two or three days ago, owing to the vagaries of our eccentric General Post Office, which seems to find some special gratification in ignoring the existence of British Central Africa, and refusing to make up its already considerable mail into special mail bags. The delight of the General Post Office in London is to shoot all our mails into Zanzibar, where they lie a greater or less time according to the degree of health and energy in which the Goanese Zanzibar Postmaster may find himself. . . . I wish you would solve the matter *more Africano* by just having the Postmaster General exposed in chains for three days at the main entrance to the Foreign Office. This is the way in which we do *not* treat natives out here. In the middle of this barbarism I feel that we cannot be too fastidiously correct in our legal procedure, and so the Habeas Corpus Act flourishes; but I often think that a rougher procedure would do a great deal of good in England. If you could arm our young men of the African Department and launch them suddenly in a raid on the Treasury, the higher officials of which being hunted from room to room at the point of the bayonet, I feel assured a much happier result would be obtained, and for months after, every suggestion of the Foreign Office as to expenditure on British interests abroad would be willingly, even slavishly, carried out.[2]

[1] In F.O. 2/54.
[2] This has been settled without rough treatment of the Postmaster-General. (Note by Anderson.)

BIBLIOGRAPHY

1. Sources[1]

The most important surviving sources are the Foreign Office dispatches in the Public Record Office. The Nyasa, Zanzibar, Mozambique, and Lisbon correspondence is in F.O. 84, except that for 1893 and later years the Nyasa correspondence is in F.O. 2. Some of the dispatches in F.O. 63 (Portugal) are also relevant.

A large number of documents, particularly those concerning the suppression of the slave-trade and the dispute with Portugal, are published in Blue Books. Specific references to these (as also to the unpublished material) are given in footnotes to the text, and the details need not be repeated here. Much of the most interesting and important information, including, of course, all that was deemed confidential, is available only in manuscript.

A semi-official publication of outstanding usefulness is the four-volume *Map of Africa by Treaty* (H.M.S.O., 1909), compiled by Sir E. Hertslet.

The material in the Public Record Office cannot be supplemented by reference to official correspondence conducted locally in Central Africa, because (as the Colonial Office ascertained in response to my inquiry) all such correspondence was destroyed by a fire at Zomba in 1923.

A similar fate befell most of the Rhodes Papers when Rhodes's house (Groote Schuur) was burned down. The papers which survive are in boxes in Rhodes House, Oxford. Also in Rhodes House are the Cawston Papers, in bound volumes; these contain much information about the Company's role north of the Zambesi, particularly in 1890. Some of the Company's own records are kept at its Cape Town office, and I have been able to use the relevant material through the generosity of Dr. Roland Oliver in allowing me to borrow his typed copies. But the records which used to be at the Company's London headquarters were completely destroyed in an air raid, except for certain legal documents (title deeds, formal agreements, &c.) which survived through being locked in a safe. Thanks to the kindness of Sir Dougal Malcolm, I have been able to use copies of the agreements with the Lakes Company, and also the Certificates of Claim. The *Reports of the Company's Proceedings, 1889–1900,* are quite useful.

The African Lakes Corporation assures me that it has not troubled to preserve the records of its predecessor, the African Lakes Company. A similar inability to recognize the importance of historical documents has been shown by the Church of Scotland, although the printed minutes of

---

[1] It is one of the limitations of this work that foreign sources (particularly Portuguese) have not been drawn upon. The British sources which I am conscious of not having used are the Salisbury Papers (Hatfield) and the Johnston Papers (Central African Archives).

its Foreign Mission Committee, and of the Free Church's Foreign Mission Committee, contain a few letters from missionaries in the field and a certain amount of other information. Duff Macdonald's diary, a very scrappy notebook, is also in the Church's possession.

The L.M.S., by contrast, has preserved its records with the greatest care. The correspondence has been placed in boxes, the contents of each box being grouped in a number of folders, and the contents of each folder in a number of paper jackets. Thus, a reference given as L.M.S., C.A., 5.2.C., means that the letter is in Jacket C of Folder 2 of Box 5 of the correspondence received from the mission to Central Africa. The outgoing correspondence of the Southern Department, and the minutes of the Southern Committee, show how the mission's affairs were managed in London. There is also in Livingstone House (the Society's London headquarters) a typescript of an unpublished book by D. P. Jones, one of the early missionaries to Tanganyika. It is interesting, though rather slight.

The U.M.C.A., too, has preserved its records, but unfortunately most of them are as yet unclassified and inaccessible. Apart from the mission's periodical publication, *Central Africa*, the only material which is both available and relevant is the letters of Bishop Smythies. I have not myself made a study of these letters, but Mr. P. Rayner, who has done so, has kindly provided me with some useful quotations.

2. *Books*

BACKGROUND

J. S. Keltie, *The Partition of Africa* (Stanford, London, 1895); Sir Harry Johnston, *The Colonization of Africa* (C.U.P., 1899); Sir Reginald Coupland, *East Africa and its Invaders* (O.U.P., 1938), *The Exploitation of East Africa, 1856–90* (Faber, London, 1939), and *The British Anti-Slavery Movement* (Home University Library, 1933); C. Lloyd, *The Navy and the Slave Trade* (Longmans, London, 1949); R. Oliver, *The Missionary Factor in East Africa* (Longmans, London, 1952); B. Williams, *Cecil Rhodes* (Constable, London, 1926); L. A. C. Raphael, *The Cape to Cairo Dream* (Columbia U.P., 1936); H. V. Livermore, *A History of Portugal* (C.U.P., 1947); M. V. Jackson, *European Powers and South East Africa, 1796–1856* (Longmans, London, 1942); A. B. Keith, *The Belgian Congo and the Berlin Act* (O.U.P., 1919); S. E. Crowe, *The Berlin West African Conference, 1884–5* (Longmans, London, 1942); M. E. Townsend, *Rise and Fall of Germany's Colonial Empire, 1884–1918* (Macmillan, New York, 1930).

EXPLORATION

D. Livingstone, *Missionary Travels in South Africa* (John Murray, London, 1857), *Narrative of an Expedition to the Zambesi and its Tributaries* (Murray, 1865), and *Last Journals* (2 vols., Murray, 1874); Sir R. Coupland, *Kirk on the Zambesi* (O.U.P., 1928), and *Livingstone's Last Journey* (Collins, London, 1945); J. P. R. Wallis (ed.), *The Zambesi Journal of James Stewart* (Chatto and Windus, London, 1952: No. 6 in the Oppenheimer Series); R. F. Burton, *The Lake Regions of Central Africa* (2 vols., Longmans, London, 1860); V. L. Cameron, *Across Africa* (2 vols., Daldy and Isbister, London, 1877); J. Thomson, *To the Central African Lakes and Back* (Sampson Low, London, 1881); J. F. Elton, *The Lakes and Mountains of Eastern and Central Africa* (London, 1879: Consul Elton's journal); and D. J. Rankin, *The Zambesi Basin and Nyassaland* (Blackwood, Edinburgh and London, 1893).

THE LIVINGSTONIA MISSION

J. Stewart, *Livingstonia, its Origin* (printed privately in 1894 by the Free Church of Scotland), and *Dawn in the Dark Continent* (Oliphant & Co., Edinburgh, 1903); J. Wells, *Stewart of Lovedale* (Hodder and Stoughton, London, 1908); W. P. Livingstone, *Laws of Livingstonia* (Hodder and Stoughton, London, 1921: an excellent biography); R. Laws, *Reminiscences of Livingstonia* (Oliver and Boyd, Edinburgh and London, 1934: a little disappointing); J. W. Jack, *Daybreak in Livingstonia* (Oliphant & Co., Edinburgh, 1901: factually reliable, but its sanctimoniousness is rather fatiguing); W. A. Elmslie, *Among the Wild Ngoni* (Oliphant and Ferrier, 1899: wholly admirable); and E. D. Young, *Nyassa* (London, 1877: useful as an account of the author's own work, but valueless except when recording personal experiences).

THE BLANTYRE MISSION

D. Macdonald, *Africana* (2 vols., Simpkin and Marshall, London, 1877: contains interesting information about the beginnings of the mission, besides much pioneer anthropological work); J. Buchanan, *The Shiré Highlands* (Blackwood, Edinburgh and London, 1885); A. Hetherwick, *The Romance of Blantyre* (J. Clarke, London, 1931); W. P. Livingstone, *A Prince of Missionaries* (J. Clarke, London, 1931: a biography of Hetherwick); and W. Robertson, *The Martyrs of Blantyre* (Nisbet, London, 1892). (All these works except Macdonald's are slight, but they are not without value.)

THE UNIVERSITIES' MISSION

The Universities' Mission is the subject of various competent though undistinguished books: G. H. Wilson, *History of the U.M.C.A.* (U.M.C.A., London, 1936); B. H. Barnes, *Johnson of Nyasaland* (U.M.C.A., 1933); W. P. Johnson, *My African Reminiscences, 1875–95* (U.M.C.A., c. 1924), and *Nyasa, the Great Water* (O.U.P., 1922); and G. Ward (ed. E. F. Russell), *Life of Charles Alan Smythies* (U.M.C.A., 1898). *The Journals and Papers of Chauncy Maples, Bishop of Likoma* (ed. Ellen Maples: Longmans, London, 1899) are clearly the work of a gifted and cultivated mind.

THE L.M.S.

The Tanganyika mission receives little attention in R. Lovett, *History of the London Missionary Society* (2 vols., Frowde, Oxford, 1899). E. C.

Hore, *Tanganyika* (E. Stanford, London, 1892) is a chronicle of the first eleven years of the mission's history; A. J. Swann, *Fighting the Slave-Hunters* (Seeley, London, 1910) is an extraordinarily vivid picture of life in the mission-field rather than an account of the mission itself.

POLITICS, ADMINISTRATION, ETC.

F. L. M. Moir, *After Livingstone* (Hodder and Stoughton, London, 1923: an account of the author's work in the service of the African Lakes Company); L. M. Fotheringham, *Adventures in Nyassaland* (Sampson Low, London, 1891); F. D. Lugard, *The Rise of Our East African Empire* (Blackwood, Edinburgh and London, 1893: almost wholly autobiographical), vol. i; Lady G. Cecil, *Life of Robert, Marquis of Salisbury* (Hodder and Stoughton, London, 1932), vol. iv; Sir H. Johnston, *British Central Africa* (Methuen, London, 1897: a substantial and informative work), and *The Story of My Life* (Chatto and Windus, London, 1923: interesting but rather smug); A. Johnston, *The Life and Letters of Sir Harry Johnston* (Jonathan Cape, London, 1929: of negligible value); Sir A. Sharpe, *The Backbone of Africa* (Witherby, London, 1921: gives little attention to Central Africa); Sir H. L. Duff, *Nyasaland under the Foreign Office* (George Bell, London, 1903: remarkably slight); R. C. F. Maugham, *Africa as I have known it* (John Murray, London, 1929), and *Nyasaland in the Nineties* (Lincoln Williams, London, 1935: both entertaining and informative books); S. S. Murray, *Handbook of Nyasaland* (Crown Agents for the Colonies, 1932: contains a good deal of solid historical information); C. Gouldsbury and H. Sheane, *The Great Plateau of Northern Rhodesia* (E. Arnold, London, 1911: gives much information about the early days of Company rule in N.E. Rhodesia, and is very well written); H. M. Hole, *The Making of Rhodesia* (Macmillan, London, 1926), and *The Passing of the Black Kings* (Philip Allan, London, 1932: both works are to some extent concerned with N. Rhodesia; they are masterly narratives and, as far as I can check their statements, thoroughly accurate).

3. *Pamphlets*

J. Stevenson, *The Civilisation of South East Africa* (Glasgow, 1877: written to point out to the public that Nyasaland existed), and *The Arabs in Central Africa and at Lake Nyassa* (Glasgow, 1888); A. Chirnside, *The Blantyre Missionaries: Discreditable Disclosures* (W. Ridgway, London, 1880); A. Riddel, *A Reply to 'The Blantyre Missionaries: Discreditable Disclosures' by Andrew Chirnside, F.R.G.S.* (Blackwood, Edinburgh, 1880: a remarkably ineffective reply); H. E. O'Neill, *The Mozambique and Nyassa Slave Trade* (British and Foreign Anti-Slavery Society, London, 1885: a careful analysis of the facts with which the consul had become acquainted while at Mozambique); H. Waller, *Nyasaland: Great Britain's Case Against Portugal* (Stanford, London, 1890: a lively piece of polemic).

INDEX